The Language of the Inuit

McGill-Queen's Native and Northern Series
(In memory of Bruce G. Trigger)
Sarah Carter and Arthur J. Ray, editors

1 When the Whalers Were Up North
Inuit Memories from the Eastern Arctic
Dorothy Harley Eber

2 The Challenge of Arctic Shipping
Science, Environmental Assessment, and Human Values
Edited by David L. VanderZwaag and Cynthia Lamson

3 Lost Harvests
Prairie Indian Reserve Farmers and Government Policy
Sarah Carter

4 Native Liberty, Crown Sovereignty
The Existing Aboriginal Right of Self-Government in Canada
Bruce Clark

5 Unravelling the Franklin Mystery
Inuit Testimony
David C. Woodman

6 Otter Skins, Boston Ships, and China Goods
The Maritime Fur Trade of the Northwest Coast, 1785–1841
James R. Gibson

7 From Wooden Ploughs to Welfare
The Story of the Western Reserves
Helen Buckley

8 In Business for Ourselves
Northern Entrepreneurs
Wanda A. Wuttunee

9 For an Amerindian Autohistory
An Essay on the Foundations of a Social Ethic
Georges E. Sioui

10 Strangers among Us
David Woodman

11 When the North Was Red
Aboriginal Education in Soviet Siberia
Dennis A. Bartels and Alice L. Bartels

12 From Talking Chiefs to a Native Corporate Elite
The Birth of Class and Nationalism among Canadian Inuit
Marybelle Mitchell

13 Cold Comfort
My Love Affair with the Arctic
Graham W. Rowley

14 The True Spirit and Original Intent of Treaty 7
Treaty 7 Elders and Tribal Council with Walter Hildebrandt
Dorothy First Rider, and Sarah Carter

15 This Distant and Unsurveyed Country
A Woman's Winter at Baffin Island, 1857–1858
W. Gillies Ross

16 Images of Justice
Dorothy Harley Eber

17 Capturing Women
The Manipulation of Cultural Imagery in Canada's Prairie West
Sarah A. Carter

18 Social and Environmental Impacts of the James Bay Hydroelectric Project
Edited by James F. Hornig

19 Saqiyuq
Stories from the Lives of Three Inuit Women
Nancy Wachowich in collaboration with Apphia Agalakti Awa, Rhoda Kaukjak Katsak, and Sandra Pikujak Katsak

20 Justice in Paradise
Bruce Clark

21 Aboriginal Rights and Self-Government
The Canadian and Mexican Experience in North American Perspective
Edited by Curtis Cook and Juan D. Lindau

22 Harvest of Souls
The Jesuit Missions and Colonialism in North America, 1632–1650
Carole Blackburn

23 Bounty and Benevolence
A History of Saskatchewan Treaties
Arthur J. Ray, Jim Miller, and Frank Tough

24 The People of Denendeh
Ethnohistory of the Indians of Canada's Northwest Territories
June Helm

25 The *Marshall* Decision and Native Rights
Ken Coates

26 The Flying Tiger
Women Shamans and Storytellers of the Amur
Kira Van Deusen

27 Alone in Silence
European Women in the Canadian North before 1940
Barbara E. Kelcey

28 The Arctic Voyages of Martin Frobisher
An Elizabethan Adventure
Robert McGhee

29 Northern Experience and the Myths of Canadian Culture
Renée Hulan

30 The White Man's Gonna Getcha
The Colonial Challenge to the Crees in Quebec
Toby Morantz

31 The Heavens Are Changing
Nineteenth-Century Protestant Missions and Tsimshian Christianity
Susan Neylan

32 Arctic Migrants/Arctic Villagers
The Transformation of Inuit Settlement in the Central Arctic
David Damas

33 Arctic Justice
On Trial for Murder – Pond Inlet, 1923
Shelagh D. Grant

34 Eighteenth-Century Naturalists of Hudson Bay
Stuart Houston, Tim Ball, and Mary Houston

35 The American Empire and the Fourth World
Anthony J. Hall

36 Uqalurait
An Oral History of Nunavut
Compiled and edited by John Bennett and Susan Rowley

37 Living Rhythms
Lessons in Aboriginal Economic Resilience and Vision
Wanda Wuttunee

38 The Making of an Explorer
George Hubert Wilkins and the Canadian Arctic Expedition, 1913–1916
Stuart E. Jenness

39 Chee Chee
A Study of Aboriginal Suicide
Alvin Evans

40 Strange Things Done
Murder in Yukon History
Ken S. Coates and William R. Morrison

41 Healing through Art
Ritualized Space and Cree Identity
Nadia Ferrara

42 Coyote and Raven Go Canoeing
Coming Home to the Village
Peter Cole

43 Something New in the Air
The Story of First Peoples Television Broadcasting in Canada
Lorna Roth

44 Listening to Old Woman Speak
Natives and Alternatives in
Canadian Literature
Laura Smyth Groening

45 Robert and Francis Flaherty
A Documentary Life, 1883–1922
Robert J. Christopher

46 Talking in Context
Language and Identity in
Kwakwaka'wakw Society
Anne Marie Goodfellow

47 Tecumseh's Bones
Guy St-Denis

48 Constructing Colonial Discourse
Captain Cook at Nootka Sound
Noel Elizabeth Currie

49 The Hollow Tree
Fighting Addiction with
Traditional Healing
Herb Nabigon

50 The Return of Caribou to Ungava
*A.T. Bergerud, Stuart Luttich,
and Lodewijk Camps*

51 Firekeepers of the
Twenty-First Century
First Nations Women Chiefs
Cora J. Voyageur

52 Isuma
Inuit Video Art
Michael Robert Evans

53 Outside Looking In
Viewing First Nations Peoples
in Canadian Dramatic
Television Series
Mary Jane Miller

54 Kiviuq
An Inuit Hero and
His Siberian Cousins
Kira Van Deusen

55 Native Peoples and Water Rights
Irrigation, Dams, and the Law
in Western Canada
Kenichi Matsui

56 The Rediscovered Self
Indigenous Identity
and Cultural Justice
Ronald Niezen

57 As affecting the fate of my
absent husband
Selected Letters of Lady Franklin
Concerning the Search for
the Lost Franklin Expedition,
1848–1860
Edited by Erika Behrisch Elce

58 The Language of the Inuit
Syntax, Semantics, and Society
in the Arctic
Louis-Jacques Dorais

59 Inuit Shamanism and Christianity
Transitions and Transformations
in the Twentieth Century
*Frederic Laugrand and
Jarich Oosten*

60 No Place for Fairness
Indigenous Land Rights and
Policy in the Bear Island Case
and Beyond
David T. McNab

61 Aleut Identity
Tradition and Modernity
in an Indigenous Fishery
Katherine L. Reedy-Mascher

62 Earth into Property
Aboriginal History and the
Making of Global Capitalism
Anthony J. Hall

63 Collections and Objections
Aboriginal Material Culture in
Southern Ontario, 1791–1914
Michelle A. Hamilton

64 These Mysterious People
Shaping History and Archaeology
in a Northwest Coast Community
Susan Roy

The Language of the Inuit

Syntax, Semantics, and Society in the Arctic

LOUIS-JACQUES DORAIS

McGill-Queen's University Press
Montreal & Kingston · London · Chicago

ISBN 978-0-7735-3646-3 (cloth)
ISBN 978-0-7735-4445-1 (paper)
ISBN 978-0-7735-8162-3 (ePDF)
ISBN 978-0-7735-8176-0 (ePUB)

Legal deposit first quarter 2010
Bibliothèque nationale du Québec

Printed in Canada on acid-free paper that is 100% ancient forest free (100% post-consumer recycled), processed chlorine free
Reprinted 2011
First paperback edition 2014, reprinted 2021

This book was first published with the help of a grant from the Canadian Federation for the Humanities and Social Sciences, through the Aid to Scholarly Publications Programme, using funds provided by the Social Sciences and Humanities Research Council of Canada. Funding was also provided by the Association Inuksiutiit Katimajiit.

Funded by the Government of Canada | Financé par le gouvernement du Canada | Canada | Canada Council for the Arts | Conseil des arts du Canada

We acknowledge the support of the Canada Council for the Arts.

Nous remercions le Conseil des arts du Canada de son soutien.

Library and Archives Canada Cataloguing in Publication

Dorais, Louis-Jacques, 1945–
The language of the Inuit: syntax, semantics, and society in the Arctic / Louis-Jacques Dorais.

(McGill-Queen's native and northern series; 58)
Includes bibliographical references and index.
ISBN 978-0-7735-3646-3 (cloth) – ISBN 978-0-7735-4445-1 (paper)
ISBN 978-0-7735-8162-3 (ePDF) – ISBN 978-0-7735-8176-0 (ePUB)

1. Inuktitut language. 2. Inuktitut language – Social aspects. 3. Inuit – Languages. I. Title. II. Series: McGill-Queen's native and northern series; 58

PM50.D669 2010 497'.124 C2009-904223-1

This book was typeset by Interscript in 10.5/13 Sabon.

Contents

Maps and Tables ix

Preface xi

Introduction 3

1 The Eskaleut Family of Languages 7

2 The Inuit Language 27

3 The Nunavik Dialect of Inuktitut 66

4 The Prehistory of the Inuit Language 88

5 Historical Sources and Linguistic Change 106

6 Semantics, Neology, and Oral Literature 135

7 Literacy and Formal Education 172

8 Language Contact and Bilingualism 215

9 The Current Status of the Inuit Language 235

10 Conclusion: Language and Identity in the Arctic 261

APPENDICES

1 The Possessive Noun Declension (Nunavik Inuktitut) 279

2 The Grammatical Endings of Verbs (Nunavik Inuktitut) 283

3 Categories of Lexical Affixes with Nunavik Inuktitut Examples 289

4 Inuit First and Home Languages in *Inuit nunaat* (Canada) in 2006 292

Notes 297

References 343

Index 387

Maps and Tables

MAPS

1 The Eskaleut World 8
2 The Alaskan Languages 12
3 Western Canadian Inuktun 33
4 Eastern Canadian Inuktitut 37
5 Greenlandic Kalaallisut 48
6 The Thule Migrations 99

TABLES

1 Eskaleut Languages and Dialects 28
2 Principal Phonological Characteristics of the Inuit Dialects 63
3 The Standard Canadian Inuit Syllabic and Roman Writing Systems 181

Preface

This book is the result of more than forty years of anthropological and ethnolinguistic research among the Inuit. Since 1965 I have had the opportunity to visit over thirty-five arctic communities, initially in Nunavik (Arctic Quebec) and later on in Nunatsiavut (Labrador), Nunavut, the Mackenzie region, Greenland, and northern Alaska. During my first trips to the North as a graduate student in anthropology, I managed to become reasonably fluent in Inuktitut. This oriented my research interests toward Inuit semantics, dialectology, sociolinguistics, and later on, questions of identity.

My research would have been impossible if a large number of Inuit men and women had not gracefully agreed, over the years, to share their linguistic and cultural knowledge with me. They are far too numerous to mention here, but I am especially grateful to the residents of Quaqtaq, Nunavik, who taught me their language and adopted me as their *inuuqati* (living companion) over four decades ago. My thanks go also to my colleagues and students in anthropology, linguistics, and Inuit studies, who were always willing to exchange ideas on our common interests, as well as to the various granting agencies that funded my research.

As far as the present book is concerned, I owe a special debt to Dr Lawrence D. Kaplan, head of the Alaska Native Language Center (University of Alaska Fairbanks), who read its opening chapters and offered very useful comments; to Birger Poppel, Carl Christian Olsen (head of the Greenland Language Secretariat), and Nuka Møller from Greenland, who answered my questions on language statistics; to the two anonymous reviewers who read my original manuscript and made very constructive suggestions; to Robert Lewis, whose copy-editing skills greatly improved my sometimes idiosyncratic English; and to Association Inuksiutiit Katimajiit, which supported the publication of the book. The maps were drawn by Mireille Sioui along a model originally designed by Johanne Levesque, and all translations into English are mine.

The Language of the Inuit

Introduction

Inuit, Inuvialuit, Inuktitut ... These are words with which we have learned to become familiar over the past two or three decades. We all know, for example, that people who were formerly referred to as "Eskimos" – the aboriginal population of arctic North America – should now be called Inuit ("human beings," the singular form being Inuk), their appellation in their own language.[1] But what about those among them who prefer to be called Inuvialuit (in the Mackenzie region of the Northwest Territories), Kalaallit (in Greenland), or Yupiit (in south-western Alaska)? The latter, for instance, never refer to themselves as Inuit, a word that does not even exist in their language. Together with the Inupiat of northern Alaska – who, like their Canadian counterparts, call a human being an Inuk – they do not object to being dubbed Eskimos.[2]

Answers to such questions are partly linguistic. "Eskimos" are largely defined as these arctic aboriginal groups whose ancestral language belongs to the Eskimo branch of the Eskimo-Aleut (or Eskaleut for short) linguistic family. As shall be seen in chapter 1, this family presently includes five different but closely related forms of speech, plus a sixth one, Unangax (also known as Aleut),[3] whose relationship is more distant. The most important Eskaleut language, in terms of number of speakers, is Inuit (sometimes called Inuit-Inupiaq), whose geographical range extends from north-western Alaska to eastern Greenland, through northern Canada. It comprises various groups of dialects – forms of the common language specific to well-defined regions – among which is Inuktitut ("[speaking] the Inuit way"), used in the eastern Canadian Arctic.

The present book deals with the Inuit language (in Inuktitut: *Inuit uqausingit*, "what the Inuit use for speaking"), although the other Eskaleut forms of speech shall be mentioned too when it becomes necessary to draw a larger geographical, historical, or sociological picture of the linguistic situation in the North American Arctic.

There already exist hundreds of studies on the Inuit dialects of Greenland, Canada, and Alaska, as well as on their linguistic relatives.[4] However, most of these books, reports, and articles limit themselves to a purely formal (phonological, grammatical, or lexical) approach to language phenomena. It is true that over the past twenty years, an increasing number of specialists have become interested in the ethnolinguistic and sociolinguistic aspects of language usage in the Arctic (i.e., in the relationship between Inuit culture, society, and linguistic expression), but there does not yet exist, at least in English, any up-to-date comprehensive description of the language situation in the North.[5]

Besides its intrinsic documentary value, such a description should be interesting and important for two main reasons. First, language plays a central part in defining contemporary Inuit identity. In Greenland, for instance, it is generally considered essential to speak Kalaallisut – the local dialect – in order to be considered a genuine Greenlander, while in Alaska and the western Canadian Arctic, substantial effort and money are invested in teaching the Inuit speech as a second language to youngsters, who, in most cases, no longer hear it at home. Learning about the structure, history, usage, and status of the language of the Inuit thus constitutes an original way of understanding more thoroughly the situation of our aboriginal northern fellow-citizens.

A second reason for showing interest in the Inuit speech is that it belongs to that vast number of minority languages whose very existence is increasingly threatened by linguistic globalization – that is, by the seemingly irresistible thrust of English and a few other world tongues (Krauss 2001). Even though it is still alive and well in Greenland and in several areas of the eastern Canadian Arctic, it has almost completely disappeared from the Inuvialuit (Mackenzie) region as well as, to a lesser extent, from Labrador and northern Alaska. If nothing is done, it might cease being spoken within a few generations.[6]

Yet, like all other linguistic minorities, the Inuit have something to tell us, in their own language, that cannot be conveyed in any borrowed form of speech. Each of the earth's languages offers its speakers a unique way, both grammatically and semantically, to express their worldview. This is why linguistic erosion has been likened to the disappearance of animal species: it amounts to the loss of a form of life – of thought in the case of language – that cannot be replicated once it is gone. In such a context, examining the historical development, current situation, and chief characteristics of Inuit can teach us a lot about the lifecycle and the conditions of preservation of minority languages in general. It should also accustom us to hearing messages whose form and contents are often quite at variance with mainstream discourse.[7]

The ambition of this book is to attempt such an examination of present-day knowledge about the geography, linguistic characteristics, history, semantics, sociology, and anthropology of the language of the Inuit, from Alaska to Canada and Greenland. The book is divided into ten chapters that deal with three main topics: the spatial localization of the language and its linguistic structure (chapters 1–3); its history and meaning (chapters 4–6); and its contemporary situation (chapters 7–10). More specifically, chapter 1 describes the geographical distribution of the various Eskaleut languages throughout the North American Arctic – and the north-easternmost tip of Russia – as well as their internal subdivisions. Chapters 2 and 3 delve in a more detailed way into the comparative phonology, grammar, and lexicon of the Inuit dialects, one of which, Nunavik (a form of Inuktitut), is the object of an in-depth description. Chapters 4 and 5 deal, respectively, with the prehistory and historical evolution of the Inuit language, while chapter 6 describes various aspects of its semantics. Finally, the last four chapters discuss topics of a sociolinguistic and anthropological nature as they apply to contemporary Inuit: literacy and formal education (chapter 7), language contact and bilingualism (chapter 8), the current demographic and administrative status of the language (chapter 9), and language and identity in the Arctic (chapter 10).

The principal danger with the type of approach here elected is its potential tendency toward being too encyclopaedic. The book consists more of a synthetic panorama of various points of view on the Inuit language than of an analytical process aiming at the confirmation of a well-defined hypothesis. It is, above all, a monograph describing the geographical, linguistic, historical, social, and cultural universe within which an aboriginal minority form of speech generates meaningful discourses.

That universe, however, is not amorphous. Its various components are linked together in a structured fashion. They influence each other in ways that both reflect and strengthen the historical and social conditions of speakers occupying a specific location in space, at a definite moment in time. For example, the nature of present-day Inuktitut-English bilingualism in the eastern Canadian Arctic cannot be explained if it is not understood as a reflection and agent of the economic, political, and cultural hegemony of southern, non-Inuit – and often global – forces that struggle to predominate over the northern aboriginal population, against frequently successful local efforts to gain some measure of social autonomy.

This is why, at the end of each chapter of the book, various aspects of the language situation in the Arctic are positioned and briefly discussed within a broader context. In this way, readers will get a better understanding of how the language of the Inuit belongs to a structured whole, whose social, cultural, and linguistic dimensions work together at enabling us to listen to – or sometimes at hiding – an eminently important speech form, that of the aboriginal people of the North American Arctic.

1

The Eskaleut Family of Languages

As everybody knows, Inuit are the northernmost population of North America. They reside principally north of the tree-line – that is, in those tundra areas where trees cannot grow due to extreme temperature and soil conditions.[1] Their habitat extends from Bering Strait in the west to the Strait of Denmark (between Greenland and Iceland) in the east.[2] This habitat is primarily limited to the seashore (map 1). In Alaska it stretches along the coasts of Norton Sound, Bering Strait, Chukchi Sea, and the Arctic Ocean. In Canada it includes the Mackenzie Delta; the shores of Beaufort Sea, Coronation Gulf, and the Arctic Straits; Hudson Bay and Hudson Strait; the northern coast of Labrador; and the Arctic Archipelago (Banks, Victoria, Baffin, Cornwallis, Ellesmere, and other islands). Finally, in Greenland, Inuit live along the north-western, western, and south-eastern coasts of the world's largest island. Only a few scattered groups dwell inland: in northern Alaska (i.e., watersheds of the Kobuk, Noatak, and Colville Rivers; Anaktuvuk Pass) and west of Hudson Bay (i.e., in the village of Qamani'tuaq/Baker Lake).

There are more than 6,500 kilometres between the westernmost Inuit community (Little Diomede Island, in the middle of Bering Strait), located more to the west than the Hawaiian Islands, and the easternmost Inuit village (Ittoqqortoormiit – or Scoresbysund – on the east coast of Greenland), at the same longitude as Reykjavik in Iceland. In a similar way, from north to south, 3,000 kilometres separate the Thule (or Avannarsuaq) District (north-western Greenland), the world's northernmost permanently inhabited area (at lat. 78°N), from the Labrador town of Happy Valley,[3] located (at lat. 53°15'N) more to the south than Edmonton, Copenhagen, or Moscow. This shows the immensity of the territory occupied by the Inuit people.

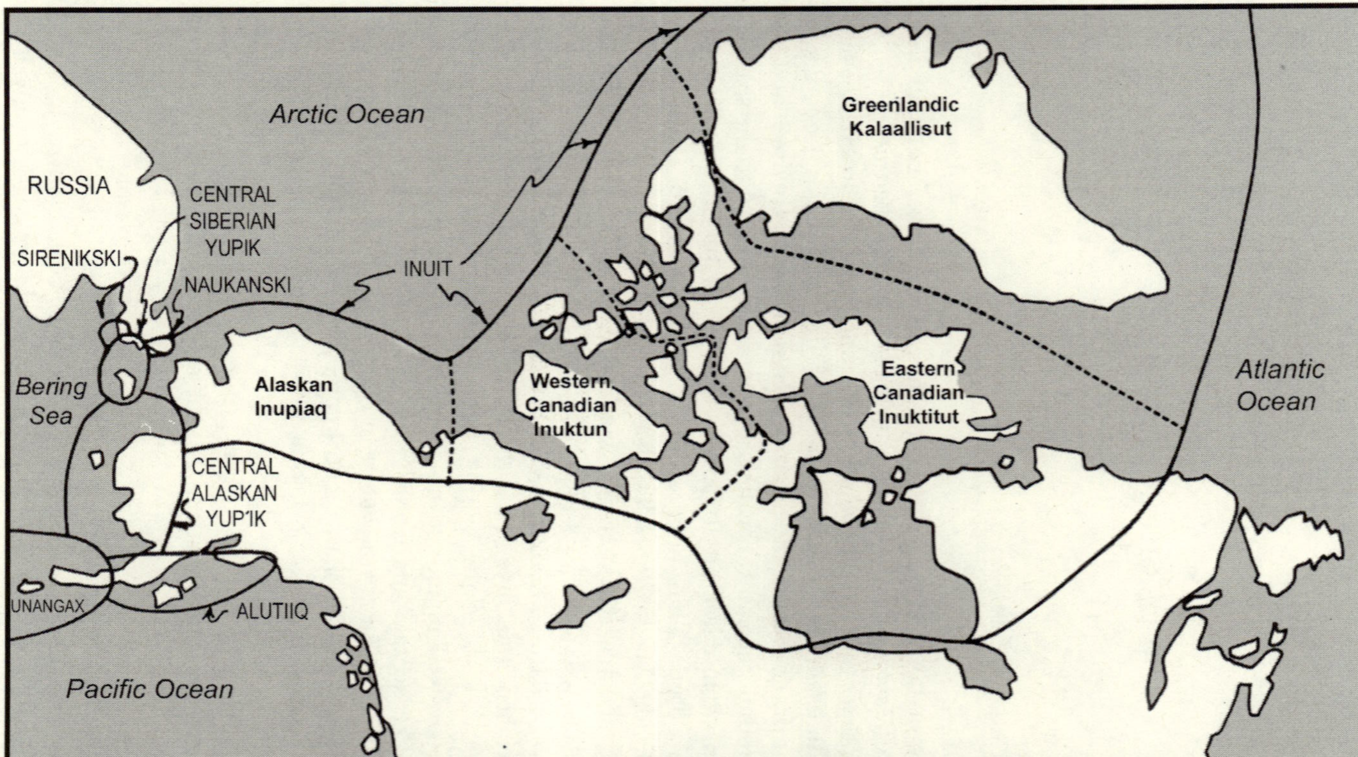

Map 1 The Eskimo-Aleut World

THE ESKIMO-ALEUT AND THEIR LANGUAGES

The Inuit, however, are not alone in the North American Arctic. As mentioned in the Introduction, south-western Alaska – and also north-easternmost Russia – are home to their close linguistic and cultural cousins, the Yupiit (Alaska) and Yupiget (Russia), as well as to more distant relatives, the Unangan (or Unangas). All these aboriginal nations, who constitute the Eskimo-Aleut people,[4] seemingly share partly common ancestors who spoke the same tongue in a more or less distant past.

Because they stem from a common source, the languages of present-day Eskimo-Aleut belong to one language group, the Eskaleut (also Eskimo-Aleut) family, and they share the same basic linguistic structure: lexemes (i.e., words) are formed by adding one or more post-bases (affixes and endings) to a word-base. This type of language, whose words must often be translated by a full English sentence (e.g., Inuktitut *illu-liu-qati-gi-laaq-tara* [house-build-mate-to have as-future-I ... him/her], "I shall have him/her as mate for building a house"), is called polysynthetic. Most North American aboriginal languages are polysynthetic, although Inuit also possesses so-called agglutinative features: each element of the word retains a specific, distinguishable meaning. In that kind of language, words are constructed as needed, which means that several thousand terms can exist. For example, in a computerized analysis of the Inuit transcription of deliberations in the Legislative Assembly of Nunavut, the computer specialist Benoit Farley (personal communication, 20 July 2004) elicited a total of 408,000 different words, only 1,000 of which occurred more than 100 times.

Up to 1997 the Eskaleut family comprised a total of seven languages. It was divided into two branches and four sub-branches:

FAMILY	BRANCH	SUB-BRANCH	LANGUAGE
Eskaleut	Aleut	Aleut	Unangax[5]
	Eskimo	Inuit-Inupiaq	Inuit
		Yupik	Central Alaskan Yup'ik
			Alutiiq
			Central Siberian Yupik
			Naukanski
		Sirenikski	Sirenikski[6]

In view of the fact that the Eskaleut family includes the speech forms used among the Yupiit, Yupiget, and Unangan, its geographical range extends beyond that of the Inuit language properly speaking. There are some 8,500 kilometres between Bering Island in the Commander Islands (which belong to Russia), the westernmost Unangan settlement, and Ittoqqortoormiit in east Greenland. The northernmost Eskimo-Aleut people, as already mentioned, are the Thule Inuit of Greenland; the southernmost ones are the Unangas of Atka Island, Alaska, who live at lat. 52°15'N, the latitude of Birmingham, England, and Saskatoon, Saskatchewan, one degree more to the south than the Inuit community of Happy Valley, Labrador.

The Eskaleut languages are spoken in four countries: Russia, the United States, Canada, and Greenland (map 1; see also Krauss 1995). In Russia, Unangax is heard in the Commander Islands, off the east coast of Kamchatka, while Central Siberian Yupik, Naukanski, and up to 1997, Sirenikski are (or were) in use in the easternmost part of Chukotka, a vast peninsula on the Russian side of Bering Strait. Central Siberian Yupik is also spoken on St Lawrence Island, off the coast of Chukotka, although it belongs to the American state of Alaska, while most Unangan speakers live in the Aleutian Islands, Alaska. Coastal Alaska is also home to the Alutiiq (south), Central Alaskan Yup'ik (southwest), and Inuit (northwest and north) languages. In Canada the Inuit language is spoken in the Inuvialuit area of the Northwest Territories, in the Kitikmeot, Kivalliq, and Baffin – or Qikiqtaaluk – regions of Nunavut, in Nunavik (Arctic Quebec), and in the Nunatsiavut region of northern Labrador (province of Newfoundland and Labrador). Inuit is also heard on the west and southeast coasts of Greenland (or Kalaallit Nunaat), a self-governing territory attached to the Kingdom of Denmark.

In the next sections, the geographical distribution and dialectal subdivisions of the Eskaleut languages are described in more detail, along with information on the status of Unangax and of the non-Inuit Eskimo forms of speech.

THE UNANGAX LANGUAGE

Unangax is spoken in the Aleutian, Pribilof, and Commander Islands (barely so in the latter), which extend from the Alaska Peninsula (south-western Alaska) to the Kamchatka Peninsula (Russia) and which mark the boundary between the Bering Sea and the

Pacific Ocean.[7] It is also in use in the westernmost part of the Alaska Peninsula. Aboriginal Unangan (or Aleuts) are not considered "Eskimos" properly speaking, but their language and traditional culture are related to those of the Yupiit and Inuit. Like them, for instance, the Unangan were – and still are, in some measure – sea-mammal hunters who used kayaks and harpoons and lived in semi-subterranean dwellings. It is highly probable that the Unangan and Inuit share the same distant ancestors.

Most Unangan (according to Krauss 1997, they totalled 2,200 people in the mid-1990s) are American citizens (the Aleutian and Pribilof Islands belong to Alaska), but some 200 live on the Commander Islands, which are part of Russia. Their ancestors were brought there by Russian fur hunters in 1826 (Russia ruled Alaska between 1741 and 1867), although a prehistoric population appears to have lived on the Commanders at some time (Fortescue 1998). During the 1790s a few hundred Unangan were also forced to move to the Pribilof Islands in the Bering Sea, where their descendants are still found. It is believed that when Russians first arrived in Alaska in 1741, there were about 16,000 Unangan but that 126 years later, in 1867, when the territory was sold to the United States, only 1,600 of them had survived the epidemics, wars, and bad treatment that had followed the arrival of Europeans (Morgan 1979).

Despite these troublesome relations with their conquerors, Unangan have been deeply influenced by Russian culture. Most of them bear Russian surnames, belong to the Orthodox Christian church, and still practise some old Russian customs (at Christmas, for instance). Until recently, a few elderly people even spoke some Russian, although this language – like English later on – never totally replaced aboriginal speech.

The Unangax language is subdivided into two dialects: Western and Eastern (map 2). Western Unangan is spoken on Atka and, historically, in the Commander Islands, while the Eastern dialect is found in a dozen settlements located in the eastern part of the Aleutians, at the tip of Alaska Peninsula, and on the Pribilof Islands. Prior to the Second World War the island of Attu, the westernmost of the Aleutians, harboured an aboriginal Unangan population (who spoke a subdialect of the Western form of speech), but in 1942 the island was invaded by the Japanese and its residents taken to Japan as prisoners. After the war, in 1945, Attuans were liberated, but for security reasons the American government did not

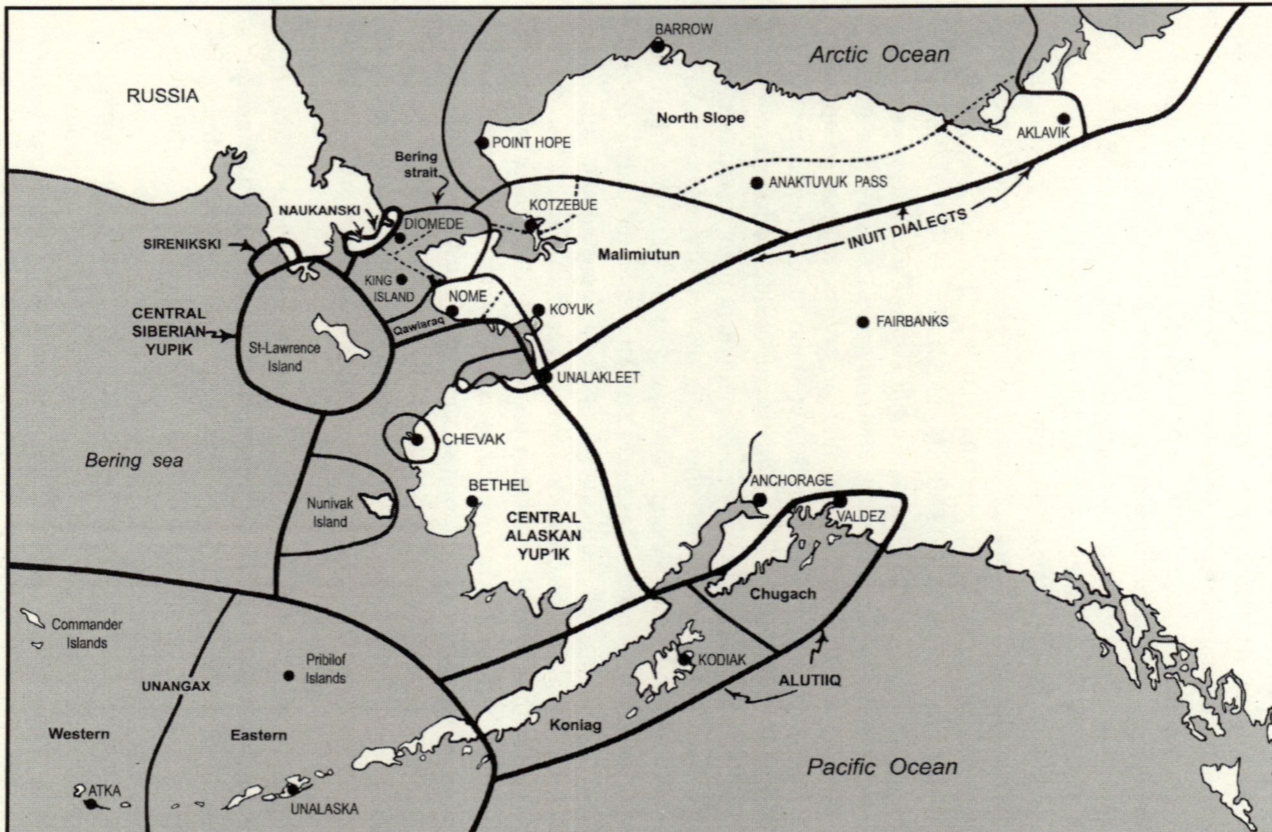

Map 2 The Alaskan Languages

allow them to go back home. They were instead resettled on Atka, on the eastern Aleutians, and in mainland Alaska.[8]

Unangax has been written for over 180 years. In 1826 the Russian Orthodox missionary Ioann Veniaminov, together with the native chief Ivan Pan'kov, had already adapted the Cyrillic (Russian) alphabet to its phonology and translated a catechism into the language. During the next forty years, thanks to the Orthodox Church and church schools, a good part of the Unangan population became literate in their own language. This literacy continued for some time after the sale of Alaska to the United States, but at the end of the nineteenth century, the area underwent tremendous social and economic changes, which entailed, among other things, increased contacts with the English language and unilingual English education. This explains why, from the 1890s on, when most young people stopped being taught to read and write their language, literacy and oral proficiency in Unangax started to decline. The only individuals who persevered in the use of written Unangax were those actively involved in one way or another with the Russian Orthodox Church. Several of them also spoke some Russian.

Things changed in the late 1960s and early 1970s, with the development of aboriginal bilingual education. Moses Dirks, an Atkan native, and Knut Bergsland, a Norwegian linguist, developed an orthography in the current (Latin) alphabet as well as school materials: a grammar, a dictionary, and several booklets. In 1972 a bilingual curriculum started being taught in the schools of Atka (Western Unangax) and Unalaska (Eastern Unangax).

In the Commander Islands (Copper Island and Bering Island), which remained Russian after 1867, the Cyrillic alphabet continued to be in use, but Unangax was not taught in the local schools, and nothing was ever published in the language. In 1931 some Soviet aboriginal teachers-in-training wrote an Unangax primer for school use, but due to the small size of the population (fewer than 500 people), it was never printed. As a matter of fact, under the influence of non-native Russian immigrants to the Commander Islands, a majority of local Unangan lost their language. When visiting the area in 1963, the Russian linguist Georgii Menovshchikov noticed that only 10% of the population over twenty years of age (and nobody under that age) still spoke Unangax. Assuming that young people comprised some 40% of the total population, this would leave us with only 6% of

Soviet Unangax speakers in 1963 (about thirty persons). Twenty-five years later, however, the language had not yet completely disappeared. When Evgeni Golovko – a young colleague of Menovshchikov – conducted fieldwork on Copper Island in 1988, he found that a dozen elderly people were using a highly Russianized form of Unangax, one that tended to add aboriginal suffixes and endings to Russian words (Golovko and Vakhtin 1990). Five of these individuals were still alive in the mid-1990s (Krauss 1997).

The language has also suffered in Alaska. In 2000 it was spoken by only 6.5% of the aboriginal population (150 speakers among some 2,300 American Unangan).[9] According to the Alaskan linguist Michael Krauss, during the late 1970s Unangax had been viable (i.e., not yet doomed to extinction) in only one community, Atka, where all children still spoke it (Krauss 1980). In the Eastern Unangan area, the youngest speakers were in their teens (they would now be in their late forties or early fifties), living in one village, Nikolski. As mentioned above, Unangax is now taught – as part of a bilingual curriculum – in at least two locations, Atka and Unalaska, but it is doubtful that it will survive into the next generation.

Despite notable differences, Unangax and Eskimo phonology share many similarities. Like the Inuit language (see chapter 2), Unangan possesses three vowels (*i*, *u*, *a*), which may be either short or long (*ii*, *uu*, *aa*). It also includes all Inuit consonants (*t*, *k*, *q*, *w* [for *v*], *m*, etc.), with the exception of *p* and *&* (voiceless *l*). The four positions of articulation of these consonants (bilabial, apical/alveolar, velar, and uvular) are identical to those of Eskimo.

The situation is not the same with Unangax grammar, which is quite different from its Eskimo counterpart. The system of grammatical endings, for instance, is much simpler. It seems that over the centuries, Unangax has developed a simplified version of the common Proto-Eskaleut morphological system. The most striking syntactical difference is the use of separate words to express grammatical notions such as tense. For example, in sentence 1 below, the lexeme *haqal* expresses the past tense. In Inuit, this notion would be rendered by an intra-word affix such as *-lauq-* or *-rataaq-*.

Despite such major divergences, similarities may be found between Unangax and the Eskimo languages. In Eastern and Western Unangax, the plural is, respectively, marked by *-n* and by *-s*, two forms close to the Eskimo plural marker *-t*. If one looks attentively at the following sentences, some common morphemes do appear:

1 *haqal axtakux* ("he/she has come")
2 *Piitrax qakux tayarum nagan qanguqaa* ("the man went to Peter who was eating")
3 *ugigan ngaan tunuxtakuu tutanarula*x ("she did not hear that her husband was talking to her")

In sentence 1, the final *-kux* in *axtakux* (he/she comes) expresses the third person singular of the indicative mood. It is very close to the equivalent Inuit morphemes: *-puq*, *-tuq*, *-kuq*, or *-quq*. In sentence 2, the final *-um* in *tayarum* ("the man") is the relative noun marker (Eskimo *-um* or *-up*). As in Yup'ik or Inuit, it is used to express that *tayaq* ("man")[10] is the subject of a double-person (transitive) verb: *qanguqaa* ("he/she comes to him/her"; the ending *-qaa*, "he/she does it to him/her," is similar to Inuktitut *-paa*, *-jaa*, or *-taa*).

Finally, as far as vocabulary is concerned, the leading specialist of Unangax, Knut Bergsland (1994), sees many similarities between the lexicons of Unangax and Yup'ik.[11] Common roots would be particularly numerous within the categories of body-part names, pronouns, and demonstratives. In the examples above, a few word-bases are clearly recognizable to Inuit speakers: *qa-* ("come"; Inuit *qai-*) in *qanguqaa* ("he/she comes to him") (sentence 2); and *ugi-* ("husband"; Inuit *ui-*) in *ugigan* ("her husband") (sentence 3). Other cognates (similar words) are *silan* or *slax* ("weather"; Inuit *sila*) and *iqyaq* ("kayak"; Inuit *qajaq*).

THE NON-INUIT ESKIMO LANGUAGES

Besides Inuit-Inupiaq, the Eskimo branch of the Eskaleut family includes two sub-branches: Yupik and Sirenikski. Whereas the former still comprises four different languages, the latter disappeared in January 1997 when its last speaker, a woman named Weyi, died at the age of eighty (Krauss 2006, 116; for an analysis of the decline of Sirenikski, see Krupnik 1991).

Distribution and Dialects

Speakers of the Yupik languages are known under various names: Yupiget in Russia and on Alaska's St Lawrence Island; Yupiit, Yupiat, or Cupiit (pronounced "Chupiit") in south-western Alaska; and Sugpiat in south-central Alaska. All these words mean the same thing, "genuine human beings," the word-bases *yug-*, *cug-*, and *sug-* being the local equivalents of the base *inuk-*. For simplicity's sake, all these people may be referred to as Yupiit, the word used by a majority of them. Two Yupik languages are exclusively spoken in Alaska, one in Russia, and another one in both Russia and Alaska. Sirenikski was spoken in Russia (see maps 1 and 2).[12]

The southernmost Yupik language is Alutiiq, or Pacific Gulf Yupik, spoken by the Sugpiat, who live on the southern (Pacific Ocean) coast of Alaska.[13] The total Yupiit population for this area reaches about 3,500 people (Krauss 2007), although the actual number of individuals now speaking Alutiiq is much smaller (see below). These "Pacific Eskimos" often call themselves "Aleut" (hence the name of their tongue), although their language is completely different from that of the Unangan (it is nearer to Central Alaskan Yup'ik). Confusion originates from the Russian period, when several Unangan (Aleuts) from the Aleutian Islands were transferred to southern Alaska. Like the Unangan, the natives of the Pacific Gulf have strongly felt Russian influence. Many of them are so-called creoles (i.e., descendants of mixed Yupiit-Russian families).

Alutiiq is subdivided into two dialects. Chugach is spoken around Prince William Sound and southern Kenai Peninsula, east and south of the city of Anchorage (which stands outside Yupiit territory, although hosting a large population of aboriginal migrants), while the Koniag dialect is used on Kodiak Island (where a few thousand non-native individuals also live) and on Alaska Peninsula, northeast of Unangan territory. In a couple of locations (such as the town of Cordova), Chugach speakers are in contact with Alaskan Indians using Dene languages.

Northwest of the Alutiiq area, in the valley of the Nushagak River as well as in the plains of the lower Kuskokwim and Yukon Rivers, and also on Nunivak Island, live the Central Yupiit, the most populous Eskimo group in Alaska (25,000 individuals in 2000, residing in some sixty-five villages). They speak Central Alaskan Yup'ik. This language is in daily use in most locations, although much less so in the largest settlement, Bethel, the principal service centre of the Yupiit territory. That the Central Yupiit had fewer contacts with early settlers (Russians and nineteenth-century Americans) than did the Unangan and Pacific Gulf Yupiit may explain why their language is still relatively strong – although, as we shall see below, it has been sharply declining since the 1970s.

Central Alaskan Yup'ik is subdivided into four dialects. The most important among them (spoken in fifty-six of sixty-five communities) is called General Central Yup'ik and is heard in the major part of the Yupiit area. The people of Mekoryuk (Miqqurjuk) on Nunivak Island have their own speech form (the Nunivak dialect), as do those living in Hooper Bay and Chevak (the Hooper Bay/Chevak – or HBC – dialect), two small coastal communities northeast of Nunivak. These two dialects share some similarities with Alutiiq, although they clearly belong to Central Alaskan Yup'ik.

The fourth dialect, called Unaliq, has a rather erratic distribution. At the end of the nineteenth century, it was in use all around Norton Sound, the large body of water south of Seward Peninsula. However, due to the southward migration of Inuit, at the beginning of the twentieth century many former Unaliq-speaking Yupiit villages became occupied by speakers of Inuit-Inupiaq. The result is that today the Unaliq dialect is heard in only six villages, somewhat isolated one from another: Kotlik, Stebbins, and St Michael, on the south shore of Norton Sound; Elim and Golovin, on the north shore; and Unalakleet (Ungalalliq), on the east shore. Unalakleet is a unique linguistic crossroads, at the junction of Yupiit and Inuit territories, where two aboriginal languages (comprising a total of three dialects) are spoken: Central Alaskan Yup'ik (Unaliq dialect) and Inuit-Inupiaq (Qawiaraq and Malimiutun dialects). This linguistic diversity may be linked to the fact that Unalakleet is considered by its inhabitants to be the "oldest Eskimo community in the world." Actually, it lies a short distance south of Cape Denbigh (which is clearly visible from the village), the site of one of the earliest prehistoric Inuit cultures (dating back to some 4,500 years ago).

West of Norton Sound, in the Bering Sea, stands St Lawrence Island. It belongs to the United States, although the nearest land is south-eastern Chukotka, in Russia. Most of the 1,400 St Lawrence Islanders (Krauss 2007) speak Central Siberian Yupik. This language is also ancestral to some three-quarters of the 1,650 Russian Yupiget (or "Asiatic Eskimos") who lived in Chukotka in the late 1990s (Vakhtin 1998).[14] In spite of political borders, the aboriginal populations of St Lawrence Island (villages of Gambell and Savoonga) and of southern Chukotka (towns of Provideniya, Novoe Chaplino, and Sireniki) constitute one social and cultural unit. They speak the same language (differences are minimal between the two areas), share a common traditional culture, and are related through kinship. Several St Lawrence Islanders still have brothers, sisters, uncles, aunts, or cousins living in Chukotka. Visits were permitted till 1948, but afterward both Russia (then the USSR) and the United States forbade them. It was only forty years later, in June 1988, that contacts resumed, and they have not stopped since.

Two other Eskimo languages are native to Chukotka: Naukanski and Sirenikski. Naukanski is a Yupik language, used by the Nevuqaq people (the Nevuqarmiit), who used to live in Naukan, at the easternmost tip of Siberia (East Cape). When their village was closed in 1957, they were transferred to other settlements in the area: Nunyamo, Uelen, and Lavrentiya. Of some 450 Nevuqarmiit, about 60 still speak their language (Jacobson 2004, vi). As far as mutual intelligibility is concerned, Naukanski stands midway between Central Siberian Yupik and Central Alaskan Yup'ik. It seems that when the latter was still spoken on the north shore of Norton Sound (southern Seward Peninsula), all the way to Bering Strait, there existed an east-west linguistic continuum that linked Central Alaskan Yup'ik with Naukanski (across Bering Strait) and Central Siberian Yupik (the south-western neighbour of Naukanski). It is quite possible that in the prehistoric past, the ancestors of present-day St Lawrence Islanders and Central Siberian Yupiget migrated from Seward Peninsula to north-eastern Chukotka, to be followed, a few generations later, by the ancestors of the Nevuqarmiit, who forced them to move farther south, to their present location.

The third Asiatic Eskimo language, Sirenikski, is now extinct. In 1990 it was still spoken by two elderly ladies who lived at Sireniki, but both of them passed away during the mid-1990s. This language was so different from Yupik and Inuit-Inupiaq that it is considered a separate sub-branch of the Eskimo languages. For instance, Sirenikski often has intervocalic consonants that do not exist elsewhere, as in *ater̲eseq* ("one") (Central Siberian Yupik *ataasiq*; Inuit *atausiq*) or *ac̲eq* ("blood") (Central Siberian Yupik *aak*; Inuit *auk*). Some Sirenikski words have no Eskimo equivalent. Such is the case with *asa* ("land"). In all other Eskimo languages, the word for land is *nuna*. Linguists speculate that Sirenikski might be the last remnant of a first wave of Eskimo migration toward Chukotka, which would have occurred before the Central Yupiget/Nevuqarmiit migration.

The Yupiget are not the sole aboriginal nation of Chukotka Peninsula. Besides the 1,650 Asiatic Eskimos, one finds some

11,300 Chukchi, whose presence there is probably more ancient than that of the Yupiit. The two populations live in the same communities, but their languages are completely different (the Chukchi language belongs to the Chukotko-Kamchadal – or Palaeo-Asiatic – family). Both speech forms, however, have borrowed several words from each other. The aboriginal presence in Chukotka is overshadowed by a population of about 60,000 Russian migrants. This population used to be much higher (it reached some 100,000 people around 1990), but after the demise of the Soviet Union, thousands of Russian settlers left Chukotka and other northern areas to move back to western Russia.

History and Current Status

In the 1840s and 1850s the Russian Orthodox missionary Ioann Veniaminov adapted Unangax orthography – in the Cyrillic alphabet – to Central Alaskan Yup'ik and to Alutiiq. Not until the end of the century, however, were religious texts published in these languages. During the 1890s the newly arrived Protestant and Catholic missionaries also started publishing in Central Alaskan Yup'ik, but instead of Cyrillic they used the Latin alphabet. Their orthography, however, was not taught in schools (where English was the unique teaching medium), and it was far from being standardized.[15]

On St Lawrence Island one missionary booklet in Central Siberian Yupik was issued in 1910 (in a non-standardized Latin orthography), but only fifty years later, in the 1960s, did a missionary-linguist from the Summer Institute of Linguistics devise a modern orthography and publish some religious material.[16] The first schools were established at the beginning of the twentieth century, but as elsewhere in Alaska, teaching was conducted solely in English.

Things were different on the Russian side. Siberian Chukotka is the only area in the Arctic not to have ever been visited by missionaries. At the arrival of the first representatives of the Soviet power, in the 1920s, shamanism was still the predominant form of religion. Because Russian officials considered religious practice to be backward, there was no question of Christian missionaries being allowed to set foot in the area.

In the early 1930s, however, the Russian government established schools in the Chukotkan Yupiget and Chukchi settlements. The official policy of the time encouraged local cultural development throughout the Soviet Union. One way to achieve this was to provide unwritten languages with writing systems and to teach them in school. This explains why, in 1932, a Russian teacher, E.P. Orlova, with the help of two Yupiget students, A. Bychkov and B. Leity, devised an orthography in the Latin alphabet for Central Siberian Yupik.[17] A schoolbook was published, but only one copy reached Chukotka. The linguist Georgii Menovshchikov, who was then teaching at the primary level, recalled later how he and his colleagues had to recopy this unique specimen by hand in order to use it in the classroom.

Fortunately, in the following years, a few more Yupik readers were published, and this time they reached Chukotkan schools. In 1937 the Latin script was replaced by the Cyrillic alphabet to facilitate the learning of Russian. This alphabet has since been standardized and is still in use today.

Between 1932 and 2004 ninety-three Yupik books have been published in Chukotka (Vakhtin 2005), including a primer titled АНХАК (*Anxaq*, "The Little Spark"), issued in 1981 by Lyudmila Ajnana and G.A. Nakazik, two local native teachers. It was reprinted in 1987 and is in current use in the three Chukotkan schools where Yupik is taught from kindergarten to grade 3. More recently, Ajnana (2003) published a small Yupik-Russian pictorial dictionary.

In Alaska it was only in the late 1960s and early 1970s, with the advent of bilingual education in the United States, that an effort was made to standardize Yupik orthographies. A few native and non-native educators devised standard writing systems for Central Alaskan Yup'ik, Central Siberian Yupik, and Alutiiq, and they struggled to have these languages taught in Alaskan schools. In 1972 a State of Alaska law obliged any school with at least fifteen children whose mother tongue was not English to provide education in these children's first language. It also established the Alaska Native Language Center (ANLC)[18] at the University of Alaska Fairbanks, whose mandate was to study the state's aboriginal speech forms and devise school materials for each of them. As Yupik languages were concerned, the original team of teachers and linguists was soon joined by new colleagues. Over the past thirty-five years, these specialists have published over 300 readers, school grammars, dictionaries, booklets, and other materials.

The main problem with Yupik orthography was that in comparison with Inuit-Inupiaq, Yupik languages possess so many phonemes[19] that it was often difficult to write them in a simple way. For example, Alutiiq, Central Alaskan Yup'ik, and Central Siberian Yupik establish distinctions between voiced and voiceless consonants (some of them labialized).[20] After discussions with native speakers, different solutions were found for symbolizing these distinctions. Generally speaking, the letters of the standard alphabet were put into use, although a few special graphemes (e.g., the apostrophe, which represents a geminate consonant and some other things in Yup'ik) had to be employed.

In spite of bilingual education – which appeared quite late in the linguistic history of Alaska – all Yupik languages have suffered from their contacts with Russian and English, some of them more than the others. At the turn of the twenty-first century, Central Alaskan Yup'ik was spoken by some 10,400 persons, a little less than 42% of the total Central Alaskan Yupiit population of 25,000 people (Krauss 2007).[21] The language had been in sharp decline since the 1970s, when its speakers accounted for 82% of the total (Krauss 1980). Outside the smaller communities, few children still have Yup'ik as their mother tongue.

Alutiiq is in much worse shape. In 2000 it was known by only 200 persons, none of them children, among a population of some 3,500 Pacific Gulf Yupiit (5.5%). As concerns Central Siberian Yupik, according to Michael Krauss (2007), it was still used by more than 71% (1,000 speakers) of the 1,400 St Lawrence Islanders, although according to other data (Koonooka 2005) several families now prefer to speak English at home. On the Russian mainland, only about 200 persons out of 1,200 (17%) still used Central Siberian Yupik in the late 1990s (Vakhtin 1998), while, as mentioned above, Naukanski had around 60 speakers (13% of the 450 Nevuqarmiit) at the turn of the twenty-first century, none of them under forty years of age.

Linguistic Characteristics

In comparison with Unangax, Yupik languages definitely sound familiar to Inuit ears. Yupik grammar is very similar to that of the Inuit dialects. If one disregards phonological variations, the morphology and syntax of both Yupik and Inuit may be considered basically similar. Like the latter, all Yupik languages possess three grammatical numbers – singular, dual, and plural – with the same endings: *-k* (dual) and *-t* (plural). Nouns can be possessed ("my ..., your ..., his/her ...") or non-possessed. Possessive endings somewhat resemble their Inuit equivalents, although some phonological peculiarities of the Yupik languages – such as the occasional prevalence of "strong" consonants (e.g., *q* instead of *r* and *c* [*ts*] rather than *s*) and the occurrence of the voiceless velar fricative *x* and of the fourth vowel *e* – may disguise their basic similarity. Look at these Central Alaskan Yup'ik (CAY) examples, compared with their South Baffin Inuktitut counterparts:

	CAY	SOUTH BAFFIN
my kayak	*qajaqa*	*qajara*
my kayaks	*qajanka*	*qajakka*
your (one of you) two lands	*nunaxken*	*nunakkik*
your (many of you) lands	*nunaci*	*nunasi*

In relation to their grammatical function within the sentence, all Yupik nouns may either occur in the basic (absolutive) form (e.g., *nuna*, "land") or be followed by one of six nominal-function endings. It should be noticed, by comparison, that Inuit possesses one supplementary ending because in Yupik languages, the modalis and ablative endings have merged into one. Here are the non-possessed singular noun endings in Central Siberian Yupik (CSY), Central Alaskan Yup'ik (CAY) and, for comparison's sake, South Baffin Inuktitut:

	CSY	CAY	SOUTH BAFFIN	
basic	*nuna*	*nuna*	*nuna*	"the land"
relative	*nunam*	*nunam*	*nunaup*	"the land's"
modalis	*nunameng*	*nunamek*	*nunamik*	"the land [direct object]"
ablative	*nunameng*	*nunamek*	*nunamit*	"from the land"
locative	*nunami*	*nunami*	*nunami*	"on the land"
allative	*nunamun*	*nunamun*	*nunamut*	"to the land"
translative	*nunakun*	*nunakun*	*nunakkut*	"by land"
simulative	*nunatun*	*nunatun*	*nunatut*	"like the land"

Yupik verbs may be followed by single-person (intransitive) or double-person (transitive) endings,[22] exactly as in the Inuit language (e.g., Central Siberian Yupik *kuuvuq*, "it spilled," and *kuuvaa*, "he/she spilled it"). These endings also convey the mood of the event expressed by the verb (i.e., the way this event is spoken about). These moods are more or less the same as in Inuit (indicative, interrogative, imperative/optative, causative/perfective, etc.), although their forms are often relatively different. Here are a few CAY examples:

	CAY	SOUTH BAFFIN
"he/she doesn't know"	*na&uuq*	*naluvuq*
"he/she doesn't know it"	*na&ua*	*naluvaa*
"he/she answers"	*kiuguq*	*kiuvuq*
"he/she answers him/her"	*kiugaa*	*kiuvaa*
"who are you?"	*kituusit?*	*kinauvit?*
"when I saw it"	*tange&xamku*	*takugakku*

Apart from nouns and verbs, the Yupik languages also possess – like Inuit – localizers (e.g., *maani*, "here"), demonstratives (e.g., *una*, "this one"), and "small words" (e.g., *aa*, "yes").

Many Yupik words are similar or quasi-similar to their Inuit equivalents. The proportion of bases and affixes shared by the two speech forms probably hovers around 50% to 60% if purely phonological differences are ignored. This often produces a peculiar situation, whereby a Yupik text looks, at the same time, both familiar and strange to Inuit readers. See, for instance, this short excerpt from the *Anxaq* Central Siberian Yupik primer, which tells about the New Year celebration in Moscow:[23]

> 31 dekabyrmi unugmi naruxlequq utuqa uksiuk.
> Moskvami kiyaxtuk kilbiagik. Takuk Kremlim kurantakak.
> (Ajnana and Nakazik 1987, 86)

Inuit speakers can understand the first line easily. In Eastern Canadian Inuktitut, it would read like this:

> 31 Decembermi unnungmi naaliqquq utuqaq ukiuq
> "On December 31, at night, the old year ends"

The second line, however, is much less intelligible. It tells about someone who lives (*kiyaxtuk*) in Moscow (*Moskvami*), but the rest of the line does not make sense to a nonspeaker of Yupik. In a general way, although most animal names, body-parts terminology, kinship terms, and several other sectors of the vocabulary are quite similar in both Inuit and the Yupik languages, some basic words such as "see" (Inuit *taku*- or *tautuk*-; Siberian Yupik *esrar*-; Yup'ik and Alutiiq *tanger*-) and "hear" (Inuit *tusaq*-; Siberian Yupik *nagaquq*-; Yup'ik and Alutiiq *niite*-) remain, nevertheless, completely different.

Some differences, however, are more apparent than real. Yupik languages have preserved several features that were formerly common to all Eskimo tongues but no longer exist in Inuit. For instance, the original Eskimo intervocalic consonant (most generally *g* or *r*) is still present within many Yupiit lexemes. With this in mind, it becomes easy, by mentally removing this consonant, to recognize a lot of familiar words. Here are a few Central Siberian Yupik (CSY) and Central Alaskan Yup'ik (CAY) examples, compared with their Kivalliq (western Hudson Bay) Inuktitut equivalents:

	CSY	CAY	KIVALLIQ
"human (shaman's word)"	*taru*	*taru*	*tau*
"sea gull"	*naruja*	*narujaq*	*nauja(q)*
"husband"	*ugi*	*ui*	*ui*
"crow-berry"	*pagunraq*	*paunraq*	*paunraq*

Some other Yupik words appear to have lost their initial vowel. This is the case, for instance, with CSY and CAY *meq* ("water"; Inuit *imiq*). Here again, an informed listener or reader can easily recognize many seemingly strange lexemes.

Finally, an interesting feature of the Alaskan Yupik languages (and also of Unangax) is the high number of words they have borrowed from Russian. See, for instance, Central Alaskan Yup'ik *kassaq* ("a white person"; from the Russian for "Cossack") and *saalaq* ("fat, shortening"; from Russian *salo*). But in Siberian Yupik, contrary to what could be expected, Russian loan-words are few and far apart. This is due to the fact that in the late nineteenth century, Euro-American material culture was introduced to Chukotka and St Lawrence Island by American whalers and traders rather than by Russians, who did not occupy the Bering Strait area till the early 1920s. In Central Siberian Yupik, for instance, the words for "butter," "cow," and "soap" were borrowed from English (*para*, *kaawa*, and *suupa*), while in Central Alaskan Yup'ik, Russian loan-words (*maslaq*, *kuluvak*, and *miilaq*) are found.

THE INUIT LANGUAGE

The Inuit – or Inuit-Inupiaq as it is also known – language forms a sub-branch by itself within the Eskimo branch of the Eskaleut family. It is currently spoken by some 100,775 people, among an Inuit (i.e., non-Yupiit and non-Unangan) population of about 133,000 persons. Although spread over a few thousand kilometres, from Little Diomede Island in the middle of Bering Strait to the east coast of Greenland, the Inuit speech clearly consists of only one language, the most important Eskaleut speech form both numerically and in terms of its geographic extension. If it were not for their bilingualism, Inupiat speakers living in Unalakleet, western Alaska, would have less difficulty understanding Greenlandic visitors than deciphering the speech of their Central Alaskan Yup'ik next-door neighbours.

Due to its dispersal, the Inuit language is subdivided into a multiplicity of dialects – sixteen of them according to most counts. These are described in detail in the next chapter. Let us simply mention here that each of them belongs to one of four groups of dialects (map 1): (1) Alaskan Inupiaq (northern and north-western Alaska), (2) Western Canadian Inuktun (Mackenzie Coast and the Kitikmeot region of Nunavut), (3) Eastern Canadian Inuktitut (Nunavik, Nunatsiavut, and the Kivalliq and Baffin regions of Nunavut), and (4) Greenlandic Kalaallisut (Greenland).

CONCLUSION

The Eskaleut language family, to which belong all languages spoken by the Inuit, Yupiit, Yupiget, and Unangan of the North American Arctic – and of north-easternmost Russia – has fared differently over the past couple centuries, according to the regions where it was spoken. Let us summarize data about the number and percentage of its speakers at the turn of the twenty-first century:

LANGUAGE	TOTAL POPULATION[24]		SPEAKERS (NO.)	SPEAKERS (%)
Unangax	(Alaska)	2,300	150	6.5
	(Russia)	200	5	2.5
Alutiiq		3,500	200	5.5
Central Alaskan Yup'ik		25,000	10,400	41.5

Central Siberian Yupik	(Russia)	1,200	200	17
	(Alaska)	1,400	1,000	71
Naukanski		450	60	13
Inuit		133,000	100,775	75.5
(Sirenikski)		0	0	(extinct in 1997)
TOTAL		167,050	112,790	67.5

These differences in the local percentages of Eskimo-Aleut individuals who have preserved their aboriginal language attest to the influence of historical and social factors on linguistic phenomena. In regions like Alaska (except for St Lawrence Island and, to a lesser extent, the Yup'ik area) and, as we shall see later in the book, western Canada and Labrador, where sustained Euro-American contact has endured for at least a century and/or was particularly authoritarian (Chukotka), the aboriginal language is now spoken by a minority of the native population. School education in particular, when it has been delivered in English or Russian for many decades, has contributed to erasing Eskaleut by persuading its speakers that using their mother tongue is not really advantageous and legitimate. Historical and social circumstances, however, were not always as brutal as they have been in Alaska and Chukotka. The following chapters, focusing on the Inuit language, show that in areas such as Greenland and, in a lesser way, the eastern Canadian Arctic, education and administrative policies were beneficial to aboriginal forms of speech or, when noxious, were implemented too recently to have destroyed the language completely.

2

The Inuit Language

North and east of where Unangax and the Yupik languages are spoken, a series of dialects are found that extend from the islands of Bering Strait and the westernmost tip of Seward Peninsula, in Alaska, to the Island of Greenland, in the North Atlantic Ocean. Despite their differences, these linguistic forms are much more intelligible to one another's speakers than they are to Yupik speakers. This is why they may be considered dialects belonging to one language, Inuit, rather than as separate languages (table 1). This means that all Inuit speakers, whether they live in northern Alaska, Canada, or Greenland, share a common means of communication and, with some adjustments, can understand each other.

With some 100,775 speakers at the turn of the twenty-first century, Inuit-Inupiaq accounts for 89% of the 112,790 users of the Eskaleut languages. This makes it, by far, the most important form of speech in the North American Arctic. In this chapter, its dialectal subdivisions are described as well as some of its linguistic characteristics.[1] Data on semantics, writing systems, sociolinguistics, and number of speakers per dialect shall be found in subsequent chapters.

THE INUIT DIALECTS

Most specialists (e.g., Fortescue 1983; Woodbury 1984a; Kaplan 1990; Dorais 1996, 2003) agree on dividing the Inuit language into four groups of dialects (map 1): Alaskan Inupiaq, Western Canadian Inuktun, Eastern Canadian Inuktitut, and Greenlandic Kalaallisut. Each of these groups is itself subdivided into subgroupings, for a total of sixteen different dialects.[2]

Table 1
Eskaleut languages and dialects

Branch	*Sub-branch*	*Language*	*Group*	*Subgroup*	*Dialect*	*Subdialect*
Aleut		Unangax			Western	
					Eastern	
Eskimo	Sirenikski	Sirenikski*				
	Yupik	Central Siberian Yupik				
		Naukanski				
		Alutiiq			Chugach	
					Koniag	
		Central Alaskan Yup'ik			General Central	
					Nunivak	
					Hooper Bay/Chevak	
					Unaliq	
	Inuit	Inuit	Alaskan Inupiaq	Seward	Bering Strait	Diomede
						Wales
						King Island
					Qawiaraq	Teller
						Fish River
				N. Alaskan Iñupiaq	Malimiutun	Kobuk
						Kotzebue
					North Slope (NS)	Common NS
						Point Barrow
						Anaktuvuk
						Uummarmiut
			Western Canadian Inuktun		Siglitun	
					Inuinnaqtun	Holman
						Kugluktuk
						Bathurst
						Cambridge Bay
					Natsilingmiutut	Natsilik
						Arviligjuaq
						Utkuhiksalik
			Eastern Canadian Inuktitut	Kivalliq	Kivalliq	Qairnirmiut
						Hauniqturmiut
						Paallirmiut
						Ahiarmiut
					Aivilik	Southampton
						Rankin Inlet
				Baffin	North Baffin	Iglulingmiut

Table 1
Eskaleut languages and dialects (*Continued*)

Branch	*Sub-branch*	*Language*	*Group*	*Subgroup*	*Dialect*	*Subdialect*
						Tununirmiut
					South Baffin	Southeast
						Southwest
				Quebec-Labrador	Nunavik	Itivimiut
						Tarramiut
					Nunatsiavut	N. Labrador
						Rigolet
			Greenlandic Kalaallisut	Greenlandic	W. Greenland	Central
						Southern
						Northern
						Upernavik
					E. Greenland	Ammassalik
						Sermilik
				Polar	Thule	

* Extinct since 1997.

Alaskan Inupiaq

In Alaska all non-Yupik Eskimo forms of speech are called Inupiaq or Iñupiaq (according to the way the word is actually pronounced).[3] This linguistic grouping includes four dialects (map 2): Bering Strait, Qawiaraq, Malimiutun, and North Slope.

The Bering Strait dialect is divided into three subdialects: Diomede, Wales, and King Island. The first, whose main characteristic is the preservation of the fourth vowel *e* (still heard in the Yupik languages; see chapter 1) is spoken on Little Diomede Island, in the middle of Bering Strait. Until the late 1940s, it was also used by the native population of Big Diomede Island, which belongs to Russia. These people were removed to the Siberian mainland after the Second World War for security reasons. They preserved their language for some time, but it was not transmitted to the young, who now speak Central Siberian Yupik or Russian.

The Wales subdialect is heard on the western Seward Peninsula mainland (in the villages of Wales, Shishmaref, and Brevig Mission), while the King Island variety was formerly spoken on King Island, a small speck of land at the entrance of Bering Strait, south of Wales. In the early 1960s the entire King Island population moved to

Nome – Seward Peninsula's main administrative centre – in order to live nearer to hospitals and other amenities of modern life and because the American federal government had decided to close the island's school in 1959. Some people still visit King Island during summer months, but their principal residence is now in Nome, where their language can still be heard (as well as in Anchorage and other places of more recent resettlement).

The Qawiaraq dialect is spoken on southern Seward Peninsula and eastern Norton Sound, in the Fish River, Shaktoolik, and Unalakleet areas. Some Qawiaraq speakers might also live in Nome and Koyuk. This speech form is divided into two subdialects: Teller (found in the villages of Teller, Shaktoolik, and perhaps Unalakleet) and Fish River (spoken at White Mountain and Golovin).[4] Some linguists contend that Qawiaraq and Bering Strait constitute only one dialect, but several local specialists prefer to classify them as two separate entities belonging to the same Seward Peninsula subgroup within Inupiaq (see Kaplan 1990).

Malimiutun and North Slope form another subgroup, North Alaskan Iñupiaq, which is characterized by the palatalization of apical consonants[5] after an etymological *i* (i.e., an *i* that does not stem from the fourth vowel *e*). The Malimiutun dialect can be heard north and west of Seward Peninsula. It includes at least two subdialects: Kobuk, in the Kobuk River valley and the village of Selawik, and Kotzebue, in the communities of Kotzebue and Noatak. Over the past 180 years, many Malimiutun speakers from both subdialects have migrated southward to Buckland, Koyuk, Shaktoolik, and Unalakleet.

The North Slope dialect is heard in northern Alaska on the coast of the Arctic Ocean, from Kivalina and Point Hope in the west to the Canadian border in the east. It is also used in the inland village of Anaktuvuk Pass. In Alaskan territory, it comprises three subdialects: common North Slope (a mix of the various speech forms formerly used in the area); Point Barrow, the original language of the Barrow Inuit (now spoken by only a few elders); and Anaktuvuk Pass, or Nunamiut, a subdialect that stands somewhat midway between the North Slope and Malimiutun dialects and that sometimes replaces *s* with *h* (e.g., *h̲avik*, "knife," rather than *s̲avik*).

At the beginning of the twentieth century, many inland families from the upper reaches of the Colville (just north of present-day Anaktuvuk) and Noatak (in the Malimiut area) river basins moved to the Mackenzie Delta in the Canadian Northwest Territories, where they became successful muskrat trappers. Their descendants now live in the communities of Aklavik (Ak&aarvik) and Inuvik (Inuuvik), which are also inhabited by Dene First Nation people. Those who still speak the language have preserved their Nunamiut North Slope dialect, but it has been influenced by Malimiutun and by Siglitun (the original speech form of the area). Mackenzie Delta Iñupiaq – or Uummarmiutun, as it is locally known – may thus be considered a fourth subdivision of the North Slope dialect.

Some linguists consider Malimiutun to be a subdialect of North Slope Iñupiaq, although differences between these two forms of speech are well marked. For example, the phonology of Malimiutun is less assimilative than that of North Slope, with the result that the allowed types of consonant clusters (groups of two consecutive consonants) are more numerous in the former than in the latter dialect. Malimiutun – and the Seward Peninsula dialects as well – distinguish between groupings that start with a stop consonant and those that begin with a nonstop, whereas in other Inuit dialects (including North Slope) the manner of the first member of a cluster (i.e., whether it must be a voiced or voiceless stop or continuant and/or nasal)[6] is always determined by the cluster's second consonant. Compare, for instance, the following Malimiutun and coastal North Slope words:

MALIMIUTUN	NORTH SLOPE	
ikniq	*igniq/ingniq*	"fire"
pangniq	*pagniq/pangniq*	"bull caribou"
qipmiq	*qimmiq*	"dog"
qapvik	*qavvik*	"wolverine"
nipliqsuq	*nivliqsuq*	"makes a sound"
uvluq	*uvluq*	"day"

It can be noticed that Malimiutun distinguishes between *kn* and *ngn* (e.g., *ikniq*; *pangniq*) or *pl* and *vl* (e.g., *nipliqsuq*; *uvluq*), whereas North Slope does not. What happens here is that Malimiutun, along with Bering Strait and Qawiaraq, preserves voiceless stops (*k*, *p*, *q*, *t*)[7] when they are etymological (i.e., when they belong to the original word-base), whereas North Slope always adapts them to the following consonant. For example, the word meaning "he/she makes a sound" is made out of the base *nipi* ("sound"), to which has been added the post-base and ending *-liqsuq* ("makes something"). In both Malimiutun and North Slope the final vowel of *nipi* disappears. In Malimiutun this combination of *nip(i)* and *-liqsuq* gives *nipliqsuq*, without any consonantal change. In the North Slope dialect, however, where regressive assimilation is more advanced than elsewhere in Alaska, the *p* of *nip(i)* becomes a voiced continuant (*v*) because it adapts to the following consonant (*l*), which is a voiced lateral (lateral consonants are a form of continuants), and the result is *nivliqsuq*.

There thus exist marked distinctions among the Alaskan Inupiaq dialects, whose distribution may be summarized as follows:

Seward Peninsula Inupiaq:	Bering Strait dialect
	Qawiaraq dialect
North Alaskan Iñupiaq:	Malimiutun dialect
	North Slope dialect (including Uummarmiutun)

Western Canadian Inuktun

The Western Canadian Inuktun group includes three dialects spoken in the western and central Canadian Arctic (map 3; see also Sontag 2007): Siglitun, Inuinnaqtun, and Natsilingmiutut. A fourth speech form, Uummarmiutun, is actually a subdialect of North Slope Alaskan Iñupiaq, and it has been mentioned as such in the preceding section. Another dialect, Kivalliq, used on the west coast of Hudson Bay (in the Kivalliq region of Nunavut), is often regarded as belonging to Western Canadian Inuktun. However, because several of its own speakers state that their language is closer to the Aivilik and North Baffin speech forms than to either Natsilingmiutut or Inuinnaqtun, and for other practical reasons, it is described later on, together with the Eastern Canadian Inuktitut dialects.[8]

Siglitun – or Inuvialuktun, as it is often called these days – is found in the Inuvialuit region (Nunaqput) of the Northwest Territories: Mackenzie Coast and Delta area, as well as Banks Island, in the villages of Tuktoyaktuk (Tuktuujaaqtuuq), Paulatuk (Paulatuuq), Sachs Harbour (Ikaasuk), and Inuvik (Inuuvik). In this last location, it is in contact with Uummarmiutun and the Dene Indian languages. Siglitun has no subdialects. Formerly spoken by a numerous population, which was diminished by epidemics at the beginning of the twentieth century, it was later thought that it had

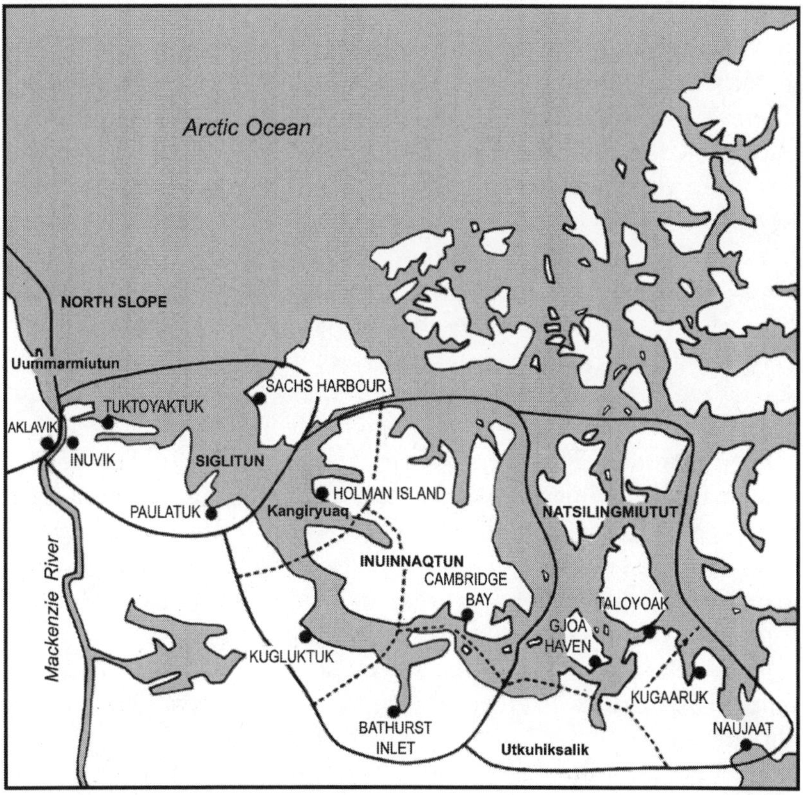

Map 3 Western Canadian Inuktun

completely disappeared and been replaced by Alaskan Inupiaq. But this assumption was far from being true. Many contemporary Mackenzie Coast Inuit descend from the original local population, and their language is still essentially the same as the one recorded by the French missionary Émile Petitot when he visited the area in the 1870s (Petitot 1876).

Inuinnaqtun is spoken by Inuit formerly known as "Copper Eskimos" on Victoria Island and the Canadian Arctic Coast, in the communities of Holman (Ulukhaktok/Ulukhaqtuuq), Kugluktuk (Qurluqtuq), Bathurst Inlet (Umingmaktuuq), and Cambridge Bay (Iqaluktuuttiaq). It comprises four subdialects – Kangiryuarmiutun (Holman), Kugluktuk, Bathurst, and Cambridge – although the differences between them are minimal.

Natsilingmiutut (or Netsilik Inuit) is spoken on the Boothia Peninsula, in Gjoa Haven (Uqsuqtuuq), and Taloyoak (Talurjuat),[9] as well as in Kugaaruk (Kuugaarjuk) and Naujaat (Repulse Bay). There are three subdialects: Natsilik (Boothia Peninsula), Arviligjuaq (Kugaaruk and, as a consequence of migration, Repulse Bay), and Utkuhiksalik. This last is spoken by people who formerly lived on Back River and Garry Lake (Hanningajuq), an inland area to the northwest of Baker Lake. In 1956 there was a famine at Hanningajuq, and its residents were transported to Rankin Inlet and Whale Cove, on Hudson Bay. Back River people resettled in Gjoa Haven and Baker Lake during the late 1960s. The Utkuhiksalik subdialect is closer to Inuinnaqtun than other Natsilingmiutut speech forms. The language of the Hanningajuq people is even considered by some Baker Lake Inuit to be quite similar to the one spoken in Bathurst Inlet. However, according to anthropologist Jean Briggs, who spent a couple of years among the Utkuhiksalingmiut in the mid-1960s and is now working on an Utkuhiksalik dictionary, Back River people assert that the Hanningajurmiut speak the same subdialect as they do (Dyck and Briggs 2005).

The three dialects of Western Canadian Inuktun show some marked phonological differences among themselves. One striking characteristic of Inuinnaqtun and Natsilingmiutut (but not of Siglitun) is that in both dialects, *h* occurs in positions where most Eastern Canadian Inuktitut, Inupiaq, and Greenlandic speech forms have *s*.[10] The phoneme *h* can appear as an initial or intervocalic consonant, and it can follow *k* or *q*.[11] The equivalent of Eastern Inuktitut *ts*, however, is either *tt* (Inuinnaqtun) or *ts/tt* (Natsilingmiutut), and *ps* occurs as *ff* in Inuinnaqtun and as *ph* or *ps* in Natsilingmiutut.[12] Here are a few examples:

SIGLITUN	INUINNAQTUN	NATSILINGMIUTUT	
savik	*havik*	*havik*	"knife"
isuk	*ihuk*	*ihuk*	"end"
pitiksivialuk	*pitikhik*	*pitikhik*	"bow"
aniqsaaq-	*aniqhaak-*	*aniqhaaq-*	"to breathe"
natchiq	*nattiq*	*natsiq/nattiq*	"seal"
pipsi	*piffi*	*piphi/pipsi*	"dried fish"

In Inuinnaqtun, *h* (or *tt* in etymological *t&* groupings) also occurs in place of *&*.[13] Compare, for instance:

SIGLITUN	INUINNAQTUN	NATSILINGMIUTUT	
I&uaqtuq	*ihuaqtuq*	*i&uaqtuq*	"is right, correct"
ak&unaaq	*akhunaaq*	*ak&unaaq*	"rope"
aq&a	*aqha*	*aq&a*	"draft of cold air"
nuu&&unga	*nuuttunga*	*nuu&&unga*	"while I moved"

Like Alaskan Inupiaq (but not Point Barrow), Siglitun distinguishes between word-final nasal and non-nasal consonants. This is not the case in Natsilingmiutut, while in Inuinnaqtun, although speakers often turn a final *-t* into *–n*,[14] this has no grammatical or semantic effect. By contrast, in Siglitun (and in Inupiaq), a functional distinction is made between a final *-t* (e.g., *qimmit*, "dogs") and a final *-n* (e.g., *qimmin*, "your dog"). Moreover, a word-final -*p* and -*k* can undergo nasalization, as in *iglum* ("the house's") and *tupaaramiung* ("because he/she wakes him/her").

Finally, Natsilingmiutut is the only Canadian dialect to make a distinction between the phonemes *j* and *J*.[15] Its speakers distinguish, for instance, between *qajaq* ("kayak") and *iJi* ("eye"), or *qajjak* ("two kayaks"; pronounced *qayyak*), *iJJak* ("two eyes"), *ugJuk* ("bearded seal"), and *arJa* ("ash"). There also exists, as in Alaskan Inupiaq, a voiceless *J*, often written *sr*, which is found in some clusters starting with *k* or *q* (e.g., *utkuhiksraq*,[16] "soapstone," and *qaqsrauq*, "red-throated loon"). Natsilingmiutut thus appears much more conservative – it preserves phonemic distinctions that have disappeared elsewhere in Canada – than other dialects. This conservatism is compounded by the fact that like Malimiutun and Seward Peninsula Inupiaq, it usually does not practise regressive consonant assimilation, thus allowing for maximum variation in the types of consonant clusters. See for instance:

SIGLITUN	INUINNAQTUN	NATSILINGMIUTUT	
tupirni	*tupirni*	*tupiqni*	"in your tent"
qimmiq	*qimmiq*	*qipmiq*	"dog"
ingniq	*ingniq*	*ikniq*	"fire"

In Siglitun and Inuinnaqtun the original stop consonant is assimilated in manner to the following one, which is not the case in Natsilingmiutut. This and other differences between the Western Canadian Inuktun forms of speech are so strong that each dialect stands by itself, subgroupings being non-relevant.

Eastern Canadian Inuktitut

The Eastern Canadian Inuktitut group of dialects includes six closely related speech forms, found in the Kivalliq and Baffin regions of Nunavut, as well as in Nunavik (Arctic Quebec) and Nunatsiavut (northern Labrador). These are: Kivalliq, Aivilik, North Baffin, South Baffin, Nunavik, and Nunatsiavut (map 4; see also Sontag 2007).[17] On phonological grounds, Inuktitut may be divided into three subgroups:

Kivalliq subgroup:	Kivalliq dialect
	Aivilik dialect
Baffin subgroup:	North Baffin dialect
	South Baffin dialect
Quebec-Labrador subgroup:	Nunavik dialect
	Nunatsiavut dialect

KIVALLIQ AND AIVILIK

The Kivalliq dialect was formerly spoken in the coastal and inland areas west of Hudson Bay by Inuit groups collectively known as "Caribou Eskimos." Nowadays, only one inland community is still in existence, Baker Lake (Qamanittuaq). Other inland groups moved to the coastal villages of Arviat (formerly Eskimo Point), Rankin Inlet (Kangiq&iniq), Whale Cove (Tikirarjuaq), and to a lesser extent, Chesterfield Inlet (Igluligaarjuk) during the 1950s and 1960s. Kivalliq may be divided into four subdialects: Qairnirmiut, Hauniqturmiut, Paallirmiut, and Ahiarmiut. A fifth one, Harvaqturmiut, disappeared about sixty years ago.[18]

Qairnirmiut Inuit used to live on the land between Baker Lake, Rankin Inlet, and Chesterfield. They now reside in the village of Baker Lake and, to a much lesser extent, in those of Rankin and Chesterfield. Hauniqturmiut generally dwelt on the coast between Rankin Inlet and Whale Cove. They have now settled in these two communities. In both locations, they are in contact with Utkuhiksalik Natsilingmiutut speakers, removed from the Garry Lake (Hanningajuq) area in 1956. It should be noted that in Rankin Inlet, Hauniqturmiut and Hanningajurmiut are much less numerous than the Aivilingmiut, who started moving to that region at the beginning of the twentieth century.

The Paallirmiut lived on the coast of southern Kivalliq, as well as on the barren grounds inland from Arviat. Ahiarmiut were found

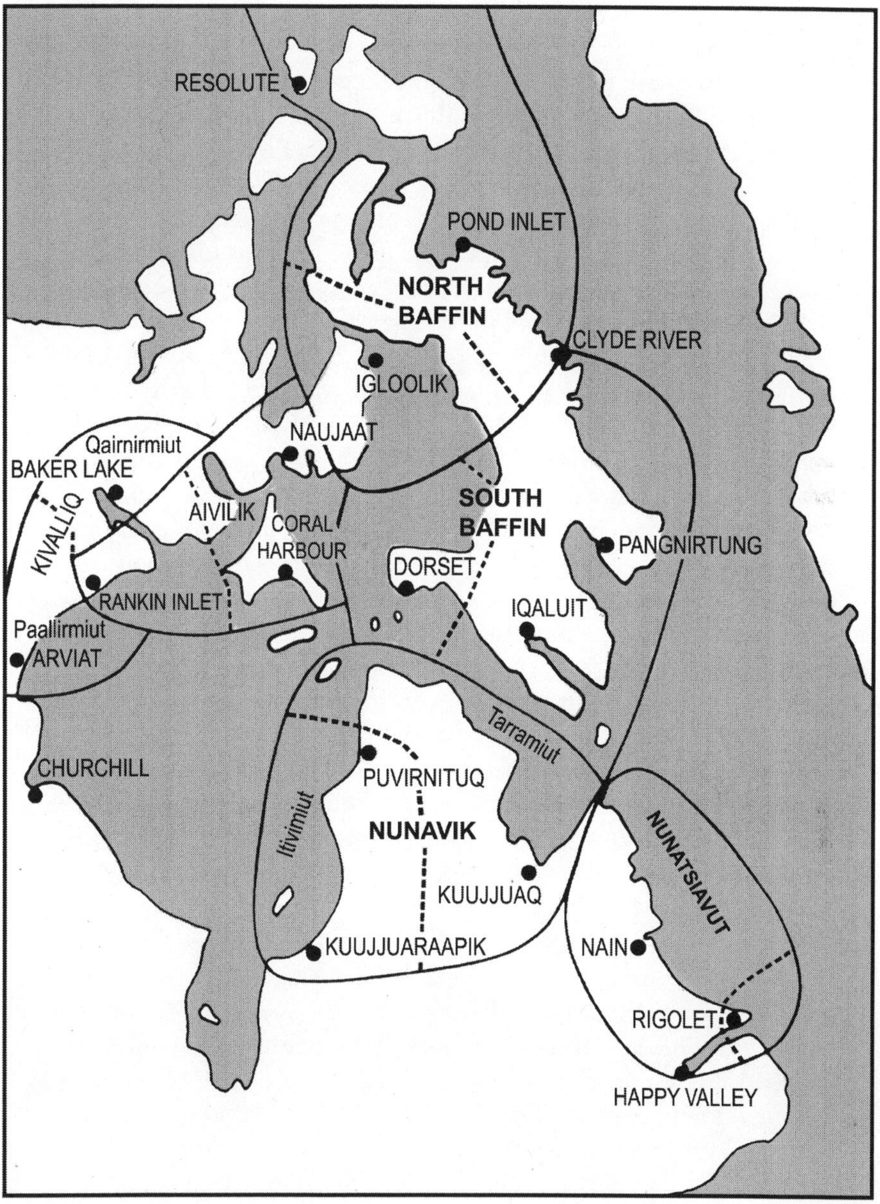

Map 4 Eastern Canadian Inuktitut

farther west, near Lake Ennadai. Living near the tree-line, both groups had contacts with Cree and Dene Chipewyan Indians. These people now dwell in the coastal village of Arviat.

The Aivilik dialect was originally spoken in the Repulse Bay and Wager Inlet areas, to the southeast of Melville Peninsula. In the first quarter of the twentieth century, with the arrival of many Natsilik families from Arviligjuaq (around present-day Kugaaruk), most Aivilingmiut left for Southampton Island (Sagliq) or migrated down the coast to Chesterfield and Rankin Inlet, where they now constitute the majority of the population.

Not long after Aivilingmiut had settled on Southampton Island (at Coral Harbour), Arctic Quebec Inuit from around Port Burwell (Killiniq) were brought there by the Hudson's Bay Company. The local form of Aivilik was thus influenced in some way by the Nunavik dialect. It is interesting to note that the original population of Southampton was a very isolated group, the Sallirmiut, who used only bone and stone to make their knife blades and harpoon heads at a time when all other Inuit had wide access to metal. It has been hypothesized that the Sallirmiut could have descended from a prehistoric population that would have survived on Southampton and other Hudson Bay islands. Whatever the truth may be, they became extinct – because of disease – in 1904, and unfortunately their language was never properly recorded.

Due to the various influences to which it has been subjected, Aivilik may be regarded as being divided into two subdialects: Southampton (spoken in Coral Harbour and Naujaat/Repulse Bay) and Rankin (in Rankin Inlet and Chesterfield).

Linguists and other specialists do not always agree on their classification of the Kivalliq and Aivilik dialects. As already mentioned, Kivalliq is often regarded as belonging to the Western Canadian Inuktun group. True enough, it shares many phonological and grammatical characteristics with western dialects: a degree of regressive consonant assimilation almost equal to that of Siglitun;[19] the occurrence of *h* (as in Inuinnaqtun and Natsilingmiutut) in place of *s*; and different sets of rules for dual and plural noun endings, based on the final consonant of the word-base (see the section below on phonological variation). Moreover, Kivalliq seems to share many more affixes with Inuinnaqtun and Natsilingmiutut than with Eastern Inuktitut dialects (Fortescue 1983).

Nonetheless, speakers of Kivalliq insist that they have less difficulty understanding Rankin Inlet, Igloolik, or even Iqaluit people than Cambridge Bay or Kugluktuk Inuit. As a matter of fact, when their word-bases are compared, more similarities are found between Kivalliq and Aivilik than between the former dialect and Inuinnaqtun. For instance, 92% of animal names and 82% of geographical terminology (words for "lake," "island," etc.) are shared with Aivilik, whereas only 83% of the former and 59% of the latter are common to both Kivalliq and Inuinnaqtun (Dorais 1990, 84). And it is also true that in at least one Kivalliq subdialect, Qairnirmiut, *h* started replacing *s* only about fifty years ago (Dorais 1988).

The classification of the Kivalliq dialect is therefore far from being settled, and linguists are not the only ones to argue about the exact ethnolinguistic position of Kivalliq Inuit. Anthropologists too are divided (see Csonka 1995). On the basis of archaeological and ethnographic evidence, some of them think that the ancestors of present-day Kivallirmiut came from the Arctic Coast area (from somewhere around Bathurst Inlet), where they belonged to the Inuinnait. But some other specialists think that the first Kivalliq Inuit migrated south along the western shore of Hudson Bay and that their original home was in the Melville Peninsula area (where Igloolik, Hall Beach, and Naujaat now stand). The Kivallirmiut would thus be more related to the Aivilik and Iglulik people than to western Inuit.

On the basis of linguistic data, it is tempting to split things a bit. On the one hand, the Qairnirmiut subdialect and, possibly, Hauniqturmiut too can be considered conservative forms of Aivilik. Many Qairnirmiut speakers now replace *s* with *h*, as is done in other Kivalliq subdialects, but this is a recent phenomenon. A couple of generations ago, Qairnirmiut always had *s* in all positions, just like Aivilik.

On the other hand, southern Kivalliq subdialects (Paallirmiut and Ahiarmiut) seem to have always had *h* instead of *s*, a truly Western Inuktun characteristic. Moreover, the Ahiarmiut system of consonant groupings is particularly conservative. Its very low degree of regressive consonant assimilation is similar in many ways to what is heard among Natsilingmiutut speakers. Would it not be possible, then, for the Kivalliq Inuit and their dialect to have had two different origins? Qairnirmiut (and perhaps Hauniqturmiut) could have come from the Aivilik area and then migrated inland to Baker Lake, whereas the ancestors of the Paallirmiut and Ahiarmiut might have crossed the barren grounds, from the Arctic Coast to the southern reaches of the Kivalliq region. Qairnirmiut would, then, be a basically Eastern Inuktitut speech form, whereas Paallirmiut and Ahiarmiut would have a Western Inuktun origin.

Due to mutual contacts during the nineteenth and early twentieth centuries, Paallirmiut (and maybe Ahiarmiut) vocabulary (word-bases more than affixes) would have felt some eastern influence, whereas Qairnirmiut (and possibly Hauniqturmiut) phonology would have been somewhat westernized. If this explanation stands true, Kivalliq would then be a genuine intermediate dialect (or even a cluster of two dialects), with both eastern and western origins. Nowadays, however, as the principal linguistic and cultural influences come from the east (the syllabic writing system, Iqaluit-produced radio and television programming, etc.), it appears more practical to consider it an Eastern Inuktitut speech form.

The classification problem of Aivilik is much simpler. This dialect is often considered a North Baffin subdialect. True enough, most grammatical endings, word-bases, and affixes used in Rankin Inlet or Coral Harbour are similar to those heard in Igloolik and Pond Inlet. And in a not-too-distant past (about seventy-five years ago), the degree of regressive consonant assimilation of the North Baffin dialect was equal to that of modern Aivilik.

There exist, however, some significant differences between the two speech forms. Aivilik has preserved many consonant groupings starting with a bilabial (*b*, *v*, *m*) that have disappeared from modern North Baffin. Moreover, like North Alaskan Iñupiaq, North Baffin assibilates (i.e., changes *t* to *s* after an etymological *i*, which is not the case in Aivilik). In order, then, to outline these – and other – important dissimilarities between the two speech forms, it seems preferable to consider Aivilik an independent dialect.

NORTH AND SOUTH BAFFIN

The North Baffin and South Baffin dialects are spoken in the Baffin (or Qikiqtaaluk) region of Nunavut (map 4). Because they share numerous similarities, they may be regarded as belonging to a common Baffin subgroup within Eastern Canadian Inuktitut.[20]

North Baffin Inuktitut is divided into two subdialects: Iglulingmiut and Tununirmiut. The former is spoken in the communities of Igloolik (Iglulik) and Hall Beach (Sanirajaq), on the Melville Peninsula to the north of Hudson Bay. Tununirmiut is principally found on northern Baffin Island, in the communities of Pond Inlet (Mittimatalik), Clyde River (Kangiqtugaapik), and Arctic Bay (Ikpiarjuk). In the 1940s about twenty Pond Inlet individuals moved to Taloyoak (then known as Spence Bay), in the Natsilik area, where some traces of their original dialect can still be heard. And in 1953 several Tununirmiut and Arctic Quebec families were incited by the Canadian federal government to relocate in the newly established villages of Resolute (Qausuittuq) and Grise Fiord (Aujuittuq), in the High Arctic. There, the North Baffin and Nunavik dialects mixed together, generating a form of speech whose phonology is closer to that of Nunavik but whose vocabulary is basically North Baffin (Dorais 1976c).[21]

The South Baffin dialect is found on the southern half of Baffin Island. It includes two subdialects: Southeast Baffin and Southwest Baffin. Southeast Baffin Inuktitut is spoken on the east coast of Baffin Island, in the communities of Clyde River (besides Tununirmiut), Qikiqtarjuaq (Broughton Island), Pangnirtung (Panniqtuuq), Iqaluit (formerly Frobisher Bay), and Kimmirut. Iqaluit, the capital of Nunavut, is a mixed community where, besides South Baffin, other dialects are heard (North Baffin, Aivilik, Nunavik, etc.) and where almost half the population are non-Inuit. Southwest Baffin Inuktitut is spoken in the community of Cape Dorset (Kinngait), on southwest Baffin Island's Foxe Peninsula. In the 1940s several Cape Dorset families moved to Taloyoak, where their dialect was still spoken two decades ago. They were replaced, in a sense, by Southeast Baffin speakers, who migrated from Kimmirut to Dorset during the 1950s and 1960s.

The principal difference between the two South Baffin subdialects lies in the way the phoneme *&* has been replaced by other consonants. It has merged with *t* in Southeast Baffin and with *s* in the Southwest speech form. Southeast Baffin also tends to substitute *s* for *t* after an etymological *i* (as is done in North Baffin), which is not the case in the Southwest subdialect. Examples may be found below.

South Baffin speakers often consider Southeast Baffin to be a dialect of its own rather than a subdialect belonging to a more encompassing South Baffin speech form. As seen from a pan-Inuit perspective, however, Southeast and Southwest (Cape Dorset) Baffin share more characteristics among each other than they do with North Baffin, even if a few elements of Southeast Baffin phonology (the assibilation – or palatalization – of *t* into *s*, for instance) may remind one of the North Baffin speech form.

North and South Baffin are decidedly eastern Inuit dialects. By comparison with western speech forms, their phonology is innovative. Their system of consonant clusters, in particular, shows a higher degree of regressive assimilation than the Aivilik or Kivalliq systems. In contrast with these dialects, clusters starting with a bilabial consonant (bilC) have become geminates (i.e., groups of two similar consonants)[22] in North and South Baffin. Compare, for instance:

AIVILIK	NORTH BAFFIN	SOUTH BAFFIN	
tusarapta	*tusaratta*	*tusaratta*	"when we heard"
takugapku	*takugakku*	*takugakku*	"when I saw it"
apqut(i)	*aqqut(i)*	*aqqut(i)*	"road"
taipsumani	*taissumani*	*taitsumani*	"formerly"
qablunaaq	*qallunaaq*	*qallunaaq*	"white person"
takugamnuk	*takugannuk*	*takugannuk*	"when we (2) saw"
imngiqtuq	*inngiqtuq*	*inngiqtuq*	"he/she sings"

Because of regressive consonant assimilation, the North Baffin dialect now possesses only two types of non-geminate groups: those starting with a velar (velC; e.g., *tuktu*, "caribou") and those whose first consonant is a uvular (uvuC; e.g., *arvik*, "right whale"). South Baffin has gone further yet in this process of assimilation. Nowadays, its speakers no longer distinguish between the velC groupings and their corresponding geminates:

NORTH BAFFIN	SOUTH BAFFIN	
akpa	*appa*	"murre"
tuktu	*tuttu*	"caribou"
iglu	*illu*	"house"
angmaluqtuq	*ammaluqtuq*	"round"

As already mentioned, one important phonemic feature that differentiates North Baffin from the southern dialect is that in the former speech form, the phoneme *&* is still in existence, whereas in South Baffin it has merged with *s* in the Southwest subdialect or with *t* (within consonant clusters) and *l* or *s* (when intervocalic) in the Southeast subdialect. Look at the following examples:

NORTH BAFFIN	SOUTHEAST BAFFIN	SOUTHWEST BAFFIN	
i&uaqtuq	*iluaqtuq* *isuaqtuq*	*isuaqtuq*	"is all right"
tiki&&uni	*tikittuni*	*tikitsuni*	"while arriving, he/she …"
ak&unaaq	*attunaaq*	*atsunaaq*	"rope, thong"
kangiq&uk	*kangiqtuk*	*kangiqsuk*	"bay, inlet"

Another marking characteristic is that North Baffin and Southeast Baffin are the only Canadian dialects to palatalize *t* (i.e., change it into *s*) after an etymological *i* (although traces of this phenomenon also exist in Natsilingmiutut). Compare, for instance, these two words:

"foot"	*is̲igak*	(the first vowel is an etymological *i*)
"palm of the hand"	*it̲imak*	(the first vowel is an etymological *e*)

Palatalization occurs either with a single intervocalic *t* or, much more infrequently (generally before the vowel *u*), when *t* is geminated (*tt*). Apparently, the clusters *kt* and *qt* are never palatalized. According to observations made in Igloolik in the mid-1970s (Dorais 1978), a palatalized *tt* is realized as *tch*, but nowadays, palatalization of *tt* occurs only with some very old speakers, if at all. It should be noticed that the extent of palatalization is much more limited in North and Southeast Baffin than in North Alaskan Iñupiaq or Greenlandic Kalaallisut, where it also occurs. Here are a few examples:

NORTH BAFFIN	SOUTHEAST BAFFIN	SOUTHWEST BAFFIN	
is̲iqpuq	*is̲iqpuq*	*it̲iqpuq*	"he/she enters"
akis̲iq	*akis̲iq*	*akit̲i*	"pillow"
is̲igak	*is̲igak*	*it̲igak*	"foot"
ivis̲aaruq	*ivis̲aaruq*	*ivit̲aaruq*	"red trout"
tikit̲c̲h̲unga (old)	*tikit̲t̲unga*	*tikit̲t̲unga*	"I arrive"
qainngit̲c̲h̲uq (old)	*qainngit̲t̲uq*	*qainngit̲t̲uq*	"does not come"

The North Baffin dialect does not have any *ts* clusters. It shares this particularity with Aivilik. Words such as South Baffin *natsiq* ("seal") and *atsaq* ("paternal aunt") become *nattiq* and *attaq*. As already mentioned, an etymological *ps* (e.g., Aivilik *ilipsi*, "many of you") is a geminate in North Baffin (*ilissi*).

NUNAVIK AND NUNATSIAVUT

The Nunavik (Arctic Quebec) and Nunatsiavut (northern Labrador) Inuit are the southernmost Eskimo populations in the world. They occupy the coastal areas of the Quebec-Labrador Peninsula (map 4), on the shores of Hudson Bay, Hudson Strait, Ungava Bay, and the Atlantic Ocean (Labrador Sea), and they are the only Canadian Inuit whose aboriginal habitat lies within provinces (Quebec and Labrador-Newfoundland) rather than in Nunavut and the Northwest Territories. Nunavik Inuit have their own dialect, as do the Nunatsiavut people. Both speech forms share some phonological features[23] that militate in favour of regarding them as belonging to the same Quebec-Labrador subgroup within Eastern Canadian Inuktitut.[24]

The Nunavik dialect comprises two subdialects, Itivimiut and Tarramiut, differentiated by a few phonological and lexical peculiarities. Itivimiut is spoken on the east coast of Hudson Bay, in the communities of Kuujjuaraapik (formerly Great Whale River), Umiujaq, Inukjuak (Inujjuaq), and Puvirnituq (formerly Povungnituk), as well as in Sanikiluaq, on the Belcher Islands (which belong to Nunavut). A few Inuit families also reside in the Cree village of Chisasibi (Mailasikkut), on James Bay. In Kuujjuaraapik too the majority of the population belong to the Cree First Nation (they call their community Whapmagoostui). Several Itivimiut speakers from the Inukjuak area migrated to the High Arctic villages of Resolute and Grise Fiord in the early 1950s. A few of them are still living there, but several families were repatriated back to Inukjuak in the 1990s.

The Tarramiut subdialect is spoken on north-eastern Hudson Bay, southern Hudson Strait, and Ungava Bay, in the communities of Akulivik, Ivujivik, Salluit, Kangiqsujuaq, Quaqtaq, Kangirsuk, Aupaluk, Tasiujaq, Kuujjuaq (formerly known as Fort Chimo), and Kangiqsualujjuaq. It was also spoken in Port Burwell (Killiniq), before the federal government closed this village in 1978.

The Nunatsiavut dialect is heard along the Atlantic coast of Labrador. It is divided into two subdialects: Northern Labrador and Rigolet. The Northern Labrador speech form is spoken principally in the communities of Nain (Naini), Hopedale, and Makkovik

(Maquuvik). After the Second World War many northern Labrador families migrated to the Goose Bay/Happy Valley (Vaali) area, in central Labrador, where they now form a community of some 300 people. A few disabled individuals were also transported to the Innu (Montagnais-Naskapi) and "Settler"[25] twin villages of North West River and Sheshatshiu, where about sixty Inuit still live. Note that in the 1950s two Inuit communities north of Nain were closed by the Government of Newfoundland: Nutak (Nutaaq), in 1956, and Hebron, in 1959. Their population was relocated to Nain, Hopedale, and Makkovik.

The Rigolet subdialect, still spoken by a few individuals in the village of Rigolet on Hamilton Inlet (central Labrador), is characterized by its unique phonemic properties (Dorais 1977a; Dresher and Johns 1996). It preserves bilC and velC consonant groupings (e.g., *igupsaq*, "bee," and *ikpasaq*, "yesterday," compared with Northern Labrador *igutsak* and *ippasak*), and syllable-final velar and uvular consonants have merged. They are always realized as a uvular after *a* and *u* and as a velar after *i*. Here are a few examples from B. Elan Dresher and Alana Johns (1996), with their Aivilik equivalents for comparison's sake:

RIGOLET	NORTHERN LABRADOR	AIVILIK	
aqpaq	*appak*	*akpa*	"murre"
tuqtu	*tuttuk*	*tuktu*	"caribou"
ingnik	*innik*	*irniq*	"son"
igupsaq	*igutsak*	*igupsaq*	"bee"

With the exception of Rigolet, the degree of regressive consonant assimilation is higher in the Nunavik and Nunatsiavut dialects than it is in the North Baffin speech form. Nunatsiavut generally assimilates more than Nunavik, whose degree of consonant assimilation is similar to that of the South Baffin dialect. As a matter of fact, the Northern Labrador subdialect of Nunatsiavut is the most assimilating of all Inuit speech forms. Even consonant clusters starting with a uvular (uvuC) have been geminated. For example, the Nunavik word for "bake-apple," *aqpik*, has become *appik*, and the common Inuit word for "woman," *arnaq*, is *annak*. Moreover, the phoneme *r* has merged with *g*, and a word-final *-q* is replaced with *-k* (see Northern Labrador *tagiuk*, "sea," instead of Nunavik *tariuq*). Another characteristic of the Nunatsiavut dialect (although absent from Rigolet) is that it has borrowed a good number of German words from the Moravian Brethren, the Protestant missionaries who, from 1771 on, came from Germany to Christianize Labrador. See, for instance: *kaattupalak* ("potato"; from *Kartoffel*) and *situnatik* ("hour"; from *Stunde*).

GREENLANDIC KALAALLISUT

Kalaallisut dialects are spoken on the Island of Greenland, the easternmost mass of land in the North American Arctic. Greenland was first settled by prehistoric Palaeo-Eskimos, but it seems that they had already disappeared when the ancestors of present-day Greenlanders entered the island – around 1,000 to 1,200 years after Christ – by crossing from Ellesmere Island to the Thule district. This wave of newcomers migrated along two different routes: the west coast of Greenland, eventually reaching down to the southernmost tip of the island; and the north and east coasts. Some east-coasters later came back from northeast Greenland, to settle in the Upernavik district (northwest Greenland). Others continued around the southern tip of the island, meeting with Inuit who had come directly along the west coast. This explains why the (sub)dialects of east, northwest, and southwest Greenland share some phonological features (e.g., *u* is often transformed into *i*) that do not exist in the central west coast language. Later on, a second wave of immigrants crossed from Ellesmere Island to the Thule district, where their descendants are still found.

In southwest Greenland, Inuit met – and sometimes clashed with – European Norse (Scandinavian) settlers, who had established farms in the region from about AD 900. The Norse disappeared during the late 1400s, and the Inuit became the only inhabitants of Greenland till the arrival of Danish missionaries and traders in 1721. When asked by the Danes who they were, eighteenth-century Greenlanders answered that they were called Kalaallit (singular Kalaaliq). The meaning of this word is obscure, but several historians think that it could come from the old Scandinavian term *Skrælling*, the name that, from the tenth to thirteenth centuries, Norse gave to the natives they met in Greenland and Newfoundland-Labrador, a region they visited from 985 on (on the history of Greenland, see Gad 1971–82). If this hypothesis stands true, Greenlanders would have preserved over several generations the memory of their contacts with the first European settlers. Whatever the case may be, the word Kalaallit became the national name of Greenland Inuit. Their country is now officially known as Kalaallit Nunaat ("the land of the Kalaallit"), and their language as Kalaallisut ("[speaking] like Kalaallit").

The Greenlandic Kalaallisut group is divided into three dialects (map 5): Thule, West Greenlandic, and East Greenlandic.[26]

The Thule dialect (also known as Polar Eskimo) is spoken in the Thule district (whose administrative centre is Qaanaaq), in northwesternmost Greenland, by the Inughuit ("big Inuit"). Because of its characteristic phonological features (in several ways, such as the use of *h* instead of *s*, it is more similar to Natsilingmiutut or Kivalliq than to Kalaallisut), it stands by itself among Greenlandic speech forms. Spoken by no more than a few hundred individuals, it is not divided into subdialects.

The West Greenlandic dialect (or Kitaamiutut) has, by far, the highest number of speakers. It is heard principally on the west coast of Greenland, but many West Greenlanders have now moved to other regions of the island or to Denmark. West Greenlandic is divided into four subdialects: Southern, Central, Northern, and Upernavik. Southern West Greenlandic is spoken in the regional municipalities (*kommunit*)[27] of Nanortalik, Narsaq, Qaqortoq, and Paamiut, in southwest Greenland.

Central West Greenlandic, which has enjoyed the status of Greenland's official language since the eighteenth century, is spoken in the regional municipalities of Nuuk (the capital of Greenland, formerly known as Godthaab), Maniitsoq, Kangerlussuaq, and Sisimiut. Northern West Greenlandic is heard in the Disko Bay area, in the regional municipalities of Aasiaat, Kangaatsiaq, Qasigiannguit, Ilulissat, Qeqertarsuaq, and Uummannaq. Finally, the Upernavik subdialect is spoken in the municipality of Upernavik, in northwest Greenland, just south of the Thule district.

The East Greenlandic dialect (or Tunumiisut) is found on the east coast of Greenland, in the regional municipalities of Ammassalik and Ittoqqortoormiit. East Greenlanders also used to dwell along the coast, north and south of Ammassalik, but they moved out of these areas during the eighteenth century. The present settlement of Ittoqqortoormiit (also known as Scoresbysund), far to the north of Ammassalik, was established only in 1925, by settlers originating from all over the Ammassalik district.

East Greenlandic was traditionally divided into two subdialects, Ammassalik and Sermilik, but differences between them have now

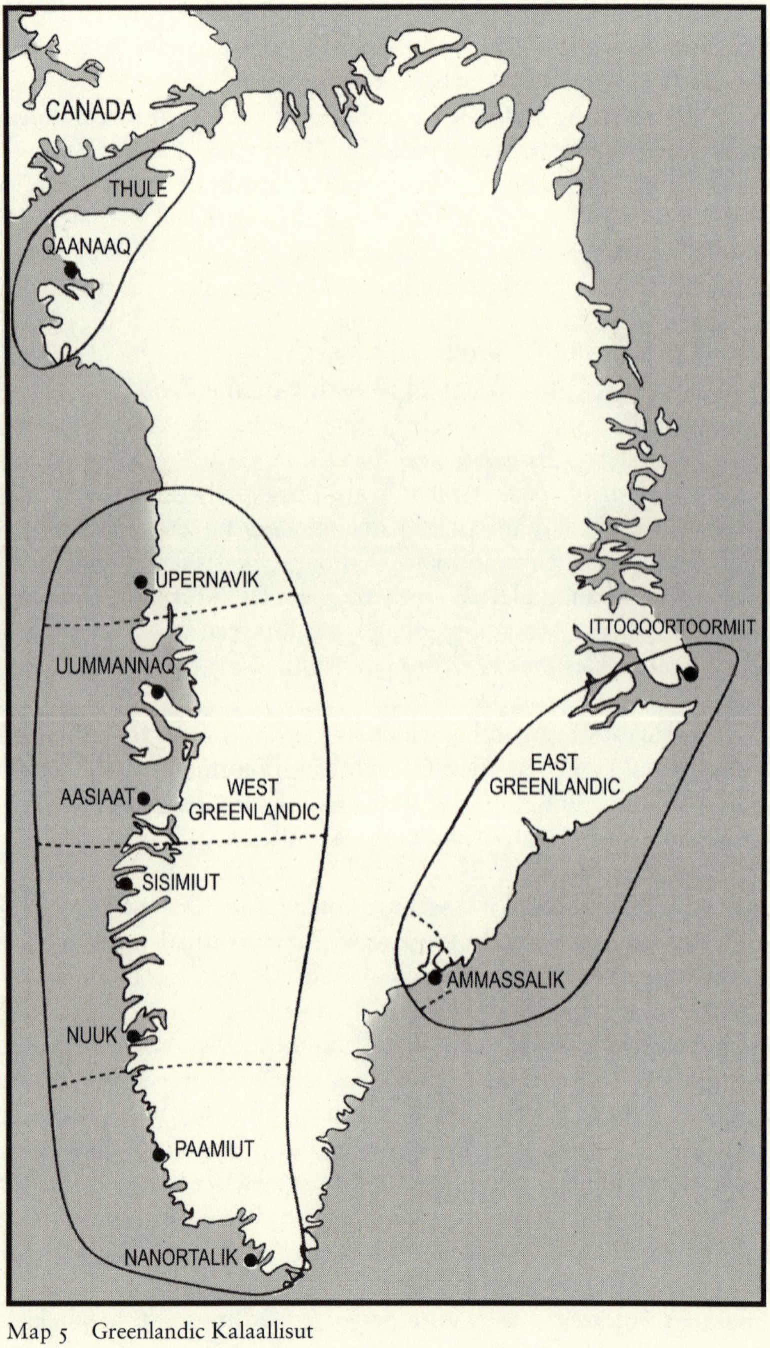

Map 5 Greenlandic Kalaallisut

almost completely disappeared. The Ammassalik subdialect was spoken in the Ammassalik and Sermiligaq fjord area, in the villages of Kulusuk and Kuummiut, among others, while Sermilik was heard in the Sermilik fjord area, as well as in the community of Tasiilaq, the administrative centre of the district.

Despite their phonological and lexical differences, West and East Greenlandic are so close that they can be regarded as belonging to the same subgroup within Greenlandic Kalaallisut. Thule is more divergent:

Polar subgroup:	Thule dialect
Greenlandic subgroup:	West Greenlandic dialect
	East Greenlandic dialect

The degree of regressive consonant assimilation of the Thule dialect is comparable to that of the North Baffin speech form (velC groupings are present), at least among older speakers, while West and East Greenlandic are at the same level as South Baffin and Nunavik.[28]

In West Greenlandic, *l* and *&* are in complementary distribution: *l* occurs intervocalically, while *&* is found within clusters. In East Greenlandic, an intervocalic *l* is pronounced as a "flap-*l*" (i.e., halfway between *l* and *d*). Within clusters, however, an etymological *l* occurs as *t*, while an etymological *&* is realized as *s*. In the Thule dialect, whether single or grouped, *l* is pronounced either as a "flap-*l*" or as *d* (single or geminate only). Here are a few comparative examples:[29]

WEST GREENLANDIC	EAST GREENLANDIC	THULE	
iluartuq	*ilivartiq*	*ilu-/iduaqtuq*	"correct, good"
ulu	*ulu*	*ulu/udu*	"woman's knife"
a&&unaaq	*atsinaaq*	*aglunaaq*	"thong, rope"
u&&u	*uttu*	*ullu/uddu*	"day"
suur&u	*suurtu*	*huurlu*	"as if, like"

Like Alaskan Inupiaq and Natsilingmiutut, Greenlandic Kalaallisut draws a phonemic distinction between the etymological consonants *J* and *j*. The latter is always realized as *y*, but the realization of the phoneme *J* is different according to dialect: *s* in West Greenlandic; *l* (intervocalic) and *t* (within clusters) in East Greenlandic; and *h* (intervocalic and within groupings) and *s* (geminate) in Thule.[30] Compare, for instance, the following words:

	WEST GREENLANDIC	EAST GREENLANDIC	THULE	
ETYMOLOGICAL *J*:	*naaja*	*naaja*	*nauja*[31]	"seagull"
ETYMOLOGICAL *J*:	*isi*	*ili*	*ihi*	"eye"
	qarsuq	*qartiq*	*qarhuq*	"arrow"
	assi	*atti*	*assi*	"likeness"

All three Greenlandic dialects palatalize *t* after an etymological *i*, although in East Greenlandic this phenomenon is not systematic. In Thule a palatalized *t* generally becomes *h*, while in West and East Greenlandic it becomes *s*, as in the following examples:

WEST GREENLANDIC	EAST GREENLANDIC	THULE	
isigak	*isigak*	*ihigak*	"foot"
isinngitsuq	*isinngitsiq*	*ihinngitsuq*	"who does not enter"
nirsurpaa	*nirsirpaa*	*nirhuraa*	"praises him/her"

By comparison with their Canadian and Alaskan equivalents, many West Greenlandic, East Greenlandic, and Thule consonant groupings have undergone metathesis (Sadock 1972). When occurring as the second element of a grouping, the continuants[32] *g*, *r*, and *v* have generally changed place with the first element of the cluster if it was an original bilabial (*m*, *v*) or apical (*n*, *l*, *J* – now fused with *s*) consonant. Moreover, *ng* has often changed place with an etymological *m*. As regressive consonant assimilation took place only after metathesis had occurred, the affected clusters often have innovative (i.e., regressively assimilated) first elements and conservative (i.e., reflecting archaic types of groupings) second elements. Here are examples of how metathesis has worked in West Greenlandic (note that as a rule, *v* becomes *f* within clusters; see below):

ETYMOLOGICAL WORD		METATHESIS		REGRESSIVELY ASSIMILATED FORM (PRESENT-DAY WORD)			
kamngit	→	*kangmit*	→	*kammit*			"boots"
kivgaq	→	*kigvaq*	→	*kivvaq*	→	*kiffaq*	"spokesperson"
umilgit	→	*umiglit*	→	*umillit*			"bearded ones"
malruk	→	*marluk*	→	*marluk*			"two"

inrutaq	→	*irnutaq*	→	*irnutaq* or *irngutaq*		"grandchild"
ilvit	→	*ivlit*	→	*illit*		"you (one)"
aqiJgiq	→	*aqigJiq*	→	*aqiJJiq*	→ *aqissiq*	"ptarmigan"
taJva	→	*tavJa*	→	*taJJa*	→ *tassa*	"here it is!"

In West Greenlandic, voiced continuant consonants (namely *v*, *l*, *j*, *g*, and *r*) become voiceless when occurring within a cluster. In East Greenlandic (and in the Upernavik subdialect of West Greenlandic), continuants are not only devoiced but also realized as stops. This explains why, within a cluster, *v* becomes *p*, *l* (which may reflect an etymological *J* – realized as *s* in West Greenlandic) becomes *t*, *g* becomes *k*, and *r* becomes *q*. Note, however, that *l* reflecting an etymological *&*, as well as *j*, are realized as *s* within clusters. Here are a few examples (including Nunavik Tarramiut for comparison's sake):

WEST GREENLANDIC	EAST GREENLANDIC	NUNAVIK TARRAMIUT	
affaq	*appaq*	*avvaq*	"half part"
arfiq	*arpiq*	*arvik*	"right whale"
qa&&unaaq	*qattunaaq*	*qallunaaq*	"white person"
a&&unaaq	*atsinaaq*	*atsunaaq*	"thong, rope"
arsat	*artat*	*arjait*	"ashes"
ixxiaq	*ikkiaq*	*iggiaq*	"throat"
taXXaq[33]	*taqqaq*	*tarraq*	"shadow"

Although Kalaallisut reinforces the strength of grouped consonants by devoicing continuants or transforming them into stops, it also has a tendency to weaken some intervocalic consonants through nasalization and/or elision. In East Greenlandic, for instance, as well as in the Northern West Greenlandic subdialect, an intervocalic *g* becomes *ng* (e.g., *ingavuq*, "he/she cooks," rather than Central West Greenlandic *igavuq*), and an intervocalic *r* is nasalized (i.e., uttered while letting air flow through the nose).

In the East Greenlandic dialect, nasalization belongs to a more general process of single-consonant weakening: word-final consonants are pronounced very faintly, if at all; the single stops *t*, *k*, and *q* become continuants (*l*, *g*, and *r*) when appearing between vowels; and several intervocalic consonants are elided when occurring at the beginning of an unstressed syllable, within the boundaries of a morpheme.[34] In the Thule dialect final consonants may be elided too. Moreover, *h*, *g*, and *r* often disappear when intervocalic. In the same position, *q* may be weakened to *r*. However, these phenomena do not seem to occur as systematically as in East Greenlandic.

Finally, in West Greenlandic, *v* is almost always elided after *u*. It may also disappear when occurring between *i* and *a*. Some East Greenlandic speakers abide by these rules, although in that dialect *v* is compulsory in many phonetic environments. Here are a few examples of consonant weakening:

WEST GREENLANDIC	EAST GREENLANDIC	THULE	
atiq	*aliq*	*atiq*	"name"
ukaliq	*ugaliq*	*ukaliq*	"arctic hare"
uqarpuq	*urarpuq*	*uqartuq*	"he/she speaks"
namminiq	*nammiiq*	*namminiq*	"self"
nirivuq	*niivuq*	*niihuq/nirihuq*	"he/she eats"
tusarpugut	*tusarpuut*	*tuhartugut*	"we hear"
takuaa	*tagivaa*	*takugaa*	"he/she sees it"
aasiak	*aasiaq/pisiisiaq*	*aahivak*	"spider"

East Greenlandic, as well as the Southern and Upernavik subdialects of West Greenlandic, are characterized by a process of vowel harmony, whereby *u* normally becomes *i*, except in some very precise phonemic environments (Rischel 1975). In East Greenlandic, vowel harmony works as follows (Dorais 1981a):

1. *u* never becomes *i* when occurring in the first syllable of a word (e.g., *nuliaq*, "wife").
2. *u* never becomes *i* when *u* already occurs in the preceding syllable (e.g., *tuttuq*, "reindeer").
3. Within the boundaries of a morpheme, *u* never becomes *i* if *u* also occurs in the following syllable (e.g., *qarungu*, "when?").
4. Within a word, when *u* is followed by a syllable containing another *u*, but belonging to a different morpheme, the first *u* changes to *i*, but the second one is kept (e.g., *pisittuq*, "one who walks").
5. *u* never becomes *i* when it belongs to a syllable initiated by a bilabial consonant (*p*, *m*, or *v*; e.g., *imirpuq*, "he/she drinks"); this

rule also applies when the preceding syllable contains an original diphthong *au* (e.g., *naasuq*, "flower"; from *nausuq*) or ends with an etymological bilabial consonant (e.g., *nunannut*, "to my country" – etymologically *nunamnut*).[35]

6 In all other cases, *u* becomes *i*, as in the following examples:

EAST GREENLANDIC	WEST GREENLANDIC	
iik	*inuk*	"human being"
naniq	*nanuq*	"polar bear"
tusartiq	*tusartuq*	"one who hears"
umiakkit	*umiakkut*	"by boat"
nunannit	*nunannut*	"to your country"

Besides harbouring vowel harmony and other phonemic characteristics, East Greenlandic is special from a lexical point of view. Over 30% of its vocabulary does not exist – or does not have the same meaning – in any other Inuit dialect, including West Greenlandic (Dorais 1981a). And this ignores differences based on purely phonological dissimilarities. The most widely accepted hypothesis for explaining this phenomenon is that of the death taboo (Thalbitzer 1921; Petersen 1975). In traditional East Greenland, after someone had died, it was strictly forbidden to utter his or her name (or names). Moreover, the objects, situations, or animals bearing the same names had to be called something else. New words (generally descriptive ones) were thus coined to avoid using the tabooed lexemes. When a child was born, he or she received the names of the deceased, but apparently, the corresponding objects kept their new appellations. By accumulating over years, these changes modified quite extensively some sectors of the vocabulary (e.g., the animal names, the terminology of body parts, the lexicon of hunting and fishing). In most areas of the Arctic, a descriptive metaphorical language was used by shamans when communicating with spirits, but in East Greenland, metaphors seem to have become a common way of speaking among the entire population.

This type of lexical change (which stopped around 1900 when East Greenlanders were converted to Christianity) is discussed more thoroughly in chapter 5. Its chief result is that the East Greenlandic dialect has now become very different from any other Inuit speech form. Look at the following examples, for instance, which illustrate the originality of East Greenlandic:

LITERAL MEANING IN EAST GREENLANDIC	EAST GREENLANDIC	WEST GREENLANDIC	NUNAVIK TARRAMIUT	
"rutting seal"	*tikkaq*	*angut*	*anguti(k)*	"man, male"
"the very small one"	*miigattak*	*natsiq*	*natsiq*	"ringed seal"
"which is dragged"	*uniarattaq*	*pamiuq*	*pamiuq*	"animal tail"
[onomatopoeia]	*qusiiq*	*naaja*	*naujaq*	"seagull"
"tool for being seen"	*saqqit*	*qajaq*	*qajaq*	"kayak"

Phonemic and lexical differences between East and West Greenlandic, however spectacular they may appear, really lie at the surface of things. By comparison with Canadian Inuktitut, these two dialects share enough similarities with each other, and also with Thule, that they truly belong to the same Kalaallisut dialectal grouping.[36]

LINGUISTIC SIMILARITIES AND DIFFERENCES

Syntax

All Inuit dialects share the same basic structure. Linguists classify them (together with the Yupik speech forms) among the so-called polysynthetic languages. Words are constructed according to one's needs. By adding one or several affixes (also called post-bases) – some of them lexical, some of them grammatical – to a word-base (also known as a radical), while respecting a certain number of rules, speakers are able to generate their own words as the conversation goes on.[37]

Inuit words are often equivalent to an English sentence. This means that they may include both verbal and nominal elements, as in *illuqaqqunga*, "I have a house" (house-to have-I). This process is called noun incorporation. According to the linguist Alana Johns (2007), Inuit words of this type exhibit a syntactic structure parallel to that of English sentences, with a subject, an object, and a verb – although only a limited number of verbal concepts are liable to be expressed through noun incorporation. The difference between Inuit and English syntax is that in the former language, rather than operating within a sentence made out of independent words, incorporated nouns are "collapsed" into a single word that includes all the morphemes required for conveying a specific meaning. As a result, syntactic relations are mostly word-external in English and word-internal in Inuit.

Radicals – which express the initial meaning of the term – always occur in the word-initial position, while affixes must follow another linguistic element. The word-final affix is generally grammatical: it marks the role played by the word within the sentence. See, for example, the following sentence (in Nunavik Inuktitut):

Inuktitut uqarumajualuujunga – "I want very much to speak Inuktitut"

Inuk-	"human being" (nominal word-base)
-titut	"like them" (grammatical affix; simulative case of the noun declension)
uqa(q)-	"to speak" (verbal word-base)
-ruma-	"to want" (lexical affix)
-ju-	"one who does something" (grammatical affix; basic case of the noun declension)
-alu-	"big" (lexical affix)
-u-	"to be" (lexical affix)
-junga	"I" (grammatical affix; first-person singular of the indicative verbal mood)

Literal meaning: "I am a big one who wants to speak like human beings"

On the whole, it may be said that about 90% of Inuit syntactic rules are common to all dialects. A similar percentage of word-bases is also shared by most forms of speech. Some differences in vocabulary are more striking than others. For instance, such a common question as "do you understand?" can be translated as *paasivit?* (in Greenland), *tukisivit?* (in eastern Canada), or *kangiqsivit?* (in western Canada and Alaska). But this should not conceal that most radicals are shared by a majority of Inuit dialects. Real – yet never insuperable – differences lie elsewhere: in phonology, in lexical affixes, and in the degree of normalization of some morphological rules.

Phonological Variation

The phonological system is basically the same in all Inuit dialects: there are three vowels, *a* (as in "f<u>a</u>ther"), *i* (as in "b<u>ee</u>"), and *u* (as in "moon"), which may be either short or long (long vowels are generally written *aa*, *ii*, and *uu*). The vocalic length is phonemic (i.e., it can distinguish between two different words; e.g., *takuvatit*, "you see them," and *takuvaatit*, "he/she sees you").

According to dialect, there are between thirteen and seventeen consonantal phonemes, distributed as follows (consonants that do not occur in all dialects appear between parentheses):

CONSONANTS	bilabial	apical			velar	uvular	aspirated
stops	p	t			k	q	
voiced continuants	v	l	j	(r) [J][38]	γ[g]	R [r]	
voiceless continuants		(l̥)[&]	s	(r̥) [sr]			(h)
nasals	m	n			η[ng]		

One interesting characteristic of Inuit phonology is the way the various dialects have coped with the disappearance – or transformation – of phonemes *e* (ə – schwa – in the phonetic alphabet) and *ð*, which belonged to the ancestral phonemic stock of the Proto-Eskimo language.[39] It seems that the phoneme *e*, still in existence in the Yupik languages, was preserved for many centuries by Inuit. In West Greenlandic, for instance, this phoneme may have been in use as late as the eighteenth century within the first syllable of some words (see Rischel 1981). Nowadays, however, *e* only survives in one Inuit speech form, the Diomede subdialect of Bering Strait Inupiaq (Kaplan 1981b). Elsewhere, it has generally merged with *i* when followed by a consonant and with *a* when followed by a vowel, and it has often disappeared when occurring in the word-final position, after the consonant *t* or *n* (otherwise, it has merged with *i*). For instance, Proto-Eskimo *angute* ("male, man") has given Inuit *angut_*, *angun_*, or *anguti(k)* (word-final position), *angutilik* ("there is a man"; followed by a consonant), and *angutauvuq* ("he is a man"; followed by a vowel).

As was mentioned in the first section of this chapter, the former existence of *e* is felt in another way. In several dialects, when following an etymological *i* (i.e., a vowel that was *i* in Proto-Eskimo), some consonants are palatalized (e.g., *t* becomes *s*), but when following a non-etymological *i* (i.e., an *i* that was originally a Proto-Eskimo *e*), these same consonants are not palatalized.

As Proto-Eskimo *δ* is concerned, it still subsists as a separate phoneme in Natsilingmiutut and in the four Alaskan Inupiaq dialects. In these forms of speech, this phoneme is realized as either *J* (voiced) or *sr* (voiceless). In other Canadian dialects, it has merged with *j* (pronounced *y*) or, more rarely, with *s* or *h* (in such cases, it corresponds to Inupiaq and Natsilingmiutut *sr*). In the Itivimiut (Hudson Bay coast) subdialect of Nunavik Inuktitut, however, it is *j* that has merged with *δ*. In West Greenlandic, *δ* was preserved for a long time – with the pronunciation *sh* – but one or two generations ago *sh* merged with *s*. In East Greenlandic, *δ* has merged with *l* (intervocalic) or *t* (within clusters) and, in Thule, with *h*. By way of example, here are the modern equivalents of the Proto-Eskimo words *naja* ("sister"), *eδe* ("eye"), and *uqδur* ("blubber"):

	"SISTER"	"EYE"	"BLUBBER"
Bering Strait, Qawiaraq, Malimiutun, North Slope, Natsilingmiutut	*naja*	*iJi* (Diomede *eJe*)	*uqsruq*
Siglitun, Inuinnaqtun, Kivalliq, Aivilik, North Baffin, South Baffin, Nunavik Tarramiut, Nunatsiavut	*naja(k)*	*iji(k)*	*uqsuq/uqhuq*[40]
Nunavik Itivimiut	*naJa*	*iJi*	*uqsuq*
Thule	*naja*	*ihi*	*urhuq*
West Greenlandic	*naja*	*isi*	*ursuq*
East Greenlandic	*naja*	*ili* (or *uitsat*)	*ursuq* (*aammaqqaaq*)

Another important phonological feature of Inuit, occasionally mentioned in this chapter's first section, is that when one moves from west to east within the Inuit area, the types of allowed consonant clusters tend to diminish. For Baffin, Nunavik, Nunatsiavut, and Greenland speakers, for instance, consonant groupings such as *lr*, *vg*, and *pq* are not acceptable. But in southern Kivalliq, the western Canadian Arctic, and Alaska, words like *malruk* ("two"), *kivgaq* ("messenger, servant"), and *apqutit* ("roads") are perfectly allowable. What happened in the eastern Arctic is due to regressive consonant assimilation: in some types of clusters, the first consonant has become the same as the second consonant. As a rule, regressive consonant assimilation increases when one moves from west to east. In Siglitun, for instance, Inuit speakers say *malruk* for "two" and *kivgaq* for a servant. But in Aivilik and North or South Baffin, they say *marruuk* because in these dialects the first consonant, *l*, has become identical to the second one, *r*. In Aivilik, however, *apqutit* is still acceptable (but *kivgaq* is not), as it is in Siglitun. This is not the case in North and South Baffin, where, because of regressive consonant assimilation, speakers instead say *kiggaq* and *aqqutit*. So, in the easternmost dialects, there is more assimilation than in western speech forms.

In total, four basic types of clusters are found, each beginning with a consonant belonging to one of the four main positions of articulation of Inuit phonology: uvular (*q*, *r*), velar (*k*, *g*, *ng*), bilabial (*p* [*b*],[41] *v*, *m*), and apical (*t*, *l*, *&*, *n*). In Inupiaq and Western Inuktun these initials may be followed by almost any consonant, whereas in Eastern Canadian Inuktitut and in Kalaallisut, the two consonants must often belong to the same position (i.e., an apical may be preceded only by an apical, a bilabial by a bilabial, etc.), as an effect of regressive assimilation. Moreover, in the western dialects, "special" consonant clusters such as *Jg*/*djg* (e.g., *aJgak*/*adjgak*, "hand") and *Jv*/*djv* (e.g., *taJva*/*tadjva*, "there!") also occur.

The various types of consonant clusters allowed by the different dialects are found below. As can be noticed, the number of geminates (two identical consonants following each other) is higher in the eastern dialects (Baffin, Nunavik, Nunatsiavut, Greenland) than in the western ones because of the higher incidence of regressive consonant assimilation. In the list below, the symbol C stands for any consonant. The following abbreviations are also used: uvu (uvular), vel (velar), bil (bilabial), api (apical), and cont (continuant consonant). For instance, the abbreviation uvuC refers to a grouping that starts with a uvular consonant, followed by any type of consonant.

DIALECTS	TYPES OF CONSONANT CLUSTERS		
Bering Strait, Qawiaraq, Malimiutun, Uummarmiutun, Natsilingmiutut	mr	*paamruqtuq*	"crawls"
	nr	*upinraaq*	"springtime" (Bering: *uvinraaq*)

	qC	*tupiqni*	"in your tent"
		iqquq	"buttock"
	uvuC	*arnaq*	"woman"
	kC	*ikniq*	"fire"
	velC	*pangniq*	"bull caribou"
		iggiaq	"throat"
	pC	*qapvik*	"wolverine" (Uumm.: *qavvik*)
	bilC	*avvaq*	"half"
		qavlu	"eyebrow"
	tC	*maatna*	"now"
	apiC	*mannik*	"egg"
		malruk	"two" (King and Diomede: *mar-luk*)
	Jcont	*aJgak*	"hand"
North Slope (coastal), Siglitun, some Natsilingmiutut	mr	*paamruqtuq*	
	nr	*upinraaq* (some Natsilingmiutut: *upin'ngaq*)[42]	
	uvuC	*tupirni*; *arnaq*; *iqquq*	
	velC	*igniq*; *pagniq*; *iggiaq* (North Slope)	
		ingniq; *pangniq*; *iggiaq* (Siglitun; Natsilingmiutut)	
	bilC	*qavvik*; *avvaq*; *qavlu*	
	apiC	*maanna*; *mannik*; *malruk*	
	Jcont	*aJgak* (North Slope, Natsilingmiutut); *adjgak* (Siglitun)	
Kivalliq	mr	*paamruqtuq*	
	nr	*upinraaq*	
	uvuC	*tupirni*; *arnaq*; *iqquq*	
	velC	*ingniq*; *pangniq*; *iggiaq*	
	bilC	*qavvik*; *avvaq*; *qablu*	
	apiC	*maanna*; *mannik*; *malruk*	
	Jg	*adjgak*	
Inuinnaqtun	mng/mr	*paamnguqtuq or paamruqtuq*	
	n'ng/nr	*upin'ngaaq* or *upinraaq*	
	uvuC	*tupirni*; *arnaq*; *iqquq*	
	velC	*ingniq*; *pangniq*; *iggiaq*	

	bilC	*qavvik*; *avvaq*; *qablu*
	apiC	*maanna*; *mannik*; *malruk*; *algak*
Aivilik	mr	*paamruqtuq*
	rng	*upirngaaq*
	uvuC	*tupirni*; *arnaq*; *marruk*; *iqquq*
	velC	*ingniq*; *pangniq*; *aggak*; *iggiaq*
	bilC	*qavvik*; *avvaq*; *qablu*
	api/api	*maanna*; *mannik*
North Baffin, Thule	rng	*paarnguqtuq*; *upirngaaq*
	uvuC	*tupirni*; *arnaq*; *marruuk* (Thule: *marluk*); *iqquq*
	velC	*ingniq*; *pangniq*; *aggak* (Thule: *aghak*); *iggiaq*
	bil/bil	*qavvik*; *avvaq*
	api/api	*maanna*; *mannik*; *qallu*
South Baffin, Nunavik	rng	*paarnguqtuq* (Nunavik: *paarngutuq*); *upirngaaq*
	uvuC	*tupirni*; *arnaq*; *marruuk*; *iqquq*
	vel/vel	*aggak*; *iggiaq*
	bil/bil	*qavvik*; *avvaq*
	api/api	*maanna*; *mannik*; *qallu*; *inniq*; *panniq*
West Greenlandic, East Greenlandic (EG)	rng	*paarnguqpuq*; *upirngaaq*
	uvuC[43]	*tupirni*; *arnaq*; *mar&uk* (EG: *martit*); *irquq/irqiq*
	vel/vel	*iggiaq*
	bil/bil	*qavvik*; *avvaq*
	api/api	*maanna*; *mannik*; *qa&&u* (EG: *qattu*); *inniq*; *panniq*; *assak* (EG: *attak*)[44]
Nunatsiavut	kq	*ikquk*
	vel/vel	*aggak*; *iggiak*; *magguuk*; *paanngutuk*; *upinngaak*
	bil/bil	*qavvik*; *avvak*
	api/api	*maanna*; *mannik*; *qalluk*; *innik*; *pannik*; *tupinni*; *annak*

The pattern of more advanced regressive assimilation in eastern dialects is relatively recent. As shall be seen in chapter 5, historical written sources from the late eighteenth and early nineteenth centuries show that the types of clusters then in use in Nunatsiavut and Greenland were similar to those that can still be heard in more western dialects. For instance, words like *qablu* (*qavlu*) and *paamruqtuq* were formerly common in Nunatsiavut Inuktitut as well as in Greenlandic. Much more recently, in the late 1950s and early 1960s, when linguist Alex Spalding was gathering linguistic data in Arctic Bay (North Baffin), old people told him that good Inuktitut speakers should say *qablunaaq* ("European"), *apqut* ("road"), and *nibliramnuk* ("when both of us uttered a sound") rather than *qallunaaq*, *aqqut*, and *nillirannuk* (Spalding 1993). Ten years later (late 1960s and early 1970s), when I was conducting research in Nunavik and South Baffin, many people in their forties and fifties said *ukpi(g)juaq* ("snowy owl") and *iglumiingmat* ("because he/she is in the house") rather than the assimilated forms *uppi(j)juaq* and *illumiimmat*, which are now in common usage. This ongoing simplification of consonant clusters shows that far from having completed its evolution, the phonology of Inuktitut is still on the move.

By measuring phonological differences between the various Inuit dialects,[45] it is possible to establish an index of phonological distance – that is, an evaluation of the extent to which different dialects are phonologically similar (Dorais 1986a). This index generally validates the division of Inuit-Inupiaq into four dialectal groups. To take one example, the South Baffin dialect appears to be closer to most other Eastern Canadian Inuktitut speech forms than to Western Canadian Inuktun, Greenlandic Kalaallisut, and Alaskan Inupiaq. Its indices of phonological distance are as follows (a higher figure means a larger distance):

Phonological distance between South Baffin and:

North Baffin	2	Nunavik	3
Aivilik	3.5	Nunatsiavut	5
Inuinnaqtun	5	Thule	5
Kivalliq	6	Siglitun	6
Natsilingmiutut	7	West Greenlandic	10.5
North Slope Iñupiaq	12	East Greenlandic	13.5
Malimiutun	15	Qawiaraq	17
Bering Strait	19.5		

The index shows that on phonological grounds, one Eastern Canadian Inuktitut dialect, Kivalliq, seems relatively distant from other Eastern speech forms (this was already discussed in the section above on Kivalliq and Aivilik). Another interesting point is that, as already mentioned, Thule Kalaallisut appears to be phonemically closer to some Canadian dialects than to West or East Greenlandic. Table 2 schematizes the principal phonological characteristics of the Inuit dialects.

Affixes and Morphology

The linguist Michael Fortescue has established an index of dialectal distance based on the percentage of lexical affixes shared by various dialects (Fortescue 1985a). He has found, for example, that an Eastern Canadian Inuktitut dialect such as Nunavik shares only 163 affixes with West Greenlandic, or 32% of its total stock of 509 post-bases. With Inuinnaqtun (Western Canadian Inuktun), the percentage of shared affixes is a little higher (35.5%), but with North Slope Iñupiaq, it is somewhat lower (30.5%).[46] Within Eastern Canadian Inuktitut, dialects share many more affixes among themselves than they do with other groups. For instance, about 75% of the total Arctic Quebec stock is shared with Nunatsiavut and South Baffin, and about 70% with the North Baffin dialect. Along with phonology, then, affixes constitute another area where variation among the four dialectal groupings appears to be important, a fact that may hamper easy communication between speakers of the Inuit language.

As grammar is concerned, even if morphology and syntax are essentially the same all over the Inuit (and Yupik) area, Eastern Canadian Inuktitut tends to simplify some grammatical forms common to other dialects. This is especially the case with nouns. The Inuit language possesses three grammatical numbers: singular, dual (two entities), and plural, as in Inuktitut *inuk* ("one person"), *inuuk* ("two persons"), *inuit* ("three or more people"). In West and East Greenlandic, the dual disappeared from most areas at the turn of the twentieth century,[47] but it is still in common use elsewhere. In most dialects, the rules of formation of dual and plural nouns, whether they be possessed ("my ..., your ..., his ..., etc.") or not, depend on the types of final vowels and consonants found within word-bases. In Inuktitut, however, the dual and the plural are

Table 2

Principal phonological characteristics of the Inuit dialects

Dialects	*apiC clusters*	*bilC clusters*	*velC clusters*	*uvuC clusters*	*j and J (s/l)*	*& or t or s (h)*	*s or h*	*palatalization*
Bering Strait	yes	yes	yes	yes	j and J	&	s	no
Qawiaraq	yes	yes	yes	yes	j and J	&	s/ch	no
Malimiutun	yes	yes	yes	yes	j and J	&	s/sr	yes
North Slope	yes	yes	yes	yes	j and J	&	s	yes
Uummarmiutun	yes	yes	yes	yes	j and J	&	h	yes
Siglitun	yes	yes	yes	yes	j only	&	s	no
Inuinnaqtun	yes	yes	yes	yes	j only	h	h	no
Natsilingmiutut	yes	yes	yes	yes	j and J	&	h	traces
Kivalliq	yes	yes	yes	yes	j only	&	h	no
Aivilik	no	yes	yes	yes	j only	&	s	no
North Baffin	no	no	yes	yes	j only	&	s	some
Southeast Baffin	no	no	no	yes	j only	l/s[a] t[b]	s	some
Southwest Baffin	no	no	no	yes	j only	s	s	no
Nunavik Itivimiut	no	no	no	yes	J only	s	s	no
Nunavik Tarramiut	no	no	no	yes	j only	s	s	no
Nunatsiavut	no	no	no	no	j only	&	s	no
Thule	no	no	yes	yes	j and h	l	h	yes
West Greenlandic	no	no	no	yes	j and s	l[a] &[b]	s	yes
East Greenlandic	no	no	no	yes	j and l/t	l[a] s[b]	s	some

a. When intervocalic.

b. Within a cluster.

always formed the same way: by lengthening the final vowel of the noun and adding *-k* (dual), or by adding *-it* to the word (plural).[48] Original rules have thus been normalized. Here are some examples (see also chapter 5):

NORTH SLOPE IÑUPIAQ	SIGLITUN	SOUTH BAFFIN INUKTITUT	WEST GREENLANDIC	
angun	*angun*	*anguti(k)*	*anguti*	"one male man"
angutik	*angutik*	*angutiik*	*angutit*	"two men"
angutit	*angutit*	*angutiit*	*angutit*	"many men"
angutaa	*angutaa*	*angutinga*	*angutaa*	"his/her man"
nagJuk	*nagjuk*	*nagjuk*	*nassuk*	"antler"
nagJuuk	*nagjuuk*	*nagjuuk*	*nassuit*	"two antlers"
nagJuitch	*nagjuit*	*nagjuit*	*nassuit*	"antlers"
nagJua	*nagjua*	*nagjunga*	*nassua*	"his/her antler"
iqaluk	*iqaluk*	*iqaluk*	*iqaluk*	"one fish"
iqalluk	*iqalluk*	*iqaluuk*	*iqaluit*	"two fish"
iqaluich	*iqaluit*	*iqaluit*	*iqaluit*	"many fish"
iqalua	*iqalua*	*iqalunga*	*iqalua*	"his/her one fish"
tupiq	*tupiq*	*tupiq*	*tupiq*	"tent"
tuppak	*tuppak*	*tupiik*	*tuqqit*	"two tents"
tupqit	*tupqit*	*tupiit*	*tuqqit*	"tents"
tupqa	*tupqa*	*tupinga*	*tuqqa*	"his/her tent"
nutaraq	*nutaraq*	*nutaraq*	*nutaraq*	"baby"
nutaqqak	*nutaqqak*	*nutaraak*	*nutaqqat*	"two babies"
nutaqqat	*nutaqqat*	*nutarait*	*nutaqqat*	"babies"
nutaqqaa	*nutaqqaa*	*nutaranga*	*nutaqqaa*	"his/her baby"
putuguq	*putuguq*	*putuguq*	*putuguq*	"big toe"
putukkuk	*putukkuk*	*putuguuk*	*putukkut*	"two big toes"
putukkut	*putukkut*	*putuguit*	*putukkut*	"big toes"
putugua	*putukkua*	*putugunga*	*putukkua*	"his/her big toe"
arviq	*arviq*	*arvik*	*arviq*	"right whale"
arvak	*arvak*	*arviik*	*arvirit*	"two whales"
arvirit	*arvirit*	*arviit*	*arvirit*	"whales"
arvira[49]	*arvira*	*arvinga*	*arvira*	"its whale"

More details on grammar shall be found in the next chapter, where the Nunavik dialect of Inuktitut is discussed.

CONCLUSION

This chapter has described some important dialectal and linguistic characteristics of the Inuit language. It has shown that despite regional differences that seem sometimes almost insuperable and that can give the impression of an extreme degree of interdialectal variation, Inuit manifests, at closer look, a high level of phonemic, grammatical, and lexical similarity. And this similarity is stronger than it may appear because a good part of present-day linguistic variation goes back only a few generations, two centuries at most. It may be presumed that when Greenland was colonized by Europeans in 1721, the Inuit language of the eastern North American Arctic was quite similar to the one spoken in western Canada and Alaska. This means that dialectal variation seems to have been accelerated, if not provoked, by historical factors linked to the Euro-American presence in the Arctic. It demonstrates once again that language is a human phenomenon operating within the confines of specific social and cultural conditions and that its development and evolution are influenced by these conditions.

3

The Nunavik Dialect of Inuktitut

In this chapter a closer look is cast at one specific form of the Inuit language, the Nunavik dialect of Inuktitut. A brief description of its phonology and grammar, as well as a few brief remarks on its lexicon, will afford us a deeper understanding of how the language operates. Some phonemic innovations set aside, Nunavik is typical of Eastern Canadian Inuktitut, which, as mentioned in the preceding chapter, is not so different from other Inuit dialectal groupings.

Spoken in the province of Quebec north of the 55th parallel, Nunavik can be subdivided into two subdialects: Tarramiut (Ungava Bay and Hudson Strait) and Itivimiut (Hudson Bay). With more than 10,000 speakers in 2006 (92% of all Inuit living in Arctic Quebec), it is, in numerical terms, the most important form of the Inuit language outside Greenland.[1]

PHONOLOGY

Like most other Eastern Canadian Inuktitut dialects, Nunavik has a high rate of regressive consonant assimilation. As seen in chapter 2, all groups of two consonants are geminates, except for some of those starting with a uvular (*r*, *q*). This leaves us with five types of clusters, three of them geminates:

rng[2] *upirngaaq* ("springtime")
uvuC *irniq* ("son"), *tarraq* ("shadow"), *aqsaq* ("football"), *aqqutik* ("road")
bil/bil *uppik* ("snowy owl"), *amma* ("and"), *ivvit* ("you one")
api/api *ittuk* ("old man"), *inniq* ("fire"), *atsa*[3] ("paternal aunt"), *illu* ("house"), *ijjuk* ("soil")
vel/vel *aggait* ("hand"), *akka* ("paternal uncle"), *anngaq*[4] ("nephew/niece")

The Nunavik dialect has a total of sixteen phonemes, three vowels (*a*, *i*, *u*, which may be either short or long), and thirteen consonants, distributed as follows:

VOWELS	a	aa	i	ii	u	uu
CONSONANTS		BILABIAL		APICAL	VELAR	UVULAR
stops		p		t	k	q
voiced continuants		v		l j/r [J]	γ [g]	R [r]
voiceless continuant				s		
nasals		m		n	η [ng]	

There is no voiceless lateral continuant (*&*), although that consonant is found in the neighbouring Nunatsiavut dialect of Labrador. In Nunavik, *&* has merged with *s*. As in most other Canadian forms of Inuit, no phonemic distinction exists between *j* and *J* (a voiced and palatalized apical, fricative continuant that is written as *r* in the phonetic alphabet). However, this voiced continuant phoneme is realized differently in the two subdialects of Nunavik. In Tarramiut it occurs as *j* (pronounced *y*), as it does elsewhere in Canada,[5] but in Itivimiut it is always realized as a palatalized consonant (*J*). Here are a few examples:

TARRAMIUT	ITIVIMIUT	
nauja	*nauJa*	"seagull"
qajaq	*qaJaq*	"kayak"
iji	*iJi*	"eye"
piujuq	*piuJuq*	"good"

Within clusters, the realization of *j* is pronounced *dj* in Tarramiut. In Itivimiut it is pronounced *J*, as when single, but many speakers utter a glottal stop[6] between the two consonants or even replace the first consonant with a stop (Massenet 1986). More largely, a glottal stop may occur in all Itivimiut clusters whose second element is a voiced continuant other than lateral *l*:

TARRAMIUT	ITIVIMIUT	
ajji	*aJ'Ji/a'Ji*	"picture"
qarjuk	*qar'Juk/qa'Juk*	"arrow"
ivvit	*iv'vit/i'vit*	"you one"
aggait	*ag'gait/a'gait*	"hand"
tarraq	*tar'raq/ta'raq*	"shadow"

These diverging realizations of the merged phoneme *j/J* show that the two subdialects of Nunavik followed different paths when they had to fuse together the etymological *j* and the etymological *J*. Like most other Canadian dialects, Tarramiut chose to retain *j* as the unique realization of the phoneme, but Itivimiut did otherwise. It instead preferred to preserve only *J*, extending its use to contexts where an etymological *j* should occur (e.g., *nauJa*, "seagull," etymologically *nauja*).

It is impossible to explain, at least in the present state of knowledge, why linguistic evolution operated in that way. Interestingly enough, however, another etymological phonemic difference evolved separately in the two subdialects. In Tarramiut the present-day reflection of the original fourth vowel *e* is *i* (except, among older speakers, before another vowel, where it becomes *a*), as it generally occurs in other Inuit dialects, but in Itivimiut an etymological *e* is sometimes realized as *a* before a uvular consonant or velar *g*. Compare, for instance:

TARRAMIUT	ITIVIMIUT	
angirraq	*anar'raq*	"home"
iniqunaqtuq	*inaqunaqtuq*	"pretty"
itigait	*itagait*	"foot"
angutaujuq	*angutaujuq*	"he is a man"

In both subdialects, the uvular stop *q* tends to be realized as a voiceless fricative, whose pronunciation sounds somewhat like Spanish *j* in *Juan* ("John"). This explains why in Nunavik schools, children are taught to write *q*-initial clusters with an *r* (e.g., *arqutik*, "road," and *ursuq*, "blubber"). Some younger speakers realize a word-initial *q* as *h* (e.g., *himmik*, "dog"), and many no longer discriminate between the geminates *gg* and *kk* on the one hand and *rr* and *qq* on the other. For them, the words *aggait* ("hand") and *akkait* ("your paternal uncle") or *tarraq* ("shadow") and *taqqaq* ("transversal rope on the kayak's deck") are homophonic.

One of the most striking characteristics of the Nunavik dialect is the so-called law of double consonants.[7] It prevents two sequences of consonant clusters from following one another by deleting one consonant from the second cluster (Dresher and Johns 1995). Concretely speaking, the first element of a cluster is always deleted when it is immediately preceded by another cluster within the same word. For example, if the grammatical ending *-kkut* ("through") is added to the word-base *illu-* ("house"), this should normally give *illukkut* ("through the house"). But in Nunavik, in accordance with the law of double consonants, the second geminate (*kk*) must be simplified because it follows another cluster (*ll*). As a result of this process of elision, the word becomes *illukut*, with a single *k*. Similarly, instead of *miqsurmat* ("when she was sewing") Nunavik speakers say *miqsumat*. The law of double consonants is also in usage in Nunatsiavut, and a basically similar, but more restricted, rule exists in the Siglitun dialect of Western Canadian Inuktun.

Some of the phonological features described above are relatively recent. Linguistic transcriptions made in Arctic Quebec by Rev. Edmund James Peck – the first Anglican missionary among the Inuit – and other visitors[8] during the last quarter of the nineteenth century show that 130 years ago velC, uvuC, and even bilC (bilabial/consonant) clusters were still in use and that the law of double consonants did not exist yet. Interestingly enough, the orthography of some entries in Rev. Peck's Eskimo-English dictionary (Peck 1925) suggests that *J* was heard in the Itivimiut area when he lived there from around 1875 to 1880. For instance, the word for "small dish" is written *poutarrook* (modern *pugutaarJuk*). The second *r* in *poutarrook* probably stands for *J*, whose pronunciation resembles that of English *r*.

GRAMMAR

The grammar of Nunavik is basically the same as that of the other Inuit dialects. Its description thus applies for a good part to all forms of the Inuit language – to Inuktitut in particular – if purely phonemic interdialectal variation is ignored. As seen in chapter 2, lexemes always start with a word-base, or radical, generally followed by one or more affixes (Cornillac 1993). Radicals express the basic meaning of the word, whereas affixes augment or specify that meaning (lexical affixes) or mark the function of the word within the sentence (grammatical affixes, or endings).

This means that morphology and internal syntax (i.e., the inner structure of the word) are more important than external syntax (i.e., the place of words within the sentence). The default word order is subject-object-verb (the verb being the lexeme expressing the event/s narrated in the sentence), but it may be modified for stylistic or other reasons because the grammatical function of each word is clearly marked by its ending. For example, the utterance "Peter has seen Paul" may be translated in different ways (although the first is usually preferred):

Piita Paulimik takulauqtuq
Piita takulauqtuq Paulimik
Paulimik takulauqtuq Piita ... etc.

In all cases, it is because the radical *Piita-* ("Peter") is not followed by any grammatical affix that this word is understood as being the subject of the sentence. Similarly, the ending *-mik* marks the radical *Pauli-* ("Paul") as a direct object. With regard to the third lexeme, *takulauqtuq* ("he/she has seen"), which expresses the event narrated in the sentence, it starts with the word-base *taku-* ("to see"), followed by the lexical affix *-lauq-* (past tense) and by the grammatical ending *-tuq* (third-person singular of the indicative mood).

In the Nunavik dialect, as in the Inuit language in general, there are four basic types of words: nouns, verbs, localizers/demonstratives, and small words.

Nouns

Nouns comprise a category of lexemes whose primary function is to denote objects, persons, and concepts. More extensive in meaning than their English equivalents, Inuit nouns express all at the same time the nature of what is denoted, its singleness, duality, or plurality, its eventual possession by someone or something, and its function in relation to the other elements of the sentence. Words may start with a nominal (i.e., denotative) radical and be followed (with or without intermediary lexical affixes) by a nominal ending that marks their grammatical function and, eventually, the fact that they belong to a possessor:

tuttu/alum/mut (caribou/big/toward): "toward a big caribou"
illu/alu/nganut (house/big/toward his/her): "toward his/her large house"

Alternatively, nouns may start with a verbal word-base, followed (immediately or not) by a lexical affix that transforms the base into a noun and by a nominal ending:

alla/uti/kkut (to write/tool for/by way of): "by way of a tool for writing" (with a pen)
alla/sia(q)/ruti/ga (to write/well/tool for/my): "my tool for writing well"

According to the part they play in the sentence, nouns can include one of eight endings that form the nominal declension. Each ending may occur in the singular, dual (two entities), or plural (three or more entities) number. Here are the eight cases of the Nunavik non-possessive declension (affixed to the radical *nuna*, "land"):

CASE	SINGULAR	DUAL	PLURAL
Basic	*nunaØ*[9]	*nunaak*	*nunait*
Relative	*nunaup*	*nunaak*	*nunait*
Modalis	*nunamik*	*nunaannik*	*nunanik*
Ablative	*nunamit*	*nunaannit*	*nunanit*
Locative	*nunami*	*nunaanni*	*nunani*
Allative	*nunamut*	*nunaannut*	*nunanut*
Translative	*nunakkut*	*nunaakkut*	*nunatigut*
Simulative	*nunatut*	*nunaattitut*	*nunatitut*

BASIC CASE

The basic (or absolutive) case expresses that the noun constitutes the principal referent of the event narrated in the sentence. This referent may be the subject of the sentence if the event is translated by a single-person verb (see the section below on verbs), or it may be the first object of the sentence with a double-person verb:

anguti takujuq: "the/a man is seeing something"
anguti takujanga: "the man, he/she sees him" ("he/she sees the man")
illuuk paaniittuuk: "(the) two houses are up there"
illuit takujakka: "the houses, I see them" ("I see the houses")

RELATIVE CASE

The relative case expresses that a noun is linked to another noun by way of a relation of ownership or that it acts as the grammatical subject of an event translated by a double-person verb:

angutiup[10] *illunga*: "of the man, his house" ("the man's house")
angutiup takujanga: "of the man, his object of seeing" ("the man sees it")

illuuk ukkuangik: "of the two houses, their two doors" ("the two houses' doors")
illuit taaqtangit: "of the houses, their objects of hiding" ("the houses hide them")

MODALIS CASE

The modalis (or secondary) case expresses that the noun to which it is affixed is the second referent of the event narrated in the sentence. This referent may be the first object of the sentence if the event is translated by a single-person verb, or it may be the second object of the sentence with a double-person verb:[11]

Piita angutimik takujuq: "Peter, a man he/she sees" ("Peter sees a man")
Piita angutimik takutitara: "Peter, a man I make him see" ("I show Peter a man")
Pauli illunik niuviqtitara: "Paul, houses I make him buy" ("I make Paul buy houses")
marruunik illuqaqtut: "two entities, they have as houses" ("they have two houses")

ABLATIVE CASE

The ablative case expresses that a noun denotes where something or someone comes from (in a literal or figurative sense). It answers the question "whence?":

angutimit pijuq: "from the/a man, it comes" ("it comes from a man")
illumit pisuttutit: "from the/a house, you (one) walk" ("you walk from the house")
angutiinnit anginiqsaq: "out of two men, something bigger" ("bigger than two men")
illunit anginiqpaaq: "out of the houses, the biggest one" ("the biggest house")

LOCATIVE CASE

The locative case expresses that a noun denotes the spatial location or the temporal period of occurrence of the event narrated in the sentence. It answers the question "where?" or "when?":

illumi sinittuguk: "in the/a house, we (two) sleep" ("both of us sleep in a house")

ullumi tikittugut: "in the day, we (many) arrive" ("we arrive today")
ulluuni marruuni tikilaaqtut: "in two days, in two entities, they shall arrive" ("they shall arrive within two days")
angutini itsivajutik: "within men, you (two) sit" ("the two of you sit among men")

ALLATIVE CASE

The allative case expresses that a noun denotes the place toward which one is going, the aim of the event narrated in the sentence, or the reason why an event happens. It answers the question "whereto?" "what for?" "by whom?" or "why?":

illumut pisuttuq: "toward the/a house, he/she walks" ("he/she walks to the house")
kiinaujanut pinasuttusi: "for monies, you (many) work" ("you work for money")
angutimut takujaujunga: "for a man, I am an object of seeing" ("I'm seen by a man")
inuunnut aliattunga: "because of two people I'm glad" ("I'm glad because of two persons")

TRANSLATIVE CASE

The translative (or vialis, or perlative) case expresses that the noun denotes the spatial location, or the period of time one passes through, or the means by which an event happens. It answers the question "whereby?" or "how?":

Aupalukkut timmisuqtutit: "through Aupaluk you fly" ("you fly by way of Aupaluk")
ullukut tikittuq: "through the day, he/she arrives" ("he/she arrives by day")
umiakkut maqaittut: "by way of a boat, they travel" ("they travel by boat")
irravitigut aannitunga: "through the bowels, I have a pain" ("my bowels ache")

SIMULATIVE CASE

The simulative (or similaris) case expresses that a noun denotes something that looks or acts like something else:

illutut angijuq: "like the/a house, it is big" ("it is big like a house")

auttut aupaqtuq: "like blood, it is red" ("it is blood-red")
angutiittitut takitigijut: "like two men, they are equally tall" ("they're as tall as two men")
inuttitut uqaqtut: "like human beings (Inuit), they speak" ("they speak Inuktitut")

POSSESSIVES

When the person, the object, or the concept denoted by the noun is regarded as belonging to someone or something, the word ends with a grammatical affix expressing, at the same time, its function in the sentence and the person of its possessor. This enables speakers to utter lexemes such as *illuga* ("my house"), *tupirni* ("in your tent"), and *umianganut* ("to his/her boat").

Like all other Inuit dialects, Nunavik has four grammatical persons. Each person can occur in the singular, dual, or plural, and the entity that is possessed can also be single (s.), double (d.), or multiple (p.). Here are the grammatical persons:

		SINGULAR	DUAL	PLURAL
1ST PERSON	S.	my one	our one (to both of us)	our one
	D.	my two	our two (to both of us)	our two
	P.	my many	our many (to both of us)	our many
2ND PERSON	S.	thy one	your one (to both of you)	your one
	D.	thy two	your two (to both of you)	your two
	P.	thy many	your many (to both of you)	your many
3RD PERSON	S.	his/her one	their one (to both of them)	their one
	D.	his/her two	their two (to both of them)	their two
	P.	his/her many	their many (to both of them)	their many
4TH PERSON	S.	his/her own one	their (both of them) own one	their own one
	D.	his/her own two	their (both of them) own two	their own two
	P.	his/her own many	their (both of them) own many	their own many

The fourth (reflexive) person occurs when the possessor is also the subject of the sentence. In all other cases, the third person is used. For example, the English sentence "she sees her house" can be translated in two ways according to whether the possessor of the house (the person represented by "her") is the one seeing the house or is someone else:

igluni takujanga	"her own house, she sees it" (4th person)
iglunga takujanga	"her (someone else's) house, she sees it" (3rd person)

Possessive endings may occur with each case of the noun declension. If the four grammatical persons are multiplied by the three numbers applying to the possessor, by the three numbers applying to the possessed entity, and by the eight cases of the declension, a total of 288 possessive endings is reached. Fortunately for language learners, the Nunavik dialect has amalgamated several forms, which reduces the total a bit. A complete list of possessive endings is found in appendix 1.

PERSONAL PRONOUNS

Personal pronouns may be considered a special category of possessed nouns. They are not needed for marking the person of the verb's subject because this information is included in verbal endings, but they can be useful in many ways (e.g., for expressing the object of a verb, as in *uvannut pisuttut*, "they walk toward me"). Pronouns occur only in the first and second persons. In the third person, demonstratives are used (see the section on localizers/demonstratives below). Their declension is quite similar to that of nouns:

1ST PERSON	SINGULAR ("I, ME")	DUAL ("BOTH OF US")	PLURAL ("WE, US")
Basic	*uvanga*	*uvaguk*	*uvagut*
Relative	*uvanga*	*uvaguk*	*uvagut*
Modalis	*uvannik*	*uvattinik*	*uvattinik*
Ablative	*uvannit*	*uvattinit*	*uvattinit*
Locative	*uvanni*	*uvattini*	*uvattini*
Allative	*uvannut*	*uvattinut*	*uvattinut*
Translative	*uvakkut*	*uvattigut*	*uvattigut*
Simulative	*uvattut*	*uvattitut*	*uvattitut*

2ND PERSON	SINGULAR ("YOU ONE")	DUAL ("BOTH OF YOU")	PLURAL ("MANY OF YOU")
Basic	*ivvit*	*ilittik*	*ilitsi*
Relative	*ivvit*	*ilittik*	*ilitsi*
Modalis	*ilinnik*	*ilittinik*	*ilitsinik*
Ablative	*ilinnit*	*ilittinit*	*ilitsinit*
Locative	*ilinni*	*ilittini*	*ilitsini*
Allative	*ilinnut*	*ilittinut*	*ilitsinut*
Translative	*ilikkut*	*ilittigut*	*ilitsigut*
Simulative	*ilittut*	*ilittitut*	*ilitsitut*

Verbs

In Nunavik, as in all Inuit dialects, verbs play the same part as in English: they express the event(s) (action, predicament, state of affairs, qualification) narrated in the sentence. However, the information they convey is more complete than that conveyed by English verbs. It may include the following data: person of the subject; person of the principal object; modalities, extent, and aspect of the event; grammatical tense; and even the specific nature of the object (as in *illuliuqtuq*, "he/she builds a house"). Contrary to nouns, Inuit verbs may constitute a sentence by themselves, and each sentence must usually include at least one verb.

Verbs usually start with a word-base denoting the event they express, eventually followed by one or more lexical affixes. They must close on a grammatical ending marking the modality (or mood) of the event, the person of the subject, and eventually, the person of the principal object, as in:

takuvunga	"I see"
taku/vunga	see/declarative, 1st-p. s. subject
takulauqtara	"I saw it"
taku/lauq/tara	see/past/indicative, 1st-p. s. subject, 3rd-p. s. object
tusannginavinga	"because you do not hear me"
tusa(q)/nngi(t)/navinga	hear/negation/perfective, 2nd-p. s. subject, 1st-p. s. object

Alternatively, through a process of noun incorporation (see chapter 2), verbs may start with a noun radical followed, immediately or not, by a lexical affix, which transforms the word into a verb and must be followed by a verbal ending:

illuliuqtut	"they build a house"
illu/liuq/tut	house/to build/indicative, 3rd-p. p. subject
illugilauqtavut	"we had it for a house"
illu/gi/lauq/tavut	house/have for/past/indicative, 1st-p. p. subject, 3rd-p. s. object
illumiippisi	"are you (many) in the house?"
illu/mi/it/pisi	house/in/to be somewhere/interrogative, 2nd-p. p. subject

There exist two types of verbal endings: single-person and double-person. The former mark the mood (or modality) of the event and the person of its subject, while the latter also indicate the person of its first object. When expressed in the sentence, the subject of a single-person verb is in the basic case and its object in the modalis. With double-person verbal lexemes, it is the object that is in the basic case, the subject being in the relative. As mentioned earlier, in both instances, emphasis lies on the noun in the basic form (see Menovshchikov 1969):

inuk illumik takujuq	"the person sees (single-person) a house"
illu inuup takuvaa	"the house, a person sees it (double-person)"

Technically speaking, single-person verbs with an object are analyzed as antipassives (Kalmar 1977), and their object (marked with the modalis) is actually indirect.[12] Double-person verbs are called "ergative" (see Bittner 1987; Bok-Bennema 1991; Johns 1987, 1992; Kalmar 1977, 1979; Klokeid and Arima 1977; Lipscomb 1993; Lowe 1978; Nowak 1993; and Woodbury 1975), a type of construction that exists in several languages (Basque, for instance). The degree to which speakers may switch between antipassive and ergative verbs varies from one Inuit dialect to another.

There also exists a passive construction (see Smith 1981) formed with the affixes *-jaq/-taq* ("the object of an event") and *-u-* ("to be"). In Nunavik, its complement is in the allative case:[13]

Piitamut takujaujuq Pauli	"Paul is seen by Peter"
Piita/mut taku/ja(q)/u/juq Pauli	for Peter / he is an object of seeing / Paul

The grammatical persons of the subjects and objects of verbs are the same as those of the possessive noun endings. The fourth (reflexive) person, however, occurs only as subject of a verb in a dependent mood. It is used when the subject of a subordinate clause is also the subject of the main clause of the sentence. Compare, for instance:

tikigami quviasuttuq	"because he (A) arrives, he (A) is glad" (4th p.)
tikimmat quviasuttuq	"because he (B) arrives, he (A) is glad" (3rd p.)[14]

The Nunavik dialect possesses ten verbal moods, which express various modalities of the events narrated in the sentence.[15] Each mood has its own single-person and double-person endings.

DECLARATIVE

The declarative mood (called "indicative" by some sources) expresses that an event is told as part of a narrative: a story, an account of something that has happened, and so forth. It shows that what one is telling about actually occurred and is not just a general statement:

anivunga	"I come out"
pinasuppunga[16]	"I am at work"
tusaqpaa	"he/she hears him/her/it"

INDICATIVE

The indicative mood (called "participial" or "attributive" by some sources) states that an event occurs or that something exists outside of any narrative consideration. It is used mainly for expressing a general situation or a chronic state rather than a unique fact or happening. Its third person – that of the subject, as single-person endings are concerned, and of the object, with double-person affixes – also has a participial meaning: "someone or something that is the subject or the object of an event." In such cases, the third-person indicative marker acts as a noun and can be affixed with nominal endings:[17]

pinasuttunga	"I have a job, I work"
tusaqtunga	"I hear"
utaqqijarma[18]	"you wait for me"
tusaqtuq	"he/she hears" – "someone who hears"

utaqqijara "I wait for him/her" – "someone for whom I'm waiting"
tusaqtunut "because of those who hear"
utaqqijaratut "like my object of waiting (the one I am waiting for)"

INTERROGATIVE

The interrogative mood expresses that the speaker is asking a question. Questioning is also marked by a slight heightening of the voice on the penultimate syllable and by the lengthening of the last vowel of the word. In the Nunavik dialect, several interrogative forms have become obsolete and are now replaced by their declarative or indicative equivalent:

tusaqpungaa? "do I hear?"
qailangaviit? "will you (one) come?"
utaqqivisiuk? "are you (many) waiting for him/her?"

IMPERATIVE-OPTATIVE

This mood expresses the utterance of an order or a wish. It is often attenuated by the use of lexical affixes *-lir-* ("to be doing something") or *-laur-* ("past tense"):

qailanga "may I come!"
nirilirit "be eating (you one)!" ("eat!")
ikajulaurliuk "may he/she have helped him/her!" ("may he/she help him/her!")

PERFECTIVE

Contrary to the preceding moods and like the following ones, the perfective mood (also called causative)[19] is a dependent modality, which cannot usually occur in a sentence without a main declarative, indicative, interrogative, or more infrequently, imperative-optative clause. It relates an effect to a cause (it is then translated as "because") or it expresses the fact (translated by "when," with the past tense) that an event has already occurred in relation to another event:[20]

aullarama "because I leave; when I left"
utaqqigakkit "because I wait for them; when I was waiting for them"

aullaravit aliasulauqtunga "because *or* when you (one) left, I was glad"

IMPERFECTIVE

The imperfective mood (also called conditional) expresses the occurrence of a condition ("if") or an eventuality ("when," with the future tense):

aullaruma "i I leave; when I leave"
utaqqigukkit "if I wait for them; when [future] I wait for them"
aullaruvit aliasulaaqtunga "if you leave *or* when you leave, I'll be glad"

DUBITATIVE

The dubitative mood expresses an indirect interrogation. If it occurs without any specific question word, it is translated by "if" or "whether" (as in "I wonder if/whether"):

aullalaarmangaarma "whether I shall leave"
takummangaaqpiuk "whether you (one) see him/her"
nalujunga qanga aullalaurmangaaqpit "I didn't know when you (one) left"

PERFECTIVE APPOSITIONAL

The perfective appositional mood is reflexive (its subject must be the same as that of the main clause) and expresses that an event occurs or has occurred at the same time as another event:

tusaqsunga aliasuttunga "while hearing, I am glad"
ikajuqsugu aliasuttuq "while helping him/her, he/she is glad"

IMPERFECTIVE APPOSITIONAL

A variant of the preceding, the imperfective appositional mood is reflexive and indicates that an event will occur at the same time as another event. It is also used as a polite equivalent of the imperative-optative:

tusarlunga aliasulaartunga "while hearing, I shall be glad"

ikajurlugu aliasulaaqtuq	"while helping him/her, he/she will be glad"
takulutit	"while you (one) are seeing" ("please see!")

When the subject of the perfective or imperfective appositional is different from that of the main clause, the affix *-tit-* occurs before the double-person imperfective appositional ending:

tusaqtilugu aliasuttunga	"while he/she is hearing, I am glad"
ikajuqtilunga aliasuttuq	"while I help (him/her), he/she is glad"
takutillutit aliasuttugut	"while you (one) are seeing, we are glad"

NEGATIVE APPOSITIONAL

When occurring in the negative, appositional endings appear under special forms, simultaneously perfective and imperfective. These forms may also express a prohibition:

tusarnanga aliasunngitunga	"while not hearing, I am not glad"
ikajurnagu aliasunngituq	"while not helping him/her, he/she is not glad"
takutinnak aliasuttut	"while you (one) are not seeing, they are glad"
tusarnak	"while you (one) are not hearing" ("don't hear!")

NEGATION

With moods other than the appositional, negation is marked by inserting the affix *-nngit-* before the verbal ending. Its presence may entail a slight modification of the ending (e.g., *takunnginama*, "because I do not see"), which is more marked with the declarative:[21]

takunngilanga, takunngilatit, takunngilaq …	"I, you, he/she … do not see"
tusanngilara	"I do not see it"

VERBAL ENDINGS

It is impossible here to give a complete list of all single- and double-person verbal affixes, which amount to some 850 different endings.

Examples are found in appendix 2. This appendix shows that in spite of their variety, verbal endings include a limited number of forms. For instance, single-person affixes always end with the following syllables or consonants:[22]

	SINGULAR	DUAL	PLURAL
1st person	*-nga*, *-ma*	*-uk*	*-ut*, *-ta*
2nd person	*-it*	*-tik*	*-si*
3rd person	*-q*, *-at*, *-a*	*-k*, *-ik*	*-t*, *-ata*
4th person	*-ni*, *-mi*	*-tik*, *-mik*	*-tik*, *-mik*

With double-person verbs, the form of the ending is often foreseeable. In the declarative and indicative moods, when the object is in the third person, it generally suffices to add to the syllables *-pa-*, *-va-*, *-ta-*, *-ja-*, and so on the basic possessive affix that corresponds to the person of the subject (e.g., *tusaq-pa-<u>ra</u>*, "<u>I</u> hear him/her").[23] With other persons and moods, a syllable expressing the person of the object is often added to the single-person ending: *-nga* for the first-person singular (e.g., *tusa-ravi(t)-<u>nga</u>*, "because you hear <u>me</u>"); *-(t)it* for the second-person singular (e.g., *tusa-runi-<u>tit</u>*, "if he/she hears <u>you</u> [one]"); *-uk* or *-gu* for the third-person singular (e.g., *tusaq-su-<u>gu</u>*, "when hearing <u>him/her</u>"); *-git* for the third-person plural (e.g., *tusaq-pi-<u>git</u>*, "do you [one] hear <u>them</u>?"); and so on.

It is worth noticing that some dependent mood endings look like possessive noun endings in the relative case (e.g., *-ga<u>ma</u>*, "because I," and *-ga<u>vit</u>*, "because you [one]," as compared with *-ma*, "of my," and *-vit*, "of thy"). It appears as though the relationship between the subordinate and the main clause (expressed by the dependent mood marker) were conceived of as analogous to the relation between possessor and possessed in the noun declension or to the connection between a double-person verb and its subject. The deeper meaning of this homology is not yet completely understood, although Lowe (1985a, 167) suggests that both the subordinate verb and the relative noun need, for their final interpretation, another word on which they depend syntactically. This could explain the formal analogy of their endings.

Localizers/Demonstratives

The function of localizers and of their semantic cousins the demonstratives is to indicate spatial position. They constitute a limited class of word-bases, with only ten of them in the Nunavik dialect.[24] Bases must be followed by special localizer or demonstrative endings, and no lexical affix can occur between the radical and the ending.[25] Localizers express the division of space as it is structured in relation to the speaker, according to complex criteria (proximity, perceptibility, etc.), which are examined in chapter 6, on Inuit semantics.

Localizers, properly speaking, correspond approximately to English adverbs of place, as they express spatial positioning per se ("here," "up there," "inside," etc.).[26] They have their own declension, which has four cases and no grammatical number. Here are the ten Nunavik localizers, each of them with its corresponding demonstrative:

	ABLATIVE	LOCATIVE	ALLATIVE	TRANSLATIVE	DEMONSTRATIVE
"here very close"	*uvanngat*	*uvani*	*uvunga*	*uvuuna*	*una*
"here"	*maanngat*	*maani*	*maunga*	*mauna*	*manna*
"there"	*ikanngat*	*ikani*	*ikunga*	*ikuuna*	*inna*
"there far away"	*avanngat*	*avani*	*avunga*	*avuuna*	*anna*
"down here"	*kananngat*	*kanani*	*kanunga*	*kanuuna*	*kanna*
"down there" (Tarra.)	*unanngat*	*unani*	*ununga*	*unuuna*	*unna*
"down there" (Itivi.)	*samanngat*	*samani*	*samunga*	*samuuna*	*sanna*
"up here"	*pikanngat*	*pikani*	*pikunga*	*pikuuna*	*pinna*
"up there"	*paanngat*	*paani*	*paunga*	*pauna*	*panna*
"outside"	*kianngat*	*kiani*	*kiunga*	*kiuna*	*kinna*
"inside"	*qamanngat*	*qamani*	*qamunga*	*qamuuna*	*qanna*

Demonstratives express that a single, double, or multiple entity is positioned in a portion of space delimited along the same criteria as those defining localizers. They can be translated by "this," "that," "that one up there," and so on. Their declension possesses all eight cases of the noun declension (in the singular and plural; dual forms have now become obsolete), although endings are different from those used with nouns. For example, the demonstrative *una* ("this, very close to the speaker") is declined as follows:

	SINGULAR	PLURAL/DUAL	
basic	*una*	*ukua*	"this/these"
relative	*uuma*	*ukua*	"of this/of these"

modalis	*uminga*	*ukuninga*	"this/these (first object)"
ablative	*umanngat*	*ukunanngat*	"from this/from these"
locative	*umani*	*ukunani*	"in this/in these"
allative	*umunga*	*ukununga*	"to this/to these"
translative	*umuuna*	*ukunuuna*	"through this/through these"
simulative	*utunaq*	*ukutitunaq*	"like this/like these"

Demonstratives may occur in apposition to a noun or by themselves. In the latter case, they function as third-person personal pronouns, whereas in the former they can predicate the existence of something, without any verb in the sentence:

illu manna angijuq	"this house is big"
illunut pakkununga pisuttunga	"I walk toward those houses up there"
qanna takunngitara	"that one inside, I do not see it"
natsiik kakkua	"two seals these down here" ("there are two seals down here")

Localizers and demonstratives can be preceded by the prefix *ta-* (the only prefix in the Inuit language) when they refer to a portion of space that is very hard to perceive (when speaking about the past, for instance) or that is in relation with someone or something other than the speaker (e.g., *tamaani*, "here in relation to someone else"; *taanna*, "that one there away hardly perceptible").

Small Words

The fourth and last class of lexemes, the "small words," never take any lexical affix or grammatical ending.[27] They summarize in one word a relatively complex notion, join together the components of a sentence, or translate an exclamation or an interrogation. They often correspond to English adverbs, conjunctions, exclamations, or question words.[28] Here are a few examples:

asuguuq	"I totally agree with you"
aatsuk	"I don't know"
immaqaa	"it is quite possible, maybe"
amma	"and, also"

uvva	"or"
aatataa	"ouch!"
qanga	"when?"
namut	"whereto?"

Nouns, verbs, localizers/demonstratives, and small words exhaust the grammatical categories of the Inuit language. There are no adjectives. Qualities and other characteristics are usually expressed by way of lexical affixes (e.g., *-tsiaq-*, "nice, good"; *-aluk-*, "big") or by verbs in the third person of the indicative. As already mentioned, the latter can either express the occurrence of an event or denote the subject or object of this event. Many English qualifiers thus correspond to Inuit verbs and/or nominal participles:

"small"	*mikijuq*	"he/she/it is small" or "something which is small"
"good" (plural)	*piujut*	"they are good" or "many which are good"
"white"	*qakuqtaq*	"which has been bleached" or "something white"

The verbal expression of qualities is limited to the third person of the single-person indicative. With other persons or moods, qualifiers function only as nouns (e.g., *mikiju-u-gama*, "because I am something small"). When in apposition to another noun, qualifiers agree with it in case and number (e.g., *illunut mikijunut aupaqtunut pisuttunga*, "I walk toward many houses, toward many small entities, toward many red entities" ["I walk toward small red houses"]).

As seen in the section above on nouns, personal pronouns constitute a category of nouns. The same can be said of numerals, which express numbered entities rather than pure mathematical notions. Thus they may be followed by all endings of the noun declension, and they agree in case with the nouns to which they are in apposition:

atausiq	"one entity"
marruunut pisuttunga	"I walk toward two entities"
inunnik pingasunik takujunga	"I see people, three entities" ("I see three persons")

With possessive endings (most generally in the third person), numerals function as ordinal numbers, as in: *sitamangat* ("their four" ["the fourth of them"]) and *sitamanganni* ("in their four" ["in the fourth of them," or "Thursday," when "them" refers to the days of the week]).

LEXICON

At the end of chapter 2, it was mentioned that the principal lexical differences among Inuit dialects concern their affixes. A comparison of the Tarramiut subdialect with other speech forms (Fortescue 1985a) shows that only about 30% to 35% of the Tarramiut stock of 509 lexical affixes are shared with dialects that do not belong to Eastern Canadian Inuktitut. Within Inuktitut, however, percentages of cognate affixes are much higher, hovering around 70% to 75%. Appendix 3 lists the twenty-seven categories of lexical affixes found in the Inuit language (according to Fortescue 1983), with Nunavik examples.

Most word-bases are shared among all Eastern Canadian Inuktitut dialects. It may happen, however, that identical words have different meanings in various dialects or subdialects. In Nunavik, for instance, the lexemes *alianaqtuq*, *tamarmik*, and *inummarik* respectively mean "pleasing," "both of them," and "adult." But in the North Baffin dialect, they are instead translated as "displeasing," "all of them," and "real Inuk." In the Tarramiut subdialect the words for "now" and "later on" are *maanna* and *siaruq*, but in Itivimiut *maanna* means "later on," and "now" is translated by *tagataga*. Itivimiut also has *turusiq* for "boy" and *taralikitaaq* for "butterfly," whereas Tarramiut speakers say *surusiq* and *saralikitaaq*. In Tarramiut a baby is called *nutaraq*, and in Itivimiut *kakkalaaq*. Such local differences in vocabulary may offer occasions for joking about how people speak in other communities, but they do not impair mutual understanding.

CONCLUSION

Described in this chapter is the formal phonological and grammatical structure of one Inuit dialect, Nunavik Inuktitut – that is, the common, artificially generalized characteristics underlying the actual performance of each speaker of the language. This structure may be considered a form of translation: it transforms semantic categories into linguistically transmissible messages. The phonological and grammatical structure of Inuktitut does not belong to the social rules and cultural worldview specific to the Inuit, but it relates to them in two ways: (1) it is narrowly linked with semantic categories, which stem directly from mental images and ideologies, that they organize into classes of signification; and (2) society perceives linguistic symbols as loaded with a social meaning that may, in the long run, generate variation and change in the form and usage of the language.

In the next two chapters, the evolution of Eskaleut and Inuit is discussed, starting with the prehistory of the language. This should provide us with a better understanding of the linguistic, social, and cultural factors that have contributed to generating the inter- and intradialectal surface variation described in this chapter and in the preceding ones.

4

The Prehistory of the Inuit Language

Languages belonging to a linguistic family generally share a common origin. This means that they stem from the same source: an ancestral speech form or a group of closely related languages or dialects that progressively diverged over the years because of migration and other factors.[1] This is what probably happened with Eskaleut. It is almost certain that the ancestors of present-day speakers of Unangax, Yupik, and Inuit formerly constituted a group of neighbouring tribes, whose language[2] began to evolve after they had started moving in different directions and losing contact with each other. By comparing archaeological and linguistic data, it is thus possible to learn about the ancient history of Eskaleut.

SEARCHING FOR THE ORIGINS

Questions and hypotheses about the origin of the Inuit and of their language are hardly new. As early as 1576, when the British mariner Martin Frobisher brought back to England three Inuit individuals whom his men had captured on south-eastern Baffin Island, many people thought them to be "Tartars" – that is, Mongolian inhabitants of the Russian Empire[3] (Oswalt 1979). The Russian ambassador to London lodged a formal complaint with Queen Elizabeth I to the effect that three subjects of the Tsar had been illegally abducted by Frobisher.

From their own point of view, Inuit also wondered who these strangers with big eyebrows (hence the name they gave them: *qallunaat*, "outstanding eyebrows") arriving in huge boats could well be. They were the first to find an answer. As recounted in a well-known myth from the eastern Arctic, the Inuit, Amerindians, *qallunaat*, and *ijiqqat* (mythical invisible beings) all share the same ancestor: a young woman who had wed her dog. Obliged as she was – according to several versions of the story – to part with her offspring, she put some of her children in makeshift craft consisting of skin boots that drifted south with the sea currents. The North Baffin Inuit believed that this event took place on Igloolik Island, which may then be considered the cradle of all human races (Rasmussen 1929).

The message is clear. Humanity appeared in Inuit territory and it is from this humanity that all of the world's peoples stemmed. Therefore, it is not surprising if some of these human beings, the *qallunaat*, wish to return to their country of origin. The Inuit myth, adjusted and adapted to historical events, thus constitutes a coherent explanation of racial diversity and ethnic relations (Sonne 1990). This explanation is neither more nor less valuable than old European theories on the origin of the North American natives, such as the one that considered some aboriginal populations of the Arctic to be descendants of the ancient Hebrews.[4]

From a more specifically linguistic perspective, Inuit do not seem to have questioned themselves much about the origin of the language spoken by *qallunaat*. Because they were apparently endowed with *isuma* (reason, thought), Europeans possessed a language in accordance with their own peculiar nature. Since this nature was different from that of Inuit, it was normal for *qallunaat* to speak differently from them. According to some testimonies, however, when first contacts occurred, eastern Canadian Inuit were surprised that *qallunaat* did not understand Inuktitut. As recounted in the novel *Sanaaq*, for instance: "When they entered, Aqiarulaaq said to the *Qallunaat*: '*Ai!* [Hi!]'. But because they cannot understand, they don't even utter a word. Inuit are really astonished that these people have lost their faculty of speech" (Nappaaluk 1984, 26).

Europeans, for their part, wondered about the origin of Inuit and other Eskaleut languages. In a paper read at the International Congress of Americanists in 1883, the French linguist Lucien Adam (1884) stated that the Eskimo languages[5] had nothing to do with the Amerindian speech forms, nor with the Uralic and Altaic linguistic families from central and northern Eurasia,[6] because all of these were polysynthetic, which was not the case with Eskimo.[7] Subsequent research would confirm Adam's intuition on the lack of any relation between the Eskaleut and American Indian languages,[8] but it would go against his rejection of a Uralo-Altaic kinship. As shall be seen below, prehistoric contacts between the ancestral speakers of the Eskaleut, Uralic, and Altaic forms of speech are now considered probable.

It makes sense indeed to believe that because the ancestors of Inuit, Yupiit, and Unangan are deemed to have migrated from Asia in a relatively recent past (see below), there could exist similarities between Eskaleut and some Asian or Eurasian languages. Over the years, such similarities have been hypothesized in regard to four different linguistic families of the Old World: Indo-European, Chukotko-Kamchatkan, Uralic, and Altaic.

In 1935 the Dutch linguist C.C. Uhlenbeck proposed the existence of a relationship between Eskaleut and the Indo-European family. To give some weight to this proposition, he drew a long list of words supposedly shared by the two families (Uhlenbeck 1935). The Danish Eskimologist William Thalbitzer later confirmed the relevance of Uhlenbeck's work (Thalbitzer 1944). But in 1951 another Dane, Louis Hammerich, after having re-examined the list, withdrew many words he did not think relevant (Hammerich 1951). Hammerich concluded, however, that there subsisted enough similarities to hypothesize the existence of common prehistoric influences on both Eskaleut and Indo-European, although it was impossible to confirm whether these influences had actually taken place.

In the wake of Uhlenbeck and Thalbitzer, Hammerich pointed out formal similarities between, for example, the following radicals:

INDO-EUROPEAN	ESKALEUT	
neu-	*nu(taq)*	"new"
teu-	*tu-*	"to hit with a long object"
doh-	*tu-*	"to give"
u - l	*ulik-*	"to wrap"

Hammerich also noted that the original Indo-European case system (nominal declension) was relatively similar to that of Inuit. Moreover, if some consonants were considered equivalent – Indo-European laryngeals and Eskaleut uvulars, for instance – more similarities could be discovered (e.g., Indo-European *anH* and Eskaleut *aniq-*, "to breathe").

At the beginning of the 1960s a new proposition made by Morris Swadesh (1962) suggested that the Eskaleut languages were probably related to the Chukotko-Kamchatkan family (also known as

Luoravetlan or Paleo-Asiatic), a group of speech forms (Chukchi, Koryak, Aliutor, Kerek, and Itelmen) spoken in Russian Chukotka and Kamchatka. One of these languages, Chukchi, had been in contact with Siberian Yupik for a few thousand years. According to Swadesh, the grammatical irregularities found in Eskaleut could be explained by referring to Chukotko-Kamchatkan grammar. He stated that this meant that both families shared a very ancient common history and that they probably constituted the only remainder of an older protofamily encompassing many more languages than Eskaleut and Chukotko-Kamchatkan do now.[9]

Eric Hamp (1976a), however, thought that Swadesh had gone too far. Nothing proved the existence of such a protofamily. There certainly exist some similarities between the Eskaleut and Chukotko-Kamchatkan consonant systems – for instance, both of them possess the uvular stop *q* – and the Yupiit languages have borrowed many words from Chukchi, but according to Hamp, this could be explained by the simple fact that the two linguistic groups, on both sides of Bering Strait, had been in contact for a few millennia and often shared the same territory. Under such circumstances, it was natural that they had influenced each other without necessarily being genetically related.

In an article published at the beginning of the 1980s, Michael Fortescue (1981a) held an identical view. For him, contacts between the Eskaleut and Chukotko-Kamchatkan languages constituted a merely surface phenomenon. In his opinion, they overlaid a much more ancient system of relations among languages whose speakers had been neighbours during some prehistoric periods of time. These languages, which did not all share a common ancestor but derived from ancestral forms that had been in narrow contact with each other, now belonged to the Eskaleut, Uralic, and Altaic families. Moreover, according to Fortescue, it was possible that Japanese, Korean, Ainu, and probably also the Chukotko-Kamchatkan languages had participated in this same prehistoric network of linguistic exchanges. It would be the existence of this network that would explain the lexical and grammatical similarities currently found among many of these speech forms.

Such a hypothetical linkage between the Eskaleut, Uralic, and Altaic families was hardly new. As early as 1576 Martin Frobisher supposed that the language of the "Tartars" he had brought back to Europe was some form of Mongolian (an Altaic language). And throughout the eighteenth and nineteenth centuries, scholars often pointed out similarities between the language of the Eskimos and those of the Hungarians, Finns, Samoyeds, and Tartars[10] (Krauss 1973, 851). It is true that the Uralic and Altaic languages, the former more than the latter, share with Eskaleut some relatively similar agglutinative features, as well as many words that look more or less alike.

Uhlenbeck was the first scholar, at the beginning of the twentieth century (see Uhlenbeck 1905), to undertake a systematic comparison of Uralic, Altaic, and Eskimo. He was followed by Sauvageot (1924) and, much later on, by Bergsland (1959b) and Fortescue. These specialists noted that in all languages they took into consideration, words were usually made out of radicals followed by affixes. Moreover, some basic morphemes appeared as quite similar. Fortescue (1981a) mentions that in Inuit, Japanese, Korean, and the Altaic languages, the affix used for enabling a verb to call for a marked first object (in the modalis case in Inuit) is *-i-* (as in Inuktitut *aittuivunga*, "I give something to someone"). In Uralic the dual is marked by *-k* (as in Inuktitut *inuuk*, "two persons") and the plural by *-t* or by the gemination of the syllable-initial consonant (e.g., Inuit *angutit*, "men," and *tulukkat*, "ravens" [s. *tulugaq*]). As concerns lexical similarities, they are relatively numerous. Here are a few examples quoted by Fortescue (1981a):

"outside, space, sky"	*sila* (Inuit); *sula* (Manchu); *sora* (Japanese)
"knife"	*savik* (Inuit); *safi* (old Japanese)
"kayak, canoe, small craft"	*qajaq* (Inuit); *kajuk* (Tungus); *qajiq* (old Turkish)
"ear"	*siun/siut* (Inuit); *seen* (Tungus)
"to stop up, to close"	*simik-* (Inuit); *shime-* (Japanese); *soom* (Tungus)
"sun"	*siqiniq* (Inuit); *sigun* (Manchu)
"long, tall"	*taki-* (Inuit); *taka-* (Japanese)
"spirit, god"	*tuunraq/tuurngaq* (Inuit); *tanri* (Turkish)
"toward the sea"	*kita-* (Inuit); *kidin* (old Turkish); *kita* (Japanese)
"winter, ice, snow"	*ukiuq* (Inuit); *zuke* (Tungus); *yuki* (Japanese)
"brother"	*ani* (Inuit); *ani* (Japanese); *enni* (Korean)
"tread on, step on, stand on"	*tuti-* (Inuit); *tata-* (Manchu); *tat-* (Japanese); *tudi-* (Korean)

It is therefore possible, although not completely proved, that the Eskaleut, Altaic, and Uralic languages, and maybe also Japanese and Korean, share a common substratum – an old set of identical and nearly identical morphemes and lexemes going back to a time when these speech forms were used by neighbouring populations. These people would have been aware of each other's languages and have communicated frequently among themselves, which would explain their sharing of linguistic material.

It is also possible that the relationship between Eskaleut and Uralic is stronger yet and that these two families share a common origin. A north-eastern Siberian language, Yukaghir, now spoken only by a few hundred people, seems to stand halfway between Uralic and Eskaleut. Its noun declension is very close to that of the Yupiit and Inuit languages, while some other grammatical characteristics are more similar to what is found in Uralic (Fortescue 1988a). The existence of Yukaghir might bear witness to a period when the linguistic ancestors of the Eskaleut, Samoyed, and Finno-Ugric populations spoke languages belonging to the same family.[11]

If this hypothesis stands true, similarities between Eskaleut and Indo-European would not be due to a common origin or substratum but to very old Uralic (or Uralo-Altaic) influences felt by both families. Indo-European languages have been in contact for thousands of years with some Uralic and Altaic speech forms, but it is very doubtful that they ever had any direct relation with the ancestors of the Eskaleut languages. As similarities with Chukotko-Kamchatkan are concerned, they might stem from direct contacts over a few thousand years between the Eskaleut speakers and the Chukchi, Koryak, and other north-eastern Siberian populations, although a closer connection is now considered possible.[12]

In a book published in 1998 and titled *Language Relations across Bering Strait: Reappraising the Archaeological and Linguistic Evidence*, Michael Fortescue summarizes the question of Eskaleut origins as it now stands. The Copenhagen linguist describes the Bering Strait area as a geographical bottleneck, more or less open to animal and human occupation at various periods in time, migrations being at their easiest when a Beringian land bridge between Asia and America and an ice-free corridor leading to the North American interior (and/or Pacific Ocean coast) were both in existence at the same time. In such a bottleneck, where human movements were facilitated or slowed down due to varying climate conditions, successive waves of migrants could meet predecessors who had not yet exited the area, a fact that favoured linguistic contact, the mingling of genes, and language shift, leftovers from earlier waves being liable to adopt the language of newcomers.

Comparison brings Fortescue to hypothesize that Proto-Eskaleut, the language(s) spoken by the last wave of Bering Strait migrants, belonged to a linguistic mesh (i.e., a network of interconnected speech forms) he calls Uralo-Siberian.[13] This web of typologically identical – at different degrees – languages, which might or might not have been genetically related, would have included present-day Uralic, Yukaghir, Chukotko-Kamchatkan, and Eskaleut families and, in a more distant past, could also have been influenced by Proto-Altaic languages, with which it shares several similarities. According to Fortescue (1998, 219):

> A comparison of the approximate time depths assignable to the individual [Uralic, etc.] proto-languages suggests, in conjunction with the light cast by the archaeological perspective, that Proto U[ralo] S[iberian] might have been spoken sometimes between 8,000 and 10,000 years ago across a wide area of the forested regions of southern Siberia centred on the region between Lake Baykal and the Sayan ... and extending eastward up the Lena/ Aldan valleys and westward almost as far as the Ob.

Languages belonging to the original Uralo-Siberian mesh would have displayed a constellation of characteristic typological features that would have included: basic subject-object-verb word order, simple agglutinating morphology (limited to suffixing), a palatal series of consonants, the distinction between singular, dual, and plural number on nouns, indicative verb forms based on participles,[14] some personal possessor suffixes on nouns, and voiceless stops and voiced fricatives only (Fortescue 1998, 220). It is the combination of all these features and more – some of which have been lost or modified in present-day languages – that would have made Uralo-Siberian different from other adjacent meshes and families.

Does this prehistoric intermeshing mean that present-day speakers of Eskaleut are the direct descendants of Uralo-Siberian populations? Fortescue is cautious about that. When one asks "who are the Inuit, Yupiit, and Unangan, and where did their languages come from?" two separate answers must be given (Fortescue 1998, 209):

> The right kind of answer ... is something like this: the Eskimo and Aleut populations are the result of a mingling of genes brought by mesolithic newcomers to the Bering Strait region during the last stage of the post-glacial thermal maximum with those of earlier, perhaps pre-Na-Dene[15] groups still present in the region from the days of the Beringian Land Bridge. Their language, on the other hand, has nothing whatsoever to do with the language of these residual Beringians (apart from certain typological features acquired from them through contact and language shift [on the part of pre-Na-Dene]), but is remotely related to Uralo-Siberian languages spoken still on the Asian side of the Beringian Gateway and as far to the west within Eurasia as Hungary.

To understand how the Eskaleut languages settled on the American side of Bering Strait and started expanding throughout the North American Arctic, Eskimo migrations must now be discussed.

LANGUAGE AND MIGRATIONS

Some 4,500 years ago small groups of hunter-gatherers technically and culturally well adapted to the arctic environment were living in west-central Alaska, on Norton Sound and the Bering Sea (map 1). If Fortescue (1998) is right, these groups may have resulted from a mixing of various populations that had crossed from Asia in different periods,[16] including newly arrived settlers who spoke Proto-Eskaleut.[17] This language appears to have rapidly replaced any other form(s) of speech that had been in use until then. Technology was microlithic: it consisted in small stone tools (this is why archaeologists call it the Arctic Small Tool Tradition).[18] It had many points in common with some prehistoric cultures of the Lena Basin in Siberia (Dikov 1979), a fact that might support the hypothesis of a Uralo-Siberian mesh.

The Arctic Small Tool Tradition seems to have been contemporary of the split between the Eskimo and Aleut branches of the Eskaleut family. Swadesh (1962) estimates that some 4,000 years ago, the two branches had already separated.[19] His technique of calculation, which is called glottochronology, consisted of comparing a basic lexicon of a hundred words originating from two different languages or groups of languages. Given that linguistic change is thought to occur at a steady pace, the percentage of lexemes still shared by the two languages or groups would indicate how long it was before they split off. For instance, if each century witnesses five lexical changes, and if the two compared languages still share fifty words out of a sample of a hundred, this might mean that they became separated a thousand years ago. Even though Swadesh's method was severely criticized (see Bergsland and Vogt 1962), it seemed to work in the case of Eskaleut because its results were in general agreement with those yielded by archaeology (Dumond 1965).

According to some specialists, however (see Fortescue 1981b), migration toward the Aleutian Islands cannot have started earlier than 4,000 years ago. This may mean three things: (1) the Eskimo-Aleut split occurred more recently than previously thought; (2) it had already started 4,500 years ago, but the ancestors of the Unangan remained for some time on the Alaskan mainland before crossing to the islands; and (3) part of these ancestors emigrated directly from Asia to the Aleutians, after other speakers of Proto-Eskaleut had entered America. Whatever the case may be, it seems that some time before or after 2000 BC, Unangax had become a separate language or linguistic branch. Due to this split with Aleut, bearers of the Arctic Small Tool Tradition living in west-central and, increasingly, northern Alaska around 2000 BC may be considered the first Eskimos, both linguistically and culturally. They most probably spoke Proto-Eskimo, the ancestor of all Yupiit and Inuit languages (Dumond 1965).

Between 4,000 and 3,000 years ago, Eskimo families – called Paleo-Eskimo by specialists – started leaving Alaska in growing numbers to enter what is now Canada. Some settled in the central and eastern Canadian Arctic, occupying most of the present-day Inuvialuit, Nunavut, Nunavik, and Labrador regions,[20] while others reached Greenland, where they established themselves on both the east and west coasts of the island. These people, who may have been joined later on by other migratory waves out of Alaska, progressively developed new cultures, known to archaeologists as the Pre-Dorset, Dorset, Independence, and Sarqaq traditions. In Alaska itself, microlithic technology evolved into the Norton and Birnirk cultures (Dumond 1984).

Migration also took place around Bering Strait. Some 2,000 years ago, the ancestors of the Sirenikski Eskimos crossed the strait to settle in Chukotka and on the western coast of Bering Sea, while other groups expanded into the Yukon and Kuskokwim deltas of south-western Alaska. These population movements were probably linked to the occurrence of a second great linguistic split, which separated the Yupiit languages (south and west of the Seward Peninsula) from the Inuit dialects (to the north). According to glottochronological counts (see Woodbury 1984a), this split occurred between 2,500 and 1,000 years ago.

Another period of intensive migration opened around 1,000 years ago. It was seemingly due to climatic change. The weather became warmer, some previously frozen marine channels started melting down, and large sea mammals such as whales and walrus, the favourite prey of Eskimo hunters, were now able to penetrate the northernmost waters of the Canadian and Greenlandic Arctic, as well as some Alaskan and Chukotkan maritime areas. The ancestors of the Alutiit settled on Kodiak Island and Prince William Sound, in south-central Alaska, and those of the Siberian Yupiget and later of the Naukanski crossed Bering Strait to settle in Chukotka. The Yupiget probably pushed the Sireńikski – who had lived in the area for a thousand years and whose language had become quite different from that of the new invaders – more to the south on the Bering Sea coast. When the Naukanski entered Chukotka, the Yupiget were themselves displaced, and some of them crossed to Saint Lawrence Island, where their descendants are still found. According to Fortescue (2004), others slowly moved down along the Bering Sea coast, finally reaching the Kamchatkan isthmus. Their language progressively disappeared when Chukchi from the interior started dwelling on the coast and assimilated them. It seems, however, that Kerek, a Chukotko-Kamchatkan language now on the verge of extinction, possesses some prosodic features that reveal a Yupik substratum (Fortescue 2004).

The principal migration movement, nonetheless, originated in northern Alaska. Over two centuries, between 1,000 and 800 years ago, small bands of hunters and their families, the ancestors of present-day Inuit, entered the western Canadian Arctic – where some of them settled down – before reaching the eastern Arctic and Greenland. Within Alaska, other bands moved to the Seward Peninsula, settling besides Yupiit speakers. All migrants spoke Proto-Inuit, the language ancestral to the Inuit dialects. The new culture they had developed, the Thule (or Neo-Eskimo) culture, increased their mobility and efficiency. The rapidity of the Thule migration explains why the Inuit language spread over the entire North American Arctic without losing its basic grammatical and lexical unity.

In some areas of Canada and Greenland, Thule Inuit met with descendants of the Paleo-Eskimo who had settled there more than 2,000 years earlier. Even though they themselves belonged to the Eskimo people, the Paleo had probably developed during their twenty or twenty-five centuries of isolation several linguistic, technological, economic, and social characteristics that made them quite different from the newcomers[21] (McGhee 1984, 369). As a matter of fact, Thule technology was far more advanced than its Paleo-Eskimo counterpart. The Neo-Eskimo were particularly good at hunting large marine mammals because they made kayaks able to sail into open sea. When entering what was to become Canada, they modified some of their social customs in order to adapt to their new environment. For example, in areas where whale hunting was not as productive as it had been back in Alaska, they split off into smaller groups. In some parts of the central Arctic, they abandoned the traditional winter dwelling – the semi-subterranean stone and sod house (*qarmaq*) – to replace it with the snow-house, until then exclusively used as a temporary travel shelter.

Archaeological and linguistic data show that the main route of Thule migration east of the Mackenzie Delta crossed Victoria Island (map 6) and reached the northernmost islands of the Canadian Arctic: Devon and Ellesmere. Some groups seem to have turned aside from this route to settle along the Arctic Coast.[22]

From the northern islands, several Thule groups entered Greenland at its northwest corner. This explains why, from a grammatical and lexical point of view, Kalaallisut is often closer to Western Canadian Inuktun (to Inuinnaqtun and Natsilingmiutut, in particular) than to Eastern Inuktitut and why one Greenlandic dialect, Thule Inuktun, lies midway between Canadian Inuktun and Kalaallisut (Fortescue 1984d).

The Inuit occupation of Greenland seems to have occurred in many stages (Petersen 1986). A first Neo-Eskimo wave reached the island around AD 1000, crossed its northern part, and progressed down along the east coast. Several decades later, around 1100, a second wave of Thule people started settling along the west coast of Greenland. This migration progressed much more slowly due, in part, to the Viking presence in the south of the country.[23] It was only around year 1500, because of unfavourable climatic changes, that the last Vikings disappeared from Greenland,[24] enabling Inuit to settle along the entire west coast.

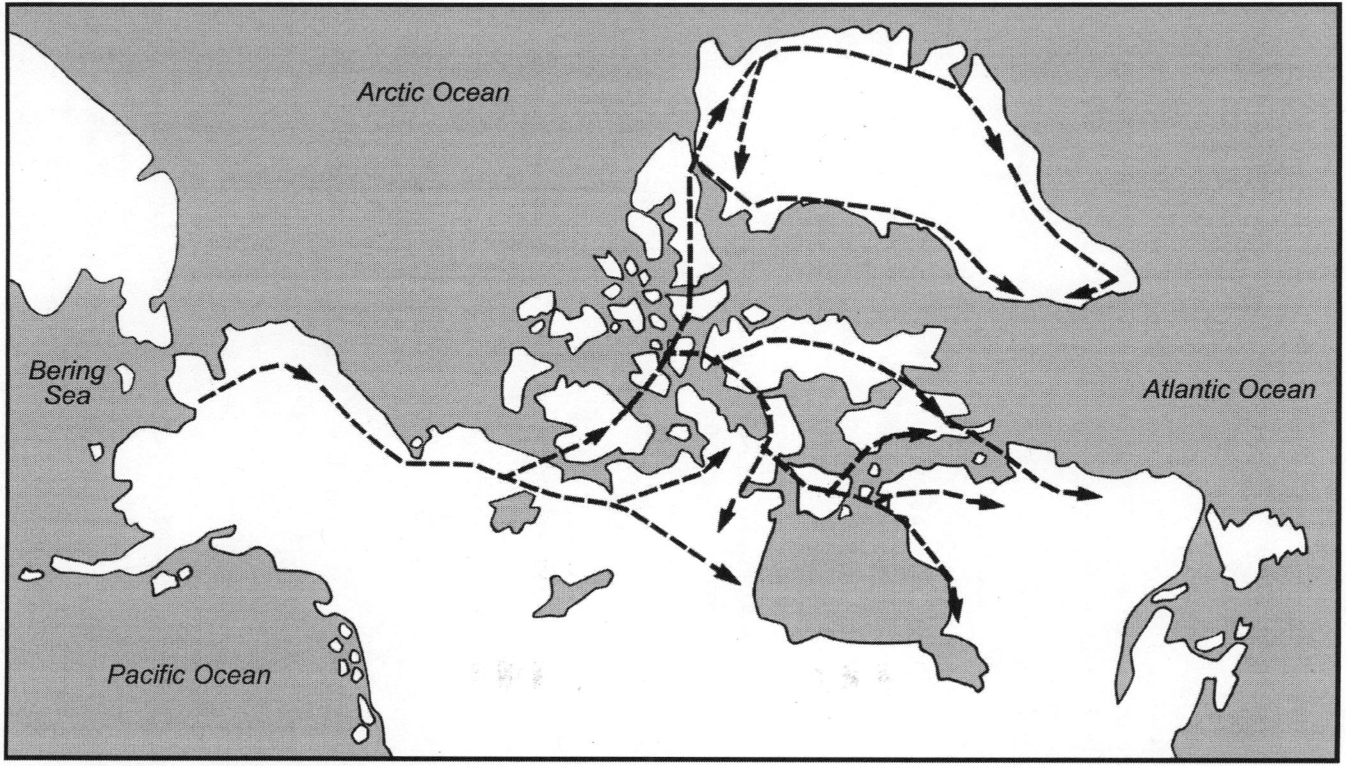

Map 6 The Thule Migrations

During the seventeenth century, some east-coasters migrated west, using both a northern and a southern route. In the north, they mixed with the Upernavik Inuit, while in the south, they settled around Kap Farvel (the southernmost point of Greenland; see Vebæk 2006). This explains why the Upernavik and southern subdialects of West Greenlandic, like the East Greenlandic dialect, replace the vowel *u* with *i* in specific contexts (as in *nan͟iq*, "polar bear," instead of *nan͟uq*). A last large-scale migration, during the eighteenth century, saw the ancestors of the present-day Polar Inuit cross from the Canadian High Arctic islands to north-westernmost Greenland (the Thule district).[25]

While these bands of Neo-Eskimo hunters were entering what would become Kalaallit Nunaat, others left the Arctic islands and moved in a southward direction, eventually reaching the Igloolik area. From there, some families continued their migration along the west coast of Foxe Basin and Hudson Bay, heading toward the Aivilik region and, probably, the northern half of Kivalliq. Other people reached south-western Baffin Island and/or crossed to Arctic Quebec, which they occupied down to the tree-line. Another route seems to have followed the eastern coast of Baffin. From the southeast corner of the island, some bands crossed Hudson Strait to reach northern Labrador, progressing down the coast toward Hamilton Inlet and the Strait of Belle-Isle. Others remained in place and mixed with people from southwest Baffin.[26] The existence of this eastern route might explain why the Nunatsiavut dialect shares some morphological and phonemic similarities with North Baffin (the presence of *&*, for instance), which are not shared by the neighbouring Nunavik dialect.

Finally, in a not-too-distant past, some Inuinnait bands from the Arctic Coast crossed the barren grounds west of Hudson Bay, to reach central and southern Kivalliq. Once there, they probably intermingled with people who had migrated along the Hudson Bay coast from the Aivilik and Igloolik regions.

Because of their superior technology, the Neo-Eskimo completely eliminated their predecessors, whose latest archaeological remains, in the Tuvaaluk area of northern Nunavik (see Plumet 1979), date back to 600 years ago. It is hypothesized that a few small groups of Paleo-Eskimo may have survived on some Hudson Bay islands till the eighteenth and even nineteenth centuries, but there is no sure proof of that. However, the memory of the Paleo-Eskimo is still preserved in the legends of present-day Inuit, who have much to tell about the Tuniit, or Tunrit (Turnit in Greenland), these strong but somewhat stupid human beings who were often the butt of practical jokes on the part of the Thule newcomers.

The migrations just described account for the progressive emergence of the present-day Eskaleut languages. The principal stages of this emergence can be schematized as follows:

NUMBER OF YEARS BEFORE PRESENT	LINGUISTIC FORMS			
1,000	Inuit dialects	Yupiit languages	Sirenikski	Unangax
	↑	↑	↑	↑
2,000	Proto-Inuit	Proto-Yupik	Proto-Sirenikski	Old Unangax
	↑	↑	↑	↑
3,000	← ← ← ←	Proto-Eskimo	→ → → →	Proto-Unangax
		↑		↑
5,000		← ← ← ←	Proto-Eskaleut	→ → → →
			↑	
6,000 (?)	Northeast Asian languages ← ← ←		Uralo-Siberian mesh	→ → → → Uralic
			↑	
8,000–10,000(?)			Proto-Uralo-Siberian mesh	

The Proto-Eskaleut language, itself probably linked to an Old World Uralo-Siberian mesh (which had hypothetically evolved from Proto-Uralo-Siberian), was ancestral to all Inuit, Yupiit, and Unangax forms of speech. About 4,500 years ago it split in two, giving birth to Proto-Unangax (which progressively evolved into old and, then, modern Unangax) and Proto-Eskimo. Some 3,000 to 2,000 years ago, Proto-Eskimo progressively divided into Proto-Inuit, Proto-Yupik, and Proto-Sirenikski, ancestors to the present-day Inuit dialects and Yupiit languages, as well as to Sirenikski, which became extinct in 1997.

PROTO-ESKIMO AND PROTO-INUIT

Because of the common origin of the Yupiit and Inuit forms of speech, specialists have been able to reconstruct the phonemic system shared between 3,000 and 2,000 years ago by the ancestors of the speakers of modern Eskimo languages (Dumond 1987), as well as part of their vocabulary. To achieve this task, they had to compare the morphemes and lexemes now found in both Yupik and Inuit. Their premise was that the most complex phonological and grammatical forms would also be the most conservative and thus the closest to original Proto-Eskimo. This was based on the fact that linguistic materials collected in the Arctic during the past three or four centuries (see next chapter) show that the phonological and grammatical systems of the Eskimo languages have had a tendency to become simplified over the years. Linguistic complexity thus reflects the preservation of a more archaic way of speaking.

Such a comparison enabled linguists to reconstruct the main features of the Proto-Eskimo language, spoken by the bearers of the Arctic Small Tool Tradition and other (Norton, for instance) Paleo-Eskimo traditions. As mentioned in the preceding section, these people were living in western and northern Alaska between 4,500 and 2,000 years ago. Their language was probably shared by the Pre-Dorset, Dorset, Independence, and Sarqaq Eskimos, the first prehistoric settlers of arctic Canada and Greenland.

Research undertaken during the late 1980s and early 1990s by a team of linguists from the University of Alaska Fairbanks (Lawrence Kaplan and Steven Jacobson) and Copenhagen University's Institute of Eskimology (Michael Fortescue) shows that Proto-Eskimo phonology was far more complex than that of the present-day Inuit dialects (Fortescue et al. 1994). It instead resembled Yupik phonology. Like modern Yupik, Proto-Eskimo possessed four vocalic phonemes, *a*, *i*, *u*, and *∂* (*e* as in "roses"), but apparently they never occurred as long vowels. By contrast, there was no *s*. In some contexts, present-day *s* was reflected by the phoneme *c* (*ch*), as in *cila* (e.g., Inuit *sila*, "outside, weather") and *citamat* (e.g., Inuit *sitamat/sisamat/tisamat*, "four").

Proto-Eskimo distinguished between a velar *k* and a uvular *q*, a voiced *l* and a voiceless *&*, and the phonemes *j* (*y*) and *δ* (whose realization resembled that of English *th* in "this"). A phonemic distinction between *j* and *J* (the modern reflection of *δ*) still exists in Alaskan Inupiaq and in the Natsilingmiutut dialect of Western Canadian Inuktun. Here is the reconstructed Proto-Eskimo phonological system (see also Fortescue et al. 1994, xi):

VOWELS	a i u	∂ [e][27]		
CONSONANTS	bilabial	apical/palatal	velar	uvular
stops	p	t c	k	q
voiced continuants	v	l j δ[28]	γ[g]	R [r]
voiceless continuants		l̥ [&]		
nasals	m	n	ŋ[ng]	

There was more variation among consonant clusters than there is now. Clusters included groupings such as *vs*, *ngt*, *lng*, *ngl*, and so on. As a matter of fact, the whole consonantal system was stronger than it is at present. Each vowel had to be separated from the next vowel by at least one consonant, as in *qur̲e-* (Inuit *qui-*; "to urinate") and *qiδ̲a-* (Inuit *qia-*; "to cry"). Moreover, many consonants now occurring as continuants were realized as stops (a stronger type of consonant) when intervocalic (e.g., *tuluk̲ar*, "raven," instead of Inuit *tulugaq*).

The grammar of Proto-Eskimo seems to have been generally similar to that of present-day Yupiit languages. There existed a distinction between single-person and double-person verbal endings (e.g., *nagattur*, "he/she hears," vs *nagatanga*, "he/she hears it"), and there were several rules for deriving the dual and plural forms of nouns.

As vocabulary is concerned, it showed many similarities to the modern lexicon – if, of course, the purely phonemic differences between Proto-Eskimo and the present-day speech forms are ignored. The unity of Eskimo vocabulary is so evident that as early as the end of the nineteenth century, specialists were already convinced about the common origin of the Yupiit and Inuit. For example, Henry Rink (1887b) noticed that words denoting a specialized adaptation to the arctic environment were the same in all Eskimo languages and dialects. These words included the names of sea mammals, the technical vocabulary of the kayak, *umiaq* (skin boat), and harpoon, and some lexemes describing arctic landscapes and natural features. On the basis of such lexical evidence, Rink concluded that Eskimo culture had come to light in a rather circumscribed territory. This Danish scholar may thus be considered a forerunner of present-day archaeologists who, as mentioned above, view the Arctic Small Tool Tradition, which flourished in western and northern Alaska four or five millennia ago, as the common ancestor of all modern Eskimo cultures.

Specialists have already identified more than 3,000 word-bases and affixes common to most Yupiit and Inuit languages. These thus belong to the basic Proto-Eskimo vocabulary. Here are a few examples from Fortescue and colleagues (1994):

	RECONSTRUCTED PROTO-ESKIMO	YUPIK	INUIT
"other side, price"	*aki*	*aki*	*aki*
"to mix"	*akut-*	*akuute-*	*akut-*
"side"	*caniqar*	*caniqaq*	*saniraq/haniraq*
"ear"	*cigun*	*ciun/siguta*	*siun/hiun/siut(ik)*

"drinking water"	*emer*	*emeq/meq*	*imiq*
"person, human being"	*inug/ingug*	*yuk/suk*	*inuk*
"two"	*malrug*	*malruk*	*malruk/marruuk/marluk*
"to ignore"	*na&u-*	*na&u-*	*nalu-/nali-*
"food"	*neqe*	*neqa*	*niqi*
"land, place"	*nuna*	*nuna*	*nuna*
"daughter"	*panig*	*panik*	*panik*
"how many?"	*qavcit*	*qafcin/qafsit*	*qapsit/qaffit/qatsit /qassit*
"oil, blubber"	*uqður*	*uquq*	*uqsruq/uqsuq/uqhuq*
"inhabitant of"	*-miru*	*-miu(q)/-mii*	*-miuq/-miutaq/-miiq*

Beyond Proto-Eskimo, a few linguists such as Knut Bergsland (1986) and Michael Fortescue (1984e) have tried to reconstruct Proto-Eskaleut, the hypothetical ancestor of the whole Eskaleut family. It is a difficult task, but some positive, although still fragmentary, results have begun to appear (see Fortescue et al. 1994). Several common Eskaleut morphemes have already been identified, such as *ku/gu*, which, when followed by a noun ending in the basic case, would have expressed the declarative mood of the verb (e.g., *-kunga*) and, when followed by a possessive relative ending, might have expressed the imperfective (e.g., *-kuma*). A few Proto-Eskaleut morphemes (mostly pronominal elements) appear to have been more mobile than their modern counterparts, being liable to occur as either radicals or affixes.

Getting closer to the present day, it has also been possible to reconstruct Proto-Inuit,[29] the language ancestral to all Inuit dialects. It was most probably spoken by the Neo-Eskimo Thule population 1,000 years ago. This language included many hundred common Proto-Eskimo lexemes, but it also comprised a number of words unknown in the Yupiit speech forms. Here are a few examples of the latter (selected from Fortescue et al. 1994):

	RECONSTRUCTED PROTO-INUIT	MODERN INUIT
"to give a present"	*aittuq-*	*aittuq-/aitsuq-*
"ball"	*aqsraq*	*aqsraq/aqsaq/aqhaq*
"to become calm"	*caima-*	*saima-/saimma-/haima-*
"to be pregnant"	*cingai-*	*singai-/hingai-*
"upper lip"	*kakkivik*	*kakkiviaq*
"land animal"	*nerJun*	*nirJun/nirjut*
"bag"	*puguq*	*puuq*

The phonology and grammar of Proto-Inuit seem to have been quite similar to those of the most conservative present-day dialects: Alaskan Inupiaq and Western Canadian Inuktun. As phonology is concerned, however, Proto-Inuit possessed several characteristics no longer found in the conservative speech forms: presence of the fourth vowel *e* (e.g., *ne̱rJun*),[30] of the consonant *c* (realized as *ch* or *ts*; e.g., *c̱ingai-*), and of some intervocalic consonants (e.g., *pugu̱q* rather than present-day *puuq*, "bag"). As shall be seen in the next chapter, Proto-Inuit appears to have survived almost unchanged up to as late as 300 to 250 years ago.

CONCLUSION

The preceding chapters enabled us to examine the geographical distribution, phonology, and grammatical mechanisms of the linguistic structures translating Inuit social and cultural ideas; chapter 4 has shown how these structures were put into place and succeeded each other over the centuries. Emerging, as it seems, from a prehistoric northeast Asian network of languages in close contact (the Uralo-Siberian mesh), Proto-Eskaleut was probably implanted on the American side of Bering Strait some 4,500 years ago, more or less at the same time as the ancestors of the Unangan were separating from those of the Eskimos. The latter's language evolved into Proto-Eskimo, a tongue that was disseminated over the whole North American Arctic during the following centuries due to large-scale migrations. Other population movements 2,000 years ago entailed linguistic transformations within Proto-Eskimo, which split progressively into three different groupings: Sirenikski, Yupik, and Inuit.

Whereas the first two groupings had a limited geographical extension (southern and western Alaska, Chukotka Peninsula, Russian coast of Bering Sea), the third one was to scatter from Bering Strait to east Greenland between 1,000 and 800 years ago. Because it was ancestral to modern Inuit dialects, its evolution is particularly interesting to examine, as the next chapter shall do.

5

Historical Sources and Linguistic Change

According to surviving historical testimonies, the language common to the Neo-Eskimo ancestors of the present-day Inuit survived well into the sixteenth and seventeenth centuries with, no doubt, some minor changes, but without losing its basic phonological, grammatical, and lexical unity. It was only over the past two or three hundred years that the rhythm of linguistic evolution seemingly increased, thus generating the sixteen Inuit dialects discussed in chapter 2. In the following pages, a number of historical descriptions of the Inuit language are first examined. It is then shown how the language evolved during a relatively recent period of time and, finally, what types of explanatory factors can account for linguistic change.

HISTORICAL SOURCES

The Inuit Language in the 1500s

During the summer of 1576 the British mariner Martin Frobisher sailed into what is now known as Frobisher Bay, on southeast Baffin Island. His party met there with a small group of Inuit with whom contact was established. Relatively smooth at first, relations between natives and Europeans rapidly turned sour. They came to an abrupt end when a few sailors who had left their boat never came back, and when Frobisher's men kidnapped three Inuit in retaliation.

This meeting nevertheless gave one of Frobisher's assistants, sailing master Christopher Hall, the opportunity to write down a list of seventeen Inuit words, the first of its kind.[1] This list is quite revealing about what the language looked like in the sixteenth century.

Here are these words (as found in Barnum 1901 and Quinn 1965) in their original orthography and translation, as well as in a standard transcription and, when needed, a more accurate translation:[2]

HALL'S LIST		STANDARD TRANSCRIPTION AND TRANSLATION	
accaskay	"boat"	*ekaagait*(?)	"they go across it"
arered	"eye"	*eJrin* or *eJrit*	"your eye" or "many eyes"
argotteyt	"a hand"	*aJgatet*	"your hand"
atoniagay	"foot"	*atungagiik*	"pair of foot-soles"
attegay	"a coat"	*atege*	"inner parka"
callagay	"breeches"	*qarligiik*	"pair of pants"
cangnawe	"nose"	*qengaq*	"nose"
chewat	"ear"	*ciut* or *siut*	"ear"
coblone	"thumb"	*kublun*	"your thumb"
comagaye	"leg"	*kamegiik*	"pair of boots"
keiotot	"tooth"	*kegutit*	"teeth"
ketteckle	"middle finger"	*qeteq&iq*	"middle finger"
mekellacane	"third finger"	*mikeliqqan*	"your third (ring) finger"
nutchatet	"head"	*nutchatet*	"your head hair"
polleuetagay	"knife"	*pilautagiik*	"pair of butchering knives"
teckkere	"forefinger"	*tekeq*	"forefinger"
yackettone[3]	"little finger"	*iqetqun*	"your little finger"

This wordlist has a lot to tell. First of all, it points to the fact that in the 1500s the phonology and morphology of the Baffin dialects were quite similar to those of present-day conservative forms of the Inuit language (i.e., Alaskan Inupiaq and Western Canadian Inuktun). For instance, a distinction was made between a word-final *-t* and *-n*. It often marked the difference between the plural (e.g., *kegutit*, "teeth") and the second-person singular of the possessive (e.g., *kublun*, "your thumb"). Moreover, Baffin Inuktitut still preserved consonant groupings no longer in use in the eastern dialects, such as apiC (apical-initial), bilC (bilabial-initial), and Jcont (J-initial) clusters, as in, respectively, *iqetqun*, *kublun*, and *aJgatet*. The phoneme *&* (the voiceless equivalent of *l*) had not yet been assimilated to *t*, as it is now in the area visited by Frobisher (e.g., *qitiq&iq* rather than present-day *qitiqtiq*).

In the transcription of Hall's list into modern orthography, it is presumed that during the sixteenth century a distinction was still made between the vowels *i* and *e* (as in "roses"). The original wordlist is not very clear on this point, although within most words containing both an etymological *i* and *e*, these two vowels are written differently (e.g., *arered* for *eJrin* or *eJrit*; *yackettone* for *iqetqun*), while two *e* belonging to the same lexeme are always written similarly (e.g., *ketteckle* for *qeteq&iq*;[4] *teckere* for *tekeq*), except in the word *attegay* (*atege*).

It is worth noticing that in the late 1500s, Inuktitut may still have preserved the word-initial *c* (pronounced *ch* or *ts*). This is what may be inferred from the transcription *chewat* for "ear" (*siut* in present-day Inuktitut).[5] Moreover, the occurrence of *w* between the two vowels of this word might reflect the existence of a fricative intervocalic consonant within the lexeme, as was the case in Proto-Eskimo, where the word for "ear" was *cigute*.[6] That *chewat* ends with a *t* rather than an *n* (in the more conservative western dialects, the word for "ear" is *siun*) further suggests that at the time of Frobisher's visit, the final vowel of Proto-Eskimo *cigute* had not yet disappeared, even though its pronunciation had become so weak that it escaped the attention of the author of the wordlist.

As morphology is concerned, one may notice the occurrence of dual forms in *-giik* (e.g., *kamegiik*, "a pair of boots") and of plural and possessive markers quite similar to those in use in the western dialects: *eJrin* or *eJrit* ("your eye" or "the eyes [plural]"; basic form *eJe* or *eje*),[7] *mikeliqqan* ("your third finger"; basic form *mikeliraq*), *nutchatet* ("your head hair"; basic form *nujaq*).

Morphological data from the same period can also be found in a list of forty Inuit words collected in 1586 by the explorer John Davis, on the central coast of West Greenland (Hakluyt 1904). Unfortunately for us, Davis and his scribe were much worse linguists than Christopher Hall. Many of their words are thus unrecognizable. Moreover, the explorer did not always understand what his informants were trying to tell him. For instance, the word for "needle" is translated *panygmah*, which evidently stands for *paningma*, "my daughter's." Davis's informant probably tried to explain whose needle it was, while the explorer thought it to be the name of the object itself.

Those words whose actual meaning can be deciphered are nevertheless interesting because their analysis offers a glimpse of old Inuit morpho-syntax. This is the case with *paningma*, which shows that 425 years ago the relative possessive morpheme *-ma-* ("of my") was used exactly as it is now. The same may be said about *ugnera* (*irnera*, "my son"),[8] which shows that in the sixteenth century the basic form of the first-person singular possessive marker ("my") was already *-ra*. Similarly, the word transcribed *sawygmeg* ("a knife") is made out of the modalis non-possessive ending *-mek* or *-meng* (present-day *-mik*), which follows the base *savik-* ("knife"),[9] as in *savingmek!* and *savingmeng!* (present-day *savingmik!*; "[give me] a knife, please!").

In contrast with Hall's compilation, the list collected by Davis includes several verbs. Among recognizable verbal lexemes, one finds *caniglow*, which Davis translates as "kiss me" but which most probably means "let both of us kiss each other" (*kunigluk*), a proof of the former existence of dual endings in Kalaallisut, a group of dialects from which the dual number has almost completely disappeared. Another word in the imperative-optative mood, *aginyok* (*a[g]eniaruk*, "go and fetch it"), constitutes a good example of a double-person ending (*-ruk*) preceded by an affix (*-nia[r]-*) still in use in Greenland with the same imperative meaning. Davis's transcription of this lexeme also seems to show that at the time of his visit, the intervocalic fricative consonant *g* (the Proto-Eskimo base is *age-*, "to go") had not yet undergone elision, thus generating a series of two-vowel clusters (e.g., modern Inuit *ai-*, "to go, to fetch").

Finally, Davis gives some examples of localizers. They are very close to what is still heard today:

DAVIS'S LIST		STANDARD TRANSCRIPTION AND TRANSLATION	
icune	"come hither!"	*ikani*	"there"
awennye	"yonder"	*avani*	"there away"
sambah	"below"	*samma*	"there it is below"
aba	"fallen down"	*avva*	"there it is far away"
gounah	"come down hither!"	*unuuna*	"by this way down there"

Despite its conservative phonology and grammar, which likens it to Inupiaq and Western Canadian Inuktun, the eastern Inuit language of the sixteenth century remains very close to present-day dialects. Its vocabulary, for instance, is quite similar to the lexicon still in use in the Baffin region and in Greenland.[10] Whereas Davis's wordlist is only partially decipherable, probably due to the poor linguistic skills of its author, Hall's compilation can be understood in a proportion of almost 100%.

The Inuit Language in the 1700s

After 1586 European visitors to the Inuit Arctic waited for over a hundred years before again producing wordlists equivalent to Hall's and Davis's compilations. From the early 1700s, however, the French merchants who had established trading posts and fishing stations on Belle-Isle Strait, the lower north shore of the Gulf of Saint Lawrence, and Hamilton Inlet (on the central Labrador coast) had ample opportunities to meet with the Nunatsiavut Inuit and inquire about their language.[11]

In 1694 the French Canadian explorer and trader Louis Jolliet met with Inuit at Bay Saint-Lewis, some 30 kilometres north of the eastern entrance to Belle-Isle Strait. On this occasion, he wrote in his logbook: "I noted down several words in their language, which seems fairly easy to learn" (quoted in Delanglez 1944, 193). Other explorers, traders, and missionaries followed his example: Augustin Le Gardeur De Courtemanche in 1705, François Martel de Brouague around 1715 to 1720,[12] Father Pierre François in 1730,[13] Louis Fornel in 1743, and Father Saint-Pié around 1745.[14] After the British conquest of Canada, the linguistic tradition was continued by Jens Haven, founder of the Moravian missions of Labrador,[15] and by George Cartwright, an English promoter and trader, who in 1770 had his lieutenant Francis Lucas compile "a very imperfect vocabulary of the Esquimaux language" (Townsend 1911, 53).

On the basis of these sources, I have tried to reconstruct the Inuit dialect of eighteenth-century Labrador (Dorais 1980). As was the case with Hall's and Davis's wordlists, the words and sentences collected by Jolliet and his followers look quite familiar to speakers of Inuktitut once the orthographic barrier has been overcome. Here are a few examples:

YEAR COLLECTED	ORIGINAL TRANSCRIPTION AND TRANSLATION		STANDARD TRANSCRIPTION AND TRANSLATION	
1694	*thou tcharacou*	"lay down arms!"	*tuksiarakku*	"because I begged him"[16]
1717	*eique*	"the eyes"	*ejiik* or *ijiik*	"both eyes"
1717	*ibiéné*	"the breast"	*iviangiq*	"breast"
1717	*qu'aplo*	"the eyebrows"	*qablu*	"eyebrow"
1720	*panna*	"peace"	*paanak*	"don't fight!"
1730	*annia*	"my brother"	*ania*	"her brother"

1730	*igliocto*	"a bed"	*igliuqtuq*	"he/she makes the bed"
1730	*matou*	"to close a cupboard"	*matu*	"cover, door"
1730	*ouriactia*	"a hammer"	*ujaratsiaq*	"hammer"
1730	*noujacte*	"the hair"	*nujait*	"head hair"
1745	*nutchade*	"the hair"	*nutchat*	"head hair"
1745	*caiackelliac*	"bark canoe"	*qajariaq*	"canoe"
1745	*tchiou*	"the ear"	*ciut* or *siut*	"ear"
1765	*memek*	"to drink"	*emeq* or *imiq*	"drinking water"
1770	*pipshy*	"dried fish"	*pipsi*	"dried fish"

The phonological, morphological, and lexical conservatism of these and similar lexemes is equal to that of present-day Alaskan Inupiaq and Western Canadian Inuktun dialects, showing:

1 occurrence of apiC consonant groupings (*mictoucs* for *mitquq*, "feather"; *ouctouchic* for *utkusik*, "kettle")
2 occurrence of bilC groupings (*qu'aplo* for *qablu*, "eyebrow"; *tibougalo* for *kivgaluk*, "muskrat"; *imiactoc* for *imngiqtuq*, "he/she sings")
3 occurrence of dual, plural, and some possessive forms marked by the occlusion[17] and doubling of the base's last intervocalic consonant (*jacquoc* for *isaqquk*, "two wings" [singular *isaruq*]; *nutchade* for *nutchat* or *nujjat*, "head hair" [plural] [singular *nujaq*]; *iticcat* for *itikkat*, "your foot" [base *itigaq*])
4 absence of the law of double consonants,[18] now in use in Nunatsiavut and Nunavik (e.g., *igliuqtuq*, "he/she makes the bed," rather than present-day *igliutuq* or *illiutuq*)
5 presence of words such as *igliacto* (*iglaqtuq*, "he/she laughs") and *tibailloc* (*tivajuq*, "he/she dances"), now unknown in Nunatsiavut but still in use in Greenland and other areas

Besides these archaisms, eighteenth-century Labrador Inuktitut displays several modern characteristics that did not yet exist in Frobisher's time. Whereas, for instance, in the 1745 wordlist published by Pehr Kalm the term for "hair" (plural) is *nutchade* (*nutchat* or *nujjat*, by consonant gemination), Father François's compilation of 1730 has *noujacte*, which seems to stand for the modern form *nujait*, where the plural is marked by adding *-it* to the base without doubling the consonant.[19] Similarly, Martel de Brouague in 1717 and Father François respectively write *eique* and *j'y que* for "the two eyes," which leads one to think that present-day dual *ijiik* had already replaced the more conservative forms *ijjak* and *iJrik*.

The orthography of the term for "eyes" also suggests that in the eighteenth century the distinction between the phonemes *J* and *j* had disappeared from Nunatsiavut speech. The etymological Proto-Inuktitut word for "eye" has *J* (*eJe*), but the transcriptions quoted above (*ei* and *j'y*) instead reflect a pronunciation that sounds like *iyi* (or *eye*), corresponding to the realization of the intervocalic phoneme *j*. The orthography of a few other words with an etymological *J* seems to confirm this hypothesis: *acquillat* (*arJat/arjat*, "ashes"), probably realized as *aryat* (*ll* being pronounced as in the French word *fille*); and *cacollia* (*qaqquJaq/qaqqujaq*, "biscuit"). The third-person singular indicative verb marker (etymologically *-Juq* when following a vowel) is rendered by *-illoc*, *-you*, *-ioc*, or *-joc*, which suggests – except perhaps in the last case – that it was pronounced *-yuq*, as in the realization of the phoneme *j* rather than of *J*.

There is very scant evidence that the fourth vowel (*e*) was still extant in eighteenth-century Labrador. Words containing an etymological *e* are generally written with *i* or *y*, as in *acquitty* (*atigi*), "inner parka" (etymologically *ateke*); *qu'amique* (*kamik*), "boot" (etymologically *kameg*); and *tigousilloc* (*tigusijuq*), "he/she grabs something" (etymologically *tegu-*). The orthography of a few lexemes, however, might indicate the presence of *e* (e.g., *eique* – *ejiik*?, "two eyes"; *memek* – *emeq*?, "drinking water"), but this is not conclusive.

The word-final *n* seems to have disappeared. For instance, the words for "pillow" and "tooth" (*akin* and *kigun* in conservative dialects) are respectively rendered by *acquitte* (*akit*) and *quigoutte* (*kigut*). By contrast, the word-initial *c* (*ch/ts*) may still have been present in eighteenth-century Nunatsiavut speech. This could explain the numerous lexemes where a present-day word-initial *s* is symbolized by *qu/k* or *tch*, as in *qui oucty* and *tchiou* (*siutik/siut*, "ear[s]"), *kinicto* (*siniktuq*, "sleeps"),[20] and so on. This means that during the eighteenth century, the Nunatsiavut Inuit spoke a fairly conservative language – by comparison with their present-day dialect – but a language that already showed some signs of evolution when compared with sixteenth-century wordlists.

At the same time that French traders and fishermen maintained sporadic contacts with Inuit in southern Labrador, Danes were in the process of settling permanently in Greenland. As soon as Danish colonization started, with the foundation of a mission and trading post at Godthaab (Nuuk) in 1721, missionaries undertook a systematic study of Kalaallisut. The dictionaries and grammars of Hans Egede and Poul Egede,[21] as well as those of Albert Top and other European authors of the eighteenth century, constitute a thorough description of the Greenlandic language as it was spoken 275 years ago.

In their analysis of these early contributions to Inuit linguistics, Knut Bergsland and Jørgen Rischel (1986) summarize the principal characteristics of old Kalaallisut. It was a language already subdivided into various dialects. In 1723 Hans Egede noticed that on the south-western coast of Greenland, pronunciation differed from that of Godthaab, where he lived. Egede also stated that women tended to use a word-final *n* (e.g., *apun*, "snow") where men used *t* (*aput*).[22]

As a general rule, eighteenth-century Kalaallisut was less conservative than was Nunatsiavut Inuktitut:

1 It still possessed bilC (and also velC and uvuC) consonant groupings, as in *iblau* (*iblauq*, "animal foetus"), but apiC clusters were not found anymore.
2 Metathesis (i.e., two consonants changing place with each other) had already occurred (e.g., *marluk*, "two," and *ivlit*, "you," instead of *malruk* and *ilvit*).
3 From the second half of the seventeenth century (Petersen 1985a), *J* was realized as *sh* (e.g., *eshi* or *ishi*, "eye," instead of etymological *eJe*).
4 The single *&* had become voiced (e.g., *iluartuq*, "comfortable," rather than *i&uartuq*).
5 The word-initial *c* was not heard anymore (this may have already been the case when Davis visited Greenland in 1586).

In contrast with modern West Greenlandic, however, fricative consonants as well as *l* remained voiced when occurring within clusters (e.g., voiceless *qitir&iq*, "middle finger," sounded different from voiced *qitirli*, "as for the middle"). The diphthongs *ai* and *au* had not yet merged with *aa* (e.g., *aiviq*, "walrus," rather than present-day

Greenlandic *aaviq*). Contrary to what had seemingly happened in Labrador, the fourth vowel *e* appears to have survived in eighteenth-century Kalaallisut but only within the first syllable of words (e.g., *eshi*, "eye"; etymological *eJe*; Nunatsiavut *iji*). Moreover, the fluctuating orthography of Top and Hans Egede sometimes suggests that *e* might have already disappeared from the speech of some individuals.

As far as morphology is concerned, the lists of verbal and nominal endings compiled by eighteenth-century grammarians are quite similar to those of present-day West Greenlandic (which remains morphologically conservative in comparison with Eastern Canadian Inuktitut) if phonemic differences are ignored. It should be noticed, however, that the markers of the dual, now generally unknown in Greenland, were in full use in the 1700s, as they had been at the time of Davis's visit. They were still in partial use a century later but had then started to disappear. In his grammar of Kalaallisut published in 1846, the missionary-linguist Samuel Kleinschmidt writes that the dual markers "are all included here for the sake of completeness and because they do sometimes occur (especially in books). In reality, however, they are rarely used and many of them do hardly ever occur" (Kleinschmidt 1981, 20).

The Inuit Language in the 1800s

In the time of Kleinschmidt, the phonology of Greenlandic had not changed much since the preceding century, as shown by the occurrence of bilC, velC, and uvuC consonant groupings, the preservation of the diphthongs *ai* and *au*, and so on. The fourth vowel, however, had completely disappeared, and all continuant consonants occurring within a cluster had now been devoiced (e.g., *arḻiq*, "whale," instead of *arviq*; *ig&u*, "house," rather than *iglu*).

In the same period (mid-nineteenth century), the phonology and grammar of Nunatsiavut Inuktitut, as described by Moravian missionaries (see Erdmann 1864; Holtved 1964; Nowak 1995), appears to have shared many characteristics with West Greenlandic:

1 occurrence of bilC, velC, and uvuC consonant groupings (apiC clusters had disappeared): for example, *qablunaaq* ("European"), *iksivavuq* ("he/she is seated"), and *arnaq* "woman") rather than present-day *qallunaak*, *itsivavuk*, and *annak*

2 devoicing of fricatives within clusters (e.g., *arfiq*, "whale") but preservation of a voiced lateral *l* (e.g., *iglu*, "house")[23]
3 preservation of conservative plural, relative, and possessive noun markers: for example, *itikkat* ("many feet" or "your foot") in place of modern *itigait*; and *siqirngup* ("the sun's") rather than *siqiniup*

In contrast with Greenlandic, however, the Nunatsiavut dialect of the 1800s still fully preserved dual markers. It did not practise metathesis[24] (compare Nunatsiavut *umngijarpuq* and Greenlandic *ungmijarpuq*, "he shaves"), and as seen above, the phoneme *J* had merged with *j* (e.g., *iji*, "eye"). The law of double consonants was not in complete use yet, although in his grammar published in 1891, the Moravian linguist Theodor Bourquin noticed some fluctuations in the pronunciation of several speakers, which could have originated from an incipient and sporadic application of this rule.

The law of double consonants was not known in Nunavik either when the Anglican missionary Edmund James Peck compiled his dictionary and grammar around 1880 (see Peck 1925; and Flint 1954). Peck had learned Inuktitut at Little Whale River, on the east coast of Hudson Bay, with an interpreter from Labrador and a young local Inuk whom he had taken into his home (Lewis 1904). He had also studied Moravian materials (his dictionary is based on Friedrich Erdmann's of 1864. Peck's orthography was thus influenced by the Labrador Moravian script, although he seemed conscious of dialectal differences between the Atlantic coast and eastern Hudson Bay speech forms, as indicated by the following: "An Eskimo grammar in the East Main [eastern Hudson Bay] dialect seemed needful. This, I have in some measure tried to supply" (quoted in Flint 1954, i).

According to Peck's data, in the late nineteenth century the Itivimiut (Hudson Bay) subdialect of Nunavik Inuktitut still preserved velC and bilC groupings (e.g., *iglumni*, "in my house") but no apiC. The existence of bilC clusters is confirmed by a manuscript wordlist compiled in the same region at the beginning of the twentieth century (Richards 1913), where words like *ublumee* (*ublumi*, "today") are found. A draft lexical and grammatical description of the Kuujjuaq (Ungava Bay) speech form, written at the end of the nineteenth century by the American natural scientist and ethnographer Lucien

Turner (1887), also bears witness to the occurrence of bilC clusters[25] and to the absence of the law of double consonants.

Peck generally wrote *l*, *kl*, *dl*, or *tdl* in places where the Labrador Nunatsiavut dialect has a voiceless lateral consonant (*&*). But he showed some hesitation. In his dictionary, for instance (Peck 1925, 22), he writes *akl̲ak* (*ak&̲ak*) for "black bear," but *aks̲ak* is also found between brackets. It is thus probable that Peck considered forms in *&* to be correct (because they had been recorded in the Moravian texts) but that from time to time he wrote down what he actually heard at Little Whale River (i.e., *s* instead of *&*, as is still the case in present-day Nunavik).

Like the Moravians, Peck generally used the letter *j* for the voiced apical-palatal fricative (e.g., *ije*, "the eye"), although in modern Itivimiut this consonant is pronounced *J*. Sometimes, however, he wrote *r* (which must be pronounced the English way) – as in *naur̲a* (*nauJa*, "seagull") – which probably means that during his time eastern Hudson Bay Inuit used a palatalized *j*, as they still do. It should be noted that Edward Richards (1913) too hesitated between *y* (*kooeeney̲ok* for *quiniJuq*, "fat") and *r* (*angar̲oka* for *angaJuqqaaq*, "chief").

Thus, in the last quarter of the nineteenth century, the eastern Inuit dialects, despite some modern characteristics, still had much in common with the western – conservative – versions of the language.[26] It was around 1900 that they started changing rapidly, progressively taking the phonemic and grammatical shape that is now theirs.[27]

LINGUISTIC CHANGE IN THE INUIT LANGUAGE

Over the past century, linguistic change has affected in a marked way the phonology, lexicon, and morphology of the Inuit language.

Phonological Change

One of the most important aspects of linguistic evolution in Inuit is the progressive reduction in the number of allowable consonant clusters as one moves from western to eastern dialectal areas. As seen in the preceding section, this reduction had already begun in the eighteenth and nineteenth centuries, with the gemination of apiC groupings (still heard in modern Inupiaq and Inuktun) in

Greenland, Nunatsiavut, and probably, the Baffin and Aivilik dialects.[28] Nonetheless, in 1900 all other types of groupings (bilC, velC, uvuC) were still in full use in the eastern Arctic.

Nowadays, however, bilC consonant clusters have completely disappeared from most dialects north and east of Hudson Bay.[29] In East and West Greenlandic, as well as in Nunatsiavut (except for Rigolet), Nunavik, and South Baffin, velC groupings are no longer heard either. Moreover, in the Nunatsiavut dialect (except, here again, for Rigolet), uvuC clusters have become full geminates,[30] whereas in Greenland they are realized as pharyngealized geminates.[31] Here are a few examples:

	AIVILIK	N. BAFFIN	S. BAFFIN/ NUNAVIK	NUNATSIAVUT	W. GREENLANDIC
GEMINATION OF BILC					
"cliff"	*imnaaruq*	*innaaruq*	*innaaruq*	*innak*	*innaq*
"weather is clearing"	*niptaqpuq*	*nittaqpuq*	*nitta(q)puq*	*nittavuk*	*nitta*^{r}*ppuq*
"morning"	*ublaaq*	*ullaaq*	*ullaaq*	*ullaak*	*u&&aaq*
GEMINATION OF VELC					
"musk-ox"	*umingmak*	*umingmak*	*umimmak*	*umimmak*	*umimmak*
"caribou"	*tuktu*	*tuktu*	*tuttu*	*tuttuk*	*tuttu*
"house"	*iglu*	*iglu*	*illu*	*illuk*	*i&&u*
GEMINATION OF UVUC					
"woman"	*arnaq*	*arnaq*	*arnaq*	*annak*	*a*^{r}*nnaq*
"he/she is afraid"	*iqsivuq*	*iqsivuq*	*iqsivuq*	*itsivuk*	*i*^{r}*ssivuq*
"killer whale"	*aarluk*	*aarluk*	*aarluk*	*aalluk*	*aa*^{r}*&&uk*

Gemination belongs to a continuing process of weakening (or simplification) of the consonant system, at work in eastern Inuit dialects.[32] VelC groupings were still in use in Nunavik during the 1960s (Schneider 1970; Dorais 1973, 88), and they could be heard in South Baffin up to the mid-1970s, at least in the speech of older speakers (Dorais 1976a). In the North Baffin, Aivilik, and Kivalliq dialects, velC clusters do exist, but many younger speakers geminate them. Canadian Inuit youngsters also tend to assimilate *gg* with *kk* and *rr* with *qq*, thus saying *kikkavik* ("falcon") and *taqqaq* ("shadow") rather than *kiggavik* and *tarraq* and obliterating the difference between *aggatit* ("your hands"; pronounced *akkatit*) and *akkatit* ("your paternal uncles").

The occurrence of the law of double consonants (e.g., *illukut*, "through the house," instead of *illukkut*) in Nunavik and Nunatsiavut[33] belongs to the same process of consonant weakening, as does the current realization of the phoneme *q* as a continuant (which sounds like Spanish *j*) rather than a stop. Some young Canadian speakers even tend to replace a word-initial *q* with *h* and a word-final *q* with *k*. In their speech, for instance, the word for "dog" sounds like *himmik* rather than *qimmiq*. Finally, weakening is also felt in Kalaallisut, where some intervocalic consonants have been elided (e.g., *nuuk*, "cape, promontory," instead of Inuktitut *nuvuk*) or transformed into continuants (e.g., East Greenlandic *sigiq*, "ice," in place of *siku*).[34]

Lexical Change

Vocabulary has been directly affected by phonological change. In several instances, the gemination and ensuing neutralization of originally different consonant groupings obliterated the distinction between lexemes. We just saw that some young speakers now confuse *aggatit* ("your hands") with *akkatit* ("your uncles"). For a majority of eastern Arctic Inuit, words such as *aglait* ("letters") and *allait* ("Indians, others") are now pronounced the same way (*allait*) due to gemination. In West and East Greenlandic, the neutralization of the diphthongs *ai* and *au* may also entail some confusion. The word *aat*, for instance, can mean either "your sleeve" (originally *ait*) or "your blood" (originally *aut*).

Potential confusion is higher in Nunatsiavut, where, in contrast with other dialects, uvuC clusters have become full geminates. For instance, the lexemes *anna* ("that one") and *annak* ("woman"; originally *arnaq*) sound almost identical. Likewise, the words for "snow owl" (*ukpik*) and "willow" (*uqpik*) have both become *uppik*. This homophony sometimes entails embarrassing confusions, to which Nunatsiavut Inuktitut has to react. For example, several older speakers still say *ibjuk* ("earth, soil") rather than *itjuk*, even though bilC groupings (e.g., *bj*) have now disappeared from their dialect. They do so in order to avoid any mismatching between this lexeme and another *itjuk* (formerly *igjuk*), which means "testicle." In a similar way, the gemination of uvuC groupings entails a potentially awkward homophony between *uqsuq* ("seal or whale blubber") and *utsuk* ("vagina"), both pronounced *utsuk*. The Nunatsiavut solution was to give *utsuk* the exclusive meaning of "blubber" and to call the vagina *aahaak* (Jeddore 1976, 5), an onomatopoeia originally belonging to the speech of young children.

Language evolution affected the lexicon in another way. All Inuit dialects were enriched by hundreds, or even thousands, of new words used for denoting objects and concepts introduced by Europeans. These words were borrowed from other languages (English, Danish, German, Russian, etc.), especially coined for the purpose, or had their original meaning modified to broaden their signification. They are discussed in the next chapter.

One corollary of this linguistic enrichment was an impoverishment of the original Inuit lexicon. The disappearance of numerous elements belonging to traditional technology, spiritual beliefs, and social organization rendered obsolete the words that designated them. For instance, few present-day Inuit know what an *ii* (a kind of hook for catching seagulls) was or what the signification of *nulajuq* ("he/she grows up suddenly by way of magical means") is. The phenomenon is not new. Research conducted in Igloolik in 1975 already showed that a sample of speakers aged eighteen to twenty-two had problems with, or ignored completely, the meaning of almost one-fifth (19.2%) of a list of 224 Inuktitut words belonging to the general lexicon (Dorais 1976c). Most of these young adults were unable to count beyond five in their native tongue.

As a general rule, bilingualism has entailed the replacement of some Inuit lexemes with their English or Danish (in Greenland) equivalents. Among several speakers, perhaps among a majority of all Inuit under forty years of age, it has also given rise to code-switching, a phenomenon whereby people constantly oscillate, often within the same sentence, between their mother tongue and their second language.

Grammatical Change

The simplification of the Inuit language has also affected syntax. The structure of words was partially modified by the expression of newly introduced ideas. Lexemes now tend to be shorter – they rarely include more than three or four morphemes – and the notions they express are more abstract than they used to be. The translation of modern concepts like "democracy," "education," "faith," and "justice" makes good use of a few key morphemes, such as the affix *-niq*, which transforms verbal bases into nouns:

niruar- ("to choose") + *-niq* = *niruarniq* ("the choosing": election, democracy)
ilinniar- ("to study") + *-niq* = *ilinniarniq* ("the fact of studying": education)
ukpir- ("to believe") + *-niq* = *ukpirniq* ("the fact of believing": faith)
iqqatui- ("to judge") + *-niq* = *iqqatuiniq* ("the action of judging": justice)

By contrast, several speakers, including many radio announcers, tend to express some fairly simple notions in a needlessly complicated way. For instance, they say *inuujut* ("those who are Inuit") and *qallunaangujut* ("those who are Europeans") instead of using the basic words *inuit* and *qallunaat*. In their mouth, a sentence like *qallunaanit pisitiuniqsait inuit* ("Inuit are more clever than Europeans") becomes: *qallunaangujunit pisitiuniqsaujut inuujut* ("those who are Inuit, they are more clever than those who are Europeans"). In the Canadian Arctic things are no longer expressed as they used to be, and this also stands true for Greenland according to the Greenlandic Eskimologist Robert Petersen (1985a).

Inuit morphology has been affected by the phonological changes described at the beginning of this section. The disappearance of phonemically functional word-final nasal consonants in Inuktitut and Kalaallisut entailed some cases of homophony among morphemes. For instance, dual and plural reflexive verbal markers now sound the same in the eastern – and some Inuktun – dialects: *tikikkamik̲* may either mean "because both of them arrive" or "because many of them arrive," while in most Alaskan Inupiaq speech forms a distinction is still maintained between *tikikkamik̲* ("because both of them arrive") and *tikikkamin̲g̲* ("because many of them arrive"; with a final nasal consonant).

Likewise, east of the Inuvialuit region, no distinction is made anymore between morphemes marking the plural number of nouns and those expressing the second-person singular of the possessive ("your"). In most Canadian and Greenlandic dialects, the word *iglut/illut* (or *igluit/illuit*) has two different meanings: "houses" or "your house." But in Siglitun and Inupiaq, speakers still discriminate between *iglut̲* ("houses") and *iglun̲* ("your house"; with a final nasal).

In Nunatsiavut the disappearance of the word-final *q* has transformed verbal radicals ending with this consonant into vowel-final bases. In consequence, declarative, indicative, and interrogative markers that follow them now start with *v* or *j* (rather than *p* or *t*), as is the rule with vowel-final radicals. This process was later extended to other verbal bases, as in the following examples:[35]

taku-	>>>	>>>	>>>	*takuvunga*	"I see"
tusaq-	>>>	*tusa-*	>>>	*tusavutit*	"you hear"
sinik-	>>>	*sini-*	>>>	*sinijuk*	"he/she sleeps"
tikit-	>>>	*tiki-*	>>>	*tikivita*	"do we arrive?"

Gemination of bilC and, sometimes, velC groupings in eastern dialects provoked a reorganization of the possessive first-person ("my") and second-person ("your [thy]") singular noun endings. The original distinction between these two sets of grammatical affixes rests for a good part on a bilC-velC contrast. Most etymological first-person markers start with a bilC cluster, whereas most second-person morphemes begin with a velC, as in the following Aivilik examples:

	"MY LAND"	"THY LAND"
basic	*nunaga*	*nunait/nunat*
relative	*nunama*	*nunavit/nunak̲p̲it*
modalis	*nunam̲n̲ik*	*nunan̲g̲n̲ik*
ablative	*nunam̲n̲it*	*nunan̲g̲n̲it*
locative	*nunam̲n̲i*	*nunan̲g̲n̲i*
allative	*nunam̲n̲ut*	*nunan̲g̲n̲ut*
translative	*nunap̲k̲ut*	*nunak̲k̲ut*
simulative	*nunap̲t̲ut*	*nunak̲t̲ut*

The difference between the two sets of endings is preserved in the North Baffin and Thule dialects, and this despite the gemination of bilC groupings, because geminate-initial first-person markers still contrast with velC-initial second-person endings:

	"MY LAND"	"THY LAND"
basic	*nunaga*	*nunait*
relative	*nunama*	*nunavit/nunakpit*
modalis	*nunannik*	*nunangnik*
ablative	*nunannit*	*nunangnit*
locative	*nunanni*	*nunangni*
allative	*nunannut*	*nunangnut*
translative	*nunakkut*	*nunakkut*
simulative	*nunattut*	*nunaktut*

In the South Baffin dialect, however, as well as in Nunavik, Nunatsiavut, and West and East Greenlandic, even velC groupings have now become geminates. This entails a complete homophony between most first- and second-person possessive endings:

	"MY LAND"	"THY LAND"
basic	*nunaga*	*nunait*
relative	*nunama*	*nunavit/nunappit*
modalis	*nunannik*	*nunannik*
ablative	*nunannit*	*nunannit*
locative	*nunanni*	*nunanni*
allative	*nunannut*	*nunannut*
translative	*nunakkut*	*nunakkut*
simulative	*nunattut*	*nunattut*

In Greenland this does not seem to have created a problem. Speakers rely on the semantic context to decide whether, for example, the correct meaning of a sentence such as *nuliannik sinippunga* is "I slept with my wife" or "I slept with your wife."[36] This is not the case in Canada, where each dialect concerned by this homophony has tried to recreate in its own way the original distinction between both sets of endings.

In South Baffin speakers use the third-person singular markers preceded by the personal pronouns *uvanga* ("I, mine") or *ivvit* ("thou, yours").[37] A distinction can thus be maintained between *uvanga nuliangani tutippunga* (literally: "I slept with [at] his wife of me") and *ivvit nuliangani tutippunga* ("I slept with [at] his wife of you"). In the Itivimiut subdialect of Nunavik, the personal pronoun is affixed at the end of the marker, with the result that two new sets of endings have been coined:

	"MY LAND"	"THY LAND"
basic	*nunaga*	*nunait*
relative	*nunama*	*nunavit/nunappit*
modalis	*nunanniuvanga*	*nunanniuvit*
ablative	*nunanniuvanga*	*nunanniuvit*
locative	*nunanniuvanga*	*nunanniuvit*
allative	*nunannuuvanga*	*nunannuuvit*
translative	*nunakkuuvanga*	*nunakkuuvit*
simulative	*nunattuuvanga*	*nunattuuvit*

In the Tarramiut subdialect of Nunavik as well as in Nunatsiavut, a new set of endings has been coined for the first person. It expands on the basic first-person singular marker (*ga-/ra-*). Geminate-initial endings are retained for the second person:[38]

	"MY LAND"	"THY LAND"
basic	*nunaga*	*nunait*
relative	*nunama*	*nunavit/nunappit*
modalis	*nunaganik*	*nunannik*
ablative	*nunaganit*	*nunannit*
locative	*nunagani*	*nunanni*
allative	*nunaganut*	*nunannut*
translative	*nunagagut*	*nunakkut*
simulative	*nunagatut*	*nunattut*

More generally, since the beginning of the twentieth century, the system of Inuktitut noun endings has been simplified, tending toward normalization (see the section on affixes and morphology in chapter 2). In the South Baffin, Nunavik, and Nunatsiavut dialects, all nominal grammatical affixes starting with a vowel are now formed in the simplest way, namely by adding a marker to the basic radical. Compare, for instance, the following Siglitun – a conservative dialect where complex rules are still in use – and Nunavik dual, plural, relative, and possessive forms:

	SIGLITUN	NUNAVIK
"child" (basic)	*nutaraq*	*nutaraq*
"two children"	*nutaqqak*	*nutaraak*
"many children"	*nutaqqat*	*nutarait*
"the child's"	*nutaqqam*	*nutaraup*

"your child"	*nutaqqan*	*nutarait*
"his/her child"	*nutaqqaa*	*nutaranga*
"boot" (basic)	*kamik*	*kamik*
"two boots"	*kammak*	*kamiik*
"many boots"	*kamngit*	*kamiit*
"the boot's"	*kamngum*	*kamiup*
"your boot"	*kamngin*	*kamiit*
"his/her boot"	*kamnga*	*kaminga*

In the Aivilik and North Baffin speech forms, only a very few older speakers still use some conservative dual and plural markers (such as *nutaqqak* and *nutaqqat*, but not *kammak* and *kamngit*). These types of markers find a more general use in the Inuinnaqtun, Natsilingmiutut, Kivalliq, and Kalaallisut dialects, but even there, speakers tend to simplify morphology. In West Greenlandic, for instance, lexemes like *tupiit* ("tents"; basic form *tupiq*) and *qajaat* ("kayaks"; basic form *qajaq*) are now much more frequently heard than their traditional equivalents *tuqqit* and *qaannat*.[39] It is only Siglitun and Alaskan Inupiaq that still resist grammatical change, but these dialects are no longer fluently spoken, at least as a first language,[40] by people under fifty years of age.

In Igloolik (North Baffin dialect), in 1975, most speakers under age twenty-five were already simplifying the irregular grammatical forms found in adult speech (Dorais 1976c). In addition to the normalization of dual, plural, relative, and possessive noun markers, they had deleted from their language some infrequent verbal endings, such as the imperative affix *-tit* (e.g., they said *tikigit* instead of *tikittit*, "do arrive!") and the perfective morpheme *-ngat* (e.g., *tikimmat* rather than *tikinngat*, "because he/she arrives"). The negation of the declarative mood was *–nngippunga*, *–nngipputit*, and so on, rather than *–nngilanga*, *-nngilatit*, and so on (e.g., *tikinngippunga*, "I do not arrive"), and young informants preferred the simpler form *tikigaviuk* ("because you reach him/her") to the more traditional *tikigaangni*. These speakers were also geminating velC consonant groupings, which compelled them to say *uvanga nunangani* ("in his/her country of me") and *ivvit nunangani* ("in his/her country of you"), because they were no longer able to distinguish between *nunanni* ("in my country") and *nunangni* ("in your country").

This Igloolik example is far from being unique. In the Southeast Baffin subdialect, speakers now assimilate the ablative ending to the modalis one (e.g., *Iqalunnik pivunga*, "I come from Iqaluit," rather than *Iqalunnit pivunga*), while in East Greenlandic *-muk* and *-nuk* are often heard instead of the modalis endings *-mik* and *-nik* (as in *qimmimuk tusarpuq*, "he/she hears a dog"). In Nunavik a majority of speakers prefer to normalize first-person plural possessive endings, saying, for instance, *tupivunni* ("in our tent"; basic form *tupivut*) rather than the original *tupittini*.

A survey of present-day phonology and morphology in Iqaluit, conducted between 1994 and 1996 on a sample of 103 school-age and 50 adult Inuktitut-mother-tongue speakers (Dorais 2002a), shows a relatively high degree of grammatical variation. For example, various solutions have been found for coping with the neutralization of the first- and second-person singular possessive endings entailed by the gemination of velC groupings. The survey elicited seven different ways of saying "toward my boat" and six for translating "toward your (thy) boat." As a rule, more regular forms (e.g., *umiannut*, "to my boat," and *umiarnut*, "to your boat") characterized older speakers and those originating from the North Baffin area, whereas the speech of younger respondents and of South Baffin natives exhibited a higher degree of linguistic variation. The overall impression, however, was that in colloquial speech, grammatical rules became relative and were easily adapted to the personal usage of each speaker.

This adaptation can even lead to the elision of morphemes. In her study of Rankin Inlet Inuktitut, Susan Sammons (1985) mentions that speakers oftentimes drop grammatical endings when these occur at the end of sentences or utterances. It is a conscious process – people know that they are dropping an ending – that is not linked to the meaning of the word or to the age or gender of the speaker (although the habit seems more frequent among women). It appears to be due to a more general restructuring of the language along a syntactical, rather than morphological, model. An identical phenomenon has also been observed in Kalaallisut (Petersen 1979) and in Nunavik (Swift and Allen 2002a).

In such a model, the relative position of words within the sentence, the semantic strength of some post-bases, and the occurrence of conjunctive lexemes like *amma* ("and") and *uvva* ("or") gain in importance at the expense of a morphological system whose original logic states that the basic meaning of the word lies with its radical, while its grammatical function is expressed in the ending. The semantic importance of some lexical affixes tends to increase, a fact that allows for the suppression of grammatical endings and – sometimes – radicals.

In the Canadian Arctic verbal endings now tend to disappear after a post-base expressing a negation (e.g., *-nngit-*) or a mental restriction (e.g., *-galuaq-*). For example, nobody says *inuugaluaqtuq* ("however, he/she is an Inuk") anymore. The current form, from which the ending *-tuq* has been dropped, is *inuugaluaq-* ("however, be an Inuk"). Likewise, speakers often say *nirigumanngi-* ("do not want to eat") rather than *nirigumanngilanga* ("I do not want to eat"). In the Nunavik dialect the base is elided if its presence is not deemed essential (see Swift and Allen 2002b), as in *-suungujunga* ("I am in the habit of") and *-jjangittuq* ("it should most probably not"). Both base and ending are sometimes suppressed within the same word, a process that generates mutilated forms such as *-gumanngi-* ("do not want"). To the ears of elders, this way of speaking Inuktitut often sounds like child language.

SOME FACTORS OF LANGUAGE EVOLUTION

It is not always possible to understand why this or that specific linguistic change occurred at all. There exist various factors of language evolution – linguistic, sociolinguistic, social, cultural – and generally speaking, more than one of the factors are at work at the same time.

Linguistic Factors

Some phenomena such as the disappearance of the fourth vowel (*e*) seem to be due to purely phonemic causes. For Jens Elmegaard Rasmussen (1979), this disappearance would have taken place in Alaska, before Neo-Eskimo migrations to Canada and Greenland. However, this hypothesis is contradicted by historical data that seem to point, as seen in the opening section of this chapter, to a survival of the vowel *e* in Baffin Island and Greenland as late as the sixteenth and seventeenth centuries. The linguist Jørgen Rischel (1981) instead believed that the assimilation of *e* to *i* (e.g., *irneq*, "son," becoming *irniq*) occurred independently in each dialect. Because *e* is a medial low-pitched vowel, it is not surprising that it became assimilated to the other medial vowel, *i*, in order to generate a well-balanced three-vowel system: front low-pitched *a*, rear low-pitched *u*, and medial high-pitched *i*.

Factors of the same type – the elimination of slighter contrasts among phonemes – may also explain why many dialects assimilate *J* to *j* (e.g., *takuJuq*, "he/she sees," becoming *takujuq*): these two consonants are articulated in quite identical ways (both are voiced palatal fricatives), which makes them more liable to neutralize each other. Likewise, the relatively widespread assimilation of *&* (as in *qitiq&iq*, "middle finger") to *s*, *h*, *t*, or *l* might be due to the fact that the phonemic contrast between *&* and *l* is the only one in any Inuit dialect to be based on the mere presence or absence of consonant voicing.[41]

Sociolinguistic Factors

The simplification (or weakening) of the consonant system, more advanced in the eastern dialects than in the western ones, is probably due to sociolinguistic factors. As seen in the section above on phonological change, this simplification is principally characterized by the gemination of consonant groupings, but it also includes the law of double consonants (in Siglitun, Nunavik, and Nunatsiavut), the transformation of *r* and a word-final *q* into velars (in Nunatsiavut), and the elision of some intervocalic consonants in East and West Greenlandic.[42]

It has long been noticed that in the central and eastern Arctic, the degree of consonantal weakening generally varies in accordance with the length of contact with Europeans. The longer the contact has lasted, the more advanced is the weakening. It reaches its maximum in Nunatsiavut and West Greenland, where permanent European presence dates back to the eighteenth century,[43] while west of Hudson Bay – where Euro-Canadians did not penetrate until the early twentieth century – the degree of simplification is very low. In the in-between areas, affected by contact since the middle or the end of the nineteenth century, consonantal weakening is either high (Nunavik, South Baffin) or low (North Baffin), in correlation with the length of contact:

DIALECTAL AREA	BEGINNING OF CONTACT	DEGREE OF CONSONANTAL WEAKENING
Inuinnait, Natsilik	early 20th century	extremely low
Kivalliq	early 20th century	extremely low
Aivilik	early 20th century	very low
Thule	early 20th century	low

North Baffin	late 19th century	low
South Baffin	mid-19th century	rather high
Nunavik	mid-19th century	high
Nunatsiavut	late 18th century	extremely high
W. and E. Greenland	early 18th century (West)[44]	very high

Some specialists believe that this coincidence between consonantal simplification and foreign presence could be due to bilingualism. The Inuit system of consonants would have collapsed under the influence of English and Danish. One should not forget, however, that in the eastern Arctic, Greenland and Nunatsiavut being no exceptions, it was only in the second half of the twentieth century that bilingualism became generalized. It would then be difficult to explain how English and Danish could have had any influence on the pronunciation of monolingual Inuit speakers.

The linguist Chet Creider (1981) has set forth the following hypothesis: the weakening of consonant groupings, leading to their progressive gemination, would have originated in Greenland and Labrador and then expanded westward to Nunavik, Baffin Island, and Kivalliq. This process of linguistic diffusion could have occurred through mutual contacts, without involving any actual migration of people. Here again, this hypothesis may be contradicted on chronological grounds. Before the middle of the twentieth century, contacts among Inuit from different regions of the Arctic were so infrequent that it is highly improbable that so important a change could have been transmitted from one group to another. Who would have been responsible for this transmittal? Why, for instance, would Nunavik speakers have adopted a phonological model imported from Nunatsiavut or Greenland? Creider does not answer such questions.

I have tried (Dorais 1985a) to find a solution to the problem, endeavouring to resolve it by way of sociolinguistics. In precontact days, the weakening of the consonant system could have already been present in the language of women and children, and this everywhere in the Arctic, but absent from the speech of men, who, as a general rule, would have firmly articulated all consonant clusters. If this hypothesis stands true, eighteenth-century male Greenlanders and Nunatsiavut residents would have said *ukpik* ("snowy owl"), *ubluq* ("day"), and *irnira* ("my son"), whereas most of their wives and children would have said *uppik*, *ulluk*, and *inniga*.

Present-day Inuit generally deny the existence of any difference in the pronunciation of men and women, but some old written sources seem to point to former discrepancies. As mentioned in the opening section, in Greenland, during the early eighteenth century, women had the reputation of nasalizing word-final consonants. Almost two centuries later, Thalbitzer (1904, 178) noticed that in West Greenland, women and young people were unable to pronounce some sounds "correctly."[45] In their speech, uvulars tended to geminate with the following consonant, and back sounds (e.g., *r*) were pronounced more to the front of the mouth (as in *inniga* instead of *irnira*). In Nunavik, some elders admit that sixty or seventy years ago, female pronunciation was more relaxed than that of males. And everyone is conscious that Inuit children and adolescents always had difficulties articulating several single or grouped consonants.

It is thus possible that before the period of intense European contact, both types of pronunciation (articulate and relaxed) coexisted. The first one, which characterized men and boys old enough to hunt, was a source of prestige because it was linked to highly valued extra-domestic hunting and travelling activities. The other type of pronunciation, the relaxed one, mostly used by women and children and linked to domestic activities, was less prestigious and, therefore, considered typical of people with speech deficiencies (*kutaktut*). The coexistence of these two types of language may have been made possible by the fact that men and women formerly constituted two separate social groups, whose activities were not the same at all. Because until recently the informants of Eskimologists were mostly men, male pronunciation would have generally been considered the "normal" one.

When contacts increased with Europeans, the growing dependency of Inuit on trading posts and missions, as well as their progressive sedentarization, encouraged the development of camp life at the expense of traditional nomadic life. Individuals possessing the abilities to function adequately within the confines of the camp and, later, of the village (two extensions of the domestic space) thus progressively became more prominent than nomadic hunters, still admired by Inuit but not deemed really adapted to the new living conditions. In the course of time, the domestic language with its more relaxed pronunciation probably became the dominant form of speech in settled camps and villages. Formerly limited to women and children, this speech form then apparently spread out through the entire sedentary population.

If this hypothesis stands true, it would explain why consonantal weakening, including cluster gemination, is more complete in areas where Inuit became settled earlier (Greenland, Nunatsiavut, and to a lesser extent, Nunavik and South Baffin)[46], whereas it is still an ongoing process in those regions where sedentarization was more recent (Thule, North Baffin, Kivalliq, and the central Canadian Arctic).

In Alaska and the Inuvialuit region, where sedentarization occurred around 1875, Inuit-European bilingualism, which progressed much more rapidly there than in the rest of the Arctic, seems to have taken precedence over consonantal weakening. It was the language of the Euro-Americans that became the dominant form of speech in settled camps and villages, thus preserving the status (language of subsistence and domestic activities) and traditional non-relaxed version of Inuvialuktun (Siglitun and Uummarmiutun) and Inupiaq. This would explain why, for instance, all types of consonant groupings (apiC as in *utkusik*, "kettle"; bilC as in *kublu*, "thumb"; Jcont as in *taJva*, "there!"; etc.) still subsist in the western dialects even though the Mackenzie and Alaska Inuit have long felt the effects of permanent Euro-American presence.

Such a sociolinguistic explanation could also account for the process of grammatical normalization discussed in the section above on grammatical change. It is probable that like any other language, Inuit naturally tends to regularize its grammar by replacing odd forms (such as *nannut*, "polar bears"; *tulukkat*, "ravens"; *kudjgit*, "rivers"; and *aivrit*, "many walrus") with more regular ones (i.e., *nanuit*, *tulugait*, *kuut*, and *aiviit*). However, this underlying tendency was thwarted by the linguistic conservatism of the dominant social group, adult men, whose way of speaking was considered the accepted norm. It was only when sedentarization occurred (and the domestic space became more important) that this norm was relaxed, thus enabling simpler grammatical rules (limited until then to the speech of young people)[47] to come into general usage.[48]

Social Factors

Christianity, schooling, and a new economic system based on trade and money also contributed to language evolution. The syntactic restructuring that characterizes most present-day Inuit dialects constitutes a good example of this evolution. Each component of the lexeme (i.e., radical, lexical affix, and grammatical ending) now seems to tend toward a degree of autonomy enabling it to function as a separate word. This explains the already mentioned elision of bases and endings (e.g., *-jjangittuq*, "it should most probably not"; *-rumanngi-*, "not want to") and the tendency to utter words that are shorter than they formerly were. This restructuring appears to be linked to the emergence of a new way of expressing and communicating current concepts, which, in turn, seems due to recent transformations of Inuit culture and society.[49] Modern ideas and activities cannot be thought of and transmitted without using a renewed language, which is easier to handle than its traditional counterpart and better suited to the rhythm of contemporary life.[50]

This deep-reaching sociocultural evolution probably explains the progressive disappearance of dual markers in West Greenlandic since the middle of the nineteenth century (modern Greenlanders say *inuit marluk*, with the first word in the plural, instead of *inuuk marluk*, "two persons"). Earlier than elsewhere,[51] the Greenlandic mind was able to dispense with a semantic category (the distinction between "two" and "many") without any real significance in the new society. Outside of Greenland, the dual is still in use, but for the past decade or two some young bilingual speakers have begun mixing it with the plural.

Linguistic modernization has also affected the lexicon, which, as mentioned before, now includes hundreds of new words but has lost a good part of its traditional corpus. In the central Canadian Arctic, the attrition of old lexemes is often due to the existence of a linguistic cleavage between elders and young people. Many older individuals consider it ridiculous and unacceptable for youngsters to use specialized words directly linked to traditional culture (they call them *uqausirjuat*, "big words"), with the result that these lexemes risk being forgotten because new generations will never acquire the cultural knowledge that would grant them the right to use them.

Several Inuit elders are conscious of this problem and have tried to resolve it by setting down their cultural and linguistic knowledge in writing so that it can be transmitted to young people. This is the case, for instance, with Taamusi Qumaq from Puvirnituq, who published an encyclopaedia of traditional life in Nunavik (Qumaq 1988) as well as a dictionary of definitions in Inuktitut (Qumaq

1991); David Uvingajaq from Arviat, in Kivalliq, author of a bilingual *Survival Manual* (Owingajak 1986); Emile Imaruittuq from Igloolik, who describes animal resources and hunting techniques in use in his area (Immaroitok 1985); Elisapee Ootoova and her team from Pond Inlet, who published a dictionary of Inuktitut definitions (Ootoova 2000); and Beverly Aqangngiq Hugo from Barrow, Alaska, who supervised the compilation of an Iñupiaq lexicon of medical terms (Hugo et al. 1991). Since 2000 the Nunatta campus of Nunavut Arctic College (Iqaluit) has published three ongoing series of bilingual Inuktitut-English books – as well as a few separate titles (e.g., Oosten and Laugrand 2007) – dealing with various aspects of arctic culture and history as seen from an Inuit viewpoint:[52] *Interviewing Inuit Elders*; *Inuit Perspectives on the 20th Century*; and *Memory and History in Nunavut*.

As a general rule, Inuit feel concerned about the lexical aspects of linguistic change. They deplore not only the disappearance of old words but also the heterogeneous composition of present-day vocabulary. With the development of air travel and electronic communication, individuals and their language now move around at a previously unknown pace. Local words thus tend to disappear, to be replaced by lexemes imported from neighbouring communities. Many people fear that their vocabulary will become a medley of various words and expressions brought in from different parts of the Arctic rather than remain a homogeneous locally produced lexicon.

Cultural Factors

Vocabulary also changes because of cultural factors. This type of language evolution was particularly felt in East Greenland, where there existed a strong taboo against the use of someone's name after his or her death. Since traditional personal appellations were drawn from the common vocabulary, animals and objects bearing the dead person's name had to be called something else. In such cases, a new metaphoric word was generally coined. The French explorer and anthropologist Paul-Émile Victor (1963, 363) mentions the case of an individual named Naaja ("Seagull"), who died in 1887 and whose death entailed a vocabulary change: the bird was thenceforth called *qusiiq*, an onomatopoeia. According to an elderly lady met in Ammassalik in 1980, the word for "kettle," *uujurturpik*, was changed to *uutsit* ("what is used for burning") some time before 1900, after the death of a person named Uujurturpik.[53]

This taboo, in force until the arrival of Christianity at the beginning of the twentieth century, was compounded by a general reluctance to utter words with a powerful meaning (e.g., animal and plant names, body parts, and hunting implements). This explains why 30% of the present-day East Greenlandic lexicon is comprised of descriptive lexemes that do not exist anywhere else, at least with the same meaning (Dorais 1981a). Here are a few examples:

LITERAL MEANING IN EAST GREENLANDIC	EAST GREENLANDIC	NORTH BAFFIN	
"which lives in the soil"	*itturmiilaq*	*airaq*	"edible root"
"which is used for scratching"	*qisiit*	*kukik*	"claw, nail"
"the smelly one"	*tiparartiq*	*tiggaaluk*	"rutting seal"
"the one which is stoned"	*nagalaraq*	*aqiggiq*	"ptarmigan"
"the one caught with a spear"	*kapurniaraq*	*iqaluk*	"trout, char"
"which is used for hearing"	*tusaat*	*siuti*	"ear"
"which is used for licking"	*alittuut*	*uqaq*	"tongue"
"projectile"	*sakkiq*	*ulu*	"woman's knife"
"thrown like a harpoon"	*naalivartaq*	*qarjuk*	"arrow"

The death taboo was also in use in West Greenland (Petersen 1976a) and the Thule district (Gilberg et al. 1978) but under a weaker form. On the west coast, it was limited to the community of the deceased, and the name reappeared after a few years. Among Polar Inuit, the taboo stopped having any effect when the dead person's name was given to a newborn.

More generally, this respect for the spoken word, this fear of provoking calamities through a careless manipulation of the language, characterized Inuit culture as a whole. Shamans, for instance, used a metaphorical language allowing them to avoid direct mention of potentially dangerous entities (e.g., spirits, animals, and human beings). This way of speaking had much in common with what was happening in Greenland. The East Greenlandic lexicon may thus be considered a kind of secular version of the shaman's language. Indeed, some East Greenlandic words are reminiscent of the shamanic vocabulary in use in Igloolik at the beginning of the twentieth century (see Rasmussen 1929). Compare, for instance:

LITERAL MEANING IN SHAMAN'S LANGUAGE	EAST GREENLANDIC	IGLOOLIK SHAMANS	
"which stands up"	*nappat*	*nappataq*	"neck"
"which ducks its head"	*punnguaq* (old)	*punnguuq*	"dog"
Proto-Eskimo for "human"	*taalaq* (in spirit language)	*tau*	"human being"

Through the centuries, such cultural phenomena probably played an important part in the evolution of the Inuit language.

CONCLUSION

This evolution, which has been partly measured thanks to written documents compiled since the sixteenth century, progressively transformed the common Proto-Inuit language – ancestor to all modern Inuit speech forms – into a series of regional dialects not so different from each other but possessing their own respective characteristics. In Inuktitut and Kalaallisut the consonant system became simpler or weaker (through the gemination of clusters, for instance) and morphology became more regular,[54] whereas in the western dialects the language remained conservative. Everywhere, however, over recent decades, syntax has been modified and vocabulary transformed in the wake of pervasive social change.

This shows that language evolution is caused by two types of interlinking factors: linguistic (disappearance of marginal phonological variation; tendency toward grammatical normalization) and sociocultural (influence of sedentary life on male and female language; introduction of new concepts and artefacts; naming taboo). The lexicon and morphology tend to change according to their own evolutionary constraints (which aim at increasing the regularity of the system), but they are also influenced by the social usage of the discourses they contribute to generating and by the evolution of the semantic structure they express. Hence the transformation of the Inuit language is due, on the one hand, to modifications to existing patterns of sociolinguistic variation (e.g., differences in the speech of men, women, and the young) and, on the other, to semantic change induced by the introduction of concepts reflecting new social and cultural realities.

6

Semantics, Neology, and Oral Literature

Semantics aims at describing and analyzing the encoded meanings that language translates into morphemes, lexemes, and syntactical rules. It helps us to understand how speakers of a specific tongue think about the world they live in. This chapter first examines some semantic areas particularly important to arctic culture and then shows how the Inuit language has coped with one of the principal challenges it has had to face since European contact: giving names to newly introduced objects and concepts (neology). The chapter concludes with a brief overview of oral literature, a privileged vehicle for expressing traditional semantic categories.

SOME SEMANTIC FIELDS

From a semantic point of view, the Inuit language is characterized by the lexical development of some fields of knowledge considered by Inuit to be of the utmost importance, notably animal names, body parts,[1] ice, and snow. Words for "snow," for instance, constitute a good example[2] of this kind of development. In Nunavik Inuktitut at least twenty-five different single words (if specific radicals and derivatives are included) can be applied to various types of snow (Schneider 1970, 271–2; Dorais 1990c, 205):

qanik	"falling snow"
qanittaq	"recently fallen snow"
aputi(k)	"snow on the ground"
maujaq	"soft snow on the ground"
masak	"wet falling snow"

matsaaq	"half-melted snow on the ground"
aqilluqaaq	"drift of soft snow"
sitilluqaaq	"drift of hard snow"
qiqsuqaaq	"refrozen snow"
kavisirlaq	"snow made rough by rain and freezing"
pukak	"crystalline snow on the ground"
minguliq	"fine coat of powdered snow"
natiruvaaq	"fine snow carried out by wind"
piiqturiniq	"thin coat of snow deposited on something"
qiqumaaq	"snow whose surface is frozen"
katakaqtanaq	"hard crust of snow giving way under footsteps"
aumannaq	"snow on the ground, ready to melt"
aniu	"snow for making water"
sirmiq	"melting snow used as cement for the snow-house"
illusaq	"snow that is fit for building a snow-house"
isiriaqtaq	"yellow or reddish falling snow"
kiniqtaq	"damp, compact snow"
mannguq	"melting snow"
qannialaaq	"light falling snow"
qanniapaluk	"very light falling snow, in still air"

In a completely different area, all Inuit dialects, except present-day Greenlandic, attach a great importance to the expression of duality by marking, as already seen, a distinction between the dual (*inuuk*, "two persons") and plural (*inuit*, "many people") grammatical numbers and by using a special affix (*-giik/-riik*) to express dyadic relations (e.g., *panigiik*, "a pair including a daughter" [i.e., a daughter and one of her parents]). To go further into the study of semantics, however, more complex techniques have to be put to use, such as componential analysis[3] or cognitive anthropology.[4]

There also exists an interesting method that proceeds from the basically polysynthetic nature of the Inuit language. The Inuit word being a composite structure (base, lexical affixe[s], grammatical affix; see Holtved 1956), complete lexemes often possess a signification going beyond that of their component parts, although being directly linked to them.[5] This characteristic of the Inuit language offers a particularly good key for analyzing its semantics because many words can be understood in two ways. They have a surface signification that allows them to make sense within a sentence, but at the same time, the semantic analysis of their morphological components (base, post-bases, ending) can yield a deeper literal meaning that grants access to their underlying semantic structure.[6] This technique is called morphosemantics.

Many lexemes cannot undergo morphosemantic analysis because their individual components do not have any understandable meaning in the present-day language.[7] A word like *nanuq* ("polar bear"), for instance, cannot be divided because its syllables (*na-* and *-nuq*) do not make sense by themselves. But consider the following lexemes, which, at first glance, may look like indivisible units. When undergoing morphosemantic analysis, they yield a new meaning:

INUIT LEXEME	SURFACE MEANING	MORPHOSEMANTIC ANALYSIS	LITERAL MEANING
pi-araq	"young animal"	thing-young	"a young thing"
pi-u-juq	"good"	thing-to be-which is	"which is something"
pi-u-nngit-tuq	"bad"	thing-be-not-which is	"which is nothing"
angu-t/angu-n	"man, male"	to catch game-used for	"used for catching game"
ata-usiq	"one (1)"	to cling to-the fact of	"clinging to something"
irni-q	"son"	to bear a child-who is	"the child who was born"[8]
ataata-tsiaq	"grandfather"	father-good	"good father"
tuki-lik	"makes sense"	axis, direction-it has	"it has a direction"

For the Canadian linguist Dirmid R. Collis, who worked at eliciting the semiotic[9] structure of Greenlandic Kalaallisut (Collis 1971), Inuit semantics is based on a visual aesthetics of spatial relations. The West Greenlandic lexeme *aappaluttuq* ("red"), for instance, is constructed upon the radical *aak* ("blood"). In a similar way, the term for "mushroom" (*pupik*) includes the root *pu-*, denoting any protuberance rising from a flat surface, and the morpheme *-pik* ("alone by itself"). A mushroom is thus literally named "solitary protuberance." For Collis (1969), understanding Inuit semantics presupposes the development of an aesthetic logic conveyed by a limited number of syllables, each syllable making sense separately or in combination. This idea is also supported by the French linguist Nicole Tersis (1994).

Thanks to morphosemantics, which allows us to reach the basic meaning of lexemes, it is possible to understand more clearly how the concepts and images that Inuit have in their minds are organized into meaningful categories. For instance, the word "good" (*piujuq*) actually means "which is something" because Inuit cannot divorce goodness from existence. Conversely, the negation of existence (*piunngittuq*, "which is nothing") is considered equivalent to evil. The following pages show what morphosemantics and other techniques of semantic analysis can reveal about various aspects of Inuit culture and experience.

Humanity, Gender, and Kinship

The concept of "human being" or "person" (*inuk*) will be the point of departure for this description of Inuit semantics. According to the linguist Michael Fortescue,[10] the word *inuk* may be related to Unangax *ing(i)yuX* ("living body") and *ingisxi-X* ("owner"). Men and women would thus be defined as animated beings who can "own" other beings. Such ownership could be either physical (as in *qimmiup inua*, "a dog's person" [i.e., master]) or spiritual (as in *sikuup inua*, "the person of the sea-ice" [i.e., its resident spirit]). In other words, a person (embodied or spiritual) would be an animated animator, in contrast with animals (*uumajuit*, "those who are alive"), which are animated but do not "own" anything else.

More at a surface level, but in accordance with what has just been said, the ethnolinguist Michèle Therrien states that the word *inuk* means "northern human being." It refers primarily to life, the supernatural, morality, and ethnic relations (Therrien 1987a). Therrien bases her assertion on the fact that this lexeme lies at the centre of a network of derivatives expressing the development, behaviour, and underlying nature of humanity. She gives the following examples (in Nunavik Inuktitut):

INUIT LEXEME	SURFACE MEANING	MORPHOSEMANTIC ANALYSIS	LITERAL MEANING
inu-u-liq-puq	"is born"	human-be-start-[s]he	"starts to be human"
inu-u-vuq	"is alive"	human-be-[s]he	"is human"
inu-viniq	"a deceased"	human-former	"a former human"
inu-ruq-puq	"is reincarnated"	human-become-[s]he	"becomes human"

inu-a	"owner of a thing"	human-its	"its human being"
inu-luk	"a bad person"	human-bad	"bad human being"
inu-qqi-tuq	"a good person"	human-be good-who	"who is a good human"
inuk-titut	"Inuit language"	human-like	"like human beings"

As far as ethnic relations are concerned, most Nunavik Inuit define themselves as *inutuinnait* ("the only real people"). This is what distinguishes them from other types of human beings. Some of these types are almost identical to the *inutuinnait*; others are different. All identical forms of humanity are Inuit (or "Eskimo") in the ethnic assertion of the term: northern Alaskan *inupiat* ("human beings *par excellence*"), western Canadian Arctic *inuvialuit* ("big human beings *par excellence*"), central Arctic *inuinnait* ("genuine humans"), south-western Alaskan *yupiit* ("human beings *par excellence*"), Greenlandic *kalaallit* ("Greenlanders," probably from medieval Scandinavian *skrællingar*, "pagans, savages"), and so on.

Non-identical types of humanity include, among others, First Nation Indians (*allait*, "others, strangers")[11] and Europeans (*qallunaat*, "outstanding eyebrows") (Therrien 1987a). *Qallunaat* may be subdivided into *qallunaatuinnait* ("only real big eyebrows"; the Anglo), *uiguit* ("[those who say] *oui-oui*"; the French), and *tariup akianiittut* ("those who are across the ocean"; Europeans), while the "others" comprise *qirnitait* ("the black ones"; blacks), *inuujaqtut* ("those who look like Inuit"; East Asians), and so on (Dorais 1988c).

The concept of "human being" (*inuk*) includes those of "man" (*angun/angut*) and "woman" (*arnaq*),[12] both genders being *inuit*. As seen above, the word *angun* (or *aṇgut[ik]*) literally means "that which is used for catching game." The etymology of *arnaq* is less evident. This term could proceed from the base *aq-* ("to be in movement") followed by the affix *-naq* ("to make it so"). The woman would then be defined as "the one who puts something in movement" (Dorais 1986b).

Other pairs of lexemes referring to gender can be analyzed the same way (e.g., *ui/nuliaq*, "husband/wife"; *ataata/anaana*, "father/mother"; *surusiq/niviaqsiaq*, "boy/girl," in Nunavik Tarramiut; and *ittuq/ningiuq*, "old man/old woman"). The word *ui*, for instance, seems to imply the idea of "distance apart" or "protuberance,"[13] and it probably refers to the erection of the penis. The term *nuliaq* means something like "the little female in heat."

From a semantic point of view, gender relations seem to be centred on the quartet of woman (*arnaq*), man (*angun/angut*), husband (*ui*), and wife (*nuliaq*). The woman puts the man into movement. With his protuberance, the husband/man catches (as though it were a game animal) the little female in heat – that is, this same wife/woman who put him into movement. All other words pertaining to gender are defined in relation to this basic quartet[14] (Dorais 1986b, 176–7).

Lee Guemple (1975) mentions that lexemes applying to the various periods of human life are often denoted in terms of social and economic activities. The status of "husband" (*ui*) or "wife" (*nuliaq*) can be reached only once one has mastered the techniques necessary to survival. Because these techniques are generally restricted to one or the other gender,[15] it is not necessary, when speaking, to specify the male or female status of those involved in activities specific to their gender. For example, the lexeme *angunasukpuq* will be understood as "<u>he</u> hunts," even though the ending *-puq* (third-person singular of the declarative mood) does not connote any grammatical gender.

As kinship terms are concerned, they are best understood by way of componential analysis, which shows, for instance, that blood relatives and in-laws are never called by the same names (e.g., *ataata/anaana*, "father/mother," versus *saki*, "father- or mother-in-law") and that relatives belonging to different generations always receive different appellations.[16] Gender too is often distinguished (e.g., *ani/naja*, "brother/sister"; and *irniq/panik*, "son/daughter"), and within the same generation, the speaker sometimes discriminates between his or her elder and younger siblings and cousins (e.g., *angajuq/nukaq*, "elder sibling/younger sibling"). According to Nelson Graburn (1964), these characteristics of kinship terminology (e.g., the relevance of gender and age) reflect some of the basic social and family attitudes of the Inuit.

Bernard Saladin d'Anglure (1967) adds that kinship relations are unequal, some positions (those of women and youngsters) being considered inferior to those of adult men. This inequality is reflected in the lexical rule stating that all lexemes expressing a dyadic relation (with the affix *-giik/-riik*) must normally start with the base referring to the "inferior" element of the relation, as in *irniriik* ("a son and his mother") rather than *anaanagiik* and in *najagiik* ("a sister and her brother") instead of *anigiik*.

The Human Body

Human beings, men and women, have a body that holds no secret for the Inuit, whose language includes several hundred words referring to the external and internal parts of anatomy (see, among others, Balt 1977b; Hugo 1991; Bordin 2003). Therrien (1987a) has analyzed this vocabulary as it occurs in Nunavik Inuktitut. According to her, the lexicon of anatomy comprises two levels: somatic (pertaining to the body) and psychic (pertaining to the mind and soul). Inuit anatomical terms describe the material body and the relationships between its various components, but at the same time, they explain how the psychic body (e.g., *tarniq*, "soul"; *anirniq*, "breath"; *atiq*, "name"; *isuma*, "thought"; and *sila*, "intelligence") acts as the motor (*aulatsiji*, "that which makes it move") of the person.

The body is seen as a metaphor[17] symbolizing the three main levels of human experience: technology (manufacturing an artefact is akin to giving and taking life); society (like the body, human groups are perceived as a combination of individual parts joined together); and religion (the masters of the universe act through the body).

As far as technology is concerned, Therrien shows how words describing the kayak (*qajaq*) and the snow-house (*illuvigaq*) reproduce the male-female dichotomy. Because of its mobility and usefulness for hunting, the kayak is considered male, whereas the house, immovable focus of domestic activities, is seen as female. Their components often assume an anatomical guise. The kayak has a penis, its forepoint, which is called *usuujaq* ("which looks like a penis"), while the sleeping platform of the snow-house, *igliq*, is compared to a uterus (*igliaq*, "the small platform"). Remembering her intra-uterine life, an Igloolik elder, Iqallijuq, describes her mother's womb as a snow-house with a platform where she sits, and from which she exits (*anivuq*, "he/she exits or is born") when she becomes too big to be comfortable any more (Saladin d'Anglure 1977).

For Therrien, such metaphors entail a reflection on women, men, procreation, this world here below, and the hereafter. They teach, for instance, that the roof of the mouth (*qilaaq*, meaning "small *qilak*") is equivalent to the dome of the snow-house (*qilak*), which is itself a microcosmic version of the canopy of heaven (named *qilak* too). They also teach that weather and human intelligence, both called *sila*, are interconnected.[18] The way Inuit talk about their bodies thus enables them to move from what is known (their immediate environment) to what is unknown (the universe), as well as to generate similarities because metaphors establish an equivalence between different levels of reality (Therrien 1987a). For example, that the sky (or heaven) is called the same thing as the dome of the snow-house and the roof of the mouth gives it a more concrete and understandable meaning (it becomes similar to very familiar entities), but it also makes all three concepts equivalent: the roof and the dome are smaller versions of the sky, and conversely, the sky is just a big dome.

The body normally coexists in harmony with the universe. It does not create space but is completely bounded by it. It is itself an organized and divisible space. The cohesion of the body (perceived as hard and firm, like earth) implies the action of the soul (seen as fluid and impalpable, like air, breath, or water). Any disruption of this harmony and cohesion entails sickness (Therrien 1995; Therrien and Laugrand 2001), which is perceived as a disorder (expressed by the post-base *-luk-*, "it is bad") provoking a situation (*-sima-*, "to be in such a state") that is suffered (*-jaq/-taq*, "who is the object of") because the body has been run through (*-kkut*, "through") by an external entity, as in:

qaritakkut tikitausimagami
"because [s]he is in the situation of having been reached through the brain [by sickness]"

isumaluktuq
"[s]he thinks badly" (i.e., suffers from a psychological disorder)

The sickness/healing process is thus understood as the occurrence of a disorder that must be put into order (*aaqqik-*, "to repair an object or heal a sick person") if life is to continue.

Emotion and Social Harmony

Disorder can be provoked by a lack of emotional balance. The Inuit vocabulary of feelings has been analyzed by Jean Briggs in the course of her research among the Utkuhiksalik Natsilingmiut (Briggs 1968, 1970). According to this anthropologist, the Back River Utkuhiksalik have names for eleven different types of emotions, each type comprising several degrees.[19] Affection, for instance, is expressed in many ways: a desire to be with someone (*unga-* "to want to be with someone"; *naglik-*, "to feel concerned with the physical or emotional well-being of someone; to want to be with him/her"); a show of sentiments (*niviuq-*, "to want to touch or hug someone"; *aqaq-*, "to communicate tenderly with someone without touching him/her"); an offer of protection (*huqu-*, "to answer the needs of someone").

Happiness (*quvia-*, "to be happy") is perceived as a lack of hatred and envy, which entails moral well-being. When they do occur, hatred and envy can take several forms: *huaq-* ("to abuse someone with words; to quarrel"), *ninngaq-* ("to abuse someone physically; to express frustration"), *pijuma-* ("to want something a lot, with envy"), *tuhuu-* ("to want for oneself something belonging to someone else"; it is the contrary of *naglik-*), and so on.

There exist numerous other feelings, all of them expressed thanks to various bases and affixes. Outside of the Natsilingmiut area, the expression of emotions follows quite similar patterns. An interesting phenomenon occurs in West and East Greenlandic, where a linguistic distinction is made between male and female jealousy (*sangiappuq*, "he is jealous," and *ningarpuq*, "she is jealous").

Such emotions constitute the basis of traditional or semi-traditional social relations. In Nunatsiavut, for instance (Collis and Dorais 1983), the expression of customary law invokes the concepts of harmony and peace or, on the contrary, that of humiliation to distinguish between good and bad deeds. What is good (*piujuk*, "it is something") is defined as *naammapuk* ("adequate"), *alianattuk* ("pleasant"), or *i&uappuk* ("comfortable, correct"). Conversely, evil (*piunngituk*, "it is not something") can be *nammangittuk* ("inadequate"), *aliananngituk* ("unpleasant"), or *i&uippuk* ("uncomfortable, incorrect").

Any inadequate or incorrect (i.e., bad) behaviour or habit tends to jeopardize harmony and break peace (defined as *saimmainik*, "the fact of being consoled"). Such behaviour is thus considered undesirable and, for this reason, felt offensive. Offences humiliate those whom they victimize by embarrassing (*kanngusuttisi-*), frightening (*quinatsaa-*), or alienating (*atsaa-*) them. Such humiliations, which increase unbalance and loss of social harmony, are intrinsically bad since evil is defined as a break with harmony and a negative relation with the natural order of things. Semantic analysis thus shows that for the Nunatsiavut Inuit, judiciary procedures and sanctions are justified only when they tend to restore harmony by reminding people what is the best way to behave in society.

Numeration

Body metaphors give form to a semantic field that at first glance seems quite far from human anatomy: the lexicon of numeration. For Inuit, the basic measuring standard is the human body with its ten fingers and ten toes. As with many other peoples of the world – the Maya, for instance – their numerical system is based on the number twenty (the sum of fingers and toes). Forty is two times twenty, fifty is two times twenty plus ten, one hundred is five times twenty, and so on.

The very names of numbers often express their affiliation with the body. "One" is *atausiq* ("the adherence, what is indivisible"). "Two" is "the following unit" (the original form is *malruk*, which seems etymologically linked to the radical *malik-*, "to follow"). Whereas the etymology of "three" (*pingasut*) and "four" (*sitamat/tisamat/sisamat*) remains unclear, that of the number five exhibits an anatomical connotation: *tallimat* means something like "an arm is complete." To reach the number five, one must count all five fingers on one hand, which allows one to "complete" an arm.

From the number six on, there must be a change of hand. This is why in most dialects, "six" is *arvinilik*, which means "there is a passage, a crossing." The following numbers, seven, eight, and nine, are respectively called: "there is a passage with two [numbers]"; "there is a passage with three"; and "there is a passage with four."[20] The number ten is translated as *qulit* ("the upper part"). This word expresses that all fingers of both hands have now been used for counting and that if one wants to continue, one must turn to the lower limbs.

The numbers eleven to nineteen are usually translated as "ten and one," "ten and two," and so forth. In Natsilingmiutut, however, the number eleven is called *qulit arvingmat* ("the upper part is put aside"), an expression of the transfer from hands to feet. This transfer was expressed even more directly in old South Baffin Inuktitut, where the word for "eleven" was *itikkanuuqtut* ("they get to the feet"), and in the Thule dialect, where, according to Kaj Birket-Smith (1928), the number eleven was formerly called *itikkani* ("on the feet") (Baillargeon et al. 1977). And even today, in Greenland, "eleven" is *aqqanillit* (West Greenlandic) or *aqqanittit* (East Greenlandic) ("they are going down [to the feet]").

According to this logic, the number twenty corresponds to a kind of completeness (as two hands and two feet make a full human being). This explains why, in several dialects, it is expressed as *avatit* ("the limbs"). Some speech forms are even more explicit. "Twenty" may be called *inuinnaq* ("only a person," in Inupiaq and Siglitun), *inuk atauhiq* ("one human being," in Inuinnaqtun), *inuk naamaJuq* ("the person is complete," in Natsilingmiutut), *inuk naajuq* ("the person is being completed," in old North Baffin), or *ii naättungu* ("completing a person," in East Greenlandic).

The Inuit numeration system can be summarized as follows:

"one"	*atausiq/atauhiq/ataasiq*	"adherence, what is indivisible"
"two"	*malruk/marruuk/marluk/martit*	"the following unit"
"three"	*pingasut/pingahut/pingasit*	?
"four"	*sitamat/hitamat/tisamat/sisamat*	?
"five"	*tallimat*	"an arm is complete"
"six"	*arvinilik/arfinillit*	"there is a passage; they have a passage"
	pingasuujuqtut	"they are three once again"
"ten"	*qulit*	"the upper part"
	tallimaujuqtut	"they are five once again"
"eleven"	*qulillu atausirlu*	"ten and one"
	qulit arvingmat	"the upper part is put aside"
	itikkanuuqtut/itikkani	"they get to the feet; on the feet"
	aqqanillit/aqqanittit	"they are going down"
"twenty"	*avatit*	"the limbs"
	inuinnaq/inuk atauhiq	"one person"
	inuk naa(ma)juq/ii naattungu	"completing a person"
"forty"	*avatit marruuk/iit naattungut martit*	"two twenties; completing two persons"

Richard Baillargeon and colleagues (1977, 122) suggest that such a system is particularly fragile because of its anthropomorphic nature. It is a fact that since the introduction of money, Inuit numbers have progressively become obsolete, except for the lower figures – one to five – and, sometimes, ten and twenty. Even monolingual Inuit speakers now count in English or Danish.[21] For Wilfried Schuhmacher (1975), this is a typical example of cultural deprivation due to the introduction of a capitalist economy.

The real nature of Inuit numeration, however, lies beyond such explanations. According to J. Peter Denny (1981a), hunters do not need high numbers.[22] Abstract mathematical concepts are thus useless for them. Such concepts appear only in societies based on agriculture and trade because they need common denominators for comparing the value of various types of goods. Hunter arithmetic is limited by the concrete context of its usage. This is why it often refers to fingers and toes or to other kinds of objects in need of being counted.

Such a situation has important effects on teaching mathematics in school. In the lower elementary grades, arithmetic should be adapted to the cognitive logic and native numerical system of children (see Pallascio et al. 1993). Asked, for instance, to classify a number of objects according to their size (from the smallest to the largest), most Inuit children spontaneously tend to divide them into two groups: small objects on one side, large ones on the other. This way of behaving may be attributed to the specificity of basic Inuit logic, which puts much emphasis on duality. Any mathematics curriculum ignoring these factors risks ending in failure.

Time and Space

The difference between European and Inuit mathematical thinking is particularly important when it comes to measuring time. Inuit perceive and express time as an extent of space through which one is moving rather than as a succession of events whose dates of occurrence can be measured with numbers (Lowe 1980).[23] This is shown by the fact that the grammatical endings *-mi* ("in, at"), *-mut* ("to"), *-mit* ("from"), and *-kkut* ("through, by") can express either space or time:

iglu-mi	"in the house"
iglu-mut	"to the house"
iglu-mit	"from the house"
iglu-kkut	"through the house"

ullu-mi	"in the day; today"
ullumi-mut	"up to this day"
ullumi-mit	"from this day on"
ullu-kkut	"by day; during the day"

The localizers and demonstratives, which point out spatial positions (see chapter 3), are also used for expressing time. This is the case, for example, with the lexeme *manna*, which has two meanings: spatial ("this one here") and temporal ("now"). Proximity in space ("here") is considered equivalent to proximity in time ("now"). Conversely, temporal distance may be expressed the same way as spatial remoteness, as in *taipsumani/taitsumani* ("formerly"), whose literal meaning is "in that one far away." In another grammatical context, the nouns *sivulliq* and *kingulliq* respectively mean "one in front" or "one who came before" and "one in the back" or "one who will come after."[24]

The semantic analysis of localizers and demonstratives has generated a copious literature. Inuit divide space in a very subtle way, which enables them to indicate precisely the actual or symbolic position of any entity in relation to the speaker or to the main topic of the ongoing conversation (see Correll 1976). For example, when a hunter in a boat spots a seal and says *natsikanna* (or *natsiq kanna*; "a seal, this down here!"), his companions immediately know that the animal has to be looked for toward the open sea. If this were not the case, the localizers *pinna* or *panna* ("upward, toward land") would be used. The hunters also know that the seal is immobile. A moving animal would be referred to as *unna* or *sanna*.

According to Raymond Gagné (1968), all objects, animals, and persons are perceived by Inuit as though they were either equidimensional (their length being roughly equal to their width) or, on the contrary, non-equidimensional (their length exceeding their width). All immobile entities are supposed to be equidimensional, whereas those in movement are considered non-equidimensional. Entities are also classified according to their position in relation to three pairs of criteria: proximity and distance, height and depth, and internality and externality. The basic singular forms of demonstratives can thus be distributed as follows (examples are in Nunavik Tarramiut):

	EQUI-DIMENSIONAL	NON-EQUIDIMENSIONAL	
near	*una*	*manna*	"this one here"
far	*inna*	*anna*	"that one there"

high	*pinna*	*panna*	"this/that one up [t]here"
low	*kanna*	*unna*	"this/that one down [t]here"
inside	*qanna*	*qanna*	"this one in here"
outside	*kinna*	*kinna*	"that one out there"

I once suggested replacing the notion of equidimensionality with that of perceptibility (Dorais 1971). Entities called equidimensional by Gagné would be more easily perceptible than others because of their shape or visibility. Another interpretation has been given by Monique Vézinet (1975), who states that localizers and place-names[25] are to be understood in relation to three main factors: their accessibility by kayak or dog team, their visibility, and the presence of game animals at some periods of the year.[26] Denny (1981c) suggests that the semantics of localizers expresses a triple network of relations: entities positioned "in" a place, "some distance" from a place, or "out of field" (i.e., out of the area perceptible to speakers).

It is difficult to decide whether an interpretation is more valid than the others. Gagné's observations seem particularly precise, however, and many linguists (e.g., Lowe 1980) have borrowed his analytical framework. In fact, only a systematic study of the natural speech of several speakers (as in Arnakak 1994) could elicit an exact and complete description of the semantics of localizers.

The French anthropologist Pierre Robbe has studied Inuit orientation in East Greenland. According to him: "Inuit hunters divide the space within which they live into four sections. The orientation of these sections may vary because it is not based on a steady system, such as the trajectory of the sun, but on a system of variable references: the direction of the seashore" (Robbe 1977, 82). Robbe adds that by referring to the various place-names distributed along the coast, this system enables hunters to localize precisely any point on the sea and to express this localization in a brief and exact way.[27]

Orientation is also discussed by John Macdonald in his book on Inuit astronomy (1998).[28] The author shows that stars play an important part in night-time navigation – especially in areas where the sun does not appear above the horizon for a number of months – but that other factors such as prevailing winds are of consequence too. The book is particularly interesting for its description and nomenclature of constellations and other celestial bodies as they are known in the Igloolik area.

Finally, Michael Fortescue (1988b) has synthesized everything that is known about Inuit and Yupik orientation systems, from Greenland to Russian Chukotka. He concludes that all these systems are organized around a few shared dimensions:

- up and down (from any landmark, in the direction of the sea coast or river shore)[29]
- left and right (along the coast when looking toward open sea)
- along the axis of the prevailing winds of the area

Fortescue suggests that the present-day orientation systems are an extension of the system of localizers originally in use inside and around prehistoric dwellings at the time the Norton culture was flourishing in the Bering Strait region some 3,000 years ago.

Colours, Plants, and Animals

The Inuit lexicon of colour, flora, and fauna has been the object of several studies that sometimes resort to cognitive anthropology. Albert Heinrich (1972, 1977), for instance, has shown that the terminology of colours as expressed in the Bering Strait dialect, as well as among Inuit of the central Canadian Arctic, proceeds from a fundamental contrast between light (white) and dark (black). All "primary" colours (red, green/blue,[30] yellow, brown, and grey) can occur within one of these two registers – that is, as a light (white) or dark (black) shade. More recently, Keiichi Omura (1998) has discussed the morphology of Natsilingmiutut colour terms, dividing them into basic, derivative, and metaphorical lexemes.

Jean-Pierre Paillet (1973) warns researchers against too narrow a use of cognitive anthropology. His own research shows that in Inuktitut most lexemes cannot be classified into well-defined taxonomies, where generic classes would systematically include less encompassing specific categories. For him, the Inuit taxonomy of plants and animals cannot be explained in purely linguistic terms because many lexemes cannot be understood without reference to culture. Michael Wilson (1978) gives the example of the words *ipiraq*, *maniq*, *kanguujaq*, and *urjuq*, which refer simultaneously to vegetal species and to the wick of the traditional lamp (*qulliq*), made from one or the other of these plants. In all cases, the Inuit word denotes at the same time the species in question and the object that uses it as raw material, a fact complicating the process of taxonomic classification.

In her master's thesis on ethnobotany in Igloolik, Polly Dritsas (1986) confirms Paillet's and Wilson's observations. She shows that plants are classified according to their use and morphological complexity rather than being put into separate, clearly distinguished categories. Inuit give much attention to the components of plants, as well as to their growth. Because they are able to grow, plants constitute a specific subcategory within the more encompassing class of *nunarait*, or *nunajait* ("things from the earth"; rocks, faeces, plants).

Also working in Igloolik, the ethnolinguist Vladimir Randa applies morphosemantics to the study of animal terminology. According to him, the zoological lexicon describes the appearance, behaviour, or habitat of the species referred to. Onomatopoeias are occasionally used (Randa 1989, 1994, 1998).

In Igloolik all animals are called *uumajuit* ("living ones"). They are divided into *nunamiutait* ("land dwellers") and *imarmiutait* ("sea dwellers"). Each of these classes includes two subcategories: *nirjutiit* ("those used for eating"; game animals) and a category without a name, that of non-edible animals. *Nunamiutait* and *imarmiutait* are also subdivided into five families: *pisuktiit* ("the walkers"; land mammals), *puijiit* ("those popping their head out of the water"; sea mammals), *iqaluit* (fish), *tingmiat* ("the flying ones"; birds), and *qupirruit* (insects and vermin). A sixth family, molluscs and shellfish (found only among *imarmiutait*), has not received any name.

Among the Belcher Islands Inuit, who speak the Itivimiut subdialect of Nunavik Inuktitut, the *qupirruit* are not considered a kind of *uumajuit* (Nakashima 1991).[31] Animals are nevertheless divided into six families: *pisuttiit* (land mammals), *puijiit* (sea mammals), *iqaluit* (trout-like and freshwater fish), *iqqamiutait* ("dwellers of the bottom"; sea fish, molluscs, and shellfish), *timmiat* (large birds), and *qupanuat* (small birds).

Zoological taxonomy is a little more complex in East Greenland (Dorais 1984), where *uumasut* ("living beings, animals") are subdivided into nine families: *nirsutit* ("those used for eating"; four-legged animals), *puilit* ("those popping their head out of the water"; seal and walrus), *timmittat* ("flying ones"; birds), *uumasuaqqat* ("small living beings"; walking insects and vermin), *timmiaaqqat* ("small flying ones"; flying insects), *qilittut* ("flexible ones"; molluscs and shellfish), *kapurniakkat* ("those that are speared"; trout-like fish), *aalisakkat* ("those caught with a line"; the other fish), and a ninth family, whales, which has not received any specific name. The designation of individual species generally follows the same rules as in Igloolik or the Belcher Islands. It refers to the appearance, behaviour, or habitat of animals, and onomatopoeias are sometimes used.

In the Inuit area as a whole, flora and fauna are perceived as being linked to human experience. Plants and animals are often named after their cultural function (e.g., *manniq*, vegetal moss or lamp wick), their use by people (e.g., *aalisakkat*, fish caught with a line) or their appearance. This confirms that Inuit semantics is anthropocentric. The human being and his or her body – in harmony with the environment – serve as models for describing the world. Even in fields generally deemed totally abstract (numeration and space categories, for instance), it is the body, considered a measuring instrument or spatial reference, that constitutes the basic standard for understanding the universe.

GIVING NAMES TO NEW CONCEPTS

For over 300 years Inuit semantics has been confronted by an enormous challenge: how to make sense of the thousands of new objects, institutions, and concepts introduced by Europeans, classify them into meaningful categories, and give them appropriate Inuit names. Each dialect tackled this task in an independent but basically similar way. Everywhere in the Arctic coining new lexemes that made use of the available stock of bases and affixes took precedence over borrowing foreign terms. Thanks to the polysynthetic structure of the language, speakers easily created Inuit neologisms (i.e., new words) describing the function or appearance of the objects and concepts they denoted.

In all dialects the percentage of words borrowed from English, Danish, or another language is very low. In Uummarmiut, for instance, of 421 terms belonging to the "culture" section of my interdialectal lexicon[32] (Dorais 1990b), only 14 (3.3%) were borrowed from English. The proportion is almost the same (3.5%) in Inuinnaqtun, where the 404 "cultural" lexemes found in the lexicon include 14 loan-words. In the North Baffin dialect the proportion of borrowings is higher: 6.6% (31/516). It is in West Greenlandic, however, that borrowing reaches its maximum. Of 500 words pertaining to culture, 45 (9%) were borrowed from Danish.

It is interesting to note that the proportion of loan-words tends to increase from west to east. In Nunatsiavut, for instance, it reaches almost 7% (35/508), more than in North Baffin but less than in Kalaallisut. It is possible that lexical borrowing was influenced by factors similar to those that caused consonant weakening in the eastern Arctic (see chapter 5). The percentage of borrowed words would be directly linked to the occurrence of sedentary life around European trading posts and missions. The earlier this process was completed, the more numerous the borrowings would have been. In the western Canadian Arctic and probably Alaska, the early introduction of bilingualism would have impaired linguistic borrowing, freezing the lexicon in the state it was at the beginning of the twentieth century, when English became the dominant language of sedentary settlements. This could explain the low proportion of loan-words in Uummarmiut and Inuinnaqtun.

Even though the designation of new realities always seems to follow the same general pattern, the choice of this or that specific lexeme for naming a new object may vary greatly from one area to another. An airplane, for example, is called *tingmisuun* ("which is used for flying frequently") in Alaskan Malimiutun but *tingmijualuk* ("the big flying one") in Siglitun, *tingmin* ("which is used for flying") in Inuinnaqtun, *tingmisuuq* ("which usually flies") in Aivilik and North Baffin, *qangattajuuq* ("which usually ascends") in South Baffin and Nunavik Tarramiut, *tingisuuk* ("which uses to fly") in Nunatsiavut, and *timmisartuq* ("which flies frequently") in West and East Greenlandic. Of 950 imported objects and concepts whose Inuktitut names I once collected in Nunavik and Nunatsiavut, only 133 (14%) were called the same in all villages of these two regions (Dorais 1983).

This situation is hardly new. As early as 1765, the Moravian missionary Jens Haven noted: "Family names, as well as names of places, animals and implements with which both nations [the Inuit of Nunatsiavut and of West Greenland] have long been acquainted are the same. Only such objects as have more recently fallen under their notice, are distinguished by different appellations which are, however, in both languages, expressive of the nature of the thing signified" (quoted in Cranz 1820, 293).

The appearance of neologisms thus dates back to the first period of contact between Inuit and Europeans. As early as the eighteenth century, Inuit were coining new lexemes – terms "expressive of the nature of the thing signified" in Haven's words – which often differed from one region to another. Of a sample of 2,153 neologisms collected in Nunavik and Nunatsiavut in 1968–69 (Dorais 1983), at least 255 (12%) had already been in use by the end of the nineteenth century. Like their present-day descendants, Inuit of the 1870s and 1880s spoke about guns (*qukiuti*, "which is used for uttering a cracking noise" or "for shooting at something"), chess and checkers (*inugait*, "small persons" [i.e., the pieces of the game]), canned beef meat (*tuttuvajaq*, "piece of big caribou" [i.e., ox]), and so on (see Turner 1887; Peck 1925).

Modes of Designation

This adaptation of the lexicon to transformations of the social and cultural environment has been called linguistic acculturation by Nelson Graburn (1965). According to him, the phenomenon can be studied under two aspects: (1) as a linguistic adaptation of foreign words and (2) as a relation between linguistic mechanisms and sociocultural change. Graburn points out that in the Inuit language, almost all neologisms refer to cultural elements introduced from the outside and that they are fashioned through semantic extension (an already existing word receives a new meaning) or a combination of morphemes (a new lexeme is coined). These neologisms generally describe the function or the appearance of the reality referred to. Borrowed words are few and apart, and they generally consist of proper names (Christian first names such as *Miaji*/Mary, *Pita*/Peter, *Saali*/Charlie, *Ulipika*/Rebecca) or terms denoting intimate contacts with Europeans (the names of some playing-card figures, for instance). The genesis of the new vocabulary is thus simultaneously linked to the circumstances of contact and to the structure of the language. Borrowing is relatively infrequent because intimate contact with Europeans is recent and because the polysynthetic structure of the language facilitates the creation of descriptive lexemes.

In 1968 and 1969 I collected in Nunavik and Nunatsiavut the already mentioned sample of 2,153 Inuit words denoting 950 objects, animals, and concrete ideas (e.g., occupations, measurement standards, games, and diseases) introduced by Europeans. The analysis of this corpus allowed the elicitation of three modes of designation used by Inuit to give names to these new realities: lexeme-coining, semantic change, and borrowing from another language (Dorais 1983).

LEXEME-COINING

Coining new lexemes by using bases and affixes already belonging to the language is, by far, the most productive mode of designation, as it accounts for 76.8% of the corpus. From a semantic point of view, these lexemes may be subdivided into three categories: (1) those expressing the function of the object or idea, (2) those describing its appearance, and (3) those equating it to an element of traditional culture. Most words produced through lexeme-coining belong to the first category (60.3% of newly coined terms; 46.4% of the corpus). Here are a few examples of these functional lexemes:

aluijarvik	carpet ("where one rubs the soles of his/her feet")
aupalutsiguti	lipstick ("which is used so that it becomes red")
itigaguti	shoe ("which is used for the foot")
kapuqqauti	fork ("which serves for thrusting a sharp instrument into meat")
nijjauti	accordion ("which is used for uttering a sound")
niuvirvik	shop, store ("the place where one trades")
puttusiuti	baking powder, yeast ("which is used so that it will inflate")
qangattajuuqti	airplane pilot ("the one whose usual occupation is flying")

Lexemes describing the appearance of the named object account for 36.1% of the mode of designation and 27.7% of the corpus. They generally delineate one salient characteristic of the object: its form, its colour, how it smells, how it is handled, and so on. The very few onomatopoeias may be attributed to this category because they aim at imitating the noise made by the object referred to.[33] Here are a few examples of descriptive words:

aukuluk	chocolate ("nice little blood")
iigaq	pill ("which is swallowed")
imialuk	alcohol ("big water")
imiraq	fruit juice, soft drink ("little water")
kiinannguaq	postage stamp ("imitation of a face")

kiinaujaq money ("which looks like a face")
qianngujuuq outboard motor ("which usually emits a crying sound")
tattataak morse (key) telegraph ("tack-a-tack")

The last category includes words referring to an element of traditional culture, which are affixed with a qualifying post-base or with a morpheme expressing the fact of being part of something. Objects designated in this way are perceived as showing similarity with some specific element of Inuit culture while pertaining to a different level.[34] Lexemes belonging to this class are not numerous: 3.6% of all coined lexemes and 2.7% of the corpus. Here are some examples:

atsunaajaq rope ("piece of leather thong")
kamialuk store-bought boot ("big *kamik* [traditional sealskin boot]")
qamutikallak snowmobile ("short sled")

SEMANTIC CHANGE

The second mode of designation, semantic change, consists of extending or replacing the original meaning of an already existing word without modifying its form. Lexemes pertaining to this mode account for 15.8% of the 1968–69 Nunavik and Nunatsiavut corpus.

Words whose meaning has been extended (which account for 50.5% of all semantic changes; 8% of the corpus) generally belong to the general vocabulary of Inuktitut. They include lexemes that, besides their original meaning, are also used for naming specific elements of present-day culture:

akutsijuk dough ("which makes a pasty mixture")
atajuq long underwear ("which is in one piece")
kiatik blouse ("trunk [body part]")
pullaq electric bulb ("air bubble")
umimmak ox, beef ("musk-ox")

Several lexemes that once referred – or still refer – to an element of traditional culture are now used, without any formal modification, to denote a modern object or idea. Some of them have lost their original meaning (which has thus been replaced by a new one), but others have preserved it. These words account for 49.5% of the second mode of designation (7.8% of the corpus):

itsivik	chest, box, suitcase ("traditional container")
kikiak	metal nail ("wood or bone peg")
pualuk	store-bought mitt, lamp chimney ("traditional mitt")
qajuuttaq	cup, mug ("old-fashioned wooden, leather, or stone drinking vessel")
uvvauti	soap ("blubber, fish roe, or secretions formerly used as detergent")

BORROWING

The third and last mode of designation includes all words borrowed from another language. Borrowings belonging to the 1968–69 corpus are perfectly adapted to the phonology of Inuktitut,[35] even though in the 1960s – and the phenomenon has not stopped increasing since then – many bilingual individuals turned to English pronunciation when uttering a word borrowed from that language (saying *coffee* instead of *kaapi*, for instance).

Loan-words account for only 7.3% of the corpus.[36] They are much more numerous in the Nunatsiavut dialect (17.2%) than in Nunavik Itivimiut (5.8%) and Tarramiut (5.1%) because the Inuit of Labrador have been in contact with Europeans for a much longer time than Arctic Quebec people.

Terms borrowed from English are the most numerous (82.3% of all loan-words). They are followed by lexemes of German origin (15.2%), whose use is restricted to Nunatsiavut (with one exception).[37] The language of the Innu (Montagnais Indians) loaned two lexemes. The same is true of West Greenlandic. French has not left any trace despite the existence of a French-Inuktitut trade pidgin on Belle-Isle Strait during the eighteenth century.[38] Here are some examples of loan-words:

BORROWED FROM ENGLISH

isipi	spades [in a deck of cards]
jaikak	jacket, sweater
maiki	monkey
puliisi	police
paniuppaaq	frying pan
siisi	cheese

BORROWED FROM GERMAN

jaari	year (from *Jahre*)
situnatik	hour, clock (from *Stunde*, "hour")
suuntaagi	Sunday (from *Sonntag*)
suvailivak	noon, midnight (from *zwölf*, "twelve")
kattupalak	potato (from *Kartoffel*)

BORROWED FROM INNU

kuukusi	pig (from *kûkus*)
pakaakuani	chicken (from *pakâkwan*)

BORROWED FROM WEST GREENLANDIC

saugaq	sheep (from *sava*, itself probably borrowed from Old Norse)

A fourth mode of designation has now appeared in the Arctic: semantic borrowing. The new object or concept is given an Inuit name that literally translates its English appellation. In Nunavik, for instance, intoxicating drugs were originally called *ujaraq*, "stone," because in English doped individuals are said to be "stoned."[39] Similarly, the person heading an assembly is its *itsivautaq*, "chair," as in colloquial English, where the president of a meeting is called its chair.[40]

The Semantic Structure of Neologisms

Establishing a typology of the modes of designation does not exhaust the study of neologisms. It does not explain, for instance, why a particular type of new object or idea is named in this or that specific way. To reach such a level of explanation, the semantic structure of various fields of experience must be analyzed – that is, the significant relationships linking words that denote cultural elements used together in different situations (e.g., the food and utensils necessary for cooking a meal, the pieces of clothing currently used to dress oneself). I undertook this kind of analysis by applying morphosemantics to the Nunavik and Nunatsiavut corpus collected in 1968–69 (Dorais 1977a, 1985b).

Analysis showed that there exist two principal types of fields of experience. Actantial fields are perceived and conceptualized as active processes within which various elements contribute, each in its own way, to the occurrence of a specific event (e.g., cooking a meal, sewing a piece of clothing, heating a house). By contrast, classificatory fields are seen as combinations of static elements playing the same basic part but being differentiated from each other thanks to their specific form or function (e.g., the various pieces of clothing and ornament, the working parts of a motor).

The varying nature of each type of field is reflected at the semantic level. When one speaks about fields that are implied in an actantial process, lexemes expressing the function of the objects and concepts belonging to these fields are generally preferred. By contrast, classificatory fields are expressed with words describing the most salient characteristics of their components. The semantic structure of the vocabulary thus reflects the type of experience referred to.

Among the Itivimiut speakers of Nunavik Inuktitut, for instance, the unfolding of the week is perceived as a building process (Dorais 1975d). The work week (*pinasuarusiq*, "the habit of working") extends from Monday to Saturday, standing in sharp contrast with Sunday, when it is forbidden to work. This is why the Lord's day is called *allitut* ("they abide by a taboo"). This taboo (the interdiction of working, hunting, travelling, and playing on Sunday) was so important to Christian Inuit that the first day of the work week, Monday, was named *alliriiqtut* ("they cease to abide by a taboo") and the last one, Saturday, *allingisungaqtut* ("they do not quite abide by the taboo yet").

Tuesday, Wednesday, and Thursday are perceived and named as though they were blocks added to each other to build an entire workable week. Tuesday is called *aippitut* ("they add a second [work day]"), Wednesday *pingatsitut* ("they add a third one"), and Thursday *sitammitut* ("they add a fourth one"). This process can be schematized as follows:

1 + 2 (tuesday)	1–2 + 3 (wednesday)	1–2–3 + 4 (thursday)
"they add a second one"	"they add a third one"	"they add a fourth one"

Friday is an exception. As in some other dialects, this day is named in reference to the fact that it was on Friday that Inuit working for the trading companies received their weekly food allowance. Accordingly, Itivimiut speakers call Friday *niritsitut* ("they make them eat").

The semantic structure of this field of experience exhibits both actantial and classificatory characteristics. The unfolding of workable days is understood as an active process of temporal construction, but the fundamental contradistinction between tabooed Sunday and the rest of the week is instead expressed in classificatory terms.

The actual linguistic form of named objects or concepts is not entirely determined by the nature of the field of experience to which they belong. It also depends on etymological constraints – that is, on the degree of proximity between traditional culture and particular aspects of present-day experience. The interaction between experience and constraints generates a series of rules governing the designation of newly introduced objects and ideas (Dorais 1985b, 16). According to these rules, when a new cultural element is perceived as similar in both form and function to a traditional one, it is given the same name as the older element. Conversely, when an element is seen as completely alien to any already existing semantic category, it may be designated with a loan-word. In most cases, however, when newly introduced notions appear as only partly linked to already existing forms or functions, speakers resort to lexeme-coining or, more rarely, to semantic change.[41] The existence of any lexeme can thus be explained in relation to the specific semantic structure within which it operates. Each structure expresses a particular type of cultural experience, while being influenced in this expression by the traditional substratum to which this experience is eventually linked.

The Modern Lexicon

My study of neologisms dealt only with nouns. In her master's thesis, Danièle Saint-Aubin examined how bilingual Inuit from three regions (Nunavik, South Baffin, and Kivalliq) translated English verbs without an Inuktitut equivalent (Saint-Aubin 1980). She discovered that the modes of designation for newly introduced verbs were the same as they were for nouns, with a sensibly lower occurrence of lexeme-coining (68%) and borrowing (3.5%) and a higher proportion of semantic change (28.5%). According to Saint-Aubin, the ease with which a speaker is able to translate a foreign meaning into Inuktitut depends first of all on whether he or she has lived in southern Canada. Familiarity with Euro-Canadian culture would thus be more important than age or level of formal education in assessing an individual's ability to give names to new realities.

Outside Canada, West Greenlandic neologisms have been studied by Catherine Enel (1982), while Niels Grann (1988) has analyzed their East Greenlandic equivalents. Both of them identified four modes of designation: lexeme-coining, semantic change, borrowing from Danish,[42] and coining hybrid words. This last mode includes all lexemes where Inuit post-bases are affixed to a borrowed radical.[43] Enel notices that several Danish loan-words were later replaced by newly coined lexemes, which tend to become increasingly numerous in Kalaallisut, although some younger speakers prefer using the Danish versions, often shorter and hence easier to handle than their Greenlandic counterparts.

Betty Harnum (1989) confirms the presence of these same four modes of designation in all Canadian dialects. She points out that lexical borrowing works in both directions: English comprises eighteen words borrowed from the Inuit language. Some of these refer to native cultural elements (e.g., igloo, kayak, anorak) and others to peculiarities of arctic geography (e.g., pingo, nunatak). Apart from that, some thirty technical geological terms (e.g., pinguite, alaskite, tugtupite) have been borrowed from one or another Eskaleut speech form.

Harnum gives a list she deems exhaustive of all languages that lent words to Yupik and Inuit. This includes Siberian Chukchi (in Central Siberian Yupik and, much less so, Central Alaskan Yup'ik), Russian (e.g., Yup'ik words such as *saalaq*, "lard"; *mas&aq*, "butter"; *kuluvak*, "cow"; *miilaq*, "soap"), the Dene Indian languages (in Yup'ik and Alaskan Inupiaq),[44] Innu (the two already mentioned words lent to Nunavik Inuktitut), Old Norse (the Greenlandic terms *Kalaaliq*, "Greenlander," and perhaps *sava*, "sheep"), Philippines Tagalog (which lent three words to Bristol Bay Yup'ik),[45] German (in Nunatsiavut), Danish (in Greenland), and English (everywhere in the Arctic – including Yupik Siberia – except for Greenland).[46] Harnum also mentions Norwegian (e.g., Greenlandic *puuluki*, "pork"), Hawaiian (e.g., *tanik* [plural *tan'ngit*], the name given to Europeans in Inupiaq and Siglitun),[47] French (e.g., *uiguit*, "French, francophone"), and Portuguese (in the South Baffin dialect, any black person is called *puatagi*, "Português").[48] One more language can be added to the list: north European Saami, which lent at least one word to Yup'ik, *lauciq* ("reindeer harness") (Jacobson 1984).[49]

Georgii Menovshchikov (1978) has studied Russian loan-words in the Alaskan languages. They generally refer to food items introduced from the outside, Christian beliefs and paraphernalia, and concepts linked to trade. At first, these words were adapted to the phonetics of the native languages, but later on populations more familiar with Russian (e.g., the Unangan) tended to use them without any modification.

For Michael Krauss (1980), the number of words borrowed from Russian reflects the influence of Russian speakers on the various Alaskan native groups. Very strong among Unangan (400 Russian loan-words) and the Pacific Alutiit (350 borrowed terms), this influence was weaker among Central Alaskan Yupiit (190 loan-words) and negligible among Bering Strait Inupiat (15 terms) and Saint-Lawrence Island Yupiget (3 terms). In Siberian Yupik, contrary to what could be expected, Russian loan-words are few and far apart. This is because European material culture was introduced to Chukotka by American whalers and traders in the late nineteenth century rather than by the Russians, who did not settle in the Bering Strait area until the 1920s.

Albert Heinrich (1971) has studied German borrowings in Nunatsiavut Inuktitut. Introduced in the eighteenth and nineteenth centuries by Moravian missionaries, they endured despite the fact that the non-native linguistic environment of Labrador was generally anglophone. According to Heinrich, German loan-words express either early borrowed concepts (e.g., Christian religious beliefs) or cultural elements without any traditional equivalent (e.g., the measurement of time). Many lexemes borrowed from German (like the numbering system) were later replaced with English loan-words. The Nunatsiavut section of my 1968–69 corpus still included some thirty terms of German origin.

Confronted by the monumental task of translating a whole new reality, the Inuit language was able to find the words necessary to express and designate the thousands of exogenous objects and concepts that now form an integral part of daily life in the Arctic. From flat-irons (*isittiriuti*, "which is used for extending something") to computers (*qaritaujaq*, "which looks like a brain"), Inuit can use their language for speaking about the present-day environment. By coining new lexemes, modifying the original meaning of already existing words, and in a lesser measure, borrowing foreign terms, they are able to express quite precisely the world that surrounds them.

One cannot but wonder, however, whether the Inuit language will be able to continue meeting the challenge. In a universe whose complexity is constantly growing, are its radicals and affixes sufficient to translate all scientific, technological, political, administrative, and economic concepts now shared by any moderately educated person? Some believe not. For the linguist Ivan Kalmar (1982), for instance, it is impossible for the language to adjust itself in a very short time to all newly introduced social and political ideas. Lexical derivations stemming from a restricted number of bases may generate concepts difficult to handle. By way of example, Kalmar mentions the Inuktitut words *angajuqqaaq* ("parent, chief") and *isumataq* ("leader"), which, according to context, can mean "store manager," "senior clerk," "chief administrator," "minister," "prime minister," and "premier," among others, and whose derivatives (*isumataaluk* and *angajuqqaaraaluk*, "big chief"; *angajuqqaaraapik*, "small chief"; *angajuqqaasuk*, "assistant chief") only add confusion.

The author suggests a Greenland-type solution for Canada: to make compulsory the use of current Inuit lexemes and borrow the rest from English, adapting it if necessary to the specificity of local phonetics. With, by far, the highest percentage of loan-words (Danish), Greenlandic is nevertheless the most successful of all Inuit dialects, having a proportion of speakers reaching almost 100%. It remains to be seen, however, whether the solution proposed by Kalmar is acceptable to Canadian Inuit, who are conscious of the creative strength of their language and reluctant to overcharge it with too heavy a mass of foreign terms. Current research on neology, based on the analysis of actual political and other discourses in Inuktitut (see Therrien 2000; Tersis 2003), confirms this strong desire to coin words that are felt to be 100% Inuit.[50]

ORAL LITERATURE

It is through oral literature that the Inuit language exhibits its full strength and beauty. From Alaska to Greenland, Inuit of yore have imagined hundreds of myths, legends, songs, and magical formulas[51] that have been transmitted orally from one generation to another. Some of these creations are known throughout the entire Arctic, with regional variations. Others have only a local scope. All of them, however, used to play an important part in the expression of the most fundamental cultural concepts and values.

Myths and Legends

Inuit from the Canadian eastern Arctic establish a distinction between two types of stories, respectively called *unikkaatuaq* and *unikkausiq* (Dorais 1990c, 201). The first term applies to any story narrating events that happened recently or in a not-too-distant past. By contrast, an *unikkausiq* is a legend or a myth (Inuit do not distinguish between the two) considered to have happened a very long time ago.[52] Stories deemed imaginary are called *unikkausinnguaq*, "a made-up *unikkausiq*." All of these lexemes derive from the radical *unipkaaq-* or *unikkaaq-*, in use throughout the Inuit area, which means "to tell a story."[53]

The ethnographers who have collected Inuit myths and legends[54] subdivide *unikkausiit* into various categories. For example, Diamond Jenness (1924) has the following subdivisions: animal and bird stories, humans and animals, quasi-historical traditions, giants and dwarves, stories of shamans, and etiological myths (explaining the origin of the universe). Stories belonging to this last category do not really tell about the creation of the world. They instead show how, thanks to the spoken word, order was progressively established in an originally incoherent universe: how, for instance, alternation between day and night replaced perpetual darkness; how a non-differentiated humanity became divided into men and women and, later on, into various races; how death appeared; and so on.

Two myths are known by a majority of Inuit. The story of the origin of the moon and the sun tells about a young man (whose name is Aningaat in some versions) who had incestuous relations with his sister. To discover who was taking advantage of her, the sister smeared her hands with soot and blotted the face of her nocturnal visitor. The next day, upon discovering the identity of her lover, she grabbed a lighted torch and started running around the house. Her brother pursued her, holding a half-lighted torch. They then ascended to the sky – one still running after the other – where the girl became the sun (*siqiniq*) and the boy the moon (*taqqiq*).[55]

The myth of the sea-woman tells the story of a girl who refused to marry.[56] After having finally accepted to wed a seabird who pretended to be a man, she left her family to live with him. After some time, however, disgusted by her husband, she asked her father to bring her back home. The father took his daughter on the deck of his kayak, but when the bird provoked a storm that risked capsizing the skiff, he threw her into the water. She tried clinging to the kayak, but the man cut her fingers phalanx by phalanx and she sank to the bottom of the sea. Her phalanxes were transformed into marine mammals, whose guardian she became. Shamans visited her when game was scarce.

Myths have a philosophical and pedagogical function. They express the worldview of traditional Inuit while facilitating the transmission of old traditions and of some rules of social life (Turquetil 1968). The story of the sun and the moon shows the dreadful consequences of incest, while that of the sea-woman teaches that refusing marriage may lead to the destruction of society.

In his in-depth study of Inuit mythology, the anthropologist Bernard Saladin d'Anglure (2006a) discusses a series of myths from the Igloolik area in the Canadian eastern Arctic. He concludes that these myths bring explanatory answers or practical solutions to five major contradictions, which were – and may still be – problematic to Inuit:

1 Sexual differences. Why are women needed, while there could be only men on earth? It is to allow humanity to multiply more rapidly.
2 Sterility. The impossibility for some women to procreate, while others bear many children. The solution is adoption and/or spouse exchange.
3 The existence of animals. They are very close to humanity (sometimes transforming themselves into human beings or vice-versa), but they must be hunted for food and raw materials. The solution is to avoid kinship relations with animals and to respect a number of rules when hunting them.
4 Aging. Human beings become old and impotent, although it is so pleasant to be young and fit. The mythical solution was the "jump of youth": old persons jumped to the floor of the house in order to regain their youth.
5 War and death. Why do people fight and die, although human existence should be based on exchange and sharing? It is to avoid overpopulation and a possible sinking of the ground due to the excessive weight of humanity. Continuity beyond death is ensured by the reincarnation of the *atiq* (name) souls of deceased people in the newborns who are named after them and by the survival of their weightless *tarniq* (immortal) souls in the hereafter.[57]

Several tales and legends recount the revenge of persecuted orphans. This is the case with a cycle of stories whose hero is often called Kaujjaarjuk. Severely mistreated by his step-family (he must sleep in the porch of the igloo and fight with the dogs to get something to eat), Kaujjaarjuk is rescued by three polar bears who make him grow through magical means. Once he has reached a size and strength superior to the average, he avenges himself by killing all his persecutors. His story shares some traits with that of the young blind boy whose mother denies he has killed a bear because she wants to keep all the meat for herself and her daughter. After having been healed by a loon (which immerses him three times in a lake), the boy takes vengeance on his mother, who is transformed into a narwhal. Another cycle of tales recounts the story of Kiviuq, whose two wives share the habit of copulating with a giant penis that comes out of a lake at their call.[58] Kiviuq performs many feats, as does his counterpart in similar tales, Atungaq, who travels around the world with his dog team.

Inuit tales and legends also include hunting stories, animal tales (in which the raven plays an important part, particularly in Alaska), and so forth. In Nunatsiavut, for instance, Edward Hawkes (1916, 141–2) listed the following tales and myths, still known after some 150 years of missionary influence:

- *tuniit* stories
- legend of the dwarf Alasuq
- stories of skirmishes with Indians
- myth of the sea-woman
- legend of the land of the caribou
- tale of the girl who wed a whalebone
- myth of the origin of the sun and the moon
- tale of the man married to a fox-woman
- legend of the blind boy

Traditionally, these tales were told in wintertime, often in the *qadjgi* or *qaggiq* (*qassi* in Greenland), a large communal stone-, turf-, or snow-house devoted to collective ceremonies and other gatherings. Anyone could tell a story. The repertoire of storytellers was generally well known, and anybody straying from the canonical version was called back to order. Myths and tales often comprised sung or mimed parts. They usually concluded on the interjection *taimak* ("it is so, it is finished") or, conversely, with a statement expressing that this kind of narration never reaches an end, *naajuujaaqtuq naanngittuugaluaq* ("it looks finished, but it is not finished"), all *unikkausiit* forming only one superstory illustrating the basic foundations of Inuit culture and society.

Songs and Magic Formulas

Songs and, to a lesser extent, magic formulas also belong to oral literature.[59] Much more easy to create and handle than myths and legends, they could be used by anybody: men, women, children, elders. Old ethnographers noted that Inuit were always singing (*atuqtuq* or *imngiqtuq/inngiqtuq*, "he/she sings"), the adults at work and the children at play. Anyone could improvise a song: a woman welcoming her husband or her son back home, a man celebrating his hunting successes or disappointments, a child teasing a friend, and so on. In Nunavik, for instance, Inuit made use of several types of musical forms: *pisiit* (or *ajajait*),[60] songs composed by men to recount various episodes of their life, often in an ironic mood; *katajjait*, throat-singing, a female game; *aqausiit*, lullabies for putting babies to sleep; *illukitaarutiit*, juggling songs; *pinnguarutiit*, playful songs; *irinaliurutiit*, magical songs; and so on.

None of these compositions was rhymed or compelled to follow prosodic or metric rules. They should, however, have some rhythm, broken or monotonous according to the type of song. People often sang in chorus. Unlike myths and legends, which were common property, songs normally belonged to their composer. They could not be used without their composer's permission, at least when he or she was present. Some types of songs were accompanied by body movements and required that a flat seal- or caribou-skin drum be used. Masks were sometimes worn. The Inupiat and Yupiit from Alaska had a very rich ceremonial life, where masks, costumes, dancing, drumming, and singing played an important part.

In most areas of the Arctic, but more so in Greenland and eastern Canada, Inuit practised singing duels. Two men who had developed a dispute confronted each other by singing alternating songs they had specially composed for the occasion. These compositions did not deal specifically with the object of the litigation but with the personality of the opponent, whose shortcomings were publicly exposed. Duels usually occurred during summer, in the presence of the whole community. The loser was the one who, having exhausted all his songs, was unable to reply to his opponent (Rouland 1979).

In Nunavik a few elders still remember – because they heard them from their parents and grandparents – songs from the turn of the twentieth century that were occasioned by opposition between Angutinnguaq and Makimmaq, two leaders living on the west coast of Ungava Bay.[61] The former used to mock his opponent by comparing him to a butterfly (*taralikitaaq*) that goes from one woman to another like the insect flies from flower to flower. Makimmaq replied by recalling the poor sexual performances of Angutinnguaq (who had no children of his own), comparing him to a child (his name means "imitation of a male"):

Piararlatitut surusirlatitut
Iqqaumajarali una ajaa ajaa ajaijaijaijaa

Like a big child, like a big boy
I remember this one ajaa ajaa ajaijaijaijaa

Singing was also used by shamans (*angakkuit*) to summon their helping spirits (*tuurngait*) when travelling to the abodes of the moon-man or the sea-woman or when trying to heal a sick person. Shamans as well as ordinary people made frequent use of magic formulas, which were generally sung. Called *irinaliuqtiit* in the Igloolik area (*irinaliurutiit* in Nunavik), these formulas often consisted of fragments of old songs or of hardly understandable sentences collected, it was said, when animals were still able to speak. Magical formulas lost their power if heard by someone who was not their owner, unless the owner had sold them or transmitted them on his or her deathbed (Rasmussen 1929). Several formulas had to do with the polar bear, whose power they exalted (Randa 1986).

Composers of songs sometimes used a poetical language in which the names of animals, body parts, and other worldly elements were replaced by metaphors. Shamans did likewise when officiating. They used a special vocabulary – akin to the already mentioned culturally motivated East Greenlandic neologisms – whose words described what they denoted, without naming things directly.

Vladimir Randa (1990, 208) gives some examples – collected in Igloolik – of both poetic speech and shaman's language:

	COMMON SPEECH	POETIC SPEECH	SHAMAN'S LANGUAGE
polar bear	*nanuq*	*qakuqturjuaq* "big white"	*uqsuralik* "the one with fat"
caribou	*tuktu*	*nagjulik* "one with antlers"	*kumaruaq* "looks like lice"[62]

bearded seal	*ugjuk*	*alaksarjuaq* "big boot sole"[63]	*mak&aq* "maker of waves"
ringed seal	*nattiq*	*qisivik* "excellent skin"	*angmiaq* "maker of holes"

A quite exhaustive list of shamanic terms collected in the central Canadian Arctic can be found in Knud Rasmussen (1930). It includes words such as *auviraksaq* ("which can be used as a structure"; bones), *inaaqtuq* ("he/she finishes something"; he/she sings), and *quatsiaq* ("which is frozen hard"; a child). For Greenlandic examples, see Paul-Émile Victor and Joëlle Robert-Lamblin (1994).

Inuit thus made use of several different levels of speech: common language, poetic speech, sacred language (used by shamans), plus the diverging speech habits of women, youngsters, and men (postulated in chapter 5).

Present-Day Oral Literature

What happened to Inuit oral literature in a world now dominated by the written word and electronic transmission of ideas and messages? At first glance, almost nothing appears to remain. Traditional myths, legends, and songs are still remembered by only a small and rapidly diminishing number of elders. Many oral literary creations have been recorded or put into print, but they no longer play the philosophical and pedagogical role that used to be theirs. Inuit education is now conducted in school, at church, and before computers and television sets rather than in the *qaggiq* or at hunting camps.

Before it is too late, modern media and institutions are trying to save what is left of this literature that they have contributed to obliterating. Several northern schools now teach *katajjait* and other forms of traditional music, and they publish compilations of myths and legends for their students. Radio and, in a lesser measure, television now broadcast recordings of elders singing *pisiit* or telling old stories. In the context of the current revitalization of aboriginal identity, oral literature has acquired a relatively important symbolic value.

In Alaska and the Canadian western Arctic, drum-dancing and singing are still performed on the occasion of holidays and other important celebrations (the catch of the season's first game, for instance). At regular intervals, international events such as the Arctic Games or the general assembly of the Inuit Circumpolar Council include cultural performances where traditional music, dance, and songs play an important part.

Besides such ancient practices,[64] there exists another form of oral literature, a more recent one, that stems directly from European contact. Its chief manifestation is vocal music.[65] In Greenland, Canada, and in a lesser way, Alaska, an impressive corpus of hymns, songs, and other chanted melodies is now in existence, whose style was borrowed from the Euro-American musical tradition.

The oldest part of this corpus is made of Lutheran, Moravian, Anglican, and Catholic religious hymns, often sung in chorus. Some of these hymns, heard in the Lutheran temples of Greenland or in the Moravian churches of Nunatsiavut and Alaska, belong to the great European classical tradition, inspired as they are by composers such as Buxtehude, Bach, or Telemann.[66] In Greenland, choral music – religious as well as secular – has known a lot of success. There exist several choirs, some of which (the Mik ensemble, for instance) have recorded a number of collections. They often interpret works by Greenlandic composers such as Jonathan Petersen, who has his statue in Nuuk, or Henrik Lund, the author of *Nunarput* ("Our Country"), Greenland's national anthem.

The largest portion of modern Inuit music, however, proceeds from singers and/or composers who work alone or within small groups of musicians. Their two favourite styles have been country and folk-rock, although more recently, northern hard-rockers and rappers have started enjoying a lot of success.

Inuit country music is particularly popular in Canada. Its best known performers are Charlie Panigoniak, William Tagoona, Willie Trasher, Tumasi Quissa, and Charlie Adams, all of whom have recorded collections that are often broadcast by northern radio stations.[67] Their songs are sentimental, humorous, or inspired by religion.

Folk-rock music, appreciated in both Greenland[68] and Canada, makes occasional use of traditional motifs (e.g., *ajaja* refrains). Two Canadian performers have reached national fame: Susan Aglukark from Nunavut and Elisapee Isaac (who sings in Inuktitut, English, and French) from Nunavik. The tremendous development of Pentecostal Christianity in the Canadian Arctic since the 1970s has given rise to a growing repertoire of country and folk music on religious themes: melodious or more rhythmical songs in Inuktitut or English, accompanied by drums and electric guitar, celebrate the Almighty and His love for sinners.

Apart from music written and interpreted by professional and semi-professional singers, there exist many dozen songs whose authors are unknown. These often consist of Inuit versions of popular ditties such as *Brother John* or *London Bridge* or of more serious pieces like the national anthem *O Canada*.

The past decades have witnessed the advent of Inuit dramatic works, which, in some measure, have replaced traditional masked dances and ceremonies. Greenland's *Tukak Teatret*, established more than thirty years ago, has become internationally famous on the stage of avant-garde theatre (Brask and Morgan 1992), and it has inspired several Greenlandic and Canadian groups. Performing in the Inuit language, these theatrical ensembles mix various forms of expression, and they generally draw some of their inspiration from traditional culture.

Finally, works created for radio, television, and more recently, cinema should be mentioned. Radio dramas, skits, programs for children, and autobiographical narratives all belong to present-day oral literature. Inuit cinema in particular is in full development in both Canada and Greenland. In the former country, Igloolik Isuma Productions has released several films in Inuktitut, including Zacharias Kunuk's award-winning *Atanarjuat the Fast Runner* (see Angilirq et al. 2002; Evans 2008).

CONCLUSION

Studying Inuit semantics opens the door to a fuller understanding of how social and cultural practices and concepts are related to their linguistic expression. As mentioned on several occasions, beyond the immediate signification of words, one can often elicit underlying meanings that appear through the words' component morphemes. Comparison of these meanings shows that Inuit share an anthropomorphic vision of the universe. Human beings and their body – in harmony with the environment – are usually taken as models for describing the world.

Confronted by the challenge of naming several thousand objects and concepts introduced by Europeans for over 300 years, the language was able to draw from its own linguistic resources the raw material necessary for expressing the diversity and richness of a world in perpetual transformation. To denote newly introduced realities, Inuit dialects have preferred, by far, to resort to lexeme-coining rather than to borrow foreign terms or to modify the meaning of already existing words.

When neologisms are analyzed, it becomes clear that the organization of the semantic categories they express reflects quite directly[69] the way – actantial or classificatory – that Inuit perceive the various domains of experience that are communicated through language. This observation, which may probably be extended to Inuit vocabulary as a whole, seems particularly important. It shows that to reach the conscious mind, cultural images and social rules must first be organized as encoded classes of meaning apt to be translated into linguistic (i.e., morphemic and syntactical) – or other – symbols.

Since the birth of language, the use of such semantic and linguistic codes has allowed the development of an oral literature expressing deep-reaching philosophical concerns and playing an important pedagogical part. Among Inuit of yore, this literature included myths, tales, legends, songs, and magical formulas that, unfortunately, were unable to withstand the attacks of modernity. Seemingly doomed to oblivion despite the symbolic value now attached to their existence, they have been replaced by creative works more adapted to the present-day context: religious hymns and secular songs, theatrical drama, radio broadcasts, and so forth. The decline of traditional oral literature may be linked to the introduction of literacy, which, as will now be seen, plays a crucial role in today's Arctic.

7

Literacy and Formal Education

Inuit did not traditionally use any writing system. Everyone shared the same gendered knowledge, and individual memory was sufficient to store the information necessary for pursuing a living and understanding the world. Occasionally, however, special events endowed with a major social or symbolic value were recorded on a material support. For instance, hunters of the Mackenzie coast tattooed a cross on their shoulder every time they killed a whale, and murderers marked their face with one or several tattooed stripes (Petitot 1876). In most, if not all Inuit groups, women tattooed their face, arms, and thighs with linear designs (*tunniit* or *kakiniit*) to show that they had reached childbearing age. Various aspects of the natural or supernatural world could also be graphically represented through the ornamentation of clothing and tools. In this way, traditional Inuit culture did not completely ignore semi-abstract graphic representations, which constitute the very basis of any writing system. Moreover, its bearers already possessed some special skills that could be put to good use when formal writing was introduced (Therrien 1990), as denoted by the following word-bases:

aglaq- "to draw a shape"
titiraq- "to mark something with dots"
atuaq- "to follow a track"
taiguq- "to give names"

In the present-day Inuit language, the first two bases mean "to write," while the third and fourth are often used for conveying the idea of reading a text.

LITERACY

Writing Systems in Greenland

Inuit literacy was initiated in Greenland. Soon after his arrival in the country in 1721, the Danish-Norwegian missionary Hans Egede started to develop a writing system for the native language. He deemed it very important that Greenlanders be able to assimilate directly what he called "the correct doctrine" through perusal of the Holy Scriptures (Petersen 1984, 640). It was not before 1742, however, that the Act of Faith became available in Kalaallisut, followed two years later by large extracts of the Bible and, in 1757, by Martin Luther's catechism. In the meanwhile, Lutheran and Moravian missionaries had translated several dozen church hymns.

As early as the 1750s, the newly established Greenlandic schools were using a writing system that aimed at adapting the European Roman (Latin) alphabet to the specificity of Inuit phonology. Long vowels were symbolized by accents and the phoneme *q* by a capital *K*. It was only after 1850, however, that the Greenlandic orthography became standardized, thanks to the efforts of Samuel Kleinschmidt, a Moravian missionary born in Greenland of German parents but fully fluent in Kalaallisut (Nowak 1987). Based on an otherwise thorough analysis of West Greenlandic phonology, Kleinschmidt's system preserved two non-phonemic vowels, *e* and *o* (representing the phonemes *i* and *u* before a uvular consonant or in the word-final position). Kleinschmidt marked a graphic distinction between *k* (*k*) and *K* (*q*), as well as between *s* (*s*) and *ss* (*ʃ* [*sh*], the local rendition of an etymological *J*). Long vowels were symbolized by a circumflex accent (*â*, *ê*, *î*, *ô*, *û*), and geminate consonants by an acute accent on the preceding vowel (as in *nérivik*, for *nirrivik*, "table"). The tilde (~) showed that a long vowel was followed by a geminate consonant. Here are a few examples:

KLEINSCHMIDT'S ORTHOGRAPHY	PHONEMIC ORTHOGRAPHY	
nerigame	*nirigami*	"because he/she eats"
isse	*iʃi [ishi]*	"eye"
iserpoK	*isirpuq*	"he/she goes in"
aKût	*aquut*	"rudder"
nóraK	*nurraq*	"young caribou calf"
ãma	*aamma*	"and, also"

Kleinschmidt's orthography served as Greenland's official writing system for over a century. During the 1960s, however, more and more people kept asking for an orthographic reform because the language had changed and, in many cases, its written version no longer corresponded to its pronunciation. For instance, Greenlanders had to write *augfik* ("caterpillar"), although that word was now pronounced *aaffik*, and *nunavtíne* ("in our country") instead of *nunatsinni*. A linguistic commission investigated the matter and proposed a new, simpler orthography, closer to the actual pronunciation of Kalaallisut.

The new system came into force in 1973 (Land Council of Greenland 1973). It replaced all accents with double vowels and geminate consonants, abandoned obsolete vocalic and consonantal groupings, and replaced *K* with *q* and *ss* (when it stood for a single phoneme) with *s*.[1] However, the vowels *e* and *o* were preserved before a uvular consonant, but not in the word-final position. For instance, Kleinschmidt's *ernerma ningaungata avKutâne* ("on the way to my son's son-in-law") was now to be written as it was pronounced: *ernerma ningaangata aqqutaani*. Orthography thus caught up with the spoken language, as in the following examples:

GREENLANDIC ORTHOGRAPHY	PHONEMIC ORTHOGRAPHY	
nerigami	*nirigami*	"because he/she eats"
isi	*isi*	"eye"
iserpoq	*isirpuq*	"he/she goes in"
aquut	*aquut*	"rudder"
norraq	*nurraq*	"young caribou calf"
aamma	*aamma*	"and, also"

Because the West Greenlandic dialect stands as Greenland's official language, the reformed orthography has been made compulsory throughout the country.[2] Since the end of the 1980s, however, local linguistic committees have set up semi-official orthographies for East Greenlandic and the Thule dialect.[3]

Writing Systems in Canada

In Canada the Inuit were first introduced to literacy at the end of the eighteenth century by German Moravian missionaries working in

Labrador. As soon as they had settled in Nain in 1771, the Moravians undertook the task of translating Christian hymns and prayers, as well as the catechism, into the Nunatsiavut dialect of Inuktitut. They adopted an orthography almost identical to that developed by their Greenlandic colleagues: *k* (*k*) was distinguished from *K* (*q*), accents marked long vowels and geminate consonants, and so on. As early as 1791, Inuit in Nain, Okak (founded in 1776), and Hopedale (in 1782) were learning to read, write, and count in their own language. The first books of the Nunatsiavut Bible were printed in 1821, and by 1843 the Moravians had completed their translation of the Scriptures. In this period, only about ten adult Christian Inuit (among 334) were still illiterate (Jeddore 1979).

For unknown reasons, the Labrador missionaries never succeeded in reaching a level of linguistic fluency equal to that of their Greenlandic co-religionists (Nowak 1995), even though the most gifted among them, Theodor Bourquin, did indeed benefit from Kleinschmidt's advice (see Holtved 1964). The Moravian orthography suffered from this situation. Not very precise, sometimes downright erroneous (useless gemination of some consonants, random distribution of the non-phonemic graphemes *e* and *o*), it was difficult to handle correctly. Moreover, as was also the case in Greenland, the progressive evolution of the spoken language entailed a growing discrepancy between orthography and pronunciation. Look, for instance, at the following citation, published at the beginning of the 1970s (Anonymous 1971, 1):

> *Kattangutigêt asserortaugalloarmatta taipsomane Kommeniuse inôjungnairmat jârime 1670ime.*
>
> The [Moravian] brethren were destroyed when Comenius died in the year 1670.

At the time of its publication, this sentence was pronounced as follows:

> *Qatangutigiit asiguttaugaluammata taitsumani Kuminiusi inuujunnaimat jaagimi 1670imi.*

Moravian orthography thus represented Nunatsiavut Inuktitut as it had been heard over a century before. Nevertheless, when reading religious texts aloud, ministers and lay preachers took great care in pronouncing them the exact way they were written, thus reviving for a moment the old Inuit language of Labrador.

At the beginning of the 1970s, some young Inuit from Nain were in favour of an orthographic reform. They wished that a phonemic orthography reflecting the actual pronunciation of Nunatsiavut Inuktitut be adopted. A few texts – including a dictionary (Jeddore 1976) – were published in the new writing system, but the religious authorities and the elders voiced their opposition to the proposed reform. At the beginning of the 1980s, the Labrador Inuit Association passed a resolution stating that the Moravian script remained the only acceptable orthography for the Nunatsiavut Inuit. It was only during the 1990s that an arrangement devised by teachers and other language specialists[4] partly modified the system. According to this arrangement, *K* still stands for the phoneme *q*, but *aa*, *ii*, and *uu* are now respectively symbolized by *â*, *e*, and *o*, single vowels being written *a*, *i*, and *u* in all positions. Moreover, the orthography respects the modern pronunciation of the language, deleting nonexisting geminates and groupings.

Until the mid-nineteenth century, Inuit literacy was limited to Greenland and Labrador.[5] In 1855, however, an Anglican missionary of the Church Missionary Society, Rev. Edwin A. Watkins, taught Inuit trading at Fort George (Chisasibi, on James Bay) and Little Whale River (on the south-eastern coast of Hudson Bay) a series of syllabic graphic symbols (each sign stood for a complete syllable) enabling them to write in their own language. That same year, one of his colleagues, Rev. John Horden, had a short collection of biblical verses printed in Inuit syllabic characters, although it was only ten years later that the two missionaries produced a definitive version of the writing system (Harper 1985).

Syllabics had originally been devised by Rev. James Evans, a Wesleyan missionary among Ojibwa Indians of central Ontario. Evans had tried without success to write the Ojibwa language in the Roman alphabet. He then developed a syllabic system inspired by shorthand writing,[6] creating nine symbols that could occur in four different positions. These thirty-six characters were sufficient to reproduce all combinations of consonants and vowels found in Ojibwa (Harper 1983, 8–9).

Transferred in 1840 among the Norway House Cree, north of Lake Winnipeg, Evans took no time learning their language (which was very close to Ojibwa) and, with a team of native speakers, adapted his syllabic system to the phonology of Cree. Despite some criticisms from religious authorities, this system spread rapidly because of its simplicity and usefulness. Nowadays, syllabics still constitutes the usual writing system of most Ojibwa, most Cree, and some Dene First Nations, from Alberta to Quebec. Moreover, thanks to Wesleyan missionaries, it has been made available to other native languages, notably in south-western China (Lewis and Dorais 2004).

Watkins and Horden share the merit of having adapted to Inuktitut a system originally conceived for Algonkian languages. But it is one of their successors, Rev. Edmund James Peck (whom Inuit called Uqammak), who transcribed the Bible in syllabic script and introduced the new writing system to the eastern Canadian Arctic (with the exception of Labrador). In 1876 Peck started preaching the Gospel in Nunavik and, subsequently, on Baffin Island, a task to which he devoted himself for some thirty years (Laugrand et al. 2005). He had several dozen religious texts printed in the aboriginal language, and it is said that he asked all travellers visiting his mission to bring these texts to outlying Inuit camps (Harper 1983, 14).

Those who had learned to read from missionaries later taught syllabics to their relatives and neighbours, and then transmitted their skills to their children. The new writing system thus spread out over Nunavik and the Baffin region. Anglican and Catholic missionaries also introduced it to Kivalliq and among the Natsilingmiut. Around 1925 most eastern Canadian Inuit could read and write in their language, even though, outside Labrador, none of them had ever gone to school. Here is what the Danish archaeologist Therkel Mathiassen wrote about the Igloolik Inuit whom he had met in 1922–23: "The Peck Syllabic Writing has spread widely among the Iglulik Eskimos, where the mothers teach it to their children and the latter teach each other; most Iglulik Eskimos can read and write this fairly simple but rather imperfect language and they often write letters to each other; pencils and pocket-books are consequently in great demand among them" (Mathiassen 1928, 233, quoted in Harper 1983, 17–19).

Over the next decades, Anglicans and Catholics published several syllabic hymnals, prayer books, and extracts from the Holy Scriptures. Until the introduction of the telephone (at the beginning of the 1970s) and of the Internet (in the late 1990s),[7] syllabics was also widely used for private correspondence. Some people started writing personal diaries or noted down important events (births, deaths, trips to hospital) on the inside covers of their family Bible. The syllabic system thus became the principal medium of written communication in the eastern Arctic, apart from Labrador.

But this type of writing never spread beyond Natsilingmiut country because in the western Arctic the Inuinnait and Inuvialuit had been exposed to the Roman alphabet by missionaries, trappers, and traders since the end of the nineteenth century. Anglicans and Catholics published a few religious texts in a non-standardized orthography, wherein no distinction was made between *k*, *q*, and, very often, *r*. Here is a short Inuvialuit (Siglitun) text written in this orthography (Anonymous 1949, 60), followed by a more phonemic transcription:

> *Suli Atanik Ekniktuakuyotin Jesus Christ. Godim Imnaigalunga: Godim Ekninga, nunamiut suinangit nangmaktutin nagligilaktigut. Ilwit nunamiut suinangit nangmaktutin tolsialtugut pigalugit.*
>
> *Suli ataniq irniqtuaqujutin Jisusi Cristusi. Guutim imnairaalunga: Guutim irninga, nunamiut suinnangit*[8] *nangmaktutin nagligilaktigut. Ilvit nunamiut suinnangit nangmaktutin tuksiaqtugut pigalugit.*
>
> Once again o Lord, you the Only Son Jesus Christ. Great Lamb of God: Son of God, bearing the sins of this earth's people, take pity on us. You bearing the sins of this earth's people, listen to us who are praying.

At the beginning of the 1950s, almost all Canadian Inuit were literate in their own language. Three writing systems were in use:

Moravian orthography (Roman alphabet)	Nunatsiavut
Syllabic characters	Nunavik, Baffin, Kivalliq, Natsilingmiut
Non-standardized Roman alphabet	Arctic Coast, Mackenzie

The syllabic system remained somewhat inaccurate. Its basic characters were identical everywhere, but many people did not use the diacritics, these smaller symbols standing for a consonant not followed by a vowel (see table 3). Moreover, syllabics did not distinguish between *k* and *q*, *g* and *ng*, *l* and *&*, and, among some Kivalliq groups, *g* and *r*.

This situation led the Canadian federal government to believe that the syllabic script was doomed to extinction and that it was time to replace it with an alphabetical (Roman) writing system common to all Inuit dialects. A linguist from Montreal, Gilles Lefebvre, was asked to develop the first version of what the government hoped would become the new Canadian Inuit orthography (Lefebvre 1957). This new system was to be based on systematic linguistic principles, its main benefit being to provide aboriginal people from the eastern Arctic with a perfectly accurate medium of written communication, which would be within reach of Inuit from Greenland, Labrador, the Mackenzie region, and Alaska (Spalding 1959).

After 1959 Lefebvre's work was continued by another linguist, Raymond Gagné, who published a report (Gagné 1961) promoting the adoption of a phonemic alphabetical orthography in which each symbol would always stand for the same phoneme and which would ban useless graphemes. The chief characteristics of the proposed orthography, the first one to be based on scientific principles, were as follows:

1 he grapheme *k* (representing the phoneme *k*) was to be distinguished from *q* (*q*).
2 Long vowels should be symbolized by geminates (*aa*, *ii*, *uu*).
3 Consonant gemination should be clearly indicated (*mm*, *nn*, *tt*, *kk*, etc.).
4 The letters *e* and *o* had no place in the new orthography.

The idea of an orthographic reform was interesting enough, but the government had underestimated the importance syllabics held for eastern Canadian Inuit. This writing system had become a major symbol of their identity. Arctic aboriginal people had not been consulted about the reform, and they generally perceived Ottawa's initiative as a bureaucratic measure that did not concern them. Moreover, the Lefebvre-Gagné orthography tended to obliterate interdialectal variation.[9] Consequently, it yielded very few practical results.[10]

But the need for orthographic standardization was still felt. In 1973 Inuit Tapirisat of Canada (ITC), the newly established national

Inuit organization, set up a Language Commission whose dual objective was to "produce a major statement on the viability of the Inuit language and ... to study the present state of the written language and recommend changes for the future" (Harper 1983, 51, 54). After 200 years of Inuit literacy in Canada, it was the first time that native speakers took the development of their language into their own hands.

During the course of 1974 and 1975, the members of the commission (all of them native speakers of Inuktitut or Inuktun) visited most Canadian Inuit communities to investigate the language situation. Their inquiry brought up two major points:

1 No dialect should prevail upon the others and be considered the unique standard form of speech.
2 All users of syllabics strongly wished to preserve their writing system.

Under the aegis of the Language Commission, a subcommittee met in March 1976 to work on a standard orthography. Its members soon realized that two parallel writing systems had to be proposed: syllabic and alphabetical (Roman). Each of these should ideally allow any Canadian Inuit dialect to be transcribed in a precise and acceptable way. As far as syllabic characters (*qaniujaaqpait*) were concerned, the use of diacritics was deemed essential, but the fourth column of symbols (*ai*, *pai*, *tai*, etc.) in the then standardized syllabic table was considered useless and thus suppressed. The subcommittee agreed on the addition of supplementary characters that would stand for *q*, *ng*, *&*, and long (double) vowels (table 3).

The proposed Roman alphabetical version (*qaliujaaqpait*) was based on the same phonemic principles as the Lefebvre-Gagné orthography, but it acknowledged variations in pronunciation among the various speech forms: *&* (or *ł*) was to stand for the voiceless lateral continuant, and users were to write *h* – which replaces *s* in some western dialects – whenever they heard it. It was also proposed that an apostrophe (') be used to symbolize the glottal stop heard in Natsilingmiutut, Kivalliq, and Nunavik Itivimiut.

The subcommittee's propositions were adopted by Inuit Tapirisat of Canada when its general assembly of members met in Iqaluit in September 1976. The double (syllabic and Roman) writing system thus became the official orthography of the Canadian Inuit (Inuit Cultural Institute 1978).

Table 3
The Standard Canadian Inuit syllabic and Roman writing systems

ᐃ	i	ᐅ	u	ᐊ	a	H	h
ᐱ	pi	ᐳ	pu	ᐸ	pa	ᑉ	p
ᑎ	ti	ᑐ	tu	ᑕ	ta	ᑦ	t
ᑭ	ki	ᑯ	ku	ᑲ	ka	ᒃ	k
ᒋ	gi	ᒍ	gu	ᒐ	ga	ᒡ	g
ᒥ	mi	ᒧ	mu	ᒪ	ma	ᒻ	m
ᓂ	ni	ᓄ	nu	ᓇ	na	ᓐ	n
ᓯ	si	ᓱ	su	ᓴ	sa	ᔅ	s
ᓕ	li	ᓗ	lu	ᓚ	la	ᓪ	l
ᔨ	ji	ᔪ	ju	ᔭ	ja	ᔾ	j
ᕕ	vi	ᕗ	vu	ᕙ	va	ᕝ	v
ᕆ	ri	ᕈ	ru	ᕋ	ra	ᕐ	r
ᕿ	qi	ᖁ	qu	ᖃ	qa	ᖅ	q
ᖏ	ngi	ᖑ	ngu	ᖓ	nga	ᖕ	ng
ᖠ	&i	ᖢ	&u	ᖤ	&a	ᖦ	&

ᐄ, ᐴ, ᑖ ... ii, puu, taa ...

' [glottal stop] ° [on ᐃ, ᐱ, ᑎ, etc.] ai, pai, tai ...

Even though it was adopted unanimously by the general assembly, what became known as ITC's standard orthography received a mixed welcome in many regions. Most Nunatsiavut Inuit rejected it completely. The Inuvialuit were generally indifferent because they did not feel really concerned.[11] Speakers of Inuinnaqtun first refused to make a written distinction between *k* and *q* and then adopted a long-stemmed *k* for the latter. In 1991 the Kitikmeot Inuit Association stated that the traditional (i.e., non-standard) Roman orthography should be the only one in use in the area (Harper 1992).[12]

In the Mackenzie region, it was only at the beginning of the 1980s that the Inuvialuit became interested in linguistic matters. Their association, the Committee for Original Peoples' Entitlement, set up its own language commission in 1981. A linguist from Quebec City, Ronald Lowe, was hired to study the three forms of speech (Uummarmiutun, Siglitun, and Kangiryuarmiut Inuinnaqtun) used in the region. With his assistance, the commission proposed a standardized version of the Roman orthography. It was generally similar to ITC's standard, except on the following points:

1 *y* was to be used instead of *j* (e.g., *nauyaq*, "seagull").
2 *r* with a circumflex accent (^) symbolized the Uummarmiutun fricative alveolar *J*.
3 The grapheme *ch* was to be used whenever needed (e.g., *natchiq*, "seal").
4 *ñ* symbolized the Uummarmiutun palatalized *n* (e.g., *iñuk*, "human being").
5 *tdj* was to be used instead of *jj* (e.g., *atdji*, "similarity").
6 In Siglitun, *dj* was to be used before some fricative consonants (e.g., *adjgak*, "hand").
7 A distinction was to be made between *n'ng* (*n* + *ng*, as in *tan'ngit*, "Europeans") and *nng* (*ng* + *ng*, as in *avinngaq*, "lemming, mouse").
8 *ff* could be used in Uummarmiutun and Kangiryuarmiutun (e.g., *iliffi*, "you" [p.]).

In Nunavik some people considered ITC's standard to be a novelty forced upon them from outside. A regional language commission, set up at the beginning of the 1980s, recommended that the *ai*, *pai*, *tai* series be reintroduced into the syllabic system (Avataq 1984). It also proposed the following changes to the orthography of consonant groupings:

rp instead of *qp* (e.g., *arpik*, "blackberry")
rt instead of *qt* (e.g., *qairtuq*, "rock")
rs instead of *qs* (e.g., *arsaq*, "ball")
rq instead of *qq* (e.g., *arqutik*, "road")
tj instead of *jj* (e.g., *atji*, "similarity, picture")
qr instead of *rr* (e.g., *taqraq*, "shadow")

This means that it is only in the Natsilingmiut area, Kivalliq, and the Baffin region that the official standard was accepted without discussion. Its actual use, however, entailed some minor modifications. The syllabic symbol ° (which was supposed to indicate that the *i*-column character over which it appeared should be pronounced as *ai*) was practically never used, and within consonant clusters, *r* – rather than *q* – now tends to occur before a voiceless consonant, as it does in Nunavik (Mallon 1985). Moreover, syllabics is unable to symbolize two single consonants and one cluster specific to the central Arctic. These are *h* (which must be written *s*),[13] *J* (found in Natsilingmiutut), and *n'ng* (which cannot be distinguished from *nng*). Some more work thus has to be done before syllabics become as precise as the Roman alphabet.

Writing Systems in Alaska

As seen in chapter 1, the history of Alaskan Eskaleut literacy goes back to 1826, when the Russian Orthodox missionary Ioann Veniaminov transcribed the Unangax language in the Cyrillic alphabet. Around 1850 he also established a standard Cyrillic transcription for Alutiiq and Central Alaskan Yup'ik. After Russia sold Alaska to the United States in 1867, Cyrillic gradually disappeared, and some Alaskan Inuit, Yupiit, and Unangan started writing their language in a non-standardized Roman orthography. It was this type of orthography that newly arrived American missionaries used for publishing several prayer books and Bible extracts in the native tongues. In contrast with Greenland and Canada, however, aboriginal literacy concerned only a minority of native Alaskans, a situation still prevalent today (Kaplan 1990).

An interesting development occurred at the turn of the twentieth century among Yupiit and Inupiat of central western Alaska. A few individuals – sons and daughters of shamans as it seems – invented a totally original form of picture writing. Consisting in realistic or symbolic images, this system was used as a mnemonic tool for reading already known texts (the Bible, for instance)[14] rather than as a complete medium of writing. Three styles were developed: that of the Kuskokwim (around 1870) and those of Kotzebue and Buckland (around 1900). This type of writing disappeared after a few decades (Ray 1981; Harper 1983).

During the 1960s the identity renewal that spread throughout the Arctic and other aboriginal territories led Alaskan Inuit and Yupiit to become more interested in writing their language and having it taught in school. In 1972 popular pressure brought the state legislature of Alaska to pass a law requiring any school with at least fifteen students whose mother tongue was not English to offer classes in these pupils' first language. This same law established a linguistic research and teaching organization, the Alaska Native Language Center (at the University of Alaska Fairbanks), whose efforts enabled every Alaskan aboriginal language to be endowed with a simple and accurate standard orthography by the mid-1970s.

As far as Inupiaq was concerned, however, the standardization process had begun as early as 1946, when a native speaker from the North Slope area, Roy Amaohgak, and an American linguist, Eugene Nida, worked together at developing a scientifically accurate transcription of Amaohgak's dialect. During the 1960s Amaohgak revised his orthography with the assistance of Donald Webster, a missionary linguist from the Summer Institute of Linguistics. A colleague of Webster, Wilfried Zibell, then adapted this revised transcription to the Malimiutun dialect. When the Alaska Native Language Center started standardizing writing systems, it just had to add a few finishing touches to Amaohgak's orthography, which thus became the official written medium of the Alaskan Inuit (Krauss 1980; Kaplan 1990).

This system is similar in many ways to the one in use in the Inuvialuit area (e.g., *y* stands for *j*), with two main differences: the symbol *ŋ* is preferred to *ng* for the nasal velar consonant (e.g., *aŋak* instead of *angak*, "uncle"), and the uvular continuant *R* is symbolized by *g* surmounted with a dot rather than by *r*. The letter *r* stands for the voiced fricative alveolar *J* (which sounds somewhat like English *r*), a fact that, from a Canadian or Greenlandic point of view, can generate some confusion. For instance, Inupiaq *iri* ("eye") is the equivalent of Inuktitut *iji* and West Greenlandic *isi* rather than of the base *iri-* ("to pull away" or "to wet something"), written *igi-* (with a dot on the *g*) in Inupiaq.

The Inupiaq orthography also needed to develop special graphemes for the voiceless fricative alveolar *r*∘ and for the palatalized consonants N, *λ*(voiced), and *ƛ*(voiceless) that occur after an etymological *i*. The respective renditions of the first two are *sr* and *ñ*, while the latter are symbolized by *l* and *ł*, both with a dot underneath.

It is from Alaska that came the idea of taking advantage of the similarities among the various modern Inuit orthographies (all based on the same phonological principles) to develop an auxiliary writing system common to all dialects. Such a system would allow Inuit to communicate internationally (or interregionally) in their own language while preserving their specific orthographies (whether syllabic or Roman) for local publishing and communication. First proposed by Edna Ahgeak MacLean of the Alaska Native Language Center (MacLean 1979), this suggestion was officially endorsed by the Inuit Circumpolar Council (1983) during its second general assembly. It has recently been revived as a way to allow Alaskan Inupiaq to benefit from the vitality of Inuktitut and Kalaallisut (Kaplan 2005).

The Mechanical Supports of Writing

For several decades, people have tried to reproduce mechanically the various Inuit orthographies, including syllabics. The typewriters of old, to which special keys or complete keyboards (in the case of syllabics) had to be added, were followed by commutable IBM spheres and custom-made daisy wheels for electronic printers.

These fell into disuse in the early 1980s with the advent of home computers. The development of word processing made it very easy for professionals and even amateurs to design new fonts adapted to any type of writing system. Several Inuit speakers, language specialists, and computer buffs rapidly set to work, developing a few dozen fonts for syllabics, the Alaskan orthographies, and those of the western Canadian Arctic.[15]

Nowadays, some software (often developed by Pirurvik, a cultural centre based in Iqaluit) have all their commands appearing on screen in the Inuit language (in syllabic or Roman characters). A few fonts allow automatic transcription from syllabics to the Roman standard or, more rarely, vice-versa. Font designers have been so prolific, indeed, that complaints are now heard about the lack of standardization on Inuit keyboards. In the case of syllabics, for instance, the position of several keys is at variance from one type of font to another. This problem was tentatively coped with by bringing frequent users together, notably in 1985 and 1991, to have them reach some sort of agreement. An inquiry undertaken under the aegis of the Canadian Ministry of Communications, which involved all organizations publishing in aboriginal languages, made some relevant recommendations (Vermeulen 1989). It proposed, for instance, reducing to only two the number of Inuit syllabic fonts. One of them would be in ITC's standard and the other would include all syllabic symbols that ever existed. Some keys would be left blank in order to allow the inclusion, at request, of purely local writing characters.

The advent of computers completely modified the long history of Inuit-language printing. As early as the middle of the nineteenth century, the Greenlandic administration and Labrador's Moravian missionaries were publishing books and periodicals in Kalaallisut and Nunatsiavut Inuktitut, while the Church Missionary Society was busy printing its first religious texts in syllabics. For a long time, publishing in the Inuit language remained an almost exclusive prerogative of missionary institutions, except in Greenland, where there existed a state printing establishment that released various types of documents.

With the development of computer science and its application to printing technology, publishing Inuit texts became easier and less expensive than it used to be. Many organizations then decided to make a start in this field. Besides school administrations, governments, and religious authorities, a few private concerns developed a specialization in Inuit language printing. As for now, the most active publishing houses are Atuakkiorfik and Pilersuiffik in Nuuk (official publishers to the Greenlandic government), Nortext from Iqaluit, the University of Alaska Press (Fairbanks), and the Alaska Native Language Center, at the same university.[16]

Computerization has also enabled a flourishing of bilingual or trilingual Internet sites with a Kalaallisut, Inuktitut (usually syllabic), Inuktun, or Inupiaq version. There even exists an online dictionary of Inuktitut (www.livingdictionary.com), which can be accessed in syllabics, English, or French.

The Effects of Literacy

Literacy does not simply consist of learning to read and write. It gives access to a new form of communication that must be used correctly. In a society influenced by Europeans, controlling the written word is a source of power. During recent Inuit history, social leadership has gradually been transferred from the great hunters, heading large families, to literate individuals (lay readers at church, for instance) and, then, to aboriginal bureaucrats schooled in southern (or southern-style) institutions. More generally, formal schooling has contributed to weakening the traditional authority of elders (Farrell 1983).

Literacy is now general in the Arctic. In Greenland and Canada, as well as in Alaska and Russian Chukotka, almost all Inuit and Yupiit know how to read and write in their native tongue, in a European language, or in both. Of course, in those areas where the language is now spoken by a minority of people (i.e., Chukotka, Alaska, the western Canadian Arctic, and Nunatsiavut), literacy in

Yupik, Inupiaq, Inuktun, or other native tongues is extremely low, but elsewhere (i.e., Greenland and the eastern Canadian Arctic) almost everyone is able to read and write his or her native language.[17] In the Canadian Northeast the syllabic system has become an important identity symbol, specially so since its teaching was included in most school curricula (Stairs 1985). It would then be dangerous and inefficient for both Greenlanders and eastern Canadian Inuit to abide by the recommendation of Barbara Burnaby, an educator who once suggested (although she changed her mind afterward) restricting native language literacy to a few adults, specialists of traditional culture (Burnaby 1982).

The mastery of written Inuit, considered a normal skill in Greenland, seems to pose some problems for many Canadian users of syllabics. Those among them who were schooled in English generally find that their second language is much easier to read than their mother tongue. Presented with a bilingual text, they prefer the English version to its Inuktitut equivalent because, as they say, English words can be read much more quickly than Inuktitut lexemes written in syllabic characters. Statements of this sort can even be heard from Inuit teachers and other language specialists.

Syllabics has been accused of being unfit for global reading (i.e., understanding a whole word at one glance) because of the shape and nature of its symbols (McCarthy 1991). This accusation, however, does not stand true. Several monolingual Inuit well trained in reading skills can read a syllabic text at the same speed an alphabetical English text is normally read. The problem lies elsewhere. Since the introduction of English at school, this second language has become the principal written language for Canadian Inuit. Taught for a longer time – and much more systematically – than Inuktitut and offering its readers an abundance and variety of reading materials infinitely superior to what the aboriginal language can offer, English is naturally considered the pre-eminent written medium.[18] It is no surprise then that many bilingual individuals, who find more occasions to read in English than in Inuktitut, have problems deciphering syllabics. Moreover, in the mind of several readers, syllabics is linked to very narrow contexts: the first grades at school, religion, and the transmission of traditional culture.

Perry Shearwood (1987, 2001) has studied the use of syllabics in Igloolik, Nunavut. In his opinion, literacy generates an ability to perform socially approved tasks via reading and writing. These tasks fill three types of functions: indexic (to give information about the speaker), communicative (to establish a social relation entailing some action), and conceptual (to express ideas). In a place like Igloolik, tasks and functions are shared between Inuktitut and English. By observing this sharing, Shearwood was able to define six types of literacy, the first four usually expressed by way of Inuktitut, the last two through English. Inuit forms of literacy have a limited scope: biblical and other religious reading, personal correspondence (now almost completely replaced by telephone calls and e-mailing in English), writing autobiography, and reading elementary school texts. In English, by contrast, mastery of the written word serves much wider goals: communication of various experiences through reading and writing stories as well as expression and development of one's own ideas by reading and writing essays. The functions of literacy are thus very different and obviously unequal in Inuktitut and in English, a normal fact in a situation where the latter language is socially predominant. Many speakers of Inuktitut, however, still believe that literacy in Inuktitut can play a major role in fostering stable bilingualism[19] in the Arctic (Hot 2008).

FORMAL EDUCATION

Taught and transmitted, at first, in the absence of any formal schooling system, literacy was later included – much earlier in Greenland and Labrador than elsewhere in the North American Arctic – within organized education projects, directly or indirectly controlled by the Danish, Canadian, or American state.[20] This involvement of governments in Inuit education meant that local languages were not always considered worthy of being formally taught and that the chief objectives of the schools were often defined in terms of linguistic and cultural assimilation. Formal education thus constitutes a privileged field for observing open manifestations of the national policies of rejection or development of aboriginal languages. All Inuit, Yupiit, and Unangan are now fully schooled, and the types of schooling they receive demonstrate how governments assess the value of their language.

Among other functions, schools are supposed to carry on the linguistic training initiated at home since early childhood. For a long period, however, northern schools were instead the scene of a sharp division between the family, where the native language was spoken, and the classroom, where teaching was partially or entirely conducted in Danish, English, or Russian. Nowadays, however, most Yupiit and Inuit children of aboriginal mother tongue are taught in their own language during the first elementary grades, a situation that lessens the linguistic and cultural shock induced by schooling.

Learning to Talk

Over the past decades, research has been conducted on how Inuit babies learn to talk and, therefore, on the way kindergarten and first-year curricula should be adjusted in order to adapt them to the children's learning habits and linguistic usage. Available data show that language learning among young Inuit is slower than with European children, adults being relatively silent when dealing with the young.[21]

According to Martha Crago (1988), who recorded on videocassettes mother-child interaction in two Nunavik villages, language teaching is mainly conducted through teasing and uttering routine phrases that the baby must repeat. Children are considered speakers as soon as they obey when asked to do something, but those who talk too much are deemed less intelligent than others because they cannot control their speech. A well-educated child learns by observing and listening rather than by asking questions.

When addressing young children, adults use a special language: *aqausiit* (lullabies), now known only by elders; *nilliujuusiit* (words of affection);[22] and *piarajausiq* (baby talk). Baby talk includes special words such as *amaama* ("breast- or bottle-feeding"), *apaapa* ("eating"), and *a'aluk* ("watch out!"), as well as morphologically truncated morphemes such as *tiitu-* ("drink tea") rather than *tiitulaurit* ("drink some tea!") or *tiitulaurlanga* ("may I drink tea!") and *mali-* ("follow") instead of *malilaunga* ("follow me!") or *malilaurlanga* ("may I come along!").[23] Crago noticed that babies are sometimes taught English words in order, it is said, to prepare them for school.

After they have reached four years of age, children are no longer addressed in baby talk, but sentences are simplified when speaking to them. Another specialist of the language of youngsters, David Wilman (1988), has observed a high level of linguistic sophistication among six year olds, together with some phonemic simplification. In Greenland, Lise Lennert-Olsen (1987) has documented the progressive development of language between the ages of two, when babies start talking, and five, when children enter school (see also Fortescue 1985b; Fortescue and Lennert-Olsen 1992). It is at school that knowledge of the mother tongue will be strengthened or, on the contrary, become endangered.

Formal Education in Greenland

In Greenland the history of formal education dates back to the first decades of the eighteenth century, when mission schools teaching in Greenlandic were established. This entailed a rapid development of literacy. At the turn of the nineteenth century, most West Greenlanders knew how to read and write in Kalaallisut,[24] and in 1845 a teacher-training college was established in Nuuk to improve education standards. Up to the 1950s, however, formal education was usually limited to the seven compulsory years during which religion, arithmetic, and Greenlandic grammar were taught (Gynther 1980). In 1925 the Danish language had been introduced as a teaching subject, but because most schools were unable to hire qualified Danish-speaking teachers, Kalaallisut remained the only language heard in the vast majority of classrooms.

After 1950 it was decided that Danish should be taught in a much more systematic way because, educators believed, modern cultural and technical data could not be translated into Greenlandic. This decision, which was rapidly enforced, entailed a severe setback for the aboriginal language. The reform of curricula conducted between 1961 and 1964 favoured the production of Danish didactical material but left teachers of Greenlandic with a limited number of outdated manuals. Compounding these problems was the fact that schools were then facing a severe shortage of aboriginal personnel. This was palliated by importing teachers from Denmark and sending promising students to complete high school in that country. Lacking qualified local personnel, many Greenlandic schools were unable to start teaching Kalaallisut before grade 3.

This way of doing things was ratified in 1967 by a law stipulating that school authorities could wait for up to three years before starting classes in Greenlandic but that Danish should be part of the curriculum from grade 1 on. Several Greenlanders then understood that their language risked being progressively set aside by the state. Danish was important to them, but it was primarily a school language that very few were able to speak fluently. People realized that formal education delivered in Greenland was more exacting than its Danish equivalent because it supposed mastering two languages instead of one (Gynther 1980).

This situation brought the local administrative body, the Provincial Council of Greenland, to engage in a public debate from 1970 on and to inquire into the role of the vernacular language in formal education. The ensuing report recommended that Greenlandic become at the same time the principal means of communication at school and the chief medium for understanding the modern world, and that adequate measures be taken to achieve this. These recommendations entailed the orthographic reform of 1973 and a complete remodelling of school manuals in Kalaallisut. It was also decided that students would have to master only one language – preferably their mother tongue – in order to complete the school curriculum and that the other form of speech (usually Danish for those born in Greenland) should be taught as a foreign language.

These reforms became really significant after Greenland achieved Home Rule (i.e., political autonomy within the Kingdom of Denmark) in 1979. Education became a local responsibility in 1980, and the new Greenlandic Parliament declared Kalaallisut the principal school language, both as a subject and as a medium of teaching. Compulsory schooling was increased to nine years, with the possibility of studying for four more years (Berthelsen 1990a, 338).

The system nevertheless preserved – and it still does – a degree of bilingualism. According to the language usually spoken at home, parents may enrol their children – at least in larger towns – in a Greenlandic or a Danish curriculum. In the former case, Danish is taught as a foreign language from grade 4 on, whereas in the latter, students learn Kalaallisut for two hours a week. Because the number of qualified Greenlandic teachers is still insufficient, the law states that Danish teaching professionals may be hired – a fact that restricts ipso facto the use of Kalaallisut at school – when it is impossible to find enough Greenlandic or bilingual[25] schoolmasters (Møller 1990, 362). Over the past two decades, however, the situation has greatly improved.

Training teachers and other professionals constitutes one of the major priorities of present-day Greenland. Nuuk's teacher college (the Seminarium or Ilinniarfissuaq, founded in 1845; see Thorleifsen 1995) has revamped its curricula. In 1980 it was offering a four-year course that included 214 Kalaallisut lessons, 158 Danish lessons,[26]

168 lessons in Inuit studies, and 364 lessons on elective matters (e.g., mathematics, English, religion, physics/chemistry). The teaching medium was Greenlandic, except for Danish lessons and some classes in science (Greenland Home Rule 1980).

In 1984 the Greenlandic Parliament established an Inuit Studies Institute (Ilisimatusarfik) whose objective was to provide high school graduates with postsecondary training in the social sciences and humanities. For several reasons, this training was soon considered inadequate, and in 1989 the institute became the University of Greenland (Ilisimatusarfik – Grønlands Universitet), which is funded by the Greenlandic Ministry of Education and headed by a rector elected for three years.[27] To be admitted, students must speak Kalaallisut, and courses are normally taught in that language by Greenlandic professors (Langgaard 1990).[28] The university comprises four departments, which offer undergraduate, master, and doctorate programs in administration; cultural and social history; language, literature, and the media; and theology (see www.ilisimatusarfik.gl).[29] Students interested in other domains of learning (e.g., medicine, architecture, or law) may receive fellowships allowing them to study in Denmark (especially at the University of Aarhus) or elsewhere (mainly in Canada and Alaska), although since the turn of the current century a science complex (Ilimmarfik) has been present in Nuuk, a fact that might entail the creation of new university departments.

Formal Education in Canada

In contrast with Greenland, the history of education in arctic Canada is short – except for Labrador – and chaotic. Here are some important dates:

1790 Moravian schools are established in Labrador; they teach a very basic curriculum in Nunatsiavut Inuktitut.[30]

1920–50 Most Anglican and Catholic missions operate government-subsidized schools (elementary English, with syllabics and some arithmetic).[31]

1929 Mission boarding schools are established in Aklavik (Mackenzie region). They teach an elementary English curriculum.

1949 Moravian schools in Labrador are ceded to the Newfoundland government after that province joins Canada;

Inuktitut is replaced with English (Jeddore 1979); elsewhere in Canada, the first federal day-schools open in the largest communities.

1950–65 Federal day-schools (and four boarding schools)[32] are established throughout Nunavik and the Northwest Territories; they offer a complete elementary – and, in a few communities, secondary – curriculum in English.[33]

1964–68 Quebec provincial kindergartens and elementary schools are established in Nunavik[34] (Inuktitut and French curricula).

1969–70 In the Northwest Territories schools are taken over by the territorial Department of Education. In Nunavik both federal and provincial schools are ceded to the Arctic Quebec School Board.

1978 In Nunavik education becomes the responsibility of the Inuit-run Kativik School Board under the James Bay and Northern Quebec Agreement.[35]

1980 All over the eastern Arctic, classes are taught in Inuktitut for the first three or four years, before pupils switch to English (English or French in Nunavik).

1984 In the Mackenzie region, Inuit take charge of their own schools under the Inuvialuit Agreement.

1999 After the establishment of the Nunavut territory, education comes under the responsibility of the territorial Department of Education.

2005 The Nunatsiavut Inuit gain full authority over their education with the establishment of the Nunatsiavut government.

2007 Agreement is reached on a Nunavik government with full control over education.

As may be seen, education in northern Canada has evolved a lot since the beginning of the twentieth century. Up to the Second World War, Inuit were generally considered unfit for formal education. The following words from a high-ranking civil servant in the federal Department of the Interior clearly express prewar views: "The educational needs of the Eskimos ... are very simple and their mental capacity for assimilating academic matters is limited" (Bethune 1935, 15).

After the war, opinions started to change and it seemed wise to give Inuit a basic education in order to make them "average Canadians"[36] while preserving their traditional lifestyle.[37] Linguistic and cultural assimilation then came into fashion. It was believed that the only way for Inuit to become full-fledged modern participants in mainstream society was to educate them in a school system whose curriculum would closely copy that in use in southern Canada and would resort to English as the exclusive teaching language.[38]

Federal bureaucrats had not considered the strength of aboriginal identity. Forcing Inuit to become anglicized did not yield the expected results. On the contrary, the first generation of young educated bilinguals entered into politics and established associations and other organizations that challenged Euro-Canadian control over the North. They were supported in their efforts by a number of non-Inuit teachers who pushed for change from within the system. Among other results, this led to the gradual takeover of education by local populations and to the introduction of Inuktitut at school.

The federal period is now judged quite severely by most Inuit (see Curley 1975; Immaroitok and Jull 1985), although many agree that those who went through the federal system speak English better than more recent students while continuing to feel at ease with their mother tongue.[39] Ethnographies of Inuit communities published during the 1960s show that there was almost no local opposition to northern schools. Nelson Graburn (1960), for instance, notes that in Salluit (Nunavik), 90% of the population were in favour of formal education in English. In Baker Lake (Kivalliq) parents were anxious to send their children to school. Using English did not entail any major difficulties, and because Inuktitut was the only language spoken at home, it was not considered endangered (Vallee 1987). In Iqaluit 72% of school-age children were at school, and the parents of the most diligent students generally exhibited a high degree of economic stability (Honigmann and Honigmann 1965). In Inukjuak (Nunavik), however, according to William E. Willmott (1961), the only positive functions of the federal school were that it freed mothers from their children, tracked down illness, and could be used as a dancehall or movie theatre. The school was supposed to help youngsters to integrate into Euro-Canadian society, but it appeared unable to meet this goal: after eight years of operation, only one graduate from Inukjuak could speak any English.

Even after the education system had begun to evolve in a direction seemingly more respectful of Inuit language and culture, it did not escape criticism (Mallon 1979, 66):

> Our school system is alien not only because it has been developed and is being run by non-Inuit: it is alien because it *is* a system. There were no places in traditional Inuit culture where children were herded together for a set number of hours a day to learn how to become functioning adults; there was no sub-set of adults who devoted their lives to instruction, or to educational administration, or to the preparation of instructional materials. To put it as extremely as possible: the mere building of a school could be said to be an alien act of cultural aggression.

Curricula often appeared unstructured (Prattis and Chartrand 1984), and Inuit frequently asserted that education would become really functional when they were able to fully participate at all levels in a teaching system that took their own values into account.

Over the past decades, the decentralization of education and its devolution into Inuit hands has indeed increased local participation, as well as the inclusion of aboriginal values in curricula and school materials (Douglas 1994). In Nunavut the school system is now run by the territorial Department of Education,[40] which functions under the Nunavut Education Act. This law includes among its objectives the assertions that "the education system should be based on Inuit societal values and the principles and concepts of *Inuit Qaujimajatuqangit* [Inuit traditional knowledge]" and that "students should be given a bilingual education in the Inuit language and another official language to enable graduates to use both languages competently" (Government of Nunavut 2002, 2). On a regional basis, schools are supervised by district education authorities, whose members of the board are elected by the population.[41]

The situation is similar in Nunavik, where the Kativik School Board is headed by elected Inuit commissioners. However, the Nunavik Agreement-in-Principle of August 2007, which provides for a regional government in Arctic Quebec, plans for the abolition of the Kativik School Board and its transformation into a regional Department of Education. In both Nunavik and Nunavut, each local community possesses its own education committee, which supervises the hiring of teachers, manages school buildings, and decides on languages to be taught in the classroom in accordance with regional or territorial laws.

In the Baffin and Kivalliq schools, Inuktitut is usually the only language taught from kindergarten to grade 3. From grade 4 on,

English becomes the principal teaching medium, but Inuktitut continues to be taught as a subject matter and, very sporadically, to be used as a teaching medium in courses with an Inuit cultural content. In the western Arctic, however, very few children speak Inuktun. Teaching is thus conducted in English, with a few classes in Inuktun as a second language in some schools.

In Nunavut the development of native language curricula and teaching materials is under the responsibility of the territorial Department of Education in collaboration with the district education authorities. Dialectal differences impose limits on the diffusion of materials outside their area of production, although some collaboration does exist between various regions. Efforts are made to give local content to Inuktitut – and also English – class material and to adapt basic learning skills to the Inuit worldview. Beyond high school, postsecondary education is offered by Nunavut Arctic College (with campuses in Iqaluit, Rankin Inlet, and Cambridge Bay),[42] which is in charge, among other programs, of Inuit teacher education and interpreter/translator training.[43]

In Nunavik the degree of local control over the education system is generally similar to what has just been described for Nunavut. Elementary, secondary, and adult education, as well as Inuit teacher training and the development of Inuktitut curricula, will continue to be under the responsibility of the Kativik School Board, up to the time of their transfer to the Government of Nunavik. The board also offers a limited range of technical courses, but postsecondary students must usually move to Montreal.[44]

In most Nunavik schools, Inuktitut is the exclusive medium of instruction from kindergarten to grade 2. From grade 3 on, parents can choose between French and English as the principal teaching language for their children, although some grammar, religion, and culture classes continue to be taught in Inuktitut. The proportion of students enrolled in the French stream may vary a lot from one village to another or, within any school, from one year to the next. It generally hovers between 25% and 60%, with an annual average of 35% to 40% of all Nunavik students learning French as their principal second language. In many cases, this language is spoken only within the confines of the classroom, and after graduation it is rapidly replaced by English (learned from older children, television, or Euro-Canadian residents of the village), the lingua franca of Inuit communities (Taylor and Wright 1989).

In Nunavik and Nunavut interest in education is generally high, but due to several factors – lack of support from some parents, language problems, lack of motivation, absence of adequate education facilities in some villages, and so on – many students drop out of the system before completing high school. However, things are improving. School attendance is increasing steadily, and as the older generation, which had no or little formal education, is replaced by younger people, the overall degree of schooling should rise.

In Nunatsiavut the level of formal education is higher than the Canadian Inuit average, but most instruction is offered in English. Inuktitut is taught only in the lower elementary grades of two or three villages, generally as a second language. Since the late 1980s Inuit teachers have been trained at the Happy Valley facilities of the Memorial University of Newfoundland. With the signing of the Nunatsiavut Agreement in late 2005 and the establishment of a regional government, Labrador Inuit have gained full control over their education system.

It must finally be mentioned that there exist a number of Inuktitut courses for non-Inuit eager to learn the language. The most complete has been created by Mick Mallon (Mallon 1991). It is offered during intensive sessions at Nunavut Arctic College (Iqaluit) and elsewhere in northern Canada and is available on videocassettes.[45] Inuktitut has also been taught to francophones since 1972 at Université Laval in Quebec City (Dorais 1975e, 1975f).[46] Other teaching methods are in existence. These are either old (Gagné 1964; Trinel 1970; Spalding 1979b) or more recent (Igloliorte 1990; Ortiz 1993).

Formal Education in Alaska

The history of formal education in Alaska goes back to the Russian period, when Orthodox missionaries taught their flocks how to read and write in their own languages. After Alaska became American in 1867, the Orthodox were joined by Catholics, Moravians, Presbyterians, Methodists, and representatives of other Protestant churches. All of them established mission schools. Whereas the Orthodox, Catholics, and Moravians offered some classes in Inupiaq, Yupik, Unangax, and Dene, the schools of the other denominations made exclusive use of English (Krauss 1980).

The appointment of the Presbyterian minister Sheldon Jackson as head of Alaskan schools in 1888 and the creation of an Education

Bureau in 1910 entailed the establishment of secular federal and territorial teaching institutions and the progressive disappearance of aboriginal-language education. From 1912 on, all schools in Alaska – including missionary establishments – taught in English only. The Inuit, Yupiit, and Unangan thus gained easy access to education, including postsecondary instruction,[47] but this occurred at the expense of their aboriginal languages, which entered a period of seemingly irreversible decline.

It was not until 1970 that experimental bilingual classes were reopened in four schools whose pupils' first language was Central Alaskan Yup'ik. Two years later, the state legislature of Alaska compelled all teaching establishments with at least fifteen students – this number was soon reduced to eight – who were not native speakers of English to offer courses at the elementary level in the local aboriginal languages (Krauss 1980). Federal schools were not subject to that law, but most of them chose voluntarily to abide by it. This was facilitated by the fact that since the end of the 1960s, the federal government had been subsidizing bilingual education for linguistic minorities. The ultimate goal of these bilingual and bicultural programs was to facilitate English-language proficiency among students. Bilingualism was thus seen by legislators as a transitory step toward more efficient monolingual English education, and the native tongues seemed reduced to play a merely instrumental role in school. In 1988, however, the Alaskan secretary for education recognized that aboriginal languages were "unique and essential elements of Alaska's heritage, and [were] thus distinct from immigrant languages" (MacLean 1990, 17s4). In such a context, it became a duty for schools to teach local native languages, provided parents agreed with the idea.

Since the late 1980s each Alaskan school district has had to develop elementary and secondary curricula adapted to the specific linguistic needs of its clientele: "In regions where children still speak their Native language, the language of instruction from Kindergarten to Fourth Grade is usually in that language. After Fourth Grade, instruction in the Native language is usually reduced, for various reasons including shortage of bilingual teachers, lack of curricular materials and, most importantly, lack of commitment by the community and school to promote the growth and enrichment of the Alaska Native language *per se*" (MacLean 1990, 174).

In those places – which are now the vast majority – where youngsters no longer speak Inupiaq, Yupik, or Unangax, children are often taught basic elements of the local aboriginal tongue as a second language. English then constitutes the principal medium of instruction from kindergarten on, and this even when instructors have to teach about native culture. But the mere presence of native topics in the curriculum may contribute to promoting Inuit identity, and many aboriginal teachers actively encourage such promotion.[48]

Barbara Harrison (1981) has studied the transmission of knowledge in a village of southwest Alaska at the end of the 1970s. Contrary to what was happening among Inupiat in the same period, all children she observed were of aboriginal (Yup'ik) mother tongue. Adults encouraged them to speak the native language by giving lessons to babies and letting young people improvise Yup'ik stories of their own. The school, however, had a somewhat negative effect. Even though it had been offering bilingual classes since 1974, English predominated after the first elementary grades, and young children started learning that language from their older siblings, even before going to school. In the Moravian church, catechism was taught in English.

Up to 1980, teenagers had to leave the village to complete high school in an anglophone boarding institution. This was detrimental to their linguistic identity and to the transmission of aboriginal culture. School teaching also stood in contradiction to education received at home because the latter was based on observation and informal speech rather than on discourse. There was thus a real risk that school could destroy a language and a culture still in good health.[49]

Postsecondary teaching institutions try the best they can to preserve these languages and cultures. Through the Alaska Native Language Center, the University of Alaska Fairbanks trains teachers of aboriginal languages, teaches these languages to students,[50] and produces school- and college-level materials in Inupiaq, Yupik, Unangax, and Dene. Other Alaskan organizations, such as the University of Alaska Anchorage, also produce language materials, some of which are available online (e.g., at www.alaskool.org).

The Linguistic Impact of Education

One cannot but wonder about the impact of bilingual education on the linguistic skills of students. In the past decades, several specialists have looked at that situation. As early as 1976 the Greenlandic educator Ingmar Egede noticed the special problems of children educated in two languages (i.e., Kalaallisut and Danish). He showed that when bilingual education was not conducted properly, it often slowed down the process of learning one's own mother tongue. In some Greenlandic schools, 80% of the teaching was conducted in Danish, but students were unable to speak that language fluently. Frequent switching from one form of speech to the other prevented many children from establishing relations between their various subject matters. They thus accumulated delays in their learning process (Egede 1976).

The situation seems to have improved in Greenland, where Home Rule has given an added value to Kalaallisut and aboriginal-language education. However, what Egede described in 1976 still occurs in most parts of the eastern Canadian Arctic: teaching is initially conducted in Inuktitut, but afterward the second language becomes predominant.

This way of doing things has good and bad effects. It has long been known that children who initially learn to read and write in their mother tongue may do better in both their first and second languages than those who start with an inadequate bilingual or, worse, second-language monolingual education (Cummins 1991). Inuit schools are thus right in making exclusive use of Inuktitut during the first elementary grades. Ideally, full-time instruction in the aboriginal language should even continue for as long as possible. Curricula should also better respect the students' learning habits and the type of linguistic code to which they are accustomed.[51] Work by the well-known education specialist Jim Cummins (see Devillar et al. 1994) outlines the importance of adapting curricula to the linguistic and cultural needs of minority children.

Research conducted in Nunavik (Stairs and Annahatak 1987) has shown that initial Inuktitut instruction was beneficial to students. Among third- and fourth-grade pupils, the schools whose performances in written Inuktitut were the highest were also those that exhibited the best academic results in written English. Moreover, students did not have the same writing style from one school to another. Where native-language literacy had been correctly taught, they were prone to use "traditional" words (i.e., lexemes comprising several post-bases) or, on the contrary, shorter but morphologically correct and well-constructed terms.

As the negative effects of poorly programmed bilingual education are concerned, let us mention a rapid increase in second-language vocabulary[52] – at the expense of the Inuktitut lexicon – as soon as children reach eleven years of age (Dorais 1989), as well as the fact that most non-Inuit teachers – who still comprise a majority in Canadian Arctic schools – are not well trained for second-language education. The latter situation often causes these teachers to lower their academic demands – by resorting to closed questioning, for instance, rather than to open discussion with pupils – in order not to overburden their students. This results in preventing students from becoming really fluent in their second language because their practice of full English conversation is infrequent (Mackay 1986). These two factors (poor bilingual programs and low academic demands) contribute to the advent and preservation of subtractive bilingualism (learning a second language diminishes one's skills in his or her mother tongue) and, in some cases, more or less severe occurrences of semi-lingualism (inadequate fluency in both first and second languages).

A survey on education in Nunavik, sponsored by the Makivik Corporation and conducted by four native Inuktitut speakers (Nunavik Educational Task Force 1992) has tried to understand the social and academic causes of these problems in order to seek solutions. Among other findings, the survey mentions the absence of norms for measuring the level of success and the rate of efficacy of linguistic programs. Parents notice a progressive decline in their children's fluency in Inuktitut as children proceed from grade to grade, as well as a general academic lag of two or three years, but they are told by the school that this is normal in a bilingual system. According to the authors of the report, this last assertion is inaccurate. One should instead put the blame on the absence of effective programs and materials and on the lack of serious education norms and parental support.

According to the report, teacher training should also be revised. Francophone and anglophone instructors should be more knowledgeable about how to teach French or English as a second language, and Inuit teachers would benefit from genuine pedagogical training, as opposed to an approach that insists on teaching only Inuktitut. Specialists supervising curriculum development and teacher training should be more critical, no longer taking the pretext of cultural differences between Inuit and Europeans as grounds for letting the former freely develop education programs without any valid scientific basis.

To solve all these problems, the report suggests tightening up the norms for defining programs, transmitting academic knowledge, training teachers, and evaluating northern schools. Students should be able to get access to high-quality Inuktitut education, and this at all levels. Moreover, the report offers the hypothesis that for bilingualism to become really additive, second-language instruction should start as early as possible (from grade 2, for instance), provided that Inuktitut plays a predominant part during the very first linguistic training of students.

This last recommendation reflects the wish of many Inuit parents that their children accede to a complete and fully functional knowledge of English or French. One should wonder, however, whether, in a situation where the second language clearly predominates over the mother tongue, bilingual education, if not carefully planned, does not risk leading to the progressive demise of the aboriginal language. One might thus fear that despite the goodwill of everybody, northern schools could be paving the way for a penetration of English that would further weaken the Inuktitut fluency of young people (see Martin 2000a for a similar view).

Since the early 1990s various attempts have been ongoing in both Nunavik and Nunavut to improve bilingual programs and teacher training. Much, however, still has to be done. In a report released in 2006 (Berger 2006), Judge Thomas R. Berger has put into light what he calls the failure of education in Nunavut, suggesting that Inuktitut be taught up to the end of high school and that the whole education system be greatly improved to avoid a social catastrophe.[53] Research conducted in Nunavik by the psychologist Donald Taylor and his colleagues has shown repeatedly that proficiency in Inuktitut among children, teenagers, and young adults is still high after three decades of bilingual schooling but that, generally speaking, this proficiency has become more conversational (ability to discuss day-to-day matters) than academic (communication of relatively abstract concepts in decontextualized settings) due to the all-pervading presence of English (Taylor et al. 2000; Wright et al. 2000; Louis and Taylor 2001; Taylor and Wright 2004).

Such research work,[54] as well as examples from Alaska, show that bilingual programs can contribute to the preservation of some form of the aboriginal language, provided that the vernacular remains the principal medium of communication in the community and, above all, at home (Orvik 1977; Wilson 1977; Cummins 1981). This is no longer the case in the major part of Alaska (Iutzi-Mitchell 1992), but it still is in the eastern Canadian Arctic, where

Inuit have manifested a clear will – in Nunavut (Couch 1992; Tulloch 2004; Dorais 2006a) as well as in Nunavik (Crago et al. 1992) – to continue doing all that is possible to preserve their language. In 2001, 89% of adult Inuit living in Nunavut felt it was very important for children to be taught Inuktitut in school (Nunavummit Kiglisiniartiit 2001, 59). There is thus no need yet to be completely pessimistic.

LITERATURE AND THE MEDIA

Literacy and formal education have entailed the emergence of a corpus of written texts that have almost completely replaced the old Inuit oral traditions. They have also allowed for the development of various media of communication, both written and electronic.

Written Literature

It is only in Greenland, however, that there exists a real literary tradition in the Inuit language. The Greenlanders' long experience with aboriginal literacy, their high level of formal education, the standardization of their language since the mid-1800s, and support from the Danish and Home Rule administrations, have all contributed to the emergence and development of a varied literature in Kalaallisut. It is impossible to describe this literature in any detail here. Robert Petersen (1984), Christian Berthelsen (1976, 1986, 1990b), Bjarne Thomsen (2007), and Karen Langgaard (2008) have summarized some of its principal trends, while Michael Fortescue (1990) provides the English translation of significant extracts from several well-known Greenlandic authors.[55]

Intellectual life in Greenland was first dominated by missionaries, who translated the catechism and Holy Scriptures into Kalaallisut. Lutherans and Moravians also compiled grammars and dictionaries to facilitate evangelization. Moreover, they wrote religious hymns, many of which are still in use.

It was only in the middle of the nineteenth century, however, with the installation of a printing press in Nuuk, that literature really started to develop. Rasmus Berthelsen (1827–1901), considered the first Greenlandic author, became famous by writing hymns and poems. In 1861 the Danish administrator and ethnologist Henrik Rink founded *Atuagagdliutit*, Greenland's oldest journal.[56] Exclusively devoted, at first, to disseminating local[57] and international information, and to publishing Inuit legends[58] and Greenlandic translations of popular literary works (*Robinson Crusoe*, for instance), *Atuagagdliutit* progressively opened its pages to young local writers.

The second decade of the twentieth century witnessed an intense debate on Greenlandic identity, which found an echo in literature. Intellectuals in their thirties, often graduates from Nuuk's teacher college (Ilinniarfissuaq), wrote poems, songs, and hymns celebrating the aboriginal tradition while encouraging Greenlanders to modernize their thinking. Two major writers, Henrik Lund and Jonathan Petersen, published their most significant works during that period. The first Greenlandic novel, *Sinnattugaq* (The Dream), appeared at the same time (1914), written by Mathias Storch, a clergyman. It was a social and philosophical novel criticizing Greenland's situation and the alleged ignorance of its inhabitants.

Seventeen years passed before a second novel was published (in 1931), *Ukiut 300–nngornerat* (The 300th Anniversary). Written by a schoolteacher, Augo Lynge, it is a work of anticipation set in 2021, three hundred years after Hans Egede founded the Danish colony. The author describes a fictional Greenland that has become an integral part of Denmark. Danes and aboriginal Greenlanders enjoy equal rights, and the capital, Nuuk, has become a thriving fishing port with huge buildings. The book's objective was to put into light some possible ways to develop the country. Like *Sinnattugaq*, it aimed at encouraging Greenlanders to modernize themselves.

The 1930s were particularly productive. They witnessed a renewal of poetry, as well as the emergence of Greenlandic drama. Works written during this period celebrate the beauty of the land, tell about its Inuit past, or describe daily life in its villages. Figureheads of Greenlandic literature in the 1930s are Pavia Petersen, Hans Lynge (also a painter and sculptor), and Frederik Nielsen. Nielsen's masterpiece, however, *Ilissi tassa nunassarsi* (This Land Shall Be Yours), a fictional trilogy relating prehistoric Inuit migrations into Greenland, appeared only in 1970.

During the Second World War, Greenland was completely cut off from German-occupied Denmark. In literature, this situation provoked a marked interest in the past, which endured till the 1970s. Many books written between 1940 and 1980 (Otto Rosing's, Ole Brandt's, or Villads Villadsen's novels, for instance) draw their inspiration from history or traditional life.

Since the 1960s the social and political situation of modern Greenland has provided another source of inspiration, expressed in the poems of Moses Olsen, Aqigssiaq Møller, Aqqaluk Lynge, and Kristian Olsen; in the novels of Hans Anthon Lynge, Inooraq Olsen, and Maaliaaraq Vebæk (the first Greenlandic woman novelist); or in the short stories of Pitaaraq Brandt and Ole Korneliussen.

Greenlandic literature has had its essayists too, including Jakob Olsen, who accompanied the anthropologist and explorer Knud Rasmussen during his expeditions and published an account of his travels in 1927; Otto Sandgreen, who wrote on traditional life in east Greenland; and Robert Petersen (the first rector of the University of Greenland) and Emil Rosing (a former chief curator at Nuuk's National Museum), who have published on Greenlandic ethnology (Petersen 1987; Rosing 1978).[59]

Greenlandic writers are very close to their public. It often happens that their novels and short stories first appear in local periodicals. Their songs, poems, and plays are widely broadcast on the national radio system. Greenland possesses an excellent network of public libraries (managed by the National Library in Nuuk), where the entire literary production in Kalaallisut can generally be found.

The young, however, seem to have lost interest in their literature (Langgaard 1990). Many of them consider it to be merely academic subject matter, which is forgotten as soon as one has left school. The numerous foreign titles translated into Kalaallisut[60] are often preferred to local works, and many readers are satisfied with newspapers, magazines, and comic strips. Langgaard attributes this loss of interest to the fact that Greenlandic literature did not evolve at the same rhythm as society in general. In consequence, young people find it old-fashioned and moralizing. Contemporary literature should thus make an effort to better adapt to the preoccupations of present-day Greenlanders.

In Canada there is no literary tradition similar to the Greenlandic one. A few Inuit texts written by talented authors in their native language can indeed be found, but there does not exist any fully developed literature. Setting religious and classroom publications aside, fewer than a dozen full-length books for adults have been published in Inuktitut and none in Inuktun. Most writers make equal use of their first and second languages, and a majority of their readers prefer English to Inuktitut. As a matter of fact, with the notable exception of school materials authored by Inuit teachers, the written production in the aboriginal tongue is more journalistic than literary, and genuine creativity must be sought elsewhere: in Inuit songs, for instance, which are thriving in the Canadian Arctic; in native radio programming, which plays an important part in most communities; or in Inuit filmmaking.

In a way, present-day Inuit literature in Canada continues a tradition of transmitting tales and various other types of information and of using singing as a privileged means for self-expression. According to Robin McGrath (1979, 1984), this relation with tradition goes deeper yet. Themes and structures characteristic of old Inuit myths are often found in written texts. For instance, several autobiographies relate how a neglected orphan was able to overcome a number of ordeals before becoming a great hunter, a family head, or a respected leader.

McGrath defines four types of contemporary Inuit prose:[61] modern tales, memoirs and recollections, descriptions of traditional culture, and articles or essays about present-day life. Children's literature should be added to this list, a genre that is now flourishing. It is best illustrated by several dozen booklets and storybooks written and published by various student and teacher groups (Iqaluit's Nunavut Teacher Education Program, for example) and by individual authors such as Michael Kusugak.

To the first type belong the only two full-length Inuktitut novels ever published in Canada. Markoosie's *The Harpoon of the Hunter* relates the ordeals of a young hunter who commits suicide after having lost his family and his fiancée. First published between 1967 and 1969 as a serial in *Inuktitut* magazine, this novel was later translated into English and appeared in book form in 1970 (Markoosie 1970). Another novel, *Sanaaq*, by Salome Mitiarjuk Nappaaluk (published in 1984 but written in 1953), narrates the deeds of a young widow (whose name gives the book its title) belonging to a semi-nomadic band of Nunavik Inuit at the time of first contacts with Europeans.[62] The book has been published in French (Nappaaluk 2002). Within a related genre, a volume of highly imaginative short stories by the author, journalist, and draughtsman Alootook Ipellie[63] appeared in English in 1993. Some stories may have been originally written in Inuktitut, but it is not clear whether this is actually the case.

Memoirs and autobiographical recollections are more numerous. Some were originally authored in English (e.g., Thrasher 1976;

Freeman 1978), but most of them were first written in Inuktitut before being published in this language (e.g., Ajaruaq 1970; Alasuaq 1981), in French (e.g., Nuligak 1972a), and/or in English (e.g., Pitseolak 1971; Nuligak 1972b; Tagoona 1975; Pitseolak 1975; Igloliorte 1976). Since 2005 Nunavut Arctic College has been publishing a bilingual (English-Inuktitut) biographical series based on interviews, titled *Life Stories of Northern Leaders* (see Okpik 2005).

Inuit descriptions of traditional culture, including several collections of myths and legends, have appeared in Inuktitut or in bilingual or trilingual editions (see Nungak and Arima 1969; Sivuaq 1972, 1973; Alasuaq 1973; Owingajak 1986; Qumaq 1988). Taamusi Qumaq's dictionary of definitions in Inuktitut (Qumaq 1991), the first of its kind in the Inuit world, belongs to a special category, as do the three bilingual series of books on Inuit culture published by Nunavut Arctic College (which are discussed in chapter 4).

Essays on present-day life were, and still are, mostly published as journal articles by a few dozen authors of all ages. Three names, from among the most prolific, should be mentioned here: Leah Idlout, Alootook Ipellie, and Rachel Qitsualik. Ipellie and Robin (McGrath) Gedalof have published an anthology of Inuit literary texts (Gedalof and Ipellie 1980). Other anthologies have been edited by Penny Petrone (1988) and John Robert Colombo (1997). There also exist two trilingual collections of testimonies on contemporary life in the Arctic, compiled, respectively, by Jusipi Padlayat (1974) and by Rhoda Innuksuk and Susan Cowan (1978).

McGrath (1984) concludes that despite their small number, books published in Inuktitut, including the Bible, have greatly influenced northern authors. The written word thus enjoys the same respect as the spoken word. For this reason, it would be important to transcribe in Inuktitut syllabics, and put at the disposal of Inuit readers, traditional oral literary texts already collected and published in English or French. This would probably improve the performance of young writers.[64] According to McGrath, the new written literature is inferior to the old oral one, but it nevertheless plays an important social role as an outlet for the traumas and frustrations generated by contact with Europeans.

Despite its embryonic state, Inuit literature in Canada attracts many young and not-so-young individuals. Several arctic communities host a literary circle where would-be authors can exercise and improve their talents. A government program enables northern and southern writers to meet and discuss their art,[65] and in Nunavut an annual Language Week includes a writing competition in Inuktitut for young authors. There is thus some chance that a genuine Canadian Inuit literary tradition will be established and developed in the future, although it risks being mostly in English rather than in Inuktitut.

Such a tradition would concern chiefly the eastern Arctic. In western Canada, as in Alaska, general bilingualism and the decline of the aboriginal language occurred before any identity revival could lead to the emergence of a native literary tradition. With the notable exception of Nuligak, on the Mackenzie coast, the few Inuvialuit or Alaskan individuals who published autobiographies or collections of tales for the general public did so in English (e.g., Brown 1987; Bodfish 1991; Oman 1995). The first and only novel to appear in an Alaskan Eskaleut language, *Elnguq* (the name of its main character, a young girl), was written in Central Yup'ik by Anna Jacobson (1990), a native teacher. If academic and religious booklets are ignored,[66] the only full-length book in Inupiaq is a bilingual (English-Bering Strait dialect) anthology of tales, collectively edited by a non-native linguist and a team of King Island residents (Kaplan 1988).[67] Beyond that, it is in the local and regional media that Alaskan Inuit and Yupiit seek to express their ideas, and they do this primarily in English. Eskaleut texts do appear from time to time, however, as evidenced by the existence of a published anthology of Alaskan literature in the native languages (Fienup-Riordan and Kaplan 2008).[68]

The Media

The oldest Inuit periodical is the national Greenlandic newspaper *Atuagagdliutit*, published out of Nuuk since 1861. This bilingual weekly (in 1952, it absorbed the Danish-speaking *Grønlandsposten*) provides its readers with a mix of national and international news, leading social and political articles, literary texts, and varied chronicles, all this being liberally interspersed with photos and illustrations. The quality of *Atuagagdliutit* is equal or even superior to that of similar newspapers published elsewhere in the world. The journal now coexists with a score of other periodicals, including *Sermitsiaq*, Nuuk's own weekly paper.[69]

In Canada the first periodical in an Inuit dialect was published out of Nain, Nunatsiavut (Labrador), by the Moravian missionaries.

Titled *Aglait illunainortut*, it appeared once a year between 1902 and 1922. After a hiatus of five decades, it was revived in 1972 by a team of young aboriginal journalists as a weekly bilingual newspaper called *Kinatuinamot illengajuk*.

Outside Nunatsiavut, no Inuit written media were published before the 1940s and 1950s, when the churches and, later on, the Canadian government decided that the northern residents should receive information in their own language. The federal Department of Northern Affairs issued an irregular *Eskimo Bulletin* between 1953 and 1956. It changed its format and title in 1959 to become *Inuktitut*, a magazine published four times a year in Baffin Inuktitut (syllabics), Nunatsiavut Inuktitut, Inuinnaqtun, English, and French. Dealing with Inuit history, language, culture, and contemporary achievements, and abundantly illustrated, this periodical was later ceded to Inuit Tapiriit Kanatami, the national Inuit association.

From the 1960s on, various community newspapers began to appear. Most of them were short-lived, but they fulfilled the major function of enabling Inuit to voice concerns that they would never have dared to mention directly to Euro-Canadians. These periodicals also encouraged people to tell about their own special interests: dogs, traditional life, and so on (McGrath 1986).[70] The most important, by far, of these community papers is Iqaluit's weekly and bilingual (Inuktitut-English) *Nunatsiaq News*, published since 1972 (initially under the title *Inukshuk*). With an online version (www.nunatsiaq.com), it has now become *the* regional newspaper for Nunavut and Nunavik.

A new generation of periodicals started to appear during the 1970s: the magazines and newsletters of national and regional Inuit associations. Their objective was to inform the public about the associations' activities and about topics deemed important by aboriginal leaders. Trilingual (Inuktitut-English-French) in Quebec and bilingual elsewhere, many of these journals have since disappeared, to be occasionally replaced by new titles. In 2007 forty-two periodicals with Inuit content were published in Canada,[71] an encouraging number, although only sixteen of them had some Inuktitut or Inuktun text besides English or French (Rankin 2008). The situation is worse in Alaska, where it is extremely infrequent that aboriginal languages make their way into written media.[72]

Journals and newspapers now have to compete with radio, television, and the Internet (see Perrot 1986; Christensen 2003; Roth

2005). In Greenland the national radio network, Kalaallit Nunaata Radioa, was established as early as 1926, but it was only in 1955 that it started offering good-quality broadcasting throughout the country. The national radio is an autonomous organization managed by a committee of sixty members, most of them Greenlanders. Its programming is almost equally divided between culture and information, and it uses Kalaallisut in a proportion of some 80%. This is not the case with television, where programs in the local language never exceed a few hours per week.[73]

In Canada the Canadian Broadcasting Corporation's (CBC) northern radio service began broadcasting throughout the Arctic in 1960. Most programs were in English, but a daily period of 45 to 60 minutes was set aside for Inuktitut. It included the news, music, interviews with elders, and a program during which letters sent by Inuit patients hospitalized in the south and addressed to their northern relatives were read on the air.

This was far from being sufficient. In 1972 a mere 17% of the northern service's programming was in Inuktitut. The Inuit wished to give more visibility to their language. New technology put into place in the early 1970s, when communication satellites were launched, gave them the opportunity to increase their presence on the radio scene (Valaskakis 1983b). A CBC plan called Accelerated Access, complemented by territorial and provincial schemes, allowed all northern communities to establish local FM radio stations that could be fed from three sources: (1) CBC's northern service (with three daily hours in Inuktitut); (2) regional broadcasts produced in Iqaluit and Salluit (chiefly in Inuktitut) or Inuvik (in Inuktun, Dene, and English); and (3) local production (almost entirely in Inuktitut). Most Inuit villages availed themselves of this plan, and by the late 1970s they were operating their own radio stations.

Initially limited to five hours a day, local radio production may now last as long as wanted. Most radio stations have become genuine community organizations, where everybody is welcome to express his or her views on the air. It often happens that a program is interrupted to broadcast local information (the arrival of an airplane, for instance) or to ask a child (supposing he or she is listening) to come back home for lunch. Community bingos are organized and voluntary taxes levied to fund the village radio, which is generally managed by the municipality. Since the programs, almost entirely in Inuktitut, are listened to by nearly all of the population, radio contributes enormously to reinforcing local identity (McComber 2001).[74]

This is not always the case with television. Available in some villages since 1972 (via the CBC's northern service), the year when the first communication satellite became operational, it offered less than one hour a week of broadcasting in Inuktitut for a decade. Several communities (including all villages in Nunavik) refused at first to receive the TV signal, fearing that this new medium would weaken their language and culture. As time elapsed, however, municipal councils changed their minds, and television became gradually available everywhere in the Arctic. In 1984 all Canadian Inuit settlements had access to the TV signal. The widening of broadcasting regulations at the end of the 1980s allowed villages to receive as many channels as they wanted. Nowadays, most Inuit homes have access to the same sixty or seventy channels available on satellite television anywhere else in Canada.

Before 1992 the only station to broadcast regularly in Inuktitut was that of the CBC's northern service. The aboriginal content of its programming had steadily increased, to reach its present level of 60 to 90 minutes a day. In January 1992 a public educational channel, Northern Canada Television (TVNC) started broadcasting in the Arctic. Its programs originated from the Northwest Territories, Yukon, and the northern part of the provinces. After a year of operation, TVNC was broadcasting from 2 to 6 hours a day in Inuktitut. In the early 2000s a new aboriginal channel, Aboriginal Peoples Television Network (APTN), also began offering a few hours a week of Inuktitut and Inuktun programming.

Inuit programs are principally produced by Taqramiut Nipingat Inc. (established in Nunavik in 1975), the Inuit Broadcasting Corporation (IBC; founded in 1983), the Inuvialuit Communication Society (in Inuvik), Labradormiut (in Nunatsiavut), and a few private concerns like Igloolik Isuma (in Igloolik, Nunavut). This production includes news reporting, interviews, sports events, cultural programs, and a few features for children. A new noticeable development, which started around the year 2000, is the establishment in some villages of community television stations, which broadcast locally produced programs, usually in Inuktitut.

In spite of its significant aboriginal content, however, Canadian Arctic television is still mostly in English. During its first few years, this medium strongly influenced the population. Gail Valaskakis (1983a) quotes a CBC survey showing that in 1979 in Kivalliq, nine out of ten households owned a television set and watched it for a daily average of three and a half hours. Another survey, completed in Nunavik in 1984 (Anonymous 1984), showed that 98% of the respondents watched television. But as time elapsed, the initial craze for this medium diminished progressively.[75] In 1974, 85% of a sample of Iqaluit students listed television as their principal leisure time activity, but by 1980 it had become the main hobby of only 45% of them (Coldevin and Wilson 1983).

In some Inuit households, the TV set is on all day long but with the sound off for most of the time. In the long run, however, the all-pervading presence of predominantly anglophone and culturally alien programming can have negative effects on Inuit language and identity, especially among young people. For example, Gary Coldevin and Thomas Wilson (1983) noticed that the favourite programs of Inuit students in Iqaluit were *Police Story*, *Happy Days*, and *Hockey Night in Canada* and that they did not mention any Inuktitut broadcast among their preferences. The 1984 Nunavik survey showed that interest in Inuit production was directly linked to the age of the audience and that it was at a minimum among the youngest part of the population.

The anthropologist Nelson Graburn asserts that the omnipresence of English on television can reinforce English at the expense of Inuktitut (Graburn 1982, 13–14):

> Even in the typical Inuit household where family conversation – at least that including the adults – is still carried on in Inuktitut, the TV set is the perfect teaching machine for pre-adapting infants to the use of English and for reinforcing the English that the children all learn in school ... It is remarkable to see infants and preschoolers who hardly speak Inuktitut yet or who are wholly addressed in Inuktitut by their parents, picking up English, with its familiar media phrases and accents, and bandying them about as well as any teenager in Peoria. Thus they are developing English-as-a-first-language, with none of the hesitancy of accent of those who have learned it in school or later.

Electronic media thus play an ambivalent part in the Canadian Arctic, although research on their current impact is clearly needed. Whereas community radio and, increasingly, community television contribute, thanks to their language and content, to enhancing aboriginal identity, such is not the case with mainstream television, which, by contrast, could constitute the perfect instrument for destroying Inuit culture, values, and language. And this says nothing about the Internet, whose meagre Inuit content cannot compete with the rest of the worldwide web[76] and where chat groups and e-mailing are conducted in English or, at best, in a mix of truncated Inuktitut and basic English (Pasch 2008).

The problem is worse in Alaska, where only one television station broadcasts from time to time in an Eskaleut language (Kaplan 1990). This station is Bethel's KYUK, which produces newscasts and cultural videos in Yup'ik. KYUK also operates a radio station whose language is partially Yup'ik. The Barrow and Kotzebue radio stations use some Iñupiaq, while in Nome native language broadcasts are few and apart. More than in Canada, the all-pervading presence of English-speaking television is detrimental to the survival of aboriginal language and culture.

CONCLUSION

Literacy, formal education, literature, and the media are social phenomena, produced by a society whose interests they reflect and help to preserve. In Greenland, as in Canada and Alaska, it was in the interest of European colonizers to preserve the language and culture of the Inuit – so that they could continue to produce the goods needed by Danish, British, and Russian traders – while teaching them to read the Scriptures in order to make good, obedient Christians out of them. In Alaska the economic development that followed the outset of American rule in 1867 soon made aboriginal cultural identity appear obsolete, thus justifying the inception of a fully anglophone education system. This also occurred later on in the western Canadian Arctic.

In eastern Canada and Greenland this insertion of the Inuit into national society occurred only after the end of the Second World War, once it was realized that the arctic regions had a tremendous strategic and economic potential. This is when the Canadian government established a complete system of public services in the North, including monolingual English schools, while Denmark made a province out of its Greenlandic colony and tried to impose Danish in place of Kalaallisut. This may have worked for a time, but at the end of the 1960s, when Greenlandic and Canadian Inuit had learned enough about mainstream society to know how it should be handled, they started organizing themselves to fight for their identity. This included the right to have their language respected in the school system, the media, and the community in general.

Alaskans reacted the same way, and by 1980 bilingual education in Canada and Alaska as well as full use of Kalaallisut in Greenlandic schools had become the rule. Inuit had gained a high enough degree of political visibility[77] that their social and cultural interests could no longer continue to be bypassed. It remains to be seen, however, whether the often deleterious influence of European-dominated formal education and media can be reversed, as far as language is concerned. For this reason, the next chapter discusses linguistic contact.

8

Language Contact and Bilingualism

For many centuries the Inuit language functioned in a kind of linguistic vacuum. The vast majority of its speakers did not have any contact with speakers of other tongues. Only those groups living at the northern edge of the boreal forest had sporadic encounters with aboriginal people speaking languages of the Athapaskan (Dene) or Algonkian families.[1] But mistrust between First Nations and Inuit was such that contacts were momentary at best.[2]

The situation completely changed with the arrival of Europeans, who progressively imposed their languages on local populations. Nowadays the North has become a multilingual area where, besides aboriginal languages, English, Danish, Russian, and French are in daily use. Thousands of Inuit, Yupiit, and Unangan have even given up the use of their native tongue in favour of an exogenous language. It is thus important to understand what is going on, which is shown in this chapter through a description of the principal modalities of linguistic contact and Inuit bilingualism.

LANGUAGE CONTACT

With Other Aboriginal Languages

Contacts – very limited as it seems – between the Inuit language and other North American aboriginal forms of speech have left few traces. As mentioned in chapter 6, fewer than a half-dozen Amerindian words have been borrowed by Inuit or Yupik. And these often consist of recent loans, like the two Nunavik terms borrowed from Innu (Montagnais): *pakaakuani* ("chicken"; from *pakâkwan*) and *kuukusi* ("pig"; from *kûkus*). Conversely, no American Indian languages have been influenced by Eskaleut, neither in their grammatical structure nor in their lexicon.

In Russian Chukotka, Chukchi and Central Siberian Yupik have exchanged a higher number of lexemes and morphemes as a consequence of a cohabitation of several centuries, or even a few millennia, between the two languages. But both forms of speech remain completely distinct from each other and totally unintelligible to monolinguals.

Bilingualism in another aboriginal language does not seem to have been common among Inuit and Yupiit.[3] Communication with Amerindians was instead facilitated by sign language or by a limited vocabulary, probably made out of elements borrowed from the two languages present. Some individuals, however, could be considered genuine bilinguals. In the Kuujjuaraapik area of Nunavik (on southeastern Hudson Bay), a few elders still remember Cree, a language learned during their youth when they were living among the James Bay First Nation people. In Chisasibi, Quebec's largest Cree village, there exists a small community of Inuit or part-Inuit residents, most of whom are fluent in the majority Amerindian language. The oldest among them also speak Inuktitut, but younger individuals know only Cree and/or English.

On the opposite side of Nunavik, Naskapi trappers and hunters who traded in Kuujjuaq until 1955 often spoke Inuktitut, and a few elders now living in Kawawachikamach (near Schefferville, Quebec) may still understand this language. It thus seems that the dominant speech form in a given area was that of the original residents of the land. On James Bay, in First Nation territory, Inuit spoke – or still speak – Cree, while in Kuujjuaq, an Inuit area, the Naskapi had learned Inuktitut.

Hugh Beach (1986, 64–5) mentions the existence of language contacts between Inuit and immigrant Saami reindeer herders on Alaska's Seward Peninsula at the end of the nineteenth century.[4] These Saami learned Inupiaq, while some Inuit adopted Saami rather than English as their second language. In herding stations, a mix of Inupiaq, Saami, and English was spoken.

Within the Eskaleut language area, contacts were – and remain – frequent between Inuit and Yupiit speakers as well as among users of various Inuit dialects. Communication does not usually entail any major problem. More difficult between Inuit and Yupiit, it occurs almost instantly among individuals speaking dialects of the Inuit language.[5] In all cases, it is visitors or residents from outside the area who adapt their language to that of their hosts.

When people from different dialectal areas settle in a hitherto uninhabited or sparsely settled region, adults usually preserve their original dialect, but their children often speak a mixed language that includes elements from all speech forms present. In Resolute Bay, for instance, in the Canadian Far North, descendants of Inuit settlers originally from Pond Inlet (North Baffin) and Inukjuak (Nunavik), who had moved there at the beginning of the 1950s, were in 1975 using a language whose phonology and morphology were those of the Nunavik Itivimiut subdialect (absence of the phoneme *&*, gemination of velČ clusters, possessive allatives on the *-nnuuvunga* model, etc.) but whose vocabulary was essentially North Baffin (Dorais 1976c).

In Greenland

Whereas contacts with other aboriginal languages did not have much impact in the North American Arctic, the situation was different with respect to European speech forms (see Van der Voort 1996). The very first encounters between Inuit and Europeans occurred in Greenland, where, at the end of the twelfth or early in the thirteenth century, the Scandinavian settlers entered into contact with local Neo-Eskimo Thule populations.[6] Nothing is known linguistically about these encounters, even if Greenlandic legends mention conversations between Inuit and Vikings (Kleivan 1984). The only linguistic testimonies from this period are a few possibly Old Norse terms preserved in Kalaallisut: *Kalaaliq*, "Greenlander" (from *Skrælling*); *sava*, "sheep"; *kuanniq*, "angelica" (a plant; from Scandinavian *kvan*); and *niisa*, "porpoise." Stories also tell the names (adapted to Inuit phonetics) of a few Viking settlers (e.g., Unngurtuq and Qasapi).

It was not before the eighteenth century, with the return of Europeans (Danes) to Greenland in 1721, that Kalaallisut entered into permanent contact with a non-Inuit language. For two centuries Danish played a relatively secondary part. Missionaries had to preach in Greenlandic (the first baptism was administered in 1724), and this language became pre-eminent in religious matters, a position it has maintained up to now (Kleivan 1979). Since education was in the hands of missionaries, Greenlandic schools naturally adopted Kalaallisut[7] as their teaching medium because their goal was to train aboriginal clergymen (who would preach in Greenlandic) and to allow the general population direct access to the Holy Scriptures translated into Kalaallisut, thanks to literacy.

It seems that the civil administration adopted the same attitude as missionaries, as far as language was concerned. Because the colonial administrators favoured total isolationism, to protect the Danish trade monopoly in Greenland,[8] they decided that the aboriginal way of life and language should be preserved. As seen in the preceding chapter, it was only in 1925 that schools were required to teach some Danish, and even then, there were not enough qualified personnel to enforce this requirement. The only ones to learn the colonial language were teachers-in-training at Nuuk's Ilinniarfissuaq (Kleivan 1970).[9]

The situation really started to change after Greenland became a province of Denmark in 1953.[10] Economic and social development attracted many Danish workers, who, in contrast with the missionaries, traders, and administrators who had preceded them, did not speak Kalaallisut and had no intention to learn it. It was then felt that Greenland's aboriginal population should become bilingual in order to communicate with newcomers and to participate as fully as possible in the modernization of the country (Kleivan 1970). At school Danish became compulsory from grade 1, and it was preferred over Kalaallisut as a teaching medium. It also gained predominance in economic and administrative matters. This alienating situation, which reflected the social inferiority of Greenlanders in their own country,[11] encouraged some aboriginal leaders to ask for political autonomy and the rehabilitation of their national language and culture. These claims were increasingly seen as justified in both Greenland and Denmark, and they finally entailed the advent of Home Rule in 1979.

The language situation then changed drastically. Kalaallisut became Greenland's first language once again, in education as well as in public and business administration. Nowadays, Danish still plays an important part on the island (15% to 20% of the country's residents were born in Denmark or have two Danish parents), but everyone agrees on recognizing the supremacy of Kalaallisut. For example, it is considered normal for children of Danish mother tongue to be taught elementary Greenlandic at school or for the aboriginal language to be given the first place in all circumstances. Some even question the need to learn Danish, maintaining that bilingualism in Kalaallisut and English would be much more useful (see Gad 2009).

In Canada

In Canada, English is the principal language with which Inuit have entered into contact, but it is not the only one. During the seventeenth and eighteenth centuries, in the vicinity of Belle-Isle Strait, the Labrador Inuit maintained more or less regular relations with Basque, Breton, and French fishermen, whalers, and traders. To communicate among themselves, these people used a trade pidgin made out of Inuit, French, Innu, and Basque elements.[12] In 1764 the Moravian missionary Jens Haven was quite surprised when the very first Inuit he met on Belle-Isle Strait, whom he was addressing in their own language (previously learned in Greenland), answered him "in broken French" (Cranz 1820, 290).

The linguist Peter Bakker has published several studies on this and other arctic pidgins (Bakker 1989, 1991, 1996). According to him, these trade languages did not comprise more than a few dozen words each. Here are some terms he has collected from eighteenth-century French archival sources:

ahé	"hello!" (Inuktitut *ai*, a common form of salutation)
memek	"to drink" (Inuktitut *imiq*, "drinking water")
camara	"friend" (French *camarade*, "mate, comrade")
troquo	"let's barter" (French *troquons!* "let us barter")
balena	"whale" (French *baleine* or Basque *balea*, "whale")
kutta	"knife" (French *couteau*, "knife")
monkoumek	"knife" (Innu *muhkumân*, "knife")
charraco	"war" (Basque *txarra*, "bad")
makagoua	"peace" (Basque *bekagoa*, "peaceful")

A manuscript dated from 1743[13] relates an encounter that had occurred in Labrador the preceding year between a French ship captain, Master Le Cour, and a group of Inuit led by a man named Amargo (probably Amaruq, "The Wolf"). This encounter had been the occasion of a short dialogue (cited in, among other sources, Dorais 1990a, 140; Bakker 1991), which the manuscript relates as follows:

Amargo:	*Bons camaras, tous camaras* ("Good friends, all friends")
Le Cour:	[says nothing]
Amargo:	*Capitaine Kellanoré* ("Captain, but who is he?")[14]
Le Cour:	[does not understand] *Kellanoré, Kellanoré* (« But who is he? »)
Amargo:	[hitting his chest] *Capitaine Amargo* (« Captain Amargo »)
Le Cour:	[who understands at last] *Capitaine Le Cour* (« Captain Le Cour »)
Amargo:	*Capitaine Le Cour, Capitaine Le Cour* (« Captain Le Cour »)
	Capitaine Amargo, Capitaine Le Cour, bons camaras, tous camaras
	(« Captain Amargo, Captain Le Cour, good friends, all friends »)

This pidgin seems to have disappeared toward the end of the eighteenth or the beginning of the nineteenth century, when the French were replaced by Moravian missionaries from Germany and by fishermen and traders from the British Isles and Newfoundland. Other trade languages, based on Inuit and English, appeared later on in the Hudson Strait and Hudson Bay areas,[15] as well as in the Mackenzie region and on Herschel Island,[16] but their life seems to have been much shorter than that of the Belle-Isle Strait pidgin.

In northern Labrador (Nunatsiavut), the German-speaking Moravian missionaries established their first mission at Nain in 1771, and they quickly learned the aboriginal language – or already spoke it when, like Jens Haven, they had previously lived in Greenland. Inuktitut thus served from the start as the principal or unique means of communication in church, at school, and even at the trading post (the Moravians had been granted a trade monopoly that endured until 1925). As seen in chapter 6, German had some limited influence on the lexicon, which borrowed a few dozen words from this language.

From the nineteenth century on, Anglo-Saxon trappers and fishers (called "Settlers" in Nunatsiavut and "Liveyeres" in southern Labrador) came to Labrador in increasing numbers, settling in Innu or Inuit territory. They adapted well to the local environment, adopting aboriginal hunting, trapping, and fishing techniques, wedding indigenous women, and in some cases, even learning the language of the native inhabitants. In Nunatsiavut, Inuit and Settlers exchanged words,[17] but each group preserved its own mother tongue.

As late as the early 1960s, bilingualism was still infrequent in Nunatsiavut. In the village of Makkovik, for instance, only 8 of 159 Settlers were bilingual (English-Inuktitut) in 1962–63 (Ben-Dor 1966). Among Inuit residents, the schoolchildren (six to fifteen years of age) spoke some English, but younger and older people were usually monolingual in the aboriginal language. Of 82 Inuit aged sixteen and over, only 14 (13 of them under age twenty-six) were bilingual. The situation changed completely over the following years. English monolingual education (in 1949 the Moravian schools had been replaced with provincial teaching institutions), the prestige of the majority language,[18] and, probably too, the longstanding presence of anglophone Settlers contributed to a marked loss of Inuktitut fluency among the new generation. As a result, in 1991 only 25% of the Nunatsiavut Inuit were still able to speak their aboriginal language.

In Nunavik, as well as in the Baffin and Kivalliq regions of Nunavut, language contact with Europeans was less brutal than it had been in Labrador. Very few non-native individuals settled permanently in these areas, and it was only during the 1950s that schools were established in a systematic way. As late as 1970, Inuit adults did not, as a rule, speak any English – except for some bilinguals living in larger communities such as Frobisher Bay (Iqaluit) and Fort Chimo (Kuujjuaq) – and Euro-Canadians who lived in the North either learned Inuktitut or used a pidgin version of that language for communicating with Inuit over twenty-five to thirty years of age.[19] It was only at the end of the 1970s that bilingualism became generalized, but this did not entail a rapid diminution in the number of individuals for whom Inuktitut was a first language, as had been the case in Nunatsiavut.

By contrast, in the western Arctic (the Mackenzie area and, in a lesser way, the Kitikmeot region of Nunavut), Inuktun sustained for over a century the repeated attacks of English, introduced by whalers, traders, and trappers who visited the area on a regular basis or even settled there for good. The establishment of boarding schools in 1929 compounded the problem because it was strictly forbidden to use any aboriginal language on the premises. Inuit were thus left with no choice. They had to speak English in order not to be excluded from the area's economic and social development (Lowe 1984c). In such a context, bilingualism made rapid progress (Dorais 1989, 201):

> The first [western Arctic] Inuit to be introduced to English, between 1850 and 1920, were local men hired by the white fur traders, whaling captains, missionaries and policemen. At the beginning of the present [i.e., twentieth] century, only these native servants were somewhat bilingual, the majority of the population still remaining Inuvialuit unilinguals. But with the tremendous growth of trapping after World War I, the white authorities (the internal colonial power, one might say) deemed it advisable to create an administrative and institutional superstructure in the area to regulate its development. Missionary hospitals and English-speaking schools were thus opened, and the presence of the police was reinforced. Linguistically speaking, this entailed a diglossic situation where, first, the biggest communities (Aklavik and Tuktoyaktuk, the "towns") and, then, the smaller settlements (such as Paulatuk) and trapping camps (the "country") gradually became bilingual, with less and less importance accorded the native tongue. After a generation, by 1950, all Inuit parents were exclusively teaching English to their children.

At present, the only Inuvialuit to speak Inuktun with some fluency are over sixty to seventy years of age. Some individuals in their fifties and sixties may understand it, but they no longer speak it, and younger people do not have any knowledge of the aboriginal language.

In Alaska

The situation is similar throughout most of Alaska. Among Inupiat the only fluent speakers are over forty years of age, with few exceptions, while the number of Alutiit and Unangan who still know their language does not exceed 200 individuals for each group (among 3,500 Alutiit and 2,500 Unangan). The south-western Alaskan Yupiit and Saint Lawrence Island Yupiget, long isolated from the rest of Alaska, have fared better, although among Yupiit the proportion of speakers amounted to only 41% at the turn of the twenty-first century, compared with 68% in 1990 and 72% in 1980.[20] As in the western Canadian Arctic, the longstanding presence of Euro-American residents (whalers, trappers, traders, and gold-diggers) and the early establishment of anglophone schools led to the demise of the vernacular forms of speech.

During the Russian period, however, colonizers had maintained a relatively favourable attitude toward local languages, finding they played a useful role. Orthodox missionaries had translated the Scriptures into Unangax, Alutiiq, and, perhaps, Yup'ik, and they had trained aboriginal priests in their own language (Krauss 1979).

The situation changed drastically in 1888, some twenty years after the purchase of Alaska by the United States government, when, as mentioned in the preceding chapter, the Presbyterian minister Sheldon Jackson took charge of education for the whole territory. Firmly convinced that aboriginal languages were detrimental to the spiritual and material development of their speakers, Jackson forbade their teaching in school. This interdiction had limited effects at first, but its enforcement over time meant that the last institution still making use of a native language (an Unangan school) would close its doors in 1912 (Krauss 1979).

Schools multiplied rapidly, a fact that improved literacy, but this came at the expense of aboriginal languages, which were progressively abandoned by younger people. In the meanwhile, the development of an economy based on trapping, commercial fisheries, reindeer herding, and mines brought thousands of non-natives to Alaska. During the Nome gold rush of 1900, for instance, 30,000 foreigners entered Inuit territory within a few weeks. It is not surprising, then, that at the beginning of the 1970s, when the aboriginal languages were reintroduced into classrooms after eighty-four years of interdiction and sixty of effective absence, few people were still able to speak them.

In the long run, the effects of contact with European languages have been disastrous for many Inuit dialects. There is no reason, however, to be totally pessimistic. On the one hand, interaction between aboriginal and European speech forms sometimes led to the emergence of new types of languages: long- or short-lived trade pidgins or, more recently, dialects whose structure and morphology are vernacular but whose lexicon borrows largely from the language of contact, thus allowing them to adapt easily to modernity (for an Innu example of this process, see Drapeau 1993). On the other hand, nothing proves that aboriginal culture and identity cannot express themselves in a language other than their own (Kwachka 1992a). This is why Inuit bilingualism will now be examined.

BILINGUALISM

Speaking a Second Language

It should be mentioned at the onset that the vast majority of present-day Inuit are bilingual. For sure, a vast number of elders and young children do not speak a second language – not yet at least – but on the whole, the situation of northern aboriginal populations is similar to that of most other linguistic minorities: to perform adequately in the world where they live, they must know the predominant language of their country of residence.

Even in Greenland, where Kalaallisut is the official language, everyone learns Danish in elementary school. High school students are also introduced to English, German (or French), and in some cases, Latin. To be admitted to the University of Greenland one must read and understand English fluently. For the vast majority of Greenlanders, however, Kalaallisut remains the first language they learn, and for want of practising Danish, many individuals lose part of their fluency in this language not long after having left school,[21] even though statistics show that between 1984 and 2003 the proportion of speakers of Kalaallisut as a first language who also had a good knowledge of Danish rose from 20% to 40% of the population (Andersen 2001, 4; Birger Poppel, personal communication, 15 March 2008). Another form of bilingualism concerns the residents of Thule and the east coast, whose mother tongue differs from official Kalaallisut. These people use their home dialect to express their daily needs, but at school, for administrative purposes, on the radio, and in all written media, only West Greenlandic is allowed. As a consequence, they must have at least a passive knowledge of this language to subsist in present-day Greenland.[22]

The situation is different in Canada, where English – and sometimes French too – is used by most Inuit on a daily basis, some people having even completely lost their ancestral language. According to the Canadian census of 2006, out of a total of 36,260 individuals able to hold a conversation in Inuktitut or Inuktun,[23] 31,550 also knew English and/or another language (usually French). The proportion of bilingual or trilingual speakers thus reached 87%, with only 13% being aboriginal-language monolinguals (4,710 individuals). The percentage of bilinguals was much higher among those under fifty-five years of age but roughly equal for both genders.[24]

Bilingualism had increased a lot since 1991, when 72.5% of Inuit speakers were bilingual (Dorais 1996a, 217), and much more so since 1981, when the proportion of bilinguals was only 53% (Robitaille and Choinière 1984, 31).

In Alaska, where at the turn of the twenty-first century 86% of all Inupiat (13,550 of 15,700) had English as their mother tongue, it goes without saying that bilingualism is universal. In the late 1980s the youngest users of Inupiaq were aged between thirty and fifty, except in the villages of Wainwright and Kobuk, where a few Inupiaq speakers in their twenties could still be found (Kaplan 1990). This means that by 2005 no Inupiaq under thirty-five could speak the language fluently.[25]

How Bilingualism Works

In daily life, bilingualism often leads to unequal knowledge and usage of the languages spoken. In an article published in 1988 (Dorais 1988d), I discuss the results of summary research[26] comparing the language situation in Igloolik, Canada (data collected in 1978), and Ammassalik, on the east coast of Greenland (data from 1980). The study shows that knowledge of the mother tongue was stronger in Ammassalik, where 21 of 22 respondents said they spoke East Greenlandic "very well," than in Igloolik, where 3 of 14 individuals spoke Inuktitut "quite well" (the balance speaking it "very well"). Knowledge of a European second language was more developed in Igloolik, where 8 respondents said they knew English "a little" (3 cases), "quite well" (4 cases), or "very well" (1 case), than in Ammassalik, where most people stated they spoke Danish "a little" (10 cases) or "not at all" (10 cases).

In Ammassalik the most important second language was West Greenlandic, which 12 individuals knew "a little," 4 "quite well," and 3 "very well." This language had been learned at school (16 of 19 cases), as was the situation with English in Igloolik (7 of 9 cases). As for Danish, the Ammassalik respondents had learned it at work (3 of 12 cases), when living in Denmark (3 cases), or through contacts with Danes (4 cases) rather than at school (2 cases only). The language usually heard in the household reflected the status of linguistic knowledge in the respective communities. In Ammassalik everyone – except for a respondent married to a Dane – made exclusive use of East Greenlandic at home, while in Igloolik a neat cleavage was to be observed between respondents aged thirty and over (7 cases), who stated they spoke only Inuktitut at home, and those under thirty, who used English "sometimes" (5 cases) or "often" (2 cases).

More extensive research, conducted in 1985 in five villages of the eastern Canadian Arctic, aimed at measuring the linguistic behaviour of a sample of 275 students of both genders, aged between nine and eighteen (Dorais and Collis 1987; Dorais 1989).[27] The study shows that among nine-year-old schoolchildren, the extent of available Inuktitut vocabulary was much larger than that of the pupils' English (or French in some Nunavik classes) lexicon. At twelve years old, however, after three or four years of second-language education, available English words had become more numerous than Inuit terms. Moreover, knowledge of the aboriginal language did not stop decreasing as children grew older. Bilingualism was thus of a subtractive[28] nature: learning a second language clearly provoked a marked weakening of the mother tongue.

This situation was reflected in language behaviour. In the three Baffin villages (Iqaluit, Igloolik, and Kimmirut), the use of Inuktitut varied markedly depending on whom respondents were speaking to. In Iqaluit, for instance, 73% of students addressed their parents in Inuktitut, but only 54% did likewise with their siblings, and only 27% did so with their friends. In the smaller and ethnically homogeneous communities of Igloolik and Lake Harbour, more than 80% of respondents usually addressed their parents in Inuktitut, but this was the case with only 77% (Igloolik) and 56% (Kimmirut) of them when addressing their siblings and with 61% (Igloolik) and 31% (Kimmirut) when speaking to friends. In the two Nunavik villages (Puvirnituq and Ivujivik), the use of Inuktitut by the young was much stronger, reaching 92% with parents and 88% with siblings and friends.

A long-term research project conducted in the same Baffin communities of Iqaluit, Igloolik, and Kimmirut from 1994 to 1997, and continued in Iqaluit[29] between 1998 and 2001, aimed at measuring the progression of bilingualism over the years and understanding the cultural and social role of both languages present, as well as of French in Iqaluit[30] (Dorais and Sammons 2000, 2002).[31] The study showed that subtractive bilingualism in favour of English had not stopped increasing since the 1990s, especially among younger people, but that it was now counteracted by a strong sentiment of identity linked to the preservation and use of Inuktitut. This led to the following conclusions (Dorais and Sammons 2002, 121–2):

1. The Baffin region [of Nunavut] should be considered a bilingual speech community (rather than a chiefly aboriginal one), because both English and Inuktitut are in constant use among a majority of Inuit. This contrasts with areas like Greenland, where the aboriginal language predominates in most spheres of activity and constitutes the almost exclusive means of communication among local people.
2. In spite of pervasive bilingualism, Inuktitut generally remains the first language spoken to young Inuit children (this is why more Inuktitut is heard in households headed by parents under thirty years of age) as well as to elders (in whose homes much more Inuktitut is used – by all age groups – than in younger households).
3. However, English tends to be spoken to children as soon as they start becoming bilingual (*i.e.* from Grades 3–4 on), "because they understand it," in [the] informants' words. This phenomenon is more widespread in Iqaluit than it is in Igloolik or Kimmirut.
4. Inuktitut and English usage are similar for men and women, but their topics of conversation at home do differ.[32] For both genders, the most important topic is food, but, then, males prefer talking about leisure and outdoor activities (including subsistence), while females talk about running the home and dealing with children.
5. As far as age is concerned, younger individuals (except for very young children) tend to speak more English than middle-aged people and elders. Conversation topics also vary with age.
6. In a more general way, English is used for expressing what many informants call the *qallunaujaniit*, the "things from the Qallunaat [European] world," *i.e.* most activities and implements that have to do with daily life in a contemporary arctic community. English is, thus, chiefly perceived as the language of modernity and practicality. Hence its prominent usage in wage work settings.
7. Inuktitut, however, is considered very important – if not essential – for preserving Inuit identity. This is why almost all informants think it is their duty to transmit the aboriginal language to younger generations.

Subsequent research in Iqaluit (2003–06) looked at the influence that the creation of Nunavut in 1999 had – or not – on discourse practices[33] and on Inuit perceptions about the usefulness of Inuktitut in relation to English (Dorais 2006a, 2006b). There were forty respondents, whose answers can be classified into two types. "Realistic" responses tell about English and code-mixing constantly increasing in Iqaluit homes and workplaces, despite the advent of Nunavut, and about young people speaking less and less Inuktitut.[34] "Idealistic" answers, often uttered by the same respondents, express what people would like to see in the future: Inuktitut being transmitted to younger generations and continuing to thrive in the North.

This dichotomy reflects the linguistic situation of the present-day Canadian Arctic. Inuktitut has become much more visible and accepted since Inuit gained political autonomy in Nunavut, thus furthering the idealization of the aboriginal language as a powerful marker of identity. But the conditions of transmission and reproduction of that language did not change after 1999. Inuktitut instruction still stops from grade 4 on, with the result that the words and meanings that most individuals under thirty to thirty-five years of age have at their command for expressing contemporary life in a modern community are English, for the good reason that English is the language in which they were taught. This explains why, despite their wish to transmit and promote Inuktitut, and their sincere assertion that the aboriginal language is essential to Inuit identity, many speakers find it easier to express themselves in English or in a mixed code[35] when they have to speak about topics other than common feelings, basic assertions (e.g., "nice day today"), or subsistence activities. They simply do not possess the required cognitive and linguistic tools to communicate fully in Inuktitut because these were never taught to them.

This means that education is the key to stable bilingualism, which would allow Inuktitut to survive and flourish rather than decrease under the influence of English. Language specialists as well as Inuit in general are conscious that the aboriginal tongue should be taught up to grade 12. In a report submitted to the Government of Nunavut, the sociolinguist Ian Martin (2000a) notes that the principal objective of the existing education model is to make English speakers out of Inuit students in order to enable them to continue their education beyond grades 4 and 5. According to Martin, the ideological orientation of such a system is seriously flawed. In another report, Nunavut Tunngavik Inc. (2004), the corporation that administers the Nunavut Agreement, reaches similar conclusions. It states that Nunavut is the only jurisdiction within Canada where a majority of the population speak an aboriginal language. But in spite of that, there does not exist any Inuktitut curriculum covering kindergarten to grade 12. This means that no barrier protects the language against ongoing erosion.

Most findings of the Baffin research discussed above generally agree with those of other specialists who worked in Nunavut at the same time. Shelley Tulloch, for instance, in her dissertation on language attitudes among young adults in Iqaluit, Pangnirtung, and Pond Inlet (Tulloch 2004), has shown that her respondents considered Inuktitut a prerequisite for participating fully in community life. They often complained, however, about their lack of fluency in the language and about the attitude of some older individuals who addressed them in English rather than in Inuktitut.[36]

In another study, Ian Martin (2000b) found that a majority of Nunavut residents believed Inuktitut should be encouraged by all means but that despite the advent of Nunavut, the number of students who spoke it had not stopped diminishing. The linguist Shanley Allen, however, in a more recent paper (Allen 2007), questioned such alarming conclusions about the decreasing usage of Inuktitut. She interprets as incipient stable bilingualism the situation that I and Susan Sammons (2002) describe for Iqaluit, Igloolik, and Kimmirut because both languages are used inside and outside the home: "Although the use of Inuktitut as a sole language of communication declines with age, Inuktitut is not typically replaced by English as a sole language, but rather by a balanced use of both languages depending on the interlocutor and the situation" (Allen 2007, 533). Allen mentions, however, that although speakers continue using Inuktitut, they may do so with decreased fluency, maintaining conversational language proficiency but gradually losing academic (i.e., more abstract and reflexive) language ability, as was observed in Nunavik (Wright et al. 2000; Allen et al. 2006).

Research conducted in 1988 in Nunavik's largest and most ethnically diversified community, Kuujjuaq,[37] showed that Inuit respondents spoke Inuktitut as well as francophones and anglophones knew their own respective languages, and this even if the distance between verbal and written abilities was markedly wider for habitual speakers of Inuktitut than it was for francophones and anglophones (Taylor

1990, 8–9). The aboriginal language occupied a lot of space in the community, but English also played an important part. Kuujjuaq's Inuit residents assessed their knowledge of English as amounting to roughly two-thirds of their performance in Inuktitut. Their fluency in French, however, was almost non-existent. Among Inuit under forty-five years of age, performance in English was almost equivalent to ability in Inuktitut, a fact that hinted at the emergence of generalized bilingualism. According to Donald Taylor, such bilingualism was unequal because even though the use of Inuktitut was still predominant in the four principal social contexts (i.e., subsistence activities, the home, the community, and wage work), in the most valued of these contexts – work – the role of English was as important as that of the aboriginal language among those under forty-five. In the long term, Inuktitut was thus at risk of losing its position as the primary language of the community.

It has already lost this position in the Kitikmeot region of Nunavut, where a survey of language conditions undertaken in the late 1990s (Aylward et al. 1998) shows that only a minority of elementary school students spoke Inuktun: 25% of the sample possessed some fluency in the aboriginal language, while 22% had only passive knowledge, understanding Inuktun but being unable to speak it. When addressing their children, parents – who were much more fluent than their offspring – used Inuktun in a mere 18% of cases, although at home the proportion was higher (30%). This low percentage of speakers did not prevent students and their parents from stating that the aboriginal language was very important for them and that they wished it to be preserved. More recently, Jean-Michel Béchard (2006) has reached similar conclusions while conducting research in Cambridge Bay, the administrative centre of the Kitikmeot region, finding reasons to believe that the shift toward English might be stopped, but not completely reversed, if the will to preserve Inuinnaqtun is translated into concrete, efficient protective measures.

Inuktitut has also lost its predominance in Nunatsiavut, where, in the early 1990s, most individuals under thirty assessed their proficiency in the aboriginal language as average or poor, even though older people considered their own abilities to be very good or excellent (Mazurkewich 1992). Parents judged the performance of their children as poor in Inuktitut but generally good or very good in English, the language most frequently spoken by the young. In the region's main centre, Nain, the performance of Inuktitut by Settlers was equivalent to that of the Inuit, although the former spoke mostly English in all circumstances. Older Inuit used both languages among themselves, but they usually addressed their children in English. In such circumstances – which have not changed over time despite several initiatives to counteract language shift (see Andersen and Johns 2005) – Irene Mazurkewich (1992) contends that teaching Inuktitut in school is not really useful and has no measurable impact.

As seen in chapter 7, research on bilingual education in Nunavut and Nunavik shows that even though early education in Inuktitut helps with the acquisition of reading and writing skills in both the first and second languages (Stairs and Annahatak 1987), the fact that instruction in the mother tongue stops after grades 2 or 3 prevents the aboriginal language from developing completely (Taylor 1990). At the same time, because the second language is often taught inadequately, many students never learn to speak it fluently. On the basis of research conducted in Igloolik, Ronald Mackay (1986) has shown that several English teachers consider their pupils "bilingual" as soon as they are able to practise a very superficial form of bilingualism, one that often resorts to non-linguistic elements (gestures, attitudes, etc.) in order to facilitate communication. Consequently, students never accede to a full knowledge of their second language, thus being at risk of developing very limited linguistic capacities.

The necessity of a good start in one's own mother tongue has been verified in Greenland, where, according to Peter Berliner (1987), college students with an excellent elementary and high school basis in Kalaallisut learn Danish words more quickly[38] than Greenlandic terms, although they forget them more rapidly. Their rate of lexical retention is very high in Greenlandic. As a consequence, they forget what they were taught in Danish more rapidly than what they learned in Kalaallisut. This demonstrates that Inuit bilingualism can be additive indeed.

Finally, data from Alaska show that even when statistics seem to point to the quasi-total demise of the language, finer research taking local opinions into account may indicate that all is not lost. In a survey of 1,328 individuals conducted in Barrow, Alaska,[39] in 2000 (Harcharek 2001), respondents were asked about their knowledge and use of Iñupiaq. Degrees of fluency were coupled with language preferences and age, yielding the following results:

DEGREE OF FLUENCY IN IÑUPIAQ	% OF SAMPLE	MEDIAN AGE
Knowledgeable and eloquent Iñupiaq speaker	2	71
Speaks Iñupiaq fluently and prefers speaking Iñupiaq	23	47
Speaks Iñupiaq fluently but prefers another language	11	39
Speaks Iñupiaq with difficulty or with minor flaws	3	28
Speaks minimal Iñupiaq with minimal comprehension	4	23
Understands Iñupiaq very well (but cannot speak much)	4	33
Understands enough to follow most conversations	4	19
Understands simple questions and directions in Iñupiaq	32	14
Understands at least two dozen words in Iñupiaq	7	12
Understands at least five or six words in Iñupiaq	5	10
Does not understand more than a few Iñupiaq words	6	4

This table shows that in Barrow, more than one-third of the Iñupiat residents (36%) spoke their language fluently, although many of them preferred another language (i.e., English). A further 40% understood at least simple questions and directions but had problems speaking Iñupiaq. The survey thus shows that contrary to what is often thought about Alaskan Inuit being monolingual in English, three-quarters of all Barrow Iñupiat of both genders had at least a basic passive knowledge of their aboriginal language. This leaves room for some optimism. However, since the degree of active and passive proficiency in Iñupiaq is higher among older people, general knowledge of the language risks diminishing as time elapses.

New technologies, however, could perhaps help to change the situation. The Greenlandic Language Commission has started developing several sophisticated electronic tools (e.g., an orthographic corrector and a parser)[40] that can be easily adapted to other Inuit dialects. These are able to generate various kinds of user-friendly lexicons, grammars, and other linguistic productions. It is surmised that such tools will contribute to accelerating the development of the language and encouraging people to use it, even when their knowledge is minimal (Langgaard 2008).

CONCLUSION

The most urgent issue for the present-day Inuit language is whether it has much chance of resisting for some more time the daily onslaught of English and other languages present in the Arctic for one or two centuries. At first, contact with these languages was rather smooth. Each group preserved its original speech form, and communication was conducted through a pidgin made out of linguistic elements borrowed from all tongues present.

This situation changed when Europeans settled permanently in Inuit territory and, above all, when they imposed economic (the fur trade and, later on, wage work), political (state administration), and ideological (school and, in a lesser way, religious missions) institutions disrespectful of aboriginal identity. From a linguistic perspective, this tutelage of Inuit by those holding economic and political power[41] entailed a situation where Inupiaq, Inuktun, Inuktitut, and Kalaallisut became dominated by European languages. Only Greenland partly escaped the effects of this situation, thanks to the functional role played by Kalaallisut, particularly at school, and thanks also to the advent of Home Rule, which endowed the country with a quasi-national status.

In Alaska and the western Canadian Arctic, schooling (in English) and economic development provoked the generalization of bilingualism and a loss in the value attributed to the aboriginal language, and this as early as the first decades of the twentieth century. Over three or four generations, this process led to a drastic decrease in the number of speakers of Inuinnaqtun, Siglitun, Inupiaq, Unangax, and some Yupik languages.[42]

By contrast, in the eastern Arctic, because of the more recent advent of formal education and wage work, Inuktitut has been well preserved up to now. But several indications, including the presence of subtractive Inuktitut-English bilingualism, call into question the long-term survival of the aboriginal language. It is to be hoped that the current revival of Inuit identity will translate into concrete and effective measures, which will prevent the dialects of Nunavik, Baffin, and Kivalliq from knowing the same fate as their western equivalents or as Nunatsiavut Inuktitut, in rapid decline since the 1960s.

9

The Current Status of the Inuit Language

As mentioned in the preceding chapters, social and cultural change undergone by the Inuit over time had a direct effect on their language. In many areas of the North American Arctic, ever-increasing economic, political, and ideological dependence on the outside resulted in the near disappearance of the aboriginal tongue. In Alaska, the western Canadian Arctic, and northern Labrador, for instance, the combined and long-lasting presence of anglophone schools, European settlers, and a low status for indigenous cultures led to the gradual demise of Inupiaq, Inuvialuktun, Inuinnaqtun, and Nunatsiavut Inuktitut. In Greenland, by contrast, native-language education, a long period of isolation from outside influences, and general support for development of a modern but specifically Greenlandic identity have contributed to making Kalaallisut a genuine national language that is now thriving. In north-eastern Canada, Inuktitut is still spoken by a majority of the population, but it might be threatened by the overwhelming economic and social predominance of English. To reach a better understanding of this rather complex situation, the present-day demography of the Inuit language,[1] as well as its administrative and social status, will now be examined.

LANGUAGE STATISTICS

It is difficult to assess the exact number of Inuit speakers, but statistical data – those of the Canadian census, for instance – and local sources of information allow for good approximations. At the turn of the twenty-first century (i.e., in the decade extending from 1997 to 2006), the grand total of people of Inuit ancestry amounted to some 133,000 individuals, distributed as follows:

Greenland (Kalaallit)[2]	50,366 (Baunbæk 2007)
Kalaallit in Denmark	13,482 (Baunbæk 2007)
Canada (Inuit and Inuvialuit)	50,480 (Canadian census of 2006)
Alaska (Inupiat)	15,700 (Krauss 2007)
Inupiat outside Alaska	3,140 (US census of 2000)
WORLD TOTAL INUIT	133,168

To this figure should be added some 31,550 Yupiit and Yupiget, as well as 2,500 Unangan, still living in their native territory (see chapter 1), for a total of 164,718 Eskimos and 167,218 Eskimo-Aleut. Moreover, when about 13,000 individuals of Yupiit, Yupiget, and Unangan ancestry residing in the United States or Russia, outside of Alaska and Chukotka (US census of 2000; Russian census of 2002), are included, a total of 180,218 Eskimo-Aleut (170,218 Eskimos and 10,000 Unangan) is reached.[3]

Percentage of Speakers

Many of these people do not speak their ancestral language.[4] As mentioned in the conclusion to chapter 1, only 67.5% of the Eskimo-Aleut[5] (112,790 individuals) could be considered speakers at the turn of the twenty-first century. The vast majority of them (89%) used an Inuit dialect, the rate of linguistic retention among Inupiat, Inuvialuit, Inuit, and Kalaallit reaching 75.5%. But the percentage of Inuit-speaking individuals was at variance across the Arctic, with an enormous difference between Greenland, where almost everyone knew Kalaallisut, and Alaska, with a very small proportion of Inupiat speaking their ancestral language:[6]

INUIT SUBDIVISIONS	NUMBER OF SPEAKERS	% OF SPEAKERS[7]
Kalaallit (Greenland and Denmark)	61,932[8]	97
Inuit and Inuvialuit (Canada)	36,260[9]	72
Inupiat (Alaska and lower United States)	2,583[10]	14

In Canada the proportion of speakers was highly variable from one political subdivision of the country to another, as may be seen in the following table showing the percentages of individuals declaring an Inuit identity who had Inuit as their first language (2006 census data):

POLITICAL SUBDIVISIONS	INUIT IDENTITY	INUIT FIRST LANGUAGE	% OF SPEAKERS
Newfoundland and Labrador	4,715	655	14
Prince Edward Island	30	15[11]	50
Nova Scotia	325	15	5
New Brunswick	185	10	5
Quebec	10,950	9,740	89
Ontario	2,035	425	21
Manitoba	565	140	25
Saskatchewan	215	50	23
Alberta	1,610	180	11
British Columbia	795	115	14
Yukon	255	60	24
Northwest Territories	4,160	800	19
Nunavut	24,640	20,760	84
CANADA	50,480	32,965[12]	65

As could be expected, the provinces and territories with the highest number of Inuit residents are those that belong entirely or in part to what may be called *Inuit nunaat*, "the land of the Inuit," namely the traditional aboriginal areas of arctic Canada: Nunavut, Quebec (Nunavik), Newfoundland and Labrador (Nunatsiavut), and the Northwest Territories (Nunaqput).[13] A total of 44,465 Inuit live in these four political subdivisions, or 88% of all Canadian residents of Inuit ancestry. If allowance is made for Inuit from Quebec, Newfoundland, and the Northwest Territories who reside outside the portion of their province/territory lying within *Inuit nunaat*,[14] we are left with 81.5% of all Canadian Inuit (41,125) still living in their aboriginal land and with 18.5% (9,355) who have moved to more southerly cities and towns (e.g., St John's, Montreal, Ottawa, Toronto, Winnipeg, Edmonton, Vancouver, Yellowknife, and Whitehorse). Apart from Newfoundland and Quebec, provinces with an Inuit population of over 1,500 in 2006 were those (Ontario and Alberta) that combined economic prosperity with direct flights from the Arctic.[15]

The highest proportions of Inuit who have the Inuit language as their mother tongue are found in Quebec (89%) and Nunavut (84%). The percentages of speakers are much lower in Yukon[16] and in those provinces lying outside *Inuit nunaat*, a fact that points to a sharp decrease in language performance and transmission[17] among people living outside their aboriginal area. The proportions are very low too in the Northwest Territories (19%) and in Newfoundland and Labrador (14%). In both cases, this is due to the already mentioned decline of, respectively, Siglitun Inuvialuktun and Nunatsiavut Inuktitut. In Labrador statistics are also blurred by the fact that a good part (perhaps half) of the Inuit population is comprised of so-called "Settlers" of Anglo-Saxon heritage, who are beneficiaries of the Nunatsiavut Agreement[18] but whose first language has always been English. If they are left out of the total number of Labradorians identifying themselves as Inuit, the proportion of Inuktitut-mother-tongue individuals climbs to 28%.

In Newfoundland and Labrador, as elsewhere in Canada, the number of persons who declared to census-takers that they were able to hold a conversation in Inuktitut or Inuktun is slightly higher than that of mother-tongue speakers. This means that the aboriginal language is still alive, able as it is to attract people – most of them presumably of Inuit ancestry – who did not learn it during childhood but acquired it later in life.[19] Here are census figures for the four provinces and territories with areas forming part of *Inuit nunaat*, as well as for the rest of the country:

POLITICAL SUBDIVISIONS	INUIT FIRST LANGUAGE	CAN SPEAK INUIT	% FIRST LANGUAGE
Newfoundland and Labrador	655	805	81
Quebec	9,740	10,170	96
Northwest Territories	800	1,030	78
Nunavut	20,760	22,945	90
Other provinces and Yukon	1,010	1,310	77
CANADA	32,965	36,260	91

In Newfoundland and Labrador the presence of bilingual Settlers might explain why 19% of those speaking Inuktitut do not have this language as their mother tongue. In the Northwest Territories, however, where, as a rule, residents from outside never learned the aboriginal languages, it is difficult to explain why 230 individuals report speaking Inuktun despite having not acquired it during their early childhood. One possible answer is that part of them might be younger individuals who were taught the language at school and had preserved some knowledge of it at census time.[20] But errors in census data cannot be ruled out. For example, the presence in southern Canada of 300 individuals who would be able to hold a conversation in Inuktitut or Inuktun without having learned it as their first language is very difficult to explain.

The percentages of Inuit-mother-tongue individuals have decreased over the past decades but not dramatically so.[21] In 1991, 69% of all Canadians identifying themselves as Inuit had Inuktitut or Inuktun as their first language (Dorais 1996a, 62), compared with 65% in 2006. The decrease seems to have been stronger in Quebec (from 94% in 1991 to 89% in 2006) and Newfoundland and Labrador (from 25% to 14%), although in the latter case, as mentioned above, if Settlers of Anglo-Saxon origin had been pulled out of statistics (as they were in 1991), the proportion of Inuktitut-mother-tongue individuals might have reached 28% in 2006.

Mother Tongue and Home Language

One perverse effect of bilingualism is that it allows bilingual speakers to use their second language, rather than their mother tongue, as their home language (i.e., as the language most often spoken at home). In areas where a vast majority of people are fluent in the local form of speech, this form normally predominates as the home language. But this is not the case when only a minority of individuals are proficient in the vernacular, or when it cannot compete, economically or otherwise, with the second language.

In Greenland, with 97% of the locally born population fluent in some form of Kalaallisut, the usual home language is West Greenlandic, East Greenlandic, or the Thule dialect. Only a few ethnically mixed families speak Danish at home. According to Robert Petersen (1990, 305), the strength of Kalaallisut is such that when speakers of different Greenlandic dialects communicate among themselves, they very rarely resort to Danish in order to be understood.[22] Research conducted by Karen Langgaard in 2000 among gymnasium (junior college) students in Nuuk (Langgaard 2001) shows that these young people always use Greenlandic among themselves, even if courses at the gymnasium are exclusively taught in Danish. Older people, however, as well as Greenlanders from smaller communities, often complain that youngsters from Nuuk prefer Danish to Greenlandic or resort to code-mixing (Sørensen et al. 2003). An association of Danish-speaking Greenlanders (GLDK) was even established in the mid-2000s (see www.gldk.gl). But this has not prevented Kalaallisut from preserving its position as the principal home and community language all over Greenland.

By contrast, in Alaska, it is the exogenous language, English, that serves as the quasi-universal home language. Only a few Yupiit and Yupiget households still communicate routinely in the vernacular. Everywhere else, including the Inupiat areas, English is almost always heard at home, except among people aged over fifty-five or sixty.[23]

In Canada the home-language situation is more contrasted. According to the census of 2006, 25,980 individuals usually spoke Inuktitut or Inuktun at home, 25,360 of them as their only home language and 620 more in combination with English and/or French. This means that 79% of the 32,965 Inuit-mother-tongue respondents[24] (and 71.5% of all those who reported being able to hold a conversation in Inuktitut or Inuktun) spoke the aboriginal language on a daily basis. But in relation to all 50,480 Canadians identifying themselves as Inuit, the proportion of Inuit-home-language speakers reached only 51.5%. In 1991 (Dorais 1996a, 219) the corresponding percentages had been 80% (of Inuit mother tongue) and 55% (of Inuit identity). The decline had been much sharper between 1981 and 1991. In the former year, 89.5% of Inuit-mother-tongue individuals and 66% of all Canadian Inuit had Inuktitut or Inuktun as their home language (Dorais 1990c, 251). It thus seems that the language situation is now showing a tendency toward stabilization. Sacha Senécal (2007, 4) mentions that in 2001 Inuit aged sixty-five and over were the most likely to report Inuktitut as their home language, while those aged twenty-five to forty-four were the least likely to do so. This might have been partly due to the latter's higher level of participation in a predominantly anglophone labour market, a fact that could have influenced the language they used with their families.

The proportions concerning language use at home in 2006 vary from one area of Canada to another, with higher ratios of habitual users of Inuktitut in Quebec (91%) and Nunavut (70%) and with lower percentages in the Northwest Territories (15.5%), Newfoundland and Labrador (23%), and the rest of the country (29%):

POLITICAL SUBDIVISIONS	INUIT SPEAKERS	INUIT HOME LANGUAGE	% HOME LANGUAGE[25]
Newfoundland and Labrador	805	185	23
Quebec	10,170	9,230	91
Northwest Territories	1,030	160	15.5
Nunavut	22,945	16,020	70
Other provinces and Yukon	1,310	385	29
CANADA	36,260	25,980	71.5

Language Use in Inuit Nunaat

To reach a finer understanding of the statistical importance of the Inuit language in Canada, we must now turn our attention to *Inuit nunaat*. As mentioned above, this traditional territory comprised of Nunatsiavut, Nunavik, Nunavut, and Nunaqput was still home in 2006 to 81.5% of all Canadian Inuit. The rates of use of Inuktitut and Inuktun within its boundaries reveal a lot about the relative strength of the various Inuit dialects spoken in Canada.[26] Appendix 4 lists all communities of *Inuit nunaat*, with their approximate numbers and percentages of Inuit-mother-tongue and Inuit-home-language residents.[27]

As may be seen in this appendix, the percentage of Inuit individuals who have Inuktitut or Inuktun as their first language is much lower in Nunaqput (20%) and Nunatsiavut (20%)[28] than it is in Nunavik (99%) and Nunavut. In the latter territory, the proportion of speakers varies from one region to another. In the Kitikmeot region, it barely reaches half the aboriginal population (49%), while it is much higher in the Kivalliq (90%) and Baffin regions (94%). Within the Kitikmeot region, there are proportionally more individuals of Inuit mother tongue in the Natsilingmiut villages of Taloyoak (70%) and Kugaaruk (72%) than in the Inuinnaqtun-speaking communities of Cambridge Bay (40%) and Kugluktuk (34%). In the Kivalliq and Baffin regions, Baker Lake (72%), Rankin Inlet (85%), Iqaluit (83%), and Resolute (75%) harbour lower percentages of Inuktitut-mother-tongue residents than the other villages, whose proportions of speakers hover between 95% and 100%.

This means that in the eastern Arctic, except for Nunatsiavut, Inuktitut is still transmitted as the first language to the vast majority – or the totality in some places – of the Inuit population. Caution is necessary, however. In 1986 (Dorais 1996b, 24–6) the proportions of Inuktitut-mother-tongue residents reached 94% in Baker Lake, 93% in Rankin Inlet, 92% in Iqaluit, and 85% (already low for that period) in Resolute. In Taloyoak, Kugaaruk, and Gjoa Haven (another Natsilingmiut community), the proportions were, respectively, 90%, 97%, and 93% in 1986, compared with 70%, 72%, and an unexplainable 48% in 2006. Even in Nain, 70% of the Inuit residents had Nunatsiavut Inuktitut as their first language in 1986, compared with 32% in 2006. This shows that the transmission of the aboriginal tongue to children can stop abruptly if pressures from the majority language and culture become too strong, without being thwarted by concrete initiatives on the part of youngsters, parents, teachers, and the community in general.

One indicator of incipient language shift may be a decline in the use of Inuktitut or Inuktun as the home language. Such a decline is already perceptible in some regions and communities. In the Kitikmeot region of Nunavut, Inuktun as the home language decreased from 46% to 31% of all mother-tongue speakers between 1986 and 2006, the reduction being stronger in the three Natsilingmiut villages (from an average of 61% in 1986 to 32% in 2006) than in the Inuinnaqtun-speaking communities (where a slight increase was even observed). In Kivalliq the decline was particularly spectacular in Baker Lake (92% of Inuktitut-home-language speakers in 1986, compared with 36% in 2006, a situation that may explain the severe decrease in Inuktitut-mother-tongue individuals also observed in this community), but it was also felt in Rankin Inlet (from 73% to 59%) and in the region in general (81% to 73%).

The proportions of Inuktitut-home-language speakers are still very high in Nunavik and in the Baffin region of Nunavut, where they generally exceed 90% to 95% (even reaching 100% in several Nunavik communities), although a decrease can be observed locally. In Iqaluit, the capital of Nunavut, those who usually spoke the language at home represented 88% of Inuit-mother-tongue residents in 1986 but only 59% in 2006. In Kuujjuaq and Kuujjuaraapik (Nunavik) the proportions dropped from over 90% in 1986 to around 80% in 2006, a smaller but significant decrease in a region where all other villages have maintained proportions of home speakers nearing 100%. As a matter of fact, Inuktitut as the home language appears to be on the decline in the larger and/or ethnically heterogeneous communities (e.g., Rankin Inlet, Iqaluit,[29] Kuujjuaq, and Kuujjuaraapik) more than in smaller places.[30]

If statistics are accurate, the proportion of Inuit-home-language individuals increased in Nunaqput (from 10% in 1986 to 24% in 2006) and decreased only slightly (from 30% to 26%) in Nunatsiavut. This might mean that a good number of the few remaining speakers of the language place great value in their mother tongue and consider its use at home to be important.[31] Absolute figures are very low, however. In both Nunaqput and Nunatsiavut the 130 individuals in each region (for a total of 260) who spoke the Inuit language at home in 2006 accounted for a mere 5% of the local Inuit population.

The figures found in appendix 4 as well as available data on the origins of residents in multidialectal communities allow us to estimate the number and proportion of first-language speakers for each Inuit dialect used in *Inuit nunaat* in 2006:

DIALECTS	PERSONS HAVING DIALECT AS ANCESTRAL LANGUAGE	NUMBER OF ACTUAL SPEAKERS	% OF ACTUAL SPEAKERS
Uummarmiut[32]	690	122	18
Siglitun (Inuvialuktun)	1,690	310	18
Inuinnaqtun	2,775	1,010	36
Natsilingmiutut	2,730	1,815	66
Kivalliq	4,170	3,735	90
Aivilik	2,990	2,655	89
North Baffin	5,215	5,170	99
South Baffin	6,600	5,975	91
Nunavik	10,350	10,215	99
Nunatsiavut	2,535	505	20

Three dialects seem to be in a very problematic condition: Uummarmiut, Siglitun, and Nunatsiavut are spoken as a first language by 20% or less of their ancestral populations. The last one, in particular, is in sharp decline, having decreased from 52% of native speakers in 1986 to 20% in 2006.[33] Inuinnaqtun still preserved over one-third (36%) of its mother-tongue speakers in 2006, but they had accounted for 56% twenty years earlier.

The decrease is much more spectacular for Natsilingmiutut, which had a rate of native fluency approaching 100% (94%) in 1986, compared with only two-thirds (66%) in 2006. The only speech forms that continue to show apparent linguistic strength are five eastern Inuktitut dialects (Kivalliq, Aivilik, North Baffin, South Baffin, and Nunavik), which had rates of native fluency of 89% to 99% in 2006, although the rates for three of them (Kivalliq, Aivilik, and South Baffin) have slightly decreased since 1986.[34]

To summarize the statistical data discussed in this section, here is how each of the four dialectal groupings of the Inuit language performed in terms of the number and proportion of speakers at the turn of the twenty-first century who resided in extended *Inuit nunaat* (i.e., the Canadian Inuit lands plus Greenland and northern Alaska):

DIALECTAL GROUPINGS	NUMBER OF SPEAKERS	% OF SPEAKERS
Kalaallisut (Greenland)	48,855	97
Eastern Canadian Inuktitut	28,255	89
Western Canadian Inuktun	3,135	44
Inupiaq (northern Alaska)	2,145	14
TOTAL, EXTENDED INUIT NUNAAT	82,390	78

To these figures must be added some 18,385 Inuit speakers living outside *Inuit nunaat* (including 13,075 Greenlanders residing in Denmark). These 100,775 people account for 75.5% of the worldwide population of individuals of Inuit origin. This means that about one-quarter of all Inuit no longer know their ancestral language. This proportion is rather low when compared to what happens with other minority languages (see Grenoble and Whaley 2006), although, as seen in the preceding pages, language shift can accelerate abruptly if nothing is done to preserve and develop aboriginal speech forms.

POLITICAL AND ADMINISTRATIVE STATUS

Greenland

Being spoken within the boundaries of duly constituted nation-states, the Inuit language is subject to various governmental authorities, and its use is often regulated by law. Greenland was probably the first Inuit territory to legislate in linguistic matters. As early as 1905, a rule stipulated that teaching should be conducted in Kalaallisut in elementary schools as well as at Nuuk's teacher training college. It was modified in 1925 to introduce Danish as a subject matter (Engell 1982). In 1950 an Education Act allowed Danish to be used as a teaching medium for subjects such as geography, science, and mathematics. The Act also created a scholarship program for sending promising students to Denmark. Finally, in 1967 the local school committees were allowed to wait until grade 3 before starting to use Kalaallisut as a teaching medium (Berthelsen 1979). Up to the 1970s, then, both Greenlandic and Danish acted as de facto official languages, the latter seeing its importance increase with the introduction of new technological and administrative concepts difficult to translate into Kalaallisut (Olsen 1979).

The 1970s witnessed a complete change. Intellectuals and the public started calling for a typically Greenlandic form of development rather than assimilatory equality with Danes. In accordance with the fact that, in Christian Berthelsen's words, "the Danish politicians have always listened to the Greenlanders' wishes" (Berthelsen 1979, 16), the political structure of Greenland rapidly evolved toward Home Rule, which became effective in 1979.

Because the country's linguistic development had always been regulated by the state, it was normal that the new administration, now under local control, revalorize the status of the aboriginal language. This explains why Paragraph 9 of the Home Rule Act states that "Greenlandic is the principal language of the land. Danish is to be taught thoroughly. Both languages may be used in matters of public concern" (quoted in Berthelsen 1990a, 339). Kalaallisut thus regained its importance and became the chief means of communication and the principal teaching medium, Danish having to be satisfied with the role of first foreign language. A Language Commission (Oqaasileriffik) was established in 1982 under the supervision of a Greenlandic Language Council. The commission became responsible for conducting research and seeing to the application of law in matters of linguistic and orthographic standardization, neology, toponymy, and personal names.

In July 2000 the Home Rule government appointed a Working Group charged with reviewing language policies. In its report (Oqaatsinut 2001), the group recommended that native Greenlanders and individuals of Danish heritage be more exposed to Kalaallisut, that added importance be granted to aboriginal-language teaching at school, that an extensive technical lexicon based on Greenlandic radicals – rather than on Danish loan-words – be developed, and that instructors apt at teaching in Kalaallisut at the postsecondary level be trained.

On 25 November 2008, 75% of Greenlanders voted in favour of a change in the political status of Greenland. They accepted, as of 21 June 2009, the replacement of Home Rule with Self Rule. This means that rather than being considered a special ethnic group within Denmark, the Kalaallit are now defined as an autonomous people with a right to self-determination (Anonymous 2008). As far as language is concerned, Kalaallisut is the official medium of communication in Greenland. A new language law will stipulate that all residents, whatever their origin, should speak it, provided this will not be detrimental to the rights of those whose principal language is Danish or another tongue (Kristensen 2009).

Canada

In Canada, up to the end of the 1960s, Inuktitut and Inuktun did not enjoy any official protection. On the contrary, they were generally considered obstacles to the modernization of arctic populations. In the eyes of the federal government, monolingual education in English was the only way to bring Inuit out of the Stone Age and transform them into average Canadians (Dorais 1988e).[35] Thus, during the 1950s, a network of anglophone federal day-schools was established across the Canadian Arctic.

It was the identity renewal and the political claims of the 1970s, combined with the promulgation of the Canadian law on multiculturalism,[36] that progressively brought politicians to recognize the linguistic rights of the Inuit and to translate these rights into law. As early as 1973, the Government of the Northwest Territories established an Interpreters' Corps, which later became a Language Bureau, to provide interpretation and translation services to the members of the territorial Legislative Assembly who were monolingual in an aboriginal language. During the same period, the federal Department of Indian Affairs devolved its responsibilities in matters of education to the territorial government, allowing Inuktitut to be taught in the first elementary grades.

In 1984, with the adoption of the Northwest Territories Official Language Act, English and French were proclaimed the official languages of the territory, while the seven indigenous tongues spoken in the region were attributed the status of "official aboriginal languages." A languages commissioner was also appointed to supervise the application of the law. When the Northwest Territories was partitioned in 1999 to establish Nunavut, all territorial laws, including the Language Act, were automatically transferred to the new government, together with the institutions already in place (that of the languages commissioner, for instance). In what became known as the "Bathurst Mandate,"[37] the newly elected leaders pledged, among other things, to make Inuktitut the working language of the territorial administration before 2020. Over the following years, the Nunavut Legislative Assembly discussed a reform of the Official Language Law, as well as the adoption of a Language

Protection Act, to adapt legislation to the current situation and to offer more support to the Inuit language (Government of Nunavut 2007a, 2007b).

Both laws were finally passed in mid-2008. The Official Languages Act stipulates that the Inuit language (i.e., Inuktitut and Inuinnaqtun), English, and French are the official languages of Nunavut, with equality of status and equal rights and privileges, while the Inuit Language Protection Act proposes various measures for supporting the use of the aboriginal tongue. It is not clear, however, up to what point the Inuit language can be legally considered equal to English and French. Because Nunavut is a federal territory rather than a province, no language other than Canada's two official tongues may be completely protected under law, even if francophones account for less than 5% of Nunavut's population and Inuit for more than 80%. According to Michelle Daveluy (2004), legislation is useless for protecting Inuktitut adequately if the federal government, which is responsible for supervising language rights in Canada, does not invest sufficient funds in its protection. Ominously enough, after the two laws were passed, the Canadian prime minister stated that his government would not necessarily recognize the official status of the Inuit language.

One domain, however, in which this language has obtained some official recognition throughout Canada is toponymy. In Nunavut several communities have recovered their original Inuit appellation (Frobisher Bay thus became Iqaluit, for instance).[38] But it is Arctic Quebec that holds the leading position as far as Inuit place-names are concerned. Besides the names of all Nunavik villages, more than 2,000 Inuit appellations have been made official by the Commission de Toponymie of the Quebec government, and they now appear on maps. This may be due to the fact that in Quebec, place-names have always acted as political instruments manipulated by those in power. In the northern area of the province, aboriginal appellations were first replaced with English names (bestowed by British explorers, the Hudson's Bay Company, and the federal administration) and then, after 1960, by French[39] toponyms emanating from a provincial government anxious to have its influence felt in the Arctic. It was only after the signing of the James Bay and Northern Quebec Agreement in 1975 that the tendency to return to original Inuit place-names became generalized, as doing so played an important political and symbolic role (Müller-Wille 1983).[40]

In Nunavik the use of Inuktitut is regulated by various federal and Quebec provincial laws, as well as by several provisions of the James Bay Agreement allowing for the establishment of a regional education authority (the Kativik School Board), under which teaching may be conducted in Inuktitut by way of locally produced curricula and school materials (Consilium 2005). Dirmid Collis (1992, 123) lists six legislative measures that have affected language use in Nunavik. The most important is Law 101 (adopted in 1977), Quebec's "Charter of the French Language," which declares French the official language of the province. In spite of the restrictions Law 101 imposes on using other tongues, it recognizes the right of aboriginal peoples to maintain and develop their indigenous language and culture, and its Clause 87 stipulates that no legislation prohibits "the use of an Amerindian language for teaching Amerindians, or of Inuktitut for teaching Inuit" (quoted in Collis 1992, 119). The law also confirms the provisions of the James Bay Agreement that make Cree, Inuktitut, English, and French the four teaching languages of the northern school boards.[41]

The Nunavik Agreement-in-Principle, signed in 2007, establishes a Nunavik regional government that should have full legislative authority over Inuit language and culture. The Nunatsiavut government of northern Labrador was granted similar powers in 2005.

Alaska and Russia

Aboriginal languages are not officially recognized in Alaska, although their use is generally accepted. According to Lawrence Kaplan (1992), the absence of any clear linguistic policy has entailed some loss of interest in indigenous speech forms, which do not carry much weight in comparison with English, the first language of a vast majority of Alaska natives. The only legal protection enjoyed by the Unangax, Yupik, and Inupiaq languages is the state law of 1972 that puts all schools with at least eight students whose mother tongue is not English under the obligation to offer start-up education in the first language of these students. Otherwise, linguistic development is left in the hands of public and private organizations, some of which are interested in devoting resources to the preservation of traditional language and culture: "For example, the North Slope Borough – the governing body of the Arctic Coast and adjoining areas – has established a Commission on Language, History and Culture. Several school districts in Native areas maintain centres devoted to the production of school materials dealing with local language and culture" (Kaplan 1990, 154).

In Russia the territories of several so-called "small peoples" (i.e., ethnic groups with a population under 100,000) are recognized as "autonomous national regions" (*okrug*), where the local language is protected by a number of rights. However, such rights are more theoretical than real. Among the Yupiget of Chukotka, who belong to the same autonomous region as the Chukchi, they amount to the possibility for schoolchildren in the first three elementary grades – all of them of Russian mother tongue – to be taught Yupik as a second language (Menovshchikov 1990b).

DIGLOSSIA

The political and administrative status of the Inuit language both reflects and influences its social position within the nation-states where it is spoken. When English, or Danish, or Russian is considered more useful for earning a living and/or more apt for expressing modernity – because of the economic, political, and cognitive strength it conveys – than Inuktitut, Kalaallisut, or Inupiaq, it tends to progressively replace the aboriginal mother tongue. Conflict thus arises between a dominant language, originally introduced from outside the indigenous linguistic community, and a dominated one, often spoken by a colonized or socially dependent population.

Such a situation of inequality and linguistic conflict is called "diglossia" (Ferguson 1959). It is characterized by the attribution to the dominant language of most tasks considered prestigious or important (the "high" communicative functions)[42] and by the relegation of the dominated language to a minor role (the "low" functions).[43] Diglossia can endure for some time, but in most cases the dominated language is finally replaced, or "swallowed" (see Calvet 1974), by its dominator. It seems evident that the Inuit are undergoing, or underwent in the past, a situation of diglossia (Dorais 1981b; 1989). As already seen, the replacement of the Inuit language with English seems well under way in Alaska, the western Canadian Arctic, and Nunatsiavut. Elsewhere in Canada the majority language seems in the process of invading all spheres of communication, even those (private conversations, for instance) usually reserved to Inuktitut.

Experiencing Diglossia

On the west coast of Greenland, diglossia is institutional rather than individual (Engell 1982). The country cannot subsist and function properly without using Danish at some higher political and administrative levels, but for ordinary people, work, domestic life, and cultural or leisure activities are almost exclusively experienced in Greenlandic. Only a few organizations operate partially in Danish: the schools, where, in the upper grades, many courses are delivered in that language; some branches of the Home Rule administration (those that have to deal with the outside world or whose upper-level employees are mostly Danes); television, where broadcasting in Kalaallisut constitutes the exception rather than the rule; and so on. In Thule, however, as well as on the east coast, there exists a genuine situation of diglossia opposing local dialects to the official west coast language. West Greenlandic Kalaallisut thus acts as the dominant language, monopolizing the "higher" functions: teaching, writing, radio broadcasts, contacts with the rest of the country,[44] and in most cases, church rituals. As for local dialects, they are chiefly limited to private conversation.[45] West Greenlanders often seem scornful toward these minority speech forms, an attitude the Greenlandic intellectual Robert Petersen (1977) has labelled cultural imperialism.

Two forms of diglossia are also found in Nunatsiavut. There is the one opposing Inuktitut to English, which, as already shown, contributed to the demise of the aboriginal language, and there is another based on the difference between the written and spoken languages. For many decades, the predominant Moravian orthography did not reflect the actual pronunciation of the Nunatsiavut dialect. It was highly valued, however, because of its intimate link with the history and religious life of the region. Moreover, the missionaries and some church elders considered the present-day language to be "bad Inuktitut" (Jeddore 1979), an attitude that explains why, during religious ceremonies, clergymen pronounced – some of them may still do so – the texts they read exactly as they had been written over a hundred years ago. Until the adoption, during the 1990s, of a standard orthography closer to modern pronunciation, two social dialects co-existed in Labrador: an extremely valued church dialect and an ordinary speech form that some people considered a degenerated language. According to Rose Jeddore (1979, 91), this internal diglossia contributed to hastening the decline of Inuktitut starting in the 1960s by strengthening the negative attitudes of young speakers toward their mother tongue.[46]

The language situation in Nunatsiavut may be dubbed triglossia because three speech forms were in interaction: ordinary Inuktitut (principally spoken), church Inuktitut (principally written), and English. Triglossia also occurs in Nunavik, where Inuktitut is confronted by two imported languages, each of them dominant in its own sphere. These are English, the traditional second language of Inuit and the most popular medium of communication with Euro-Canadians (including francophones), and French, the official language of Quebec.[47] In Kuujjuaq, for instance, according to Donald Taylor and Stephen Wright (1989), Inuktitut is "intact and vibrant" among the Inuit, who use it daily and attribute to it a high value.[48] But among other linguistic groups – francophones and anglophones account for 20% of the local population – this language is not predominant enough to make it the lingua franca of the community. This function is instead filled by English, the only language common to all residents, whatever their mother tongue.

English serves as the lingua franca because its predominant position within Canada and Quebec[49] enables it to assert itself at the expense of the other two languages, and this even though English-mother-tongue residents account for less than 10% of the Kuujjuaq population. For many young people, the ever-increasing importance of English as the language of the workplace augments its prestige and endows the anglophone minority with a central position within the community. Due to these circumstances, several of Taylor's (1990) Inuit informants wonder whether aboriginal language and culture are not in jeopardy. They feel simultaneously optimistic and anxious about the situation:[50] optimistic because Inuktitut possesses an inner strength – stemming from the mere number of its speakers – and enjoys the general support of the population; anxious because of the predominant position of English – particularly on the labour market – which, it is feared, might generate among the young some lack of interest in their own language and culture. The prevalent feeling of the Kuujjuaq Inuit is thus ambivalence. Taylor (1990, 54) concludes that to prevent this situation from having perverse effects (such as the generalization of subtractive bilingualism), Inuktitut must become a language of prestige in northern communities. Its position should be equal to that of English at work, in the administration, at school, and in the media.

Diglossia is also present,[51] although it seems less stressful, in the smaller villages of Nunavik. In Quaqtaq, for instance (with 235 residents in 1991), the principal community language is Inuktitut (Dorais 1997, 79–80):

> To the casual visitor, everyday life in Quaqtaq appears to be almost totally conducted in Inuktitut. This is the language most often heard on the street, in the stores, at church, or in the town hall, as well as in all Inuit homes, including those headed by a mixed couple. A majority of the local written messages and radio programmes are in Inuktitut too. In fact, the only really multilingual environment is to be found at school, where most of the teaching is conducted in English or French, and where pupils are requested to speak their second language at all times, except, of course, during classes dealing with Inuit language and culture.

School is usually perceived as the place where one learns Canada's majority languages, as well as other *kiinaujaliurutiit* ("tools for making money"), the skills necessary for earning a living in the modern world. Some Quaqtaq residents believe that Inuit language and culture are bound to disappear in the long run. Others maintain that they can be preserved but only if special efforts are made. In this community, where Inuktitut is spoken daily by almost everyone,[52] the position of the aboriginal language appears to be strong, although possibly fragile. The overall weight of diglossia in the Arctic might eventually contribute to its decline.

The past decades, however, have witnessed an increase in the prestige accorded to Inuktitut by both Inuit and non-Inuit, a fact that could partly counteract diglossia. According to the sociolinguist Donna Patrick (2003), this occurred because a consensus arose on the hierarchy of values linked to linguistic choice. One language (English) was considered more useful in practical situations (linked to the *kiinaujaliurutiit*), the other (Inuktitut) being principally efficient in the maintenance of identity. On the basis of her field research in Kuujjuaraapik, a quadrilingual (Inuktitut, Cree, English, and French) community of Nunavik, Patrick has shown that competing sets of values (e.g., Inuktitut and English each becoming equally important in its own sphere) may create a strong pressure in favour of an alternative market for the originally dominated language.[53] In the eastern Canadian Arctic, it became progressively possible from the late 1970s on to earn a living – as a teacher, translator, cultural agent, specialist of subsistence activities, or even politician – by using Inuktitut professionally. There thus developed a second, Inuit-language market, in addition to the main one, where English was predominant. One may wonder whether, nowadays, the two markets are not merging into a larger, bilingual one.

Except for the presence of French in Nunavik, the diglossic situation there also applies to Nunavut. In a study of diglossia in Iqaluit, Björn Eriksson (1998) has outlined the dichotomy between young Inuit, who increasingly use English among themselves, and elders, who speak almost exclusively in Inuktitut, even though both groups say they prefer expressing their emotions, feelings, and intimate thoughts in their mother tongue. Their first language thus helps them to assert their identity, English being used primarily for communicating with the outside world. Nonetheless, even those who are very much attached to their mother tongue employ English words from time to time because Inuktitut lacks adequate terminology in some domains.[54] It seems, however, that English occasions problems when speakers want to articulate the Inuit way of thinking. Anything connected with the expression of one's own innermost self is usually uttered in Inuktitut.

Broadly speaking, then, to borrow Pierre Bourdieu's (1991) – and Patrick's (2003) – terminology, English is still predominant on the Iqaluit (and Nunavut in general) language market (Dorais 2006a, 56–7).[55] This is due to the fact that: (1) English is most often required when one is searching for a job, (2) it is the principal vehicle of popular culture (television, music, the Internet), and (3) contacts with non-Inuit occur exclusively in English. Inuktitut is starting to carve itself a place, however, mostly because it has become more visible and important since the creation of Nunavut and because its market value has been augmented in consequence. Moreover, Inuktitut is also valorized as the most fitting language for expressing oneself in informal contexts and for symbolizing that one is an Inuk. This means that even though the Nunavut Agreement has nothing to say about language, and despite the Legislative Assembly's problems defining a language law adapted to the territory, the existing linguistic practices have some positive consequences. The establishment of Nunavut has thus had a nation-building effect that could perhaps bend diglossia in favour of the aboriginal language. The linguistic and cultural policies proposed by the territorial government contribute to transforming Inuktitut and Inuit culture into emblems of the specificity of the Inuit people within Canada and thus of their innate right to govern their own territory.[56] This might constitute a good example of the resilience of Inuit language and society (see Daveluy 2005).

At the community level, the use of Inuktitut and English occurs in various societal contexts. These are numerous, but in Nunavut five important contexts can be identified:

1 *Preserving the ethnic community*: using language to preserve the ethnic identity (as an Inuk, a francophone, etc.) of one's group of belonging
2 *Continuing tradition*: using language to preserve one's cultural identity
3 *Political power*: using language in the context of obtaining, preserving, and increasing administrative and political control for one's group of belonging, within Nunavut and Canada in general
4 *Labour market*: using language to earn a living
5 *Wider communication*: using language to learn about and communicate with the outside world

Research in the Baffin region (Dorais and Sammons 2002, 124–5) shows that the two principal languages spoken are not used the same way in each of these contexts.[57] Inuktitut plays a very strong part in preserving the aboriginal ethnic community and in continuing tradition (contexts 1 and 2), and with the development of Inuit organizations and the advent of Nunavut, it is also important for gaining political power (context 3). For the time being, it is not very present on the labour market (context 4) – especially in Iqaluit, less so elsewhere – but if, as envisioned by the Bathurst Mandate, Inuktitut ever becomes the working language of the Government of Nunavut, its economic importance should increase. It is only in the field of wider communication (context 5) that the Inuit language is almost completely absent.

By contrast, English is not really useful for preserving the ethnic community (anglophones do not need it to assert their identity) or for continuing tradition. It plays some part in the political arena – for instance, debates in the Legislative Assembly often occur in that language[58] – but with the advent of Nunavut, Inuktitut is probably more useful than English for addressing northern political matters.

In contexts 4 and 5 (the labour market and wider communication), however, English remains very strong, occupying most available linguistic space.

The unequal distribution of language use according to context can be schematized as follows (dotted lines and brackets indicate weaker ties):

	SOCIAL CONTEXTS	
	Preserving ethnic community →	Inuktitut
	Continuing tradition =======→	Inuktitut
(English) ←------------	Political power ===========→	Inuktitut
English ←========	Labour market -------------------→	(Inuktitut)
English ←========	Wider communication	

Due to this unequal distribution of language use, the cultural meaning attributed to discourses uttered in Inuktitut and English varies. Many people envision English as being principally a language of practicality that has a relatively weak value in terms of identity. This value is stronger, however, among younger people. Conversely, Inuktitut acts as a very strong marker and component of Inuit identity, but its practical value is generally considered inferior to that of English. This can be schematized as follows:

English	+practicality/-identity
Inuktitut	+identity/-practicality

The existence of various social contexts explains why different language choices are made. According to circumstances (and to their own linguistic fluency), speakers will choose, generally unconsciously, to speak in Inuktitut or in English (or in French), or in a mix of these languages, in order to express, at the same time, both what they intend to communicate and the cultural meaning – in terms of practicality and identity – that they impart via their discourse.

In the Inuvialuit region and in Alaska, where only a small minority of Inuit are still proficient in their ancestral language, it is English that seems to reign supreme, and the diglossic situation may have reached the stage that precedes the disappearance of a vernacular. In the late 1970s, however, during a period when a larger proportion of the population still spoke aboriginal languages, the Finnish ethnolinguist Pekka Sammallahti (1981) had the opportunity to study the linguistic behaviour of native residents in six Yupiit and Inupiat Alaskan communities, defining three different ways of experiencing diglossia. In the first type, now completely obsolete, all generations communicated among themselves in the aboriginal language, except at school, where the principal or unique medium of communication was English. In communities of the second type, parents spoke to each other in their native tongue or in both languages. They generally addressed their children in Yupik or Inupiaq, but the children always answered in English and spoke English among themselves. In the third type, the most common in Alaska even at that time, everybody spoke only English, except for a few adults who occasionally communicated among themselves in the native language.

Sammallahti stresses that the transition to English monolingualism can occur very rapidly. In English Bay (a southern Alaskan village), for instance, everybody spoke Alutiiq Yupik in 1960, but in 1980 half the residents (all of them young) spoke only English, and this despite the fact that the school had been teaching Alutiiq since the early 1970s. Among Inupiat, the King Island people started addressing their children in English a few years after their relocation to Nome in the 1960s. The researcher attributes this situation to the fact that the respective positions of the native and non-native languages in a given community are determined by their role and by their social value. In Alaska, until 1920, very few Inuit and Yupiit knew any English. Everyone spoke native languages at home, and these had an indispensable part to play in daily life. However, their value was so low that as soon as it became possible, they were replaced with English. This language thus gradually fulfilled all communicative functions, from the highest to the humblest. In most regions, Eskaleut speech forms were finally confined to ritual roles useless for practical communication, such as traditional singing or native-language courses, delivered to monolingual anglophone children in villages where even the oldest residents were fluent in English.[59] According to Sammallahti, once the replacement process has started in a community, it takes between sixty and seventy years for that community to become monolingual in English.

The dominant language can sometimes be another aboriginal speech form (as in East Greenland and the Thule district). Among the Yupiget of Chukotka, Igor Krupnik (1991) has documented with much precision how the Sirenikski language (totally extinct since 1997) gradually disappeared because of daily contacts and intermarriage with a majority population speaking Central Siberian Yupik. It was within the exclusively male teams of sea-mammal hunters that Sirenikski survived longest as the principal medium of communication. The dispersal of these teams during the 1930s, due to the relocation of several villages, seemingly hastened the disappearance of the language.

Diglossia and Dependence

Conflict between the Inuit language and those languages that try to prevail over it is the linguistic consequence of unequal social relations between aboriginal and Euro-American societies. The situation of the present-day Inuit may be analyzed as a process of (hopefully decreasing) economic, political, and ideological dependence on an external power – the predominant social and economic forces – that they initially could little influence but that they are now able to manipulate in some way. This process of European domination of northern territories was established when Inuit started participating in economic relations of production (whaling and the fur trade) and in political, social, and religious structures (government administration, missions, and schools) over which they had no control, even though they were able to adapt them partially to their own worldview and cultural practices: "Because all social phenomena are linked one to another, it is normal for the economic and social dependence of northern populations to generate linguistic subordination. As the residents of the Canadian Arctic are now dependent on economic transfers and political decisions originating in the south of the country, they also depend on English (and, to a lesser extent, French in Arctic Quebec) to operate in a world whose parameters they do not really contribute to defining" (Dorais 1988e, 240).

Diglossic phenomena thus reflect the general social and economic situation of the Inuit. Because the North was colonized by southern economic and political interests, the aboriginal populations became dominated in their own territory, where they underwent very strong assimilatory pressures. According to J. Iain Prattis (1986), it is only in those regions where the social division of labour resulted in de facto segregation (Europeans occupying the leading positions and Inuit the unskilled jobs) that native languages survived. Elsewhere (i.e., in Nunatsiavut, the Inuvialuit region, and northern Alaska), the presence of lower-class Euro-Americans (trappers, fishermen, etc.) with whom aboriginal people could identify more easily entailed the partial suppression of ethnic boundaries and thus the linguistic assimilation of the Inuit.

At present, however, the aboriginal peoples of the North American Arctic have become conscious of their special identity and have started reclaiming their territorial, political, and cultural rights. The Inuit language seems to play an important part in this process. All Inuit administrations and organizations, even in regions where the native language has almost disappeared, assess that it is necessary to preserve and develop Kalaallisut, Inuktitut, Inuktun, or Inupiaq. When questioned on this topic, individual Inuit generally share similar opinions.[60] The governments have followed suit and important – yet insufficient – sums are now set aside for aboriginal-language education and translation.

It should be wondered, however, whether this is not only a surface phenomenon. Beyond political talk and praiseworthy but useless initiatives,[61] language often appears to be an ideological object, an image whose manipulation can be profitable to those in power. Among Inuit politicians, for instance, the importance of Inuktitut, Inuktun, or Inupiaq is related more to its role as a symbol of aboriginal political and territorial rights than to its intrinsic value as a legitimate medium of communication. Inuit interviewed in Iqaluit in 2003–04, especially the elders, were often critical of the role of politicians, whose promises to protect Inuktitut were, they believed, forgotten as soon as they were elected (Dorais 2006a, 57).

On the part of the Canadian, Alaskan, or Quebec state, granting cultural and linguistic rights to aboriginal minorities might contribute to weakening the legitimacy of more encompassing political and social claims. For example, the Nunavik Agreement-in-Principle endows the Quebec Inuit with exclusive legislative power over aboriginal language and culture, but any other decision of the Nunavik government must abide by existing federal and provincial laws, a fact that sets severe limitations on political autonomy. This means that the actions of the indigenous as well as exogenous politicians may not really contribute to furthering the interests of the basic Inuit population, for whom the native language often constitutes the privileged instrument for expressing one's own deepest cultural identity (Dorais 1991, 2006a; Dorais and Sammons 2002; Eriksson 1998). In the future, such actions could even be prejudicial to the aboriginal tongue because they do not generate anything effective – formal education in the Inuit language up to grade 12, for instance – for overcoming basic linguistic inequalities.

If a systemic perspective (all aspects of social life are related one to another) is adopted, it becomes clear that social inequality and the diglossic phenomena that it entails will disappear only when Inuit stop being economically dependent. Any measure aimed at the preservation and development of Inuit language and culture is thus useless and bound to fail (and this despite the goodwill of all involved) as long as the fundamental inequality endures – that is, the control exerted on the North by external economic and political interests and/or by local leaders for whom language and culture do not hold much practical importance.[62] This control will disappear only when residents of the Arctic gain access to a real measure of political autonomy, one based on the self-management of northern resources, and only when they are provided with all that is needed for developing efficient and truly Inuit cultural, linguistic, and education programs.

CONCLUSION

The preceding pages show that the nature of the economic and political relations structuring the environment within which the speakers of languages in contact operate influences their perception of the types of discourse they have to emit as well as of the language in which to emit them. If the relations they maintain with a labour market, a school system, or an administration introduced from outside have persuaded them that their mother tongue has little value, they will be tempted to replace its semantics, syntax, and lexicon with those of the predominant language. This process of replacement will first take the form of subtractive bilingualism, whereby any acquirement in the second language provokes a loss in the mother tongue, before it evolves toward the disappearance of the original speech form, which is swallowed, one might say, by the language of those in power. This is what is happening in Nunatsiavut, the western Canadian Arctic, and Alaska, and the same might happen to Eastern Canadian Inuktitut in the not-too-distant future.

If, on the contrary, as seems to be the case in Greenland, the reinforcement of national identity and the Inuit people's accession to political autonomy translate into an increased importance being accorded to their vernacular language, its transmission and development will be ensured thanks to effective legal measures and public cultural and education initiatives. As shall be seen in the next chapter, reinforcing identity might thus be one of the keys to the survival of the Inuit language.

10

Conclusion: Language and Identity in the Arctic

The role played by language in defining Inuit identity is mentioned in passing in the preceding chapters. To give identity the importance it deserves, this book now concludes with a more thorough examination of what the Inuit language really means to the Inuit in terms of their worldview and self-definition.

INUIT CONCEPTIONS ABOUT LANGUAGE

The Meaning of Speech

In all Inuit dialects, the lexemes dealing with speech and language start with the word-base *uqaq-* ("to speak, to talk, to tell").[1] Taamusi Qumaq's[2] dictionary of Nunavik Inuktitut defines the word that means "he/she speaks or talks" as follows (Qumaq 1991, 101):

> *Uqaqtuq*:
> *Inuk suliniraqsuni isumaminik uqatuarami tagga uqaqtuq piujumik piunngitumigluuniit.*
>
> He/she speaks or talks:
> A person saying that he/she tells the truth because he/she only tells his/her idea, thus this person says something good or bad.

It is the individual (*inuk*) who speaks. By doing this, he/she discloses his/her inner thoughts. Speech is thus a way of sharing what one has in his/her mind. This sharing is highly moral because speakers "say that they tell the truth"; through their very acts of speaking, they disclose what they are actually thinking.[3] By way of consequence, these speech acts may be good or bad, depending on the good or bad contents of the ideas they express and because of the correspondence – or lack of correspondence – between the speakers' thoughts and the words used for sharing them with other people.

Speech being a human characteristic, animals are unable to talk.[4] However, they have lost language, as revealed by myths and stories that tell about conversations among animals and between human beings (shamans in particular) and animals in older times, and some communication might still by possible (Therrien 1987b). But only dogs can fully understand what they are told,[5] provided they are addressed in a special idiom.[6] Dog commands, which include a sound unknown in the Inuit phonetic system (apical *r*), are uttered as follows in Nunavik:

uit "let's go!"
aau "stop!"
rauk "turn right!"
aja "turn left"
ii piujuq "that's good, keep running!"

Speech, words, and language are called *uqausiq* ("what is used for speaking"), defined by Qumaq (1991, 100) as follows:

Uqausiq:
Inuk uqarunnapuq qanutuinnaq uqarumajaminik qaninga qausiqtuumat uqausirmik qanutuinnaq.

Speech, words, language:
The individual can say anything he/she wants to say; because his/her mouth is moist, [he/she can utter] a word in any way.

According to this definition, speech consists of the faculty of stating something freely thanks to the mouth, whose moistness enables phonation to occur. The most important speech organ is the tongue, *uqaq* (this radical is the same as the one meaning "to speak"),[7] defined by Qumaq (1991, 102) as follows:

Uqara:
Uvanga namminiq uqara qaningma iluaniittuq sauniqanngituq uqaagunnarutiga tukilingmik uqara.

My tongue:
My own thing, my tongue, it is inside my mouth, it has no bone, my tongue [is] my tool for telling something that makes sense.

Thanks to the tongue, it is possible to speak in a meaningful way.[8] These meaningful messages (*uqausiksait*, "materials for talking") are addressed to those with whom one wants to communicate. For Qumaq (1991: 101), communication is as eminently social as it is moral:

Uqausiksalik:
Inuk kinatuinnaq uqarumajuq inungmut asiminut uqausiksaqarami inuuqatiminut asiminut.

He/she has a message or something to say:
Anyone wants to talk to someone else because he/she has something to say to another one, to his/her fellow.

The receptor of the message first hears it (*tusaq-/tuhaq-*) – that is, perceives it through his/her ears (Qumaq 1991, 232):

Tusaqtuq:
Kinagulutuinnamik sunagulutuinnamilluuniit nillitumik siutimigut tusaqtuq siutiqarami sunalimaanik survaluktunik.

He/she hears:
He/she hears with his/her ears anyone or anything uttering a sound; because he/she has ears, [he/she hears] anything making a noise.

For a message to be understood, however, it must not only be heard but also listened to[9] (*tusaa-/tuhaa-*, "to hear attentively"), a phenomenon that Qumaq (1991, 233) defines as follows:

Tusaajuq:
Inuk uqausirnik amisuinik ajjigiinngitunik tukisigunnarami tagga tusaajuuniraqtaugunnamijuq ...

He/she listens:
Because someone can understand many different groups of words, it may be said of him/her that he/she listens ...

The communication process thus reaches its completion. Speech, defined as a significant and truthful reflection of the speaker's thinking, is transmitted to the receptor of a message, who hears and listens to it. Listening allows the receptor to understand the message – that is, to integrate it into his or her own thinking. For Qumaq, this process is not indifferent. It is based on moral and social values that cannot be dissociated from Inuit culture.

Mythology as well as shamanic vocabulary and various other elements from oral literature also help to explain how Inuit culture defines language. For example, the analysis of words used by shamans for communicating with spirits has enabled the ethnolinguist Michèle Therrien (1987a, ch. 5) to outline the three major characteristics of speech:

1 To name something is to reach it;[10] words give a privileged access to the world.
2 Speech reveals the intimate nature of men and women.[11]
3 Language enables communication with the sacred.

Words are powerful[12] and should be used with care.[13] They can hurt and even kill people, both in a symbolic and in a real way. According to the anthropologist Edmund Carpenter, it is with words that Inuit – for whom sight is subordinated to hearing – construct a human universe on the basis of the natural world. When someone speaks, language exists in a virtual state,[14] as does the universe that the speaker tries to describe with words (Carpenter 1973). The missionary and anthropologist Guy Mary-Rousselière (1992) gives several examples of the power of words: magic formulas,[15] the naming taboo (some names must not be pronounced), and shaman's language, among others. According to him, the use of language in sacred circumstances has allowed the preservation of many old lexemes. It has also endowed speech with an emotional content that it might not have possessed otherwise.

The linguist Thomas Correll (1974) states that the Inuit define language as a mode of communication fulfilling four main functions: (1) identifying people and objects, (2) extending and preserving social relations, (3) granting symbolic ownership over what is named, and (4) establishing a process of sincere exchange with the other. This definition includes the same three components of speech – functional, moral, and social – disclosed by Qumaq in his dictionary.

Personal Names

The personal name (*atiq*) figures among the most powerful words in existence. Across the Arctic, names are much more than mere appellations. They are a form of soul that is transmitted from an eponym (one who gives his or her name) to a homonym (one who receives the name). Traditional Inuit names being asexual, they may be given to either boys or girls. They are drawn from the common language: Ittuq ("Old Man"), Kumaq ("Louse"), Arnaittuq ("Who Has No Woman"), Usuarjuk ("Little Penis"), Qulliq ("Lamp"), Atiittuq ("Who Has No Name"), Jaakkak ("My Two"), and so forth. Christian first names are normally, but not always, gender-specific. Present-day Canadian and Alaskan Inuit usually bear one or several traditional names, one or several Christian names, as well as a family name. In Canada the family name is often the first name of one's father or grandfather, imposed on the family by the federal government during the 1960s (see Williamson 1988; Alia 1994, 2006; Okpik 2005). The Greenlanders generally bear Danish first and family names (e.g., Gudrun Jonathansen), although some use a nickname (e.g., Naja, "Little Sister"; Ammalurtuq, "The Round One") as their given name.

Several of the eponym's flaws, qualities, and characteristics are transmitted through his/her name. In a certain way, the eponym revives in the homonym, as demonstrated by the intra-uterine memories of Iqallijuq, a woman from Igloolik who recounted how she had once been her own grandfather, already dead when she was born and whose name she bore (Saladin d'Anglure 1977). Even when the eponym is still alive, it is believed that part of his or her personality is transmitted to the newborn who receives the name. In exchange, the eponym shares in the vitality of the baby.

Because names are a kind of soul, they cannot be uttered with impunity. Individuals rarely address each other by name, and older Inuit find it impolite to be asked who they are.[16] It is preferable to get the information from someone else. People often bear several names, thus maintaining multiple links with a number of persons. If such is the case, interlocutors are addressed by the term expressing the kinship relation that existed between the speaker and the interlocutor's eponym (or between one's own eponym and the interlocutor). For example, a man who gave his mother's name to his son calls the son *anaana* ("mom"). Conversely, the son addresses his father as *irniq* ("son"). Better yet, if two individuals, even unrelated, have, for instance, two sisters as their respective eponyms, they address each other as though they were sisters, or as their eponyms addressed each other when they were alive (Dufour 1977). Two persons sharing the same eponym call each other *atira* ("my name"), *atitsiara* ("my good name"), *qumnaasiara* ("my beautiful little slit"), *saunira* ("my bone"), or *avvara* ("my half"), according to the dialect they speak.

Because of the symbolic importance of the name, its use formerly entailed several prescriptions and interdictions. In East Greenland, after the end of the mourning period, the name of a deceased person could no longer be pronounced. Even if it was transmitted to newborns, it was never uttered, the individual who had received it being called by a nickname (Robbe 1981). Those already bearing the name had to modify it, and as already mentioned, the appellations of objects, animals, or phenomena denoted by tabooed names were changed (Holm 1914). In West Greenland the name of the deceased was not pronounced as long as it had not been given to a newborn. Similar practices also existed in Canada and Alaska (among both Inupiat and Yupiit). Knud Rasmussen (1931) notes that because human beings are continually called after their predecessors, there exists an unbroken chain of bearers of the same name, who grant their protection to the latest among them. Eponymy allows deceased people to be revived, and out of gratitude, they give strength to their homonyms. It also enables spirits to transmit their names to human beings, who become shamans and whom the spirits help in their functions (Saladin d'Anglure 2006b).

Identifying Speakers

Speech is an instrument of cognition and recognition: a cognitive tool because it allows speakers to explore their universe and to establish distinctions, often very subtle ones, between various entities and phenomena; a means of recognition because it helps to mark the origin and identity of speakers. According to the anthropologist Chase Hensel (2001), identity must be envisioned as a set of social resources upon which individuals constantly draw when interacting with one another. All resources drawn upon during social interaction act as markers of a person's various identities: they show who one is or pretends to be. Talk (or speech, or discourse) is one such marker, but it differs from all others because of its real-time fluidity.

Linguistic utterances are generated on the spot, according to the needs of the moment, which makes them more readily available for immediate expression and response to other people. This means that what is actually discussed (the topics of conversation) and the way it is discussed (the language or style used by the speakers) constitute fundamental identity markers.

The Baffin Island Inuit state that linguistic usage enables identification of at least three types of speakers (Brody 1975, ch. 7): those who talk *surusiqtitut* ("like children"), *inuktitummarik* ("completely like human beings"), and *inungmariktitut* ("like complete Inuit"). The first have problems uttering grammatically acceptable sentences, and their lexicon is seriously limited. By contrast, those in the second category speak correctly and possess an extensive vocabulary. However, they do not reach the level of the third group of speakers, whose speech is particularly sophisticated and elegant and who use refined words (*uqausirjuat*, "big terms") and complex grammatical forms. Those who speak *inungmariktitut*, the *inungmariit* ("complete Inuit"), are the elders who have experienced nomadic life. They can subsist almost totally on local resources because they have mastered the techniques allowing for an optimal exploitation of the environment.[17] *Inungmariit* are now on the decline, by contrast with individuals speaking like children, whose number is rapidly increasing because of the disappearance of traditional activities. Genuine Inuktitut thus appears to be severely threatened.

Language enables recognition of the geographical origin of its speakers. Inuit are usually very sensitive about dialectal differences and often regard as alien a form of speech that differs only slightly from their own.[18] More generally, speech is a marker of humanness. In some special circumstances, it is by speaking and telling their names that people succeed in being recognized by their fellow Inuit. Davidialuk Alasuaq from Puvirnituq tells how, at the beginning of the twentieth century, some Inuit who had gone adrift on a slab of broken sea-ice had been able to survive and, finally, to flee in a makeshift skin-boat when the ice started to melt during the spring. The skiff drifted for a long time before coming within sight of the Ottawa Islands in Hudson Bay. It was then spotted by three families who were camping on the islands. Wondering whether these unexpected arrivals – Inuit never sailed so early in the season – were Indians, Europeans, or spirits, the family heads seized their weapons and took a threatening attitude: "Then, with a strong voice, Aullaq [a woman aboard the boat] started shouting: 'We are Inuit! *Ai* [hello]! We are not *allait* [Indians]! We are not *qallunaat* [Europeans]! We went adrift with the floe!' Then, as they were approaching the shore, because many of them were related to the three families on the island, she told the names of all those on board" (Alasuaq, quoted in Saladin d'Anglure 1978, 24).

Inuit are conscious of the power of speech and of its eminently social character. This is why they respect it and consider it a primordial attribute of their humanness.

LANGUAGE AND IDENTITY

Kalaallisut, Inuktitut, Inuktun, and Inupiaq often constitute essential components of Inuit identity. A resident of Quaqtaq (Nunavik) expresses the idea as follows: "My thoughts (*isumakka*) and my heart (*uummatiga*) can only be expressed through Inuit words" (Dorais 1997, 86). Many people contend that one cannot be a genuine Inuk (*inutuinnaq* or *inummarik*) without speaking the Inuit language, and they regard this language as intimately linked to *maqainniq* ("going away from the community [chiefly for subsistence activities]"), the complex of traditional techniques and knowledge (*qaujimajatuqait*) that constitutes the core of Inuit culture (Dorais 1991).

Identity can be defined in at least two ways (Dorais 1994): as the consciously perceptible aspects of the cognitive system that enables individuals to understand the world where they live in order to make good use of it[19] (cultural identity); and as an appraisal of the social and political position these individuals' ancestral community[20] occupies within a specific nation-state (ethnic identity). In both cases, identity is based on the knowledge one has of his or her natural and social surroundings, as well as on one's personal and collective relations with these surroundings. As mentioned above, identity is a social resource – it can be drawn upon at will when one needs to communicate whom he or she is – rather than an ascription, and it is multifaceted and prone to change (Hensel 2001).

Language and Cultural Identity

Inuit often state that language cannot be dissociated from culture. For Qumaq (1988, 3), for instance, language and culture constitute the two bases of social communication:

> *Inuit piusirminik uqausirminillu aturmata tukisiutigunnasiaqsutik pijumajaminik pijumanngitaminillu uqaqattautigunnasutik qanutuinnalimaaq.*
>
> Inuit use their own customs and their own words, thus being able to understand each other well and to discuss what they want and what they do not want, and this on any topic.

According to Qumaq, traditional Inuit culture (*piusituqait*, "longstanding habits") possesses four main components: specific customs (*piusiit*), a special language (*uqausiit*), mutual support (*ikajuqattaniq*), and transactions that are free of charge[21] (*akiqanngituq*). This culture can thus be subdivided into ways of doing things (customs), modes of communication (language), and rules of behaviour (mutual aid and absence of monetary transactions). Its historical role has been to allow Inuit to survive up to now: "*Taimailuurasualaunngipata inuit ikittuapiugajaqput* – If people had not tried to act in that way [according to their culture], Inuit would [now] be very few" (Qumaq 1988, 3).

Nowadays, even if the context has changed, Inuit language and culture are still relevant, and efforts should be made to preserve them: "Nonetheless, we shall continue to progress in our efforts to avoid the disappearance of words and customs that used to be common in Inuit camps. In our country, in fact, we should look after our own needs, collecting our food [*maqainniq*] or working for money [*kiinaujaliurutiit*]" (Qumaq 1996, 257).

It is only through the aboriginal language that Inuit culture can express itself at its fullest level. According to the Inupiaq linguist and educator Edna Agheak MacLean (1990, 169), words as common as *siqiniq* ("sun") and *uvlugiaq* ("star") reflect, through their mere form, the deeper structure of the Inuit worldview. The former lexeme starts with the base *siqi-* ("to splatter, to splash outward"), followed by the affix *-niq* ("the action of"). Properly speaking, the word for "sun" means "splashing" or "explosion." MacLean notes that *siqiniq* thus expresses a way of thinking quite akin to the modern theory of the Big Bang,[22] which postulates a universe generated by an initial explosion and unceasing expansion.

Similarly, the literal meaning of *uvlugiaq* is "pathway for light." Here again, Inuit views recall present-day astrophysics, according to which the light emanating from stars travels through space at a constant speed. It should be mentioned here that a myth from the eastern Arctic, that of Atungaq, describes a universe where time and space mingle together as in the theory of relativity.[23] The myth relates the story of a man and his wife who travel around the world with their dog team. When they come back home, they are under the impression of having travelled for a year or two, until they discover that their daughter, who had been a child when they left and for whom they had bought a doll during their journey, has now become an old lady.

Language differences can be a source of mutual misunderstanding between Inuit and Europeans because both groups live in separate semantic universes that do not have much in common. In Canada bilingual Inuit often state that English is useful for discussing economic, administrative, or technical topics or for talking about television programming, electronic games, or their favourite websites but that when they want to express their most intimate feelings and ideas, they are more at ease in Inuktitut (Dorais and Sammons 2002). The situation is changing, however, as a growing number of young bilinguals prefer using English in all circumstances (Dorais 2006a). Things are no longer as they were during the mid-1970s, when, according to a sociolinguistic study conducted in Taloyoak by the anthropologist Robert Williamson (1977), 70% of bilingual adults considered traditional Inuktun to be their normal mode of expression.[24] The Inuit language is now apparently losing ground as a conveyor of cultural identity.

On Baffin Island this identity is embodied in the already mentioned *inungmariit*, the "complete Inuit," those male and female elders whose sophisticated language evokes the pleasures of life in the hunting camps of old (Brody 1975). According to some *inungmariit* – and younger people too – recordings of traditional speech should be carefully preserved to avoid a drastic transformation of the language and its eventual dissolution into English. In order not to lose their identity, Inuit of the future must have the possibility of listening to recordings of the voices of their ancestors.

It is not surprising, then, that surveys conducted in Inuit-speaking areas generally disclose very positive opinions about the importance of the ancestral language, at least when it comes to discussing family or community matters, and about the necessity to preserve it (Avataq

1990, 2006; Aylward et al. 1998; Harcharek 2001; Langgaard 2001; Nunavummit Kiglisiniartiit 2001; Dorais and Sammons 2002; Tulloch 2004). Respondents to these surveys deem it evident that Inupiaq, Inuktun, Inuktitut, or Kalaallisut form an integral part of their cultural identity.

Other opinions are also heard. For the authors – all of them Inuit – of a report on education in Nunavik (Nunavik Educational Task Force 1992), the relationship between language and identity is a complex one. Even if several Inuit contend that the current decrease in the use of Inuktitut entails a loss of identity, they must realize that language is just one component of identity among many others. What really matters is the social function of the vernacular speech form, not this form by itself. Bluntly stated, if Inuktitut stops being functional in contemporary society, it is useless to preserve it. A number of individuals interviewed in eastern Nunavut in the late 1990s expressed similar opinions (Dorais and Sammons 2002).

Some specialists go further yet. For them, it is normal that people do not always show much interest in their mother tongue. In such a context, one should not be surprised – or worried – by its disappearance. For the Alaskan anthropologist Patricia Kwachka, during periods of rapid social and cultural change, preserving the aboriginal language is often less important than maintaining traditional patterns of subsistence: "What you eat plays a symbolic part in your identity that is more complex than what you say" (Kwachka 1992b, 8). In this type of situation, "replacement languages" (English, for instance) can be substituted efficiently for the aboriginal tongue. Kwachka gives Yup'ik and Dene examples of the maintenance of fundamental native traditions and values that are now expressed in English. Because people from different areas of Alaska speak various types of English, this language remains useful for maintaining geographical and social distinctions rooted in aboriginal speech forms now almost completely extinct. An anglophone Dene Indian, for instance, can still be differentiated from a Yup'ik or Inupiaq individual on the basis of his or her accent and vocabulary.

Kwachka is probably right. Inuit identity appears to be as strong in Alaska, Nunaqput, the Kitikmeot region, and Nunatsiavut as it is in those areas (i.e., eastern Nunavut, Nunavik, and Greenland) where a majority of people still speak their aboriginal language. One may wonder, however, whether this is not an ethnic identity, one based on the social and political relations a native group maintains with the majority society, and whether the more fundamental cultural identity will not grow weaker and weaker for want of its ancestral linguistic support. In other words, the loss of the aboriginal language could eventually contribute to leaving us with individuals who would be nominal Inuit but whose thinking and behaviour would be indistinguishable from those of Euro-Americans.

Language and Ethnic Identity

During the 1960s and early 1970s the Inuit of Alaska, Canada, and Greenland were progressively recognized by their respective nation-states (i.e., the United States, Canada, and Denmark) as belonging to aboriginal populations that possessed special territorial and cultural rights. In Alaska this recognition led to the Alaska Native Claims Settlement Act of 1971, whereby the Inupiaq, Yupik, and Unangan territories were allocated to eight regional profit-making native corporations.[25] In Canada it allowed for the signing of the James Bay and Northern Quebec Agreement of 1975 and for the subsequent establishment of semi-autonomous administrations and/or governments in Nunaqput (1984), Nunavut (1999), Nunatsiavut (2005), and Nunavik (2007). Finally, in Greenland the Kalaallit were recognized as a separate (i.e., non-Danish) ethnic entity when they achieved Home Rule (internal political autonomy) in 1979 and as a full-fledged nationality when granted Self Rule (quasi independence) in 2009.

Wherever they live, the Inuit now form separate regional populations within larger nation-states, with the arguable exception of Greenland, whose link with Denmark is increasingly tenuous and whose native residents are deemed to form an autonomous nation.[26] In relation to their respective governments and to the general population of their countries of residence, the Inuit thus have to define themselves as ethnic groups – that is, as social entities whose specificity (and the rights it entails) stems from their original territorial, historical, and cultural position within the United States, Canada, or to a much lesser extent, the Kingdom of Denmark.[27]

To achieve public recognition, ethnic identities must be symbolized by visible markers, usually drawn from ancestral culture (Briggs 1997; Searles 2001). Language is one such marker. In Greenland, for instance, "knowledge of Greenlandic is considered the most important cultural characteristic which marks the boundary between the two groups [Kaḷaallit and Danes]" (Kleivan 1970, 236). Children from mixed families sometimes identify themselves as Greenlanders, sometimes as Danes, but if they do not speak fluent Kalaallisut, chances are that they will never be considered genuine Greenlanders.

In Greenland, as elsewhere, language is not the unique marker of identity (Petersen 1985b). Even though fluency in Kalaallisut is a necessary condition for being identified as a Kalaaliq, it is not the only one. A Kalaaliq must be born in Greenland,[28] preferably of Greenlandic parents, and, more generally, must consider oneself a Greenlander and be considered such by other Kalaallit. The importance of language as an identity symbol has changed over time. Before 1970 several Greenlandic parents preferred to speak Danish to their children in order to bestow a Danish identity upon them and to enable them, so they thought, to earn a better living. This way of doing things was a failure, and youngsters reared in Danish had to relearn Kalaallisut in order to be able to claim an aboriginal identity.

Even among Greenlanders, language serves as a marker of difference in those regions (i.e., Thule and the East Coast) where a minority dialect is in use. On the East Coast, for instance, street names, commercial signboards, and public notices, formerly in West Greenlandic, the official language, are increasingly written in the local dialect. In Thule people refer to themselves as Kalaallit ("Greenlanders") when addressing Danes, but they prefer being known as Inughuit ("Big Inuit") by other inhabitants of Greenland (Søby 1979).

Local identities also play an important part in West Greenland. According to Susanne Dybbroe (1991), rather than being based on a genuine national sentiment, "Greenlandicity" (*kalaaliusuusiq*, "being *kalaaliq*") stems from the fact that an individual belongs to a regional social network – that is, to a group of relatives and friends living in a limited number of communities. It includes a symbolic dimension whereby, thanks to language, relations between individuals, their social networks, and the territory are encoded in a significant semantic structure. This has been verified in Greenland (Le Mouël 1984; Nuttall 1991, 2001) as well as in Canada (Correll 1976).

In the Canadian North, language is generally considered an important symbol of ethnic identity. All existing Inuit-led governments and administrations (Nunavut, for instance) draw their legitimacy from the fact that because the Inuit possess their own language and culture,[29] the territories where they constitute the majority of the population are entitled to some form of political autonomy (see

Légaré 2001). Aboriginal leaders routinely mention language as an essential component of Inuit identity, although, as seen in chapter 9, this is sometimes considered a merely symbolic statement aimed at justifying the specificity of the people they represent. Canada's arctic citizens usually agree on the importance of Inuktitut, but when they want to communicate among themselves, what is primordial for them is to be sure they will be understood. Proper comprehension thus predominates over ethnic assertion, and among bilinguals, this often leads to conversations in English or in a mixed code (Dorais 2006a, 57–8).

During the 1970s and early 1980s, in those areas where the Inuit language had started to decline, Inuit identity seemed on the verge of being subsumed by more encompassing forms of aboriginal identification (Schafer 1977; Prattis 1986), namely "Labrador Native" (Inuit and "Settlers" of Anglo-Saxon heritage) in Nunatsiavut, "Mackenzie Native" (Inuvialuit and Dene) in Nunaqput, and "Alaska Native" (Inupiat, Yupiit, Unangan, and Dene) in Alaska. But this tendency did not last long,[30] and nowadays each Inuit group values its own ethnic and regional identity.[31] Lawrence Kaplan (2001) has shown that in Alaska the main markers of Inupiaq identity may now be the traditional cultural values rather than language and subsistence but that the aboriginal tongue – taught as a second language in most Inupiat schools – is still considered important in defining regional ethnicity.[32] Discourse can also be used for conveying to non-natives – and to fellow natives as well – that one is an Inupiaq or a Yup'ik rather than a white Tanik or Kas'aq. Chase Hensel (1996) has described how southwest Alaskan Yupiit manipulate conversation[33] about subsistence to convey the extent of their Yup'ik ethnicity to their interlocutors.

CONCLUSION

As can be gathered from this chapter and the preceding ones, the present-day Inuit have reached a linguistic crossroads of sorts. Some Eskaleut languages and dialects are now spoken by only a small minority of those who have them as their ancestral tongue. Some others, however, still constitute the usual means of communication of a vast majority of the aboriginal population. What can be inferred from this situation? Will the language of the Inuit continue to decline and finally disappear, or on the contrary, will it be reinvigorated thanks to the current social, political, and cultural revival of arctic societies? The answer is complex and uncertain.

According to the percentage of individuals who still retain some command of their ancestral language, the Unangax, Yupik, and Inuit speech forms can be grouped into various categories, ranging from that of languages apparently on the verge of extinction (e.g., Unangax and Alutiiq Yupik, with some 5% to 6% of speakers at the turn of the twenty-first century)[34] to that of very healthy dialects (e.g., Kalaallisut, spoken by about 97% of native Greenlanders). All languages in good health (i.e., with more than 90% of mother-tongue speakers) are found in the eastern Canadian Arctic and Greenland. These two areas harbour about 57% of the world's Eskimo-Aleut population and 72% of all individuals of Inuit (rather than Yupik or Unangan) ancestry, but they are home to 94% of all speakers of the Inuit language and to 85% of those who speak Eskaleut. It thus seems reasonable to be moderately optimistic.

Even in these regions, however, nothing is won. Although the aboriginal language appears to be solidly implanted in Greenland,[35] the situation is somewhat different in eastern Canada, where the ubiquity and predominance of English constitute a serious threat to Inuktitut. As previously discussed, current research as well as language statistics disclose a seemingly unstoppable increase in the proportion of Inuit who prefer to speak English (or mixed codes) among themselves and a parallel decrease in the percentage of homes – and also workplaces – where Inuktitut is the preferred language for addressing each other.

What should be done about such a situation? Observers of the Inuit scene agree that the survival of the aboriginal language depends on common action involving the school and the community. For Roy Iutzi-Mitchell (1992), an Alaskan anthropologist, the revival and preservation of the arctic speech forms are unthinkable without total linguistic immersion during the elementary grades and without teaching indigenous languages at least half of the time in high school and college. To reach such a goal, communities and organizations must make it very clear that Inupiaq, Inuktun, or Inuktitut are essential components of their identity and that they are committed to doing everything possible for the survival and development of their ancestral language. This may sound idealistic, however. Even though politicians and other leaders often pay lip service to the importance of the Inuit language, financial and structural barriers[36] might impede it from being protected in an efficient way.

This is why the question must be asked under a different guise: should we be optimistic or pessimistic about the future of Inuktitut – and of the other Inuit and Eskaleut languages? On the one hand, much progress has been made since the 1960s, when Diamond Jenness, an otherwise sensible and knowledgeable anthropologist, was not ashamed to write: "They [Inuit] are a fragmented amorphous race that lacks all sense of history, inherits no pride of ancestry, and discerns no glory in past events or past achievements ... Now at last, they are emerging; but with their long background of fragmentation it seems to me very doubtful that any school instruction, or any educational 'propaganda', can revive their drooping morale, or save their language from extinction – if in the end extinction is to be its fate" (Jenness 1964, 128). Twenty years after Jenness published these lines, the Inuit language was already taught in most arctic schools. Since then, its symbolic value has not stopped growing, in concert with increasing administrative and political power devolved to its speakers.

On the other hand, outside of Greenland the Inuit of today live in a world dominated by English. Taking education as an example, even though the Inuit language is highly valued as a marker of identity, it is rarely taught beyond grades 2 or 3, except, sporadically, as a relatively unimportant subject matter. This means that for one or two generations – longer in Alaska and the western Canadian Arctic – Inuit speakers, or descendants of speakers, have been partly or entirely schooled in English by predominantly non-aboriginal teachers.[37] No wonder then that many individuals, albeit bilingual, find expressing themselves easier in English or in a mixed code than in their mother tongue.

Should we be pessimistic or optimistic? It may well happen that within two generations, three at most, English will predominate in communities where Inuktitut is still strong, as it has done for a few decades in Alaska, Nunaqput, and Nunatsiavut. The aboriginal language might survive anyway but only for expressing trivialities or, on the contrary, when being used in highly symbolic circumstances (e.g., special church events and important political ceremonials).[38] And Kalaallisut might follow the same path later on, especially if English ever replaces Danish as Greenland's second language.

The Inuit, however, generally prefer to remain optimistic, even though they are increasingly concerned with the future of their language (Dorais and Sammons 2002; Tulloch 2004; Dorais 2006a). For Taamusi Qumaq, who has pondered these questions for a long time, there is no doubt that Inuktitut will be preserved if the elders and adults contribute to the task: "The Inuit language and culture will not disappear soon. And although many words of the language of the past – not too many though – have dropped out of use, I know that some of them will be used again by the young Inuit. Even if people adopt many new words, there is no reason for alarm if we, the elders, take things in hand by explaining to the others the meanings of the old words of our language" (Qumaq 1996, 256–7).

If special efforts are made in favour of the Inuit language, in the fields of education, public communication, cultural development, and personal language attitudes, a situation of stable, additive bilingualism can indeed be established in the North American Arctic. One may be an Inuk without speaking Inupiaq, Inuktun, Inuktitut, or Kalaallisut, but if the language continues to decline, a whole original way of envisioning the world risks disappearing for good, together with the cultural identity it contributes to nurturing. Like any other form of speech, the Inuit language can easily be adapted to the expression of contemporary life, provided appropriate means are taken to fully educate its speakers in their mother tongue. Will the language of the Inuit still be heard and, hopefully, listened to at the turn of the twenty-second century? *Immaqa*, maybe!

APPENDIX ONE

The Possessive Noun Declension (Nunavik Inuktitut)

WORD-BASE *NUNA* ("LAND")

		SINGULAR	DUAL	PLURAL
"my"	basic	nunaga	nunaakka	nunakka
	relative	nunamma	nunaamma	nunamma
	modalis	nunaganik (T)*	nunaakkanik	nunakkanik
		nunanniuvanga (I)*		
	ablative	nunaganit (T)	nunaakkanit	nunakkanit
		nunanniuvanga (I)		
	locative	nunagani (T)	nunaakkani	nunakkani
		nunanniuvanga (I)		
	allative	nunaganut (T)	nunaakkanut	nunakkanut
		nunannuuvanga (I)		
	translative	nunagagut (T)	nunaakkakut	nunakkatigut
		nunakkuuvanga (I)		
	simulative	nunagatut (T)	nunaakkatut	nunakka[ti]tut
		nunattuuvanga (I)		
"our (2 of us)"	basic	nunavuk	nunaappuk	nunavuk
	relative	nunannuk	nunaannuk	nunannuk
	modalis	nunattinik	nunaattinik	nunattinik
	ablative	nunattinit	nunaattinit	nunattinit
	locative	nunattini	nunaattini	nunattini
	allative	nunattinut	nunaattinut	nunattinut
	translative	nunattigut	nunaattigut	nunattigut
	simulative	nunattitut	nunaattitut	nunattitut

		SINGULAR	DUAL	PLURAL
"our"	basic	nunavut	nunaavut	nunavut
	relative	nunatta	nunaatta	nunatta
	modalis	nunattinik	nunaattinik	nunattinik
	ablative	nunattinit	nunaattinit	nunattinit
	locative	nunattini	nunaattini	nunattini
	allative	nunattinut	nunaattinut	nunattinut
	translative	nunattigut	nunaattigut	nunattigut
	simulative	nunattitut	nunaattitut	nunattitut

Also: -vunnik, -vunni, -vunnut, -vunnit, -vutigut, and -vutitut.

		SINGULAR	DUAL	PLURAL
"your (1 of you)"	basic	nunait	nunaakkik	nunatit
	relative	nunavit/ppit	nunaappit	nunavit/ppit
	modalis	nunannik (T)	nunaakkinik	nunannik (T)
		nunanniuvit (I)		nunanniuvit (I)
	ablative	nunannit (T)	nunaakkinit	nunannit (T)
		nunanniuvit (I)		nunanniuvit (I)
	locative	nunanni (T)	nunaakkini	nunanni (T)
		nunanniuvit (I)		nunanniuvit (I)
	allative	nunannut (T)	nunaakkinut	nunannut (T)
		nunannuuvit (I)		nunannuuvit (I)
	translative	nunakkut (T)	nunaakkikut	nunattigut (T)
		nunakkuuvit (I)		nunakkuuvit (I)
	simulative	nunattut (T)	nunaakkitut	nunattitut (T)
		nunattuuvit (I)		nunattuuvit (I)

In Tarramiut, also: -tinnik, -tinni, -tinnut, and -tinnit in the plural.

		SINGULAR	DUAL	PLURAL
"your (2 of you)"	basic	nunatik	nunaattik	nunatik
	relative	nunattik	nunaattik	nunattik
	modalis	nunattinik	nunaattinik	nunattinik
	ablative	nunattinit	nunaattinit	nunattinit
	locative	nunattini	nunaattini	nunattini
	allative	nunattinut	nunaattinut	nunattinut
	translative	nunattikut	nunaattikut	nunattikut
	simulative	nunattitut	nunaattitut	nunattitut

		SINGULAR	DUAL	PLURAL
"your (many of you)"	basic	nunasi	nunaasi	nunasi
	relative	nunatsi	nunaatsi	nunatsi
	modalis	nunatsinik	nunaatsinik	nunatsinik
	ablative	nunatsinit	nunaatsinit	nunatsinit

		SINGULAR	DUAL	PLURAL
	locative	nunatsini	nunaatsini	nunatsini
	allative	nunatsinut	nunaatsinut	nunatsinut
	translative	nunatsigut	nunaatsigut	nunatsigut
	simulative	nunatsitut	nunaatsitut	nunatsitut
"his/her"	basic	nunanga	nunaangik	nunangit
	relative	nunangata	nunaangitta	nunangita
	modalis	nunanganik	nunaanginnik	nunanginnik
	ablative	nunanganit	nunaanginnit	nunanginnit
	locative	nunangani	nunaanginni	nunanginni
	allative	nunanganut	nunaanginnut	nunanginnut
	translative	nunangagut	nunaangittigut	nunangitigut
	simulative	nunangatut	nunaangittitut	nunangi[ti]tut
"their (2 of them)"	basic	nunanga[k]	nunaangik	nunangit
	relative	nunangata	nunaangitta	nunangita
	modalis	nunanga[n]nik	nunaanginnik	nunanginnik
	ablative	nunanga[n]nit	nunaanginnit	nunanginnit
	locative	nunanga[n]ni	nunaanginni	nunanginni
	allative	nunanga[n]nut	nunaanginnut	nunanginnut
	translative	nunangakkut	nunaangittigut	nunangitigut
	simulative	nunanga[t]tut	nunaangittitut	nunangititut
"their"	basic	nunangat	nunaangik	nunangit
	relative	nunangata	nunaangitta	nunangita
	modalis	nunangannik	nunaanginnik	nunanginnik
	ablative	nunangannit	nunaanginnit	nunanginnit
	locative	nunanganni	nunaanginni	nunanginni
	allative	nunangannut	nunaanginnut	nunanginnut
	translative	nunangatigut	nunaangittigut	nunangitigut
	simulative	nunangatitut	nunaangittitut	nunangititut
"his/her own"	basic	nunani	nunaanni	nunani
	relative	nunami	nunaammi	nunami
	modalis	nunaminik	nunaamminik	nunaminik
	ablative	nunaminit	nunaamminit	nunaminit
	locative	nunamini	nunaammini	nunamini
	allative	nunaminut	nunaamminut	nunaminut
	translative	nunamigut	nunaammigut	nunamitigut
	simulative	nunamitut	nunaammitut	nunamititut

		SINGULAR	DUAL	PLURAL
"their own	basic	nunanni	nunaanni	nunanni
(two or	relative	nunamik	nunaammik	nunamik
many)"	modalis	nunaminnik	nunaamminik	nunaminnik
	ablative	nunaminnit	nunaamminit	nunaminnit
	locative	nunaminni	nunaammini	nunaminni
	allative	nunaminnut	nunaamminut	nunaminnut
	translative	nunamigut	nunaammikut	nunamittigut
	simulative	nunamittut	nunaammitut	nunamittitut

* T = Tarramiut subdialect; I = Itivimiut subdialect

APPENDIX TWO

The Grammatical Endings of Verbs (Nunavik Inuktitut)

SINGLE-PERSON ENDINGS

“to see” (*taku-*)	“to arrive” (*tikit-*)	“to sleep” (*sinik-*)	“to hear” (*tusaq-*)
DECLARATIVE			
1s takuvunga	tikippunga	sinippunga/kunga*	tusaqpunga/qunga
2s takuvutit	tikipputit	sinipputit/kutit	tusaqputit/qutit
3s takuvuq	tikippuq	sinippuq/kuq	tusaqpuq/quq
1d takuvuguk	tikippuguk	sinippuguk/kuguk	tusaqpuguk/quguk
2d takuvutik	tikipputik	sinipputik/kutik	tusaqputik/qutik
3d takuvuuk	tikippuuk	sinippuuk/kuuk	tusaqpuuk/quuk
1p takuvugut	tikippugut	sinippugut/kugut	tusaqpugut/qugut
2p takuvusi	tikippusi	sinippusi/kusi	tusaqpusi/qusi
3p takuvut	tikipput	sinipput/kut	tusaqput/qut

* Endings starting with *k*- assimilate the base-final consonant (e.g., *sinikkunga*).

NEGATION OF THE DECLARATIVE			
1s takunngilanga	tikinngilanga	sininngilanga	tusanngilanga
2s takunngilatit	tikinngilatit	sininngilatit	tusanngilatit
3s takunngilaq	tikinngilaq	sininngilaq	tusanngilaq
1d takunngilaguk	tikinngilaguk	sininngilaguk	tusanngilaguk
2d takunngilatik	tikinngilatik	sininngilatik	tusanngilatik
3d takunngilaak	tikinngilaak	sininngilaak	tusanngilaak
1p takunngilagut	tikinngilagut	sininngilagut	tusanngilagut
2p takunngilasi	tikinngilasi	sininngilasi	tusanngilasi
3p takunngilat	tikinngilat	sininngilat	tusanngilat

INDICATIVE

1s takujunga*	tikittunga	sinittunga	tusaqtunga
2s takujutit	tikittutit	sinittutit	tusaqtutit
3s takujuq	tikittuq	sinittuq	tusaqtuq
1d takujuguk	tikittuguk	sinittuguk	tusaqtuguk
2d takujutik	tikittutik	sinittutik	tusaqtutik
3d takujuuk	tikittuuk	sinittuuk	tusaqtuuk
1p takujugut	tikittugut	sinittugut	tusaqtugut
2p takujusi	tikittusi	sinittusi	tusaqtusi
3p takujut	tikittut	sinittut	tusaqtut

* In Itivimiut, *j* is pronounced *J* (e.g., *takuJunga*).

INTERROGATIVE

1s takuvungaa?	tikippungaa?	sinippungaa/kungaa?	tusaqpungaa/qungaa?
2s takuviit?	tikippiit?	sinippiit/kiit?	tusaqpiit/qiit?
3s takuvaa?	tikippaa?	sinippaa/kaa?	tusaqpaa/qaa?
1d takuvinuuk?	tikippinuuk?	sinippinuuk/kinuuk?	tusaqpinuuk/qinuuk?
2d takuvitiik?	tikippitiik?	sinippitiik/kitiik?	tusaqpitiik/qitiik?
3d takuvaak?	tikippaak?	sinippaak/kaak?	tusaqpaak/qaak?
1p takuvitaa?	tikippitaa?	sinippitaa/kitaa?	tusaqpitaa/qitaa?
2p takuvisii?	tikippisii?	sinippisii/kisii?	tusaqpisii/qisii?
3p takuvaat?	tikippaat?	sinippaat/kaat?	tusaqpaat/qaat?

IMPERATIVE-OPTATIVE

1s takulanga!	tikillanga!	sinillanga!	tusarlanga!
2s takugit!	tikigit!	sinigit!	tusarit!
3s takuli!	tikilli!	sinilli!	tusarli!
1d takuluk!	tikilluk!	sinilluk!	tusarluk!
2d takugittik!	tikigittik!	sinigittik!	tusarittik!
3d takulik!	tikillik!	sinillik!	tusarlik!
1p takuta!	tikita!	sinitta!	tusaqta!
2p takugitsi!	tikigitsi!	sinigitsi!	tusaritsi!
3p takulit!	tikillit!	sinillit!	tusarlit!

PERFECTIVE

1s takugama	tikigama	sinigama/kkama	tusarama
2s takugavit	tikigavit	sinigavit/kkavit	tusaravit
3s takummat	tikimmat	sinimmat	tusarmat
4s takugami	tikigami	sinigami/kkami	tusarami

1d takugannuk	tikigannuk	sinigannuk/kkanuk	tusarannuk
2d takugattik	tikigattik	sinigattik/kkatik	tusarattik
3d takummatik/mmanik	tikimmatik/manik	sinimmatik/manik	tusarmatik/manik
4d takugamik	tikigamik	sinigamik/kkamik	tusaramik
1p takugatta	tikigatta	sinigatta/kkata	tusaratta
2p takugatsi	tikigatsi	sinigatsi/kkasi	tusaratsi
3p takummata	tikimmata	sinimmata	tusarmata
4p takugamik	tikigamik	sinigamik/kkamik	tusaramik
IMPERFECTIVE			
1s takuguma	tikiguma	siniguma/kkuma	tusaruma
2s takuguvit	tikiguvit	siniguvit/kkuvit	tusaruvit
3s takuppat	tikippat	sinippat	tusaqpat
4s takuguni	tikiguni	siniguni/kkuni	tusaruni
1d takugunnuk	tikigunnuk	sinigunnuk/kkunuk	tusarunnuk
2d takuguttik	tikiguttik	siniguttik/kkutik	tusaruttik
3d takuppatik/ppanik	tikippatik/panik	sinippatik/panik	tusaqpatik/panik
4d takugutik	tikigutik/kkutik	sinigutik/kkutik	tusarutik
1p takugutta	tikigutta	sinigutta/kkuta	tusarutta
2p takugutsi	tikigutsi	sinigutsi/kkusi	tusarutsi
3p takuppata	tikippata	sinippata	tusaqpata
4p takugutik	tikigutik	sinigutik/kkutik	tusarutik
DUBITATIVE			
1s takummangaarma	tikimmangaarma	sinimmangaarma	tusarmangaarma
2s takummangaaqpit	tikimmangaaqpit	sinimmangaaqpit	tusarmangaaqpit
3s takummangaat	tikimmangaat	sinimmangaat	tusarmangaat
4s takummangaarmi	tikimmangaarmi	sinimmangaarmi	tusarmangaarmi
1d takummangaannuk	tikimmangaannuk	sinimmangaannuk	tusarmangaannuk
2d takummangaattik	tikimmangaattik	sinimmangaattik	tusarmangaattik
3d takummangaatik	tikimmangaatik	sinimmangaatik	tusarmangaatik
4d takummangaarmik	tikimmangaarmik	sinimmangaarmik	tusarmangaarmik
1p takummangaatta	tikimmangaatta	sinimmangaatta	tusarmangaatta
2p takummangaatsi	tikimmangaatsi	sinimmangaatsi	tusarmangaatsi
3p takummangaata	tikimmangaata	sinimmangaata	tusarmangaata
4p takummangaarmik	tikimmangaarmik	sinimmangaarmik	tusarmangaarmik
PERFECTIVE APPOSITIONAL			
1s takutsunga	tikitsunga	sinitsunga	tusaqsunga
2s takutsutit	tikitsutit	sinitsutit	tusaqsutit
3s takutsuni	tikitsuni	sinitsuni	tusaqsuni

1d	takutsunuk	tikitsunuk	sinitsunuk	tusaqsunuk
2d	takutsutik	tikitsutik	sinitsutik	tusaqsutik
3d	takutsutik	tikitsutik	sinitsutik	tusaqsutik
1p	takutsuta	tikitsuta	sinitsuta	tusaqsuta
2p	takutsusi	tikitsusi	sinitsusi	tusaqsusi
3p	takutsutik	tikitsutik	sinitsutik	tusaqsutik

IMPERFECTIVE APPOSITIONAL

1s	takulunga	tikillunga	sinillunga	tusarlunga
2s	takulutit	tikillutit	sinillutit	tusarlutit
3s	takuluni	tikilluni	sinilluni	tusarluni
1d	takulunuk	tikillunuk	sinillunuk	tusarlunuk
2d	takulutik	tikillutik	sinillutik	tusarlutik
3d	takulutik	tikillutik	sinillutik	tusarlutik
1p	takuluta	tikilluta	sinilluta	tusarluta
2p	takulusi	tikillusi	sinillusi	tusarlusi
3p	takulutik	tikillutik	sinillutik	tusarlutik

NON-REFLEXIVE APPOSITIONAL (WITH AFFIX *-TIT-*)

1s	takutillunga	tikitillunga	sinittilunga	tusaqtilunga
2s	takutillutit	tikitillutit	sinittilutit	tusaqtilutit
3s	takutillugu	tikitillugu	sinittilugu	tusaqtilugu
1d	takutillunuk	tikitillunuk	sinittilunuk	tusaqtilunuk
2d	takutillutik	tikitillutik	sinittilutik	tusaqtilutik
3d	takutillugik	tikitillugik	sinittilugik	tusaqtilugik
1p	takutilluta	tikitilluta	sinittiluta	tusaqtiluta
2p	takutillusi	tikitillusi	sinittilusi	tusaqtilusi
3p	takutillugit	tikitillugit	sinittilugit	tusaqtilugit

NEGATIVE APPOSITIONAL

1s	takunanga	tikinnanga	sininnanga	tusarnanga
2s	takunak	tikinnak	sininnak	tusarnak
3s	takugani	tikigani	sinigani	tusarani
1d	takuganuk	tikiganuk	siniganuk	tusaranuk
2d	takugatik	tikigatik	sinigatik	tusaratik
3d	takugatik	tikigatik	sinigatik	tusaratik
1p	takugata	tikigata	sinigata	tusarata
2p	takugasi	tikigasi	sinigasi	tusarasi
3p	takugatik	tikigatik	sinigatik	tusaratik

NEGATIVE NON-REFLEXIVE APPOSITIONAL (WITH AFFIX -*TIT*-)

1s	takutinnanga	tikittinanga	sinittinanga	tusaqtinanga
2s	takutinnak	tikittinak	sinittinak	tusaqtinak
3s	takutinnagu	tikittinagu	sinittinagu	tusaqtinagu
1d	takutinnanuk	tikittinanuk	sinittinanuk	tusaqtinanuk
2d	takutinnatik	tikittinatik	sinittinatik	tusaqtinatik
3d	takutinnagik	tikittinagik	sinittinagik	tusaqtinagik
1p	takutinnata	tikittinata	sinittinata	tusaqtinata
2p	takutinnasi	tikittinasi	sinittinasi	tusaqtinasi
3p	takutinnagit	tikittinagit	sinittinagit	tusaqtinagit

SOME EXAMPLES OF DOUBLE-PERSON ENDINGS

DECLARATIVE	INDICATIVE	
utaqqivara	utaqqijara*	"I wait for him/her"
utaqqivagit	utaqqijagit	"I wait for you (1)"
utaqqivait	utaqijait	"you (1) wait for him/her"
utaqqivarma	utaqqijarma	"you (1) wait for me"
utaqqivaa	utaqqijanga	"he/she waits for him/her"
utaqqivaatit	utaqqijaatit	"he/she waits for you (1)"
utaqqivaanga	utaqqijaanga	"he/she waits for me"
ikajuqpara/qara	ikajuqtara	"I help him/her"
ikajuqpagit/qagit	ikajuqtagit	"I help you (1)"
ikajuqpait/qait	ikajuqtait	"you (1) help him/her"
ikajuqpama/qama	ikajuqtama	"you (1) help me"
ikajuqpaa/qaa	ikajuqtanga	"he/she helps him/her"
ikajuqpaatit/qaatit	ikajuqtaatit	"he/she helps you (1)"
ikajuqpaanga/qaanga	ikajuqtaanga	"he/she helps me"

* In this and all other examples, *j* is pronounced *J* in Itivimiut.

INTERROGATIVE

utaqqivingaa?	"do you (1) wait for me?"
takuniaqpiuk/qiuk?	"will you (1) see him/her?"
ikajuqpigiit/qigiit?	"do you (1) help them?"
tusaqpajuuk/qajuuk?	"do they hear him/her?"

IMPERATIVE-OPTATIVE

takunnga!	"look at me!"
qaiguk!	"bring it here!"
ikajukkit!	"help them!"
takulagu!	"may I see him/her!"
tusarlijuk!	"may they hear him/her!"

PERFECTIVE

tikigakku	"when *or* because I reached him/her"
takugavinga	"when *or* because you (1) saw me"
ikajuraviuk	"when *or* because you (1) helped him/her"
tusaramigit	"when *or* because he/she heard them"

IMPERFECTIVE

tikigukku	"when I reach him/her, if I reach him/her"
takuguvinga	"when you (1) see me, if you see me"
ikajuruviuk	"when *or* if you (1) help him/her"
tusarunigit	"when *or* if he/she hears them"

DUBITATIVE

tikimmangaakku	"[I wonder] if I reach him/her"
takummangaasi	"[I wonder] if he/she sees you (many)"
takummangaagik	"[I wonder] if they see both of them"
tusarmangaarmitit	"[they wonder] if they hear you (1)"

PERFECTIVE APPOSITIONAL

takutsugu	"seeing him/her"
ikajuqsugit	"helping them"
tusaqsunga	"hearing me"
tikitsutit	"reaching you"

IMPERFECTIVE APPOSITIONAL

takulunigit	"seeing them, he/she will..."
tusarluninga	"hearing me, he/she will..."
utaqqilutigut	"waiting for us, you (1) will..."
takulugu	"seeing him/her in the future"
tusarluta	"hearing us in the future"

NEGATIVE APPOSITIONAL

takunanga	"not seeing me"
takunagu	"not seeing him/her/it"
tikinnagik	"not reaching both of them"

APPENDIX THREE

Categories of Lexical Affixes* with Nunavik Inuktitut Examples

1 Being and becoming
-u- ("to be something") — arnaujuq ("it is a woman")

2 Lacking
-irut- ("not to have anymore") — imairuttuq ("there is no more water")

3 Feeling
-nngu- ("to ache") — niaqunngujunga ("I have a headache")

4 Having
-qaq- ("to have something") — illuqaqtutit ("you have a house")

5 Acquiring
-siuq- ("to search for") — puijisiuqtuq ("he is searching for seals; he hunts seals")

6 Movement
-liaq- ("to go to") — Quaqtaliaqtugut ("we go to Quaqtaq")

7 Acting and seeming like
-ujaaq- ("to look like") — angutaujaaqtuq ("he/she looks like a man")

8 Doing with and providing
-liri- ("to occupy oneself with") — sulirivit ("what do you occupy yourself with?")

9 Judging and saying
-juri-/-turi- ("to think that") — qaijurivagit ("I think that you are coming")

10 10 Wishing and wanting
-guma-/-ruma- ("to want") — tusarumajuq ("he/she wants to hear")

11 Causation and request
-tit- ("to cause, to let") takutippara ("I make him/her see")

12 Striving and intending
-gasuaq-/-rasuaq- ("to strive to") aullarasuaqtunga ("I try to leave")

13 Potentiality
-gunnaq-/-runnaq- ("to be able to") qaigunnatuq ("he/she can come")

14 Relation shifters
-qatigi- ("do something with someone") sanaqatigijara ("I work with him/her")

15 Degree
-kainnaapik- ("a little") ingirrakainnaapittutit ("you move on a little")

16 Manner
-llarik- ("really") uqallarittuq ("he/she really speaks; is a real speaker")

17 Phase of completion
-vallia-/-pallia- ("more and more") piruqpaliajutit ("you grow more and more")

18 Frequency and duration
-qattaq-/-rattaq- ("oftentimes") pulaarattatuq ("he/she frequently goes on visits")

19 Tense
-langa- ("near future") tikilangajuq ("he/she will arrive soon")

20 Modality
-gajaq-/-rajaq- ("conditional") tikigajaqtunga ("I would arrive")

21 Negation
-nngit- ("negation") qainngituq ("he/she does not come")

22 Subjective coloration
-kuluk- ("gently, softly") qiakulupputit ("you are crying softly")

23 Conjunctional
-galuaq-/-raluaq- ("however, though") inuugaluaqtutit ("you are an Inuk, though")

24 Nominalizers
-niq- ("fact of, action of, state of") aullaniq ("the action of leaving; departure")

25 Nominal extenders

-lik- ("one who has, there is")	illulik ("one who has a house; there is a house")

26 Nominal modifiers

-aluk- ("big")	illualuk ("a big house")

27 Enclitics

-guuq/-ruuq ("it is said")	qailangajungaguuq ("I shall come, it is said")
-luunniit- ("even, or")	sininngiturluuniit ("he/she doesn't even sleep")
	ivviluunniit uvangaluunniit ("or you, or I")

* According to Fortescue 1983.

APPENDIX FOUR

Inuit First and Home Languages in *Inuit nunaat* (Canada) in 2006

NOTE: Tables are based on data from the Canadian census of 2006, except for the Inuvik and Aklavik figures (extrapolated from Northwest Territories statistics, 2004–07). In view of the ethnic homogeneity of most Inuit communities, census figures concerning individuals whose first language is neither English nor French have been interpreted as applying to Inuit-first-language speakers, with three exceptions: Inuvik, Aklavik (both localities being part-Dene and part-Inuvialuit), and the ethnically diverse town of Iqaluit (for which local approximations have been resorted to). In a similar way, data on home languages other than English or French have been regarded as applying to Inuit-home-language households, except, here again, for in the same three communities. Data found in this appendix are thus indicative but most probably not too far from reality.

1 COMMUNITY NAME	2 PRINCIPAL DIALECT SPOKEN	3 TOTAL POPULATION	4 INUIT POPULATION	5 INUIT 1ST LANGUAGE	6 % 5/4	7 INUIT HOME LANGUAGE	8 % 7/5
INUVIK	Siglit/Uummarmiut	3,354	981	166	17	30	18
AKLAVIK	Uummarmiut	597	297	56	19	10	18
TUKTOYAKTUK	Siglitun	870	730	150	21	50	33
SACHS HARBOUR	Siglitun	122	105	25	24	0	0
PAULATUK	Siglitun	294	265	35	13	0	0
HOLMAN	Inuinnaqtun	398	365	120	33	40	33
TOTAL INUVIALUIT (NUNAQPUT)		5,635	2,743	552	20	130	24
KUGLUKTUK	Inuinnaqtun	1,302	1,195	410	34	115	28
CAMBRIDGE BAY	Inuinnaqtun	1,477	1,215	480	40	130	27
GJOA HAVEN	Natsilingmiutut	1,064	995	480	48	150	31
TALOYOAK	Natsilingmiutut	809	745	525	70	170	32
KUGAARUK	Natsilingmiutut	688	635	460	72	155	34
TOTAL KITIKMEOT (NUNAVUT)		5,340	4,785	2,355	49	720	31
REPULSE-NAUJAAT	Natsilingmiutut/Aivilik	748	715	700	98	620	89
CHESTERFIELD INLET	Aivilik	332	295	280	95	165	59
CORAL HARBOUR	Aivilik	769	735	725	99	610	84
BAKER LAKE	Kivalliq	1,728	1,560	1,125	72	405	36
RANKIN INLET	Aivilik/Kivalliq	2,358	1,955	1,655	85	975	59
WHALE COVE	Kivalliq	353	340	340	100	310	91
ARVIAT	Kivalliq	2,060	1,915	1,915	100	1,825	95
TOTAL KIVALLIQ (NUNAVUT)		8,348	7,515	6,740	90	4,910	73

1 COMMUNITY NAME	2 PRINCIPAL DIALECT SPOKEN	3 TOTAL POPULATION	4 INUIT POPULATION	5 INUIT 1ST LANGUAGE	6 % 5/4	7 INUIT HOME LANGUAGE	8 % 7/5
HALL BEACH	North Baffin	654	630	625	99	595	95
IGLOOLIK	North Baffin	1,538	1,445	1,445	100	1,420	98
RESOLUTE	N. Baffin/Nunavik	229	200	150	75	65	43
GRISE FIORD	N. Baffin/Nunavik	141	120	120	100	80	67
ARCTIC BAY	North Baffin	690	640	640	100	610	95
POND INLET	North Baffin	1,315	1,215	1,215	100	1,140	94
CLYDE RIVER	S. Baffin/N. Baffin	820	790	790	100	760	96
QIKIQTARJUAQ	South Baffin	473	450	450	100	445	99
PANGNIRTUNG	South Baffin	1,325	1,240	1,240	100	1,185	96
IQALUIT	S./N. Baffin	6,184	3,650	3,030	83	1,805	59
KIMMIRUT	South Baffin	411	385	385	100	345	90
CAPE DORSET	South Baffin	1,236	1,130	1,125	99	1,040	92
SANIKILUAQ	Nunavik	744	710	700	99	685	98
TOTAL BAFFIN (NUNAVUT)		15,760	12,605	11,915	94	10,175	85
NAIǸ	Nunatsiavut	1,034	950	300	32	80	27
HOPEDALE	Nunatsiavut	530	475	155	33	40	26
POSTVILLE	(Nunatsiavut)[a]	219	200	0	0	0	0
MAKKOVIK	Nunatsiavut	362	320	20	6	10	50
RIGOLET	Nunatsiavut	269	250	5	2	0	0
NORTH WEST RIVER	Nunatsiavut	492	340	25	7	0	0
TOTAL NUNATSIAVUT (LABRADOR)[b]		2,906	2,535	505	20	130	26

1 COMMUNITY NAME	2 PRINCIPAL DIALECT SPOKEN	3 TOTAL POPULATION	4 INUIT POPULATION	5 INUIT 1ST LANGUAGE	6 % 5/4	7 INUIT HOME LANGUAGE	8 % 7/5
KUUJJUARAAPIK	Nunavik	568	515	505	98	405	80
UMIUJAQ	Nunavik	390	370	370	100	370	100
INUKJUAK	Nunavik	1,597	1,340	1,330	99	1,300	98
PUVIRNITUQ	Nunavik	1,457	1,390	1,390	100	1,360	98
AKULIVIK	Nunavik	507	500	500	100	500	100
IVUJIVIK	Nunavik	349	340	340	100	340	100
SALLUIT	Nunavik	1,241	1,155	1,155	100	1,120	97
KANGIQSUJUAQ	Nunavik	605	560	560	100	550	98
QUAQTAQ	Nunavik	315	295	295	100	295	100
KANGIRSUK	Nunavik	466	425	425	100	425	100
AUPALUK	Nunavik	174	155	155	100	155	100
TASIUJAQ	Nunavik	248	230	230	100	230	100
KUUJJUAQ	Nunavik	2,132	1,655	1,560	94	1,265	81
KANGIQSUALUJJUAQ	Nunavik	735	710	700	99	670	96
TOTAL NUNAVIK (QUEBEC)[c]		10,784	9,640	9,515	99	8.985	94

a The entire aboriginal population of Postville is comprised of English-speaking Settlers of Anglo-Saxon heritage. Settlers also form the vast majority of the population in Makkovik, Rigolet, and North West River.

b Inuit also live in the central Labrador town of Happy Valley-Goose Bay, whose 7,470 residents include 2,720 individuals of Inuit, Settler, or Innu heritage (they reported an aboriginal identity in 2006), but figures on the number of Inuktitut speakers are unavailable.

c Over a hundred Inuit live in the Cree village of Chisasibi, south of Kuujjuaraapik. Except for three or four elders, they do not speak Inuktitut.

Notes

INTRODUCTION

1 "Inuit" is also the term they use as an ethnonym for naming their international association, the Inuit Circumpolar Council.

2 The word "Eskimo" was borrowed by French ("Esquimaux") and English from the Algonkian Amerindian languages, where it meant either "speakers of a foreign tongue" (Mailhot 1978; Mailhot et al., 1980), "makers of snowshoes" (Goddard 1984), or according to an enduring but unproved popular etymology, "raw meat eaters." Interestingly enough, the name Hurons gave to Inuit (with which they were not in contact) was *oku8chronon*, "people of the raw meat." This suggests that they might have translated into their language the Algonkian word for "Eskimo" and that this word would have actually meant "raw meat eaters" (John Steckley, personal communication).

3 In the standard orthography, there is a circumflex accent (^) over the final *x*. Unangax ("Aleut") is in the singular. The plural is Unangan or Unangas, according to the area where the word is used.

4 Krauss (1973) presents a very detailed panorama of Eskaleut studies up to the beginning of the 1970s. To inquire about what has been done since that period, one should consult the bibliographies in Dorais (1996a, 2003), as well as the list of references at the end of the present book.

5 Dorais (1996a) proposes a synthesis, in French, of available knowledge about the language situation in the North American Arctic up to the mid-1990s. That book expands on a more basic three-volume textbook series published in Iqaluit by Nunavut Arctic College (Dorais 1990a, 1993, 1996b; some material drawn from this series is reproduced in the

present book with permission from the original publisher). Another interesting general presentation of the Eskaleut languages is Tersis and Therrien's (2000) collection of essays on various, although somewhat scattered, aspects of arctic linguistics (an earlier publication of the same type is Hamp 1976b). For an encompassing panorama of all circumpolar aboriginal languages, see Collis (1990).

6 One Eskaleut language from the north-eastern tip of Russia, Sirenikski, disappeared in 1997 when its last speaker died (Krauss 2006, 116).

7 The French sociologist Pierre Bourdieu (1991) discusses these languages, which, because of the social or numerical inferiority of their speakers, are heard without being necessarily listened to by those who belong to the ruling majority.

CHAPTER ONE

1 Technically speaking, there are trees in the Arctic, but they consist either of dwarf species – dwarf birch, for instance – which creep on the ground rather than growing upright, or of bunches of willow, which rarely exceed one metre in height. The present tendency toward climate change seems to contribute to extending the tree-line in a northerly direction.

2 This is the case for Inuit properly speaking (see Introduction). Information on their linguistic and cultural relatives – the Yupiit, Yupiget, and Aleut – can be found below.

3 Together with the aboriginal communities of the Mackenzie Delta and of the Kobuk and Noatak Rivers, central and northern Labrador villages belong to the short list of Inuit establishments located in a forest environment. Happy Valley is home to the world's southernmost permanent Inuit community.

4 The Inuit, Yupiit, and Yupiget are classified as "Eskimos," whereas the Unangan were called "Aleuts" until recently.

5 Native speakers call their language *Unangam tunuu* ("the language of Unangax"), but for brevity's sake, it will be referred to as Unangax.

6 As mentioned in the notes to the Introduction, the last speaker of Sirenikski died in 1997, thus reducing to six the number of Eskaleut languages still in existence.

7 On the Unangan and their language, see Berge and Dirks (2006), Bergsland (1959a, 1994, 1998), Bergsland et al. (1978), Bergsland and Dirks (1978, 1990), Geoghegan (1944), Golovko and Vakhtin (1990), and Snigaroff and Bergsland (1986).

8 As a matter of fact, during the Second World War, all aboriginal inhabitants of the Aleutian and Pribilof Islands were removed elsewhere. With the exception of the Attuans (under Japanese control), Unangan were relocated in south-eastern Alaska as ordered by the American government. There, they "were compelled to live for three years in internment camps unfit for human habitation without proper medical treatment, adequate food, or basic human rights" (Madden 1992).

9 The figure of 2,300 is Krauss's (2007) estimate for Unangan residing in their aboriginal territory. The total number of individuals – living all over the United States – who identified themselves as Unangan in the American census of 2000 exceeded 10,000 (a figure that may have included some Alutiiq Yupiit who identified as "Aleuts").

10 *Tayaq* seems related to *tau*, the word for "man" in the old Igloolik and Kivalliq Inuit shamanistic language.

11 Bergsland (1994) also sees similarities between the phonological systems of Unangax and Yup'ik.

12 On Sirenikski and the Yupik languages, see Ajnana (2003), Ajnana and Nakazik (1987), Amos and Amos (2004), Badten et al. (2008), DeReuse (1994), Hinz (1944), A. Jacobson (1996, 1998), S. Jacobson (1984, 1987, 1995, 1998, 2001, 2004), Krauss (1985), Krupnik (1991), Krupnik and Chlenov (1977), Leer (1982), Menovshchikov (1960, 1964, 1975), Menovshchikov and Vakhtin (1984), Mithun (1998), Reed et al. (1977), Rodionova (2006, 2007a), Rubtsova (1971), Vakhtin (1995), Vakhtin and Emelianova (1988), Woodbury (1984b).

13 On Sugpiat history and culture, see Crowell et al. (2001).

14 According to the Russian census of 2002 (quoted in Csonka 2007), 1,534 "Eskimos" were then living in Chukotka and 216 more elsewhere in the Russian federation.

15 On the linguistic history of Alaska and Chukotka, see Krauss (1980).

16 The Summer Institute of Linguistics, now known as SIL International, is a fundamentalist Christian organization based in the United States whose objective is to document as many languages as possible in order to translate the Bible into all of them and to teach "Bibleless tribes" to read the Scriptures in their own tongue.

17 Naukanski and Sirenikski, spoken by a minority of people, were never written down.

18 The centre's founder and first director was Professor Michael E. Krauss, a well-known specialist of Alaskan and other aboriginal and minority languages. In 2000 he was succeeded as ANLC head by Dr Lawrence D. Kaplan.

19 Most of them are consonants. There are only four vowels (compared with three in Inuit): *a*, *i*, *u*, and *e* (as in *roses*). The first three can be either short or long (*aa*, *ii*, *uu*).

20 Consonants are voiced when air is breathed out through the throat, making the vocal cords vibrate, and voiceless when air is blocked up in the throat, without any vibration of the vocal cords (e.g., the distinction between English voiced *b* and voiceless *p*). This distinction is phonemic (i.e., the consonants in question are considered separate phonemes) when pronunciation is the chief criterion for distinguishing between two different words (e.g., English *bark* and *park*). Labialized consonants are pronounced with rounded lips.

21 Krauss's estimates apply only to those Yupiit – and other Eskimo groups – still living in their native territory. According to US census data, in 2000 more than 54,000 Americans identified themselves as Eskimo, whereas Krauss's total (Yupiit, Yupiget, Alutiit, and Inupiat) reaches 45,600 individuals for 2000.

22 Single-person verb endings mark the person of the subject. Double-person verb endings mark the person of both the subject and the direct object.

23 I am grateful to Steven Jacobson from the University of Alaska Fairbanks for having helped me to transliterate these sentences from the Cyrillic alphabet to Latin orthography.

24 For Alaskan and Russian Yupiit, Yupiget, and Unangan, the figures indicate the total aboriginal population still residing in their native territory.

CHAPTER TWO

1 On the Inuit language in general, see Birket-Smith (1928), Collis (1970), Dorais (1986a, 1990b, 1990c), Fortescue (1983, 1985a), Hammerich (1936), and Miyaoka (1978). On Inuit culture, see Birket-Smith (1924, 1929), Boas (1964), Burch (1998), Holm (1914), Jenness (1923), Murdoch (1892), Rasmussen (1929, 1931), Rink (1887b), and Turner (1979).

2 There are only fourteen dialects according to some authors (e.g., Fortescue 1983), for whom Alaskan Qawiaraq, on the one hand, and eastern Canadian Aivilik, on the other, are mere subdialects of, respectively, the Bering Strait and the North Baffin forms of speech.

3 On Alaskan Inupiaq, see Alvanna-Stimpfle (1987), Barnum (1901), Hugo et al. (1991), Kaplan (1981a, 1981b, 1988, 1990, 2000), Lowe

(1984a, 1985a), MacLean (1980), Menovshchikov (1980), Rasmussen and Ostermann (1941), Seiler (2005), and Webster and Zibell (1970).

4 Originally spoken in the Teller and Nome areas, Qawiaraq later expanded along the Norton Sound coast toward Fish River, Shaktoolik, and Unalakleet, where it replaced, or was added to, the local Central Alaskan Yup'ik Unaliq dialect (which still subsists, although barely so, in Golovin and Unalakleet).

5 The palatalized consonants *l*, *&* (voiceless *l*), *n*, and *t* are pronounced with the tongue touching (or nearly touching) the roof of the mouth. For example, *n* is pronounced *ñ* (as in Spanish), and *t* becomes *s* (when between two vowels) or *ch* (at the end of a word or within a cluster of two consonants). Palatalized *l* and *&* are pronounced as liquids.

6 A stop (or plosive) consonant has air exploding when exiting the mouth (e.g., *p*, *t*), a continuant lets air glide through the entrance of the mouth (e.g., *v*, *l*), and nasal consonants send air through the nose (e.g., *m*, *n*).

7 The consonant *q* is a uvular stop, articulated at the back of the mouth near the uvula.

8 On Western Canadian Inuktun, see Angulalik et al. (2000), Dyck and Briggs (2005), Harnum et al. (1982), Jenness (1928), Lowe (1983, 1984b, 1985b, 1985c, 1991, 2001), Mallon (1977), Métayer (1953, 1973), Petitot (1876), Omura (1997), and Rasmussen (1931, 1942).

9 Some families from Cape Dorset and Pond Inlet, on Baffin Island, migrated to Taloyoak in 1947, with the consequence that Baffin Inuktitut has influenced the local speech.

10 As seen in the preceding section, *h* also occurs in the Anaktuvuk (and Uummarmiutun) subdialect of North Slope Iñupiaq.

11 The grouping *kh* is realized as a long voiceless velar continuant (more or less like *ch* in the German word *ich*, "I"), and *qh* sounds like a long voiceless uvular continuant (like a strong *ch* in German *machen*, "to do," or a strong *j* in Spanish *Juan*, "John").

12 In Siglitun, *ts* occurs as *tch*. Variations in Natsilingmiutut (*tt/ts*, *ph/ps*) are subdialectal.

13 The voiceless lateral consonant *&* (also written *ł*) occurs in all Alaskan – and many Canadian – dialects. Its voiced counterpart is *l*. It sounds like Welsh *fl/ll* (as in the name Floyd or Lloyd).

14 And, sometimes too, speakers turn a final *-k* into *-ng*.

15 Such a distinction exists in Alaskan Inupiaq. The phoneme *j* is realized as a *y*, while the realization of *J* (a palatalized consonant written *r* in Alaska and *r* with a circumflex accent in some Canadian transcriptions) sounds somewhat like English *r*.

16 The consonant *sr* may also be written *s*, as in Utkuhiksalik. In that subdialect, an etymological *kJ* seems to be realized as *ks* (*iqaluksaq*, "fish fry"), while the original *ks* becomes *kh* (*iqalukhiuqtuq*, "he/she is fishing").

17 On Eastern Canadian Inuktitut in general, see Bok-Bennema (1991), Bordin (2003), Dorais (1976a), Kalluak (1987), Mallon (1991), Nowak (1996, 2008), Petersen (1970), Schneider (1985), and Utatnaq et al. (1989).

18 On the Kivalliq and Aivilik dialects, see Balt (1977a), Dorais (1976b, 1988a), Johns (1987), Sammons (1985), Spalding (1969, 1982, 1998), Thibert (1970), and Turquetil (1928).

19 Kivalliq preserves clusters starting with an apical consonant (e.g., *tatqiq*, "moon"; *ilvit*, "you one"). These have been regressively assimilated in all other Inuktitut dialects (*taqqiq*, *ivvit*).

20 On North and South Baffin, see Dorais (1975a, 1975b, 1978), Gagné (1964), Harper (1974, 1979), Immaroitok et al. (1985), Kalmar (1979), Ootoova (2000), and Spalding (1993).

21 On the Inuit relocations to the High Arctic during the 1950s, see Tester and Kulchyski (1994), Marcus (1995), and for a direct testimony, Amagoalik (2007).

22 The only exception is the cluster *ps*, which is geminated (*ss*) in North Baffin but incompletely so (*ts*) in South Baffin.

23 One feature is the law of double consonants (two groups of consonants cannot follow each other within the confines of a word), which is discussed in the next chapter.

24 On the Nunatsiavut dialect (references on Nunavik are listed in the next chapter), see Bourquin (1891), Erdman (1864), Iglolioorte (1990), Jeddore (1976), Johns and Tuglavina (2004), Nochasak and Pigott (2005), Nowak (1999), Peacock (1974a, 1974b, 1974c), Smith (1975, 1977, 1979), and Smith and Metcalfe (1973).

25 The Settlers of northern and central Labrador are descendants of Euro-American fishermen and trappers of Anglo-Saxon origin, who immigrated to the Labrador coast during the nineteenth century. Some of them married aboriginal women and adopted many elements of the Inuit and Innu way of life.

26 On Greenlandic Kalaallisut, see Bergsland (1955), Berthelsen et al. (1990), Bugge et al. (1960), Dorais (1981a), Enel (1984), Fortescue (1984a, 1984b, 1984c, 1986, 1991), Gessain et al. (1986), Holtved (1951), Jacobsen (1991), Janussen (1987), Kleinschmidt (1981), Mennecier (1995), Nowak (1987), Ostermann (1938), Petersen (1975,

1980, 1990), Rink (1887a), Rischel (1974, 1975, 1981), Robbe and Dorais (1986a), Sadock (2003), Schultz-Lorentzen (1927, 1945), Swadesh (1942), Thalbitzer (1904, 1921), Tersis (2008), Tersis and Mahieu (2006), Vebæk (2006), and Vibæk (1905). Kalaallisut was one of the first non-European and non-Oriental languages to be described by linguists (Bergsland and Rischel 1986). Early descriptions include Egede (1750, 1760) and Fabricius (1801).

27 In 2008 the eighteen *kommunit* of Greenland were merged into four supermunicipalities. The names listed here are those of the original *kommunit*.

28 Or West and East Greenlandic are at a level between Nunavik and Northern Labrador. Their uvuC clusters are realized as "pharyngealised geminates of the second consonant" (Dorais 1986a, 40) rather than as full-fledged groupings of a uvular and another consonant.

29 Even though the symbol *&* never appears in Greenlandic texts (the phoneme *l/&* is always written *l*), it is used here, and in a few other examples, in order to emphasize the distinction between the two realizations of *l*.

30 In Alaskan Inupiaq and Natsilingmiutut, the realization of *J* sounds somewhat like English *r*.

31 In West and East Greenlandic, the etymological diphthongs *au* and *ai* become *aa*, which is not the case in Thule.

32 In Greenlandic, as in other Inuit dialects, the graphic symbol *g* stands for the phoneme *γ* (whose realization sounds like Greek *gamma*), a voiced velar continuant. In Canada and Greenland, as well as in the Alaskan examples found in this book, the grapheme *r* represents the phoneme *R*, a voiced uvular continuant realized like Parisian French *r*.

33 The clusters *xx* and XX stand respectively for a geminate voiceless velar continuant and a geminate voiceless uvular continuant.

34 A morpheme is a minimal unit that makes sense within a word. In English, for example, the word *houses* includes two morphemes: *house-*, "dwelling"; and *-s*, "plural number."

35 Such an etymological explanation is valid for linguists who know about comparative phonology, but native speakers do not "preserve" *u*. They speak the way they do because it is how they have learned to pronounce words.

36 The "fringe" dialects of Greenland – Thule, East Greenlandic, and most subdialects of West Greenlandic – are also drawn nearer to a common form of Kalaallisut by the overwhelming influence of school, radio, and written texts, which make almost exclusive use of the official language, based on Central West Greenlandic.

37 On Eskaleut polysynthesis, see Tersis and Mahieu (2009). On syntactic theory as it applies to Inuktitut, see Berge (1992).

38 Square brackets show the graphemes used in this book when they differ from the usual phonetic symbol representing the phoneme (e.g., the realization of the phoneme *r* is written *J*; that of *R* is written *r*).

39 Proto-Eskimo is the reconstructed language ancestral to the Eskimo branch (the Inuit and Yupik dialects) of the Eskaleut family (see chapter 4). In Proto-Eskimo the phoneme *e* was realized as in the English word "ros<u>e</u>s," and the realization of the apical fricative *ð* sounded somewhat like English *th* in "this."

40 Inuinnaqtun and Kivalliq: *uqhuq*; Nunatsiavut: *utsuk*.

41 The bilabial *p* is realized as a voiced *b* (or rather *β*, as in Spanish *ca<u>b</u>o*, "cape") when it is regressively assimilated by a voiced consonant.

42 The grouping written *n'ng* starts with the consonant *n*, followed by *ng* (*ŋ*). It must be distinguished from the cluster *nng*, which represents a geminate *ng* (*ngng* or *ŋŋ*).

43 In West and East Greenlandic, the uvuC clusters are realized as uvularized geminates of the second consonant rather than as full combinations of a uvular and another consonant.

44 *Assak* and *attak* are the Greenlandic renditions of *aJgak/aggak* ("hand").

45 The phonological distance between any two dialects is measured by counting the phonemic traits – of a possible thirty-two – whose occurrence follows different patterns in these dialects (Dorais 1986a, 48). Each divergence is assigned one point (a half-point when only partial). The higher the figure, the larger the phonological distance between two dialects.

46 According to Fortescue (1983), 302 affixes are shared by all Inuit dialects, but only 151 of them also occur in the Yupik languages and 41 in Unangax.

47 The dual survives in a limited number of inflections in the northernmost communities where West Greenlandic is spoken.

48 When a noun's final vowel is already long or double, the dual and plural are simply marked by *-k* and *-t*.

49 This is an archaic form; it has now been normalized to *arvinga*.

CHAPTER THREE

1 On the Nunavik dialect, see Dorais (1973, 1975c, 1977b, 1979a, 1983, 1988b), Flint (1954), Lefebvre (1964), Massenet (1986), Ortiz (1993),

Peck (1925), Qumaq (1991), Schneider (1970, 1972–76, 1979, 1986), and Trinel (1970).

2 The grouping *rng* is set apart from the uvuC class of consonant clusters because it constitutes the only occurrence of a uvular consonant (*r*) followed by a velar (*ng*).

3 Although incompletely assimilated, the cluster *ts* is regarded here as a geminate.

4 The grapheme *nng* stands for a geminate *ng* (*ηη*).

5 It should be remembered, however, that in Natsilingmiutut a phonemic distinction exists between *j* and *J*.

6 A glottal stop is an abrupt constriction of the throat, followed by a sudden release (as in English "uh oh!"). In current writing, it is symbolized by an apostrophe.

7 This is also known as Schneider's law, after the late Reverend Lucien Schneider, who was the first to discuss it (Schneider 1970, vii).

8 An example is the American naturalist and anthropologist Lucien Turner, who collected in Fort Chimo (Kuujjuaq) a still unpublished Inuktitut lexicon (Turner 1887).

9 Ø stands for a "zero ending." It symbolizes that the word does not end with a visible affix. This absence of ending is significant, however, because it can mean only one thing: the noun acts as the principal referent of the sentence. In any other function the noun would end with an explicitly visible grammatical affix.

10 Older speakers may say *angut<u>a</u>up* because in the word *anguti* the final *i* reflects an etymological *e*, which is often realized as *a* before a vowel.

11 In the former case, the principal referent (with a basic ending – often Ø) is the subject of the sentence; in the latter, it is the sentence's first object.

12 These verbs are sometimes called "intransitive" (Schneider 1972–76), but this is misleading because like their double-person ("transitive") counterparts, they can be endowed with an object. The only intransitive Inuit verbs are those whose meaning does not allow them to call for a semantically direct object (e.g., *sinittuq*, "he/she sleeps"; or *silaqqituq*, "the weather is good").

13 In most other dialects, the complement of the passive is marked by the ablative case.

14 The sentence could also be translated as: "because he (A) arrives, he (B) is glad."

15 Other Inuit dialects have between eight and eleven verbal moods. The grammatical tense (essentially past and future) is marked by lexical affixes rather than being included in the grammatical endings.

16 Declarative – and interrogative – endings start with *v-* when following a vowel and with *p-* (or sometimes *k-* or *q-*) after a consonant.

17 The only difference with nouns is that single-person indicative endings cannot occur in the possessive form. In Kalaallisut the indicative preserves only its participial meaning, and this in all persons. Its verbal functions have been devolved to the declarative (e.g., *tusartunga*, "I, hearing"; and *tusarpunga*, "I hear"). In Inupiaq there are two forms of the indicative: past (*niriJuanga*, "I was eating") and present (*niriJunga*, "I eat"). On the difference between the indicative and the declarative, see Hofmann (1978) and Lowe (1988).

18 Indicative endings start with *j-* (pronounced *J-* in Itivimiut) when following a vowel and with *t-* after a consonant.

19 Use of the term "perfective" (a completed action) and of its antonym "imperfective" (an action not yet completed) refers to the fact that in the first case the event expressed by the verb is considered to have definitely happened, whereas in the second case it is seen as a merely possible occurrence. Such terminology is current in Nunavik grammar (see Dorais 1988b; Ortiz 1993), which is why it is used here. More accurate appellations for "perfective" and "imperfective" might be "contingent" and "conditional" (Swift 2004).

20 The perfective may occur without an explicit main clause when the content of this main clause is already known to the speaker and his or her interlocutor (e.g., *ikkiinaqtualuulirmat*, "because the weather is very cold [I am cold, I have put many clothes on, I've caught a cold, etc.]").

21 The negation of the declarative is also used with negative interrogation (e.g., *takunngilatit?* "don't you see?").

22 The lengthening of the ending-final vowel in the interrogative mood is ignored here because it is prosodic rather than grammatical.

23 This formal analogy between possessive nominal endings and third-person-object verbal endings has led some linguists (e.g., Thalbitzer 1911; Lowe 1981) to regard the Inuit language as including only nouns and no verbs. It is true that in a few cases the analogy is total – for example, *inuup tusaqtanga*, which means both "the person's object of hearing" (i.e., "what the person hears") *and* "the person hears him/her/it." But this is exceptional. Sadock (1999) has demonstrated convincingly that the Inuit language differentiates altogether between nouns and verbs (see also Lipscomb 1993).

24 The maximum number of Inuit localizers is twenty-three, found in the Siglitun dialect.

25 The so-called enclitic affixes, however, which occur at the very end of words – even after the grammatical ending – may be attached to localizers (e.g., *maunali*, "but through here"). Their meaning is often similar to that of "small words" (see below).

26 Location can also be expressed by nouns denoting specific portions of space (e.g., the fore part, the rear part, the other side, etc.) in relation to someone or something. These nouns must end with a possessive affix (e.g., *saattini*, "in our front part; in front of us"; *tunuani*, "in his/her rear part; back of him/her").

27 However, small words can be followed by enclitic affixes (e.g., *immaqaalu*, "maybe also").

28 The pronominal question words (i.e., "who?" "what?" "which one?") are translated by nouns that can occur in the singular, dual, or plural in each case of the nominal declension (e.g., *kina*, "who? [singular]"; *sunaak*, "two what? [dual]"; *nallianut*, "because of which ones?").

CHAPTER FOUR

1 For example, the Indo-European family, which includes most languages now spoken in Europe, Iran, Afghanistan, Pakistan, Bangladesh, and northern India, stems from a group of adjacent speech forms used about 10,000 years ago somewhere north of the Black Sea – and perhaps also the Caspian Sea.

2 As shall be seen below at the end of the section on language and migrations, this language may have been native to some tribes but borrowed by other groups. This means that the linguistic ancestors of modern Eskaleut speakers did not necessarily share a unique genetic origin.

3 It was evidently believed that North America was attached to the Asian continent.

4 Scholars defending this theory thought that the "Lost Tribes of Israel," told of in the Bible, had taken refuge in the North American Arctic. One chief proponent of the hypothesis was Father Émile Petitot, who, in one of his books on the Dene First Nations of the Mackenzie basin (Petitot 1888), mentioned he was working on an article titled "Les Juifs arctiques" (The Arctic Jews), in which he planned to expose alleged evidence of the Hebraic origin of Dene culture (Savoie 1970).

5 In 1883 the linguistic unity of the Inuit language and its close kinship with the Yupiit speech forms had long been recognized. It was much later, however, at the beginning of the 1950s, that the Norwegian

linguist Knut Bergsland and other specialists (see Bergsland 1951; Marsh and Swadesh 1951) proved without doubt that Unangax also belonged to the same family, although the idea had been suggested by Rasmus Rask as far back as 1819 (Bergė 2005).

6 The Uralic family includes the Finno-Ugric (Finnish, Saami, Hungarian, etc.) and Samoyedic (Nenets of north-western Russia) languages, while the Altaic group comprises the Turkic (Turkish, etc.), Mongolian, and Manchu-Tungusic (eastern Siberia and north-eastern China) languages. Both families are sometimes regarded as belonging to a more encompassing Uralo-Altaic ensemble.

7 Modern linguistics regards the Eskaleut languages as polysynthetic (several concepts can be amalgamated into one word), although not in the same degree as most Amerindian languages. The latter often incorporate different radicals within one lexeme, which is not the case with Eskaleut, where, as already mentioned, a single word-base is followed by a number of affixes. This type of polysynthesis, which characterizes Eskaleut as well as the Uralic and Altaic families, is called "agglutination."

8 In 1953 the Canadian anthropologist Diamond Jenness hypothesized that Inuit might be related to the language of the Yahgan Indians of Tierra del Fuego, at the southernmost tip of South America (Jenness 1953). But nobody seemingly took this hypothesis seriously.

9 Besides the Chukotko-Kamchatkan and Eskaleut languages, this protofamily could have included Ainu (the aboriginal tongue of northern Japan), the Uralic and Altaic languages, and the Wakashan speech forms of Canada's coastal British Columbia.

10 In 1746, for instance, the Danish theologian Marcus Wöldike suggested that the only European language related to Greenlandic Kalaallisut was Hungarian, and in 1818 the linguist Rasmus Rask (also a Dane) posited that there existed a genetic link between Eskimo and the Finno-Ugric languages (Fortescue 1998). The French missionary Émile Petitot thought that Western Canadian Inuktun was related to the Altaic languages (Petitot 1876).

11 A distinction should be drawn, however, between linguistics and genetics. The ancestral speakers of a hypothetical common protoform of Uralic, Yukaghir, and Eskaleut were not necessarily the ancestors of present-day Inuit and Yupiit (or Uralic) individuals. At some point in time, their language(s) may have been adopted by populations with which they were not genetically related (see below).

12 According to the American linguist Merritt Ruhlen (1994), however, who draws his inspiration from Joseph Greenberg's theories on the

origin of the world's languages (see Greenberg 1987), Eskaleut would belong to a "Eurasiatic" macrofamily – one of a total of twelve such macrogroupings – which would also include the Indo-European, Uralic, Altaic, Korean, Japanese, Ainu, and Chukotko-Kamchatkan languages. Needless to say, such an encompassing classification is far from being accepted by all specialists.

13 Besides being a co-author of the *Comparative Eskimo Dictionary* (Fortescue et al. 1994), Michael Fortescue has also published a *Comparative Chukotko-Kamchatkan Dictionary* (Fortescue 2005), whose preliminary version dates from 1995, and a *Comparative Wakashan Dictionary* (Fortescue 2007a), which posits that the Wakashan languages of British Columbia might be distantly related to the Uralo-Siberian mesh. On his experience as a comparatist, see Fortescue (2007b).

14 See the *-tuq/-juq* indicative endings of Inuktitut (in chapter 3, under the section on verbs), which may act both as verbs ("he/she does something") and as participles ("someone doing something").

15 The Na-Dene speakers of Athapaskan languages (spoken in northwestern Canada, the interior of Alaska and British Columbia, and the American Southwest) descend from the last wave of Amerindian migrants to have entered America.

16 Some areas of Alaska that are now home to Eskaleut speakers were already inhabited long before the alleged arrival of the Proto-Eskaleut language in America. In the Prince William Sound and Kodiak regions, for example, human settlement dates back some 10,000 years (Crowell et al. 2001). This probably means that the ancestral speakers of the present-day Alutiiq language joined a previously established population to which they transmitted their tongue.

17 The entrance date of Proto-Eskaleut in America was formerly estimated (including by myself; see Dorais 1993, 1996a) as being much earlier (7,000 to 8,000 years ago) than it is now.

18 One of the oldest sites belonging to this tradition is the Denbigh Flint Complex, near Unalakleet on Norton Sound.

19 Woodbury (1984a) and Bergsland (1986) state that four millennia ago, there probably existed several languages and dialects occupying an intermediate linguistic position between the two branches. The later disappearance of these intermediate forms of speech now gives the false impression that Eskimo and Aleut were suddenly cut off from each other.

20 Paleo-Eskimo even reached the island of Newfoundland, occupying most of its coasts. Some Paleo-Eskimo also settled on the present-day French islands of Saint-Pierre et Miquelon (see LeBlanc 2000).

21 Over the centuries, the Paleo- and Neo-Eskimo languages had probably become too different from each other to be mutually intelligible at first hearing. However, because both speech forms had evolved from the same Proto-Eskimo linguistic ancestor, it must have been relatively easy for their speakers to learn each other's language.

22 This hypothesis, now shared by all specialists, directly refutes an earlier proposition of Birket-Smith and Rasmussen (see Birket-Smith 1929), whereby the ancestors of the Canadian Inuit could have been Indians of the northern woodlands who would have migrated toward the Arctic Coast.

23 Scandinavian Vikings from Norway and Iceland had settled in southern Greenland (then deserted by its Paleo-Eskimo population) at the same time as the Inuit were entering the island through the north.

24 The weather became colder, which destroyed the agricultural and pastoral base of the Scandinavian economy. Many Viking settlers died of epidemics and chronic illnesses, whereas some others may have been assimilated – or killed – by Inuit.

25 During the early 1860s, a small group of Inuit from North Baffin migrated to the Thule district of Greenland. Some came back to Canada after a few years, but others settled for good in Thule. This is the last recorded Neo-Eskimo migration (see Mary-Rousselière 1980).

26 The Southeast Baffin subdialect shares phonological similarities with both North Baffin (*t* often becomes *s* after an etymological *i*) and Southwest Baffin (the voiceless lateral fricative *&* is absent from the inventory of phonemes).

27 The graphemes between square brackets are those used in common writing.

28 The phoneme *ð* could also be realized as a voiceless fricative continuant.

29 It has been further possible to reconstruct Proto-Yupik, the ancestor of the four Yupiit languages.

30 However, as mentioned in chapter 2, the Diomede subdialect of Bering Strait Inupiaq still preserves the phoneme *e*.

CHAPTER FIVE

1 Earlier contacts between Europeans and Inuit had occurred in Greenland from the twelfth or thirteenth centuries on, but no linguistic material from that period appears to have survived in written form.

2 The modern transcriptions and translations are based on Erik Holtved's and Kaj Birket-Smith's comments on Hall's list (cited in Quinn 1965), as well as on Thalbitzer's (1904) and my own analyses.

3 Thalbitzer (1904) writes *yacketrone*, which is closer to the standard spelling *iqetqun*.

4 That the vowel *i*, in *-liq*, is also written *e* may be due to the quality of *i* before *q*. When preceding a uvular consonant, the phoneme *i* is realized as *I* – that is, somewhat halfway between *i* and *e*.

5 At the end of the nineteenth century, Petitot (1876) wrote *tch* at the beginning of all Siglitun words now starting with *s* (e.g., *Tchiglit*, "Siglit [Inuit]"; *tchiqiniq*, "sun [*siqiniq*]"). This might stem from an orthographic mistake, but it could also well be a testimony to the late survival of the word-initial *c* in this Inuktun dialect.

6 "Ear" is still *siguta* in Central Siberian Yupik and *sigeta* in Sirenikski.

7 It is impossible to say whether, in Frobisher's time, an etymological *J* had already merged with *j*, as it has done in the contemporary Baffin speech forms. Either consonant, followed by the markers *-rin* (possessive) or *-rit* (plural), can generate a *Jr* (or *djr*) consonant grouping after the final *e* of the base has been elided.

8 Here again, I suppose that a distinction still existed between the phonemes *i* and *e*, often transcribed by Davis with different letters when both of them occur within the same word (as in *ugnera/irnera*).

9 It should be noticed that this base seems to start with *s* rather than with *c* (e.g., Proto-Eskimo *cavig-*, "knife"). This might mean that at the end of the 1500s, the word-initial *c* would have already disappeared from Central West Greenlandic while still being present in the Baffin speech form.

10 By way of example, the word that Davis translates as "seal," *ataneg*, might well be the lexeme *aataaq*, the current West Greenlandic name of the harp seal, perhaps followed by the modalis plural ending *-nek* or *-neng*.

11 As can be seen in chapter 8, the local French traders-cum-fishermen, Basque whalers, Inuit, and Innu even developed a common pidgin, a trade language made out of Inuit, Innu, French, and Basque words.

12 Martel de Brouague learned Inuktitut from a woman named Acoutsina (Akutsinaaq), who was a prisoner at Fort Pontchartrain, Bradore Bay (on Belle-Isle Strait).

13 Father François compiled a list of 144 words collected from an Inuk woman prisoner at Beauport, near Quebec City.

14 Father Saint-Pié gave to the Swedish naturalist Pehr Kalm a list of forty Inuit words that Kalm later included in a book about his journey to Canada in 1749 (Kalm 1772).

15 Haven, who had lived in Greenland and already spoke the language, met with his first Canadian Inuit in 1764 and 1765, on Belle-Isle Strait.

16 It shall be seen in chapter 8 that the word *tcharacou* might also have a Basque origin.

17 Occlusion consists of the transformation of a continuant into a stop consonant.

18 It should be recalled that this law (see chapter 3) prevents two sequences of consonant clusters from following one another by deleting one consonant from the second cluster.

19 This could mean that various linguistic norms coexisted and that various speakers sometimes used different words and morphemes to express the same meaning.

20 An initial *k* or *qu* might indicate that the compilers of some wordlists heard *ch* as a palatalized velar (*ksh*).

21 Hans Egede, a Lutheran minister born in Norway (then under Danish sovereignty), established the Godthaab Mission. Poul Egede was his son.

22 This means that in Greenland the *n/t* distinction at the end of words was no longer phonemic (i.e., linguistically functional). It instead underlined social differences between genders.

23 Nunatsiavut Inuktitut also possessed – as it still does – the voiceless lateral *&* (e.g., *i&uittuk*, "uncomfortable").

24 An exception existed for etymological *nr* groupings, which had become *rng* (e.g., *ir̲ngutaq*, "grandchild," instead of etymological *inr̲utaq*).

25 Other texts from around 1900 show that bilC clusters were also in use in the Baffin dialects.

26 These western dialects had their own evolution (disappearance of the fourth vowel *e*; partial regressive consonant assimilation; neutralization of *J* and *j* in Siglitun and Inuinnaqtun; transformation of the word-initial *c* into *s* or *h*), but it is not possible to describe it in detail due to the lack of available data.

27 Peck's (1925) and Turner's (1887) writings, as well as some present-day place names (which preserve old linguistic forms), show that at the end of the nineteenth century, the Nunavik and Baffin dialects still harboured a conservative morphology. On the Quebec coast of Hudson Strait, for instance, the toponym Iqalukkat ("many small fish") bears witness to a time when one had to modify and geminate the initial

consonant of the affix *-gaq* ("small") in order to put it in the plural. Nowadays, the equivalent plural form would be Iqalugait.

28 For example, *mitquq* ("feather, animal hair"), *tikinmata* ("because they arrive"), and *utkusik* ("kettle") had been geminated into *miqquq, tikimmata*, and *ukkusik*.

29 Two exceptions are the Thule dialect of northwest Greenland, where bilC groupings subsisted until the 1950s and are probably still heard from time to time in the speech of a few elders (Jacobsen 1991), and the Rigolet subdialect of Nunatsiavut, where they are still in use.

30 This is due to the disappearance of the syllable-final *q* and to the assimilation of *r* to *g* (e.g., *isaguk*, "wing," in place of *isaruq*). A similar phenomenon has also occurred in two communities speaking the Itivimiut subdialect of Nunavik: Kuujjuaraapik and Umiujaq.

31 With these geminates, the voice sounds as though it were coming from the throat.

32 This process has actually been in progress – in all Inuit dialects – for over 2,000 years. It is the most recent manifestation, particularly evident in Inuit, of the progressive simplification of the original Proto-Eskimo phonemic system.

33 According to the linguist S.T. Mick Mallon (personal communication), the law of double consonants now exists under an incipient form in the South Baffin dialect. A restricted version of the law (only geminates are simplified; see Dorais and Lowe 1982) is also found in Siglitun.

34 By comparison with most Canadian and Alaskan dialects, a counter-process of consonant strengthening also exists in Greenland (and, in a lesser way, in Nunatsiavut), whereby geminate voiced continuants have been devoiced (West Greenlandic, Nunatsiavut) or transformed into stops (East Greenlandic). By contrast, in Greenland, over the past century or so, the vocalic groupings *ai* and *au* have become long vowels (e.g., modern *aaviq*, "walrus," and *aak*, "blood," instead of *aiviq* and *auk*), and *sh*, the reflex of etymological *J*, has merged with *s* (e.g., present-day *isi*, "eye," instead of nineteenth-century *ishi* and etymological *eJe*).

35 It did not extend, however, to affixes expressing grammatical tense, as in *tusanniaqunga* (and not *-vunga*), "I shall hear."

36 If the context is not clear enough, a personal pronoun can be added, as in *uanga nuliannik sinippunga* ("of me, with my wife I slept") as opposed to *illit nuliannik sinippunga* ("of you, with your wife I slept").

37 However, as shall be seen below, other solutions have been found for coping with homophony.

38 In Nunatsiavut, speakers also resort to the Greenlandic solution: adding a personal pronoun and inflecting the noun at both persons with the geminate-initial possessive endings (e.g., *uvanga nulianni*, "of me, with [at] my wife").

39 These lexemes, however, are still current in printed texts, hinting at an incipient discrepancy between spoken and written language.

40 In Alaska some young Inuit learn Inupiaq as a second language at University of Alaska Fairbanks, a few of them becoming fluent speakers.

41 The assimilation of *&* to another consonant is still an ongoing process in some dialects. In North Baffin, for instance, several young speakers now realize *&* as though it were *s* (they say *qitiqsiq* instead of *qitiq&iq*). It is thus possible that within a few generations, the contrast between *&* and *l* will have disappeared from this dialect.

42 In the Seward Peninsula dialects of Alaskan Inupiaq, consonants are weakened after an unstressed vowel (*s* becomes *z*, *p* becomes *v*, *v* becomes *w*, etc.). This phenomenon seems due to the presence of Yup'ik-type prosodic rules dating back to a time when local people spoke Central Alaskan Yup'ik rather than Inupiaq.

43 The first modern European implantation in West Greenland dates back to 1721. In Nunatsiavut, after seventy-five years of sporadic contacts around Belle-Isle Strait, a Moravian mission-cum-trading post was established in Nain in 1771. In East Greenland, Danish colonization began only in 1894, but people living in the southern part of the area had always been in contact with south-western Greenlanders (Vebæk 2006). This might account for the equivalent degree of consonantal simplification in West and East Greenlandic. In the Thule district (northwest Greenland), however, where before 1910 there had been neither any permanent foreign presence nor regular contacts with the outside world, consonantal weakening – equivalent to that of the North Baffin dialect – is much lower than anywhere else in Greenland.

44 In East Greenland contact began in the late nineteenth century, but there were previous sustained contacts with south-western Greenlanders.

45 In both Inuktitut and Kalaallisut, this phenomenon is called *kutan(g)niq*.

46 Within Nunavik, the southeast coast of Hudson Bay (Little and Great Whale Rivers), being the region that first witnessed a permanent European presence (at the very beginning of the nineteenth century), now exhibits a degree of consonantal weakening equal to that of Nunatsiavut and thus higher than in the rest of Nunavik. In Kuujjuaraapik (Great

Whale River), for instance, uvuC groupings are now geminates and the word-final *q* is pronounced *k* (e.g., *annak* rather than *arnaq*, "woman"), as it is in Nunatsiavut.

47 Simpler grammatical rules may also have characterized the language of women. At the beginning of the eighteenth century, Martel de Brouague and Father François collected southern Labrador Inuit lexemes with innovative grammatical endings from female informants, although more conservative forms (like those collected by Father Saint-Pié) were still in usage.

48 The norm can be codified and imposed by an external authority, a fact that contributes to its artificial preservation. This is what happened in Greenland, where the conservative morphology of Kleinschmidt's time (mid-nineteenth century) was made official by Danish authorities, compulsorily taught in all schools, and widely used by the administration, the church, and written literature.

49 Syntactic change is also influenced by now pervasive contact with English, Danish, and to a much lesser extent, French.

50 As can be seen in chapter 8, this need for a "modern" language now often entails the downright replacement of Inuktitut with English when discussing non-traditional topics.

51 This was probably because of compulsory schooling and the importance of literacy.

52 These series are under the general editorship of Susan Sammons, head of the Language and Culture Program of Nunavut Arctic College, in collaboration with Alexina Kublu and Maggie Kakkiq. Some of the books are accessible on the Internet (http://nac.nu.ca/OnlineBookSite), and a few of them have been translated into French. A fourth Inuktitut-English series (Life Stories of Northern Leaders) publishes biographies of Inuit politicians.

53 Due to its metaphoric meaning, the word *uujurturpik* ("where cooked meat is eaten") might have itself replaced in a distant past the common Inuit appellation of the kettle, *utkusik/ukkusik*.

54 The only exception was West Greenlandic, where the school, the church, and written literature contributed to the preservation of a conservative morphology.

CHAPTER SIX

1 David Niviaxie, an elder from Umiujaq, Nunavik, notes that in Inuktitut the head can be divided into fifty-three different parts and that the

anatomy of the duck includes ninety-two elements, each with its own name (Avataq 1984).

2 The words for snow also constitute a well-known example. In anthropology and linguistics classes, Inuit appellations for snow are often overused as an instance of a supposed adequacy between language and environment. There is now a tendency to denounce this example as inadequate (see Martin 1986; Pullum 1991; Newsweek 1991; Kaplan 2003; Steckley 2008). Although it is true, as has often been repeated, that the Inuit vocabulary does not have fifty or one hundred words for "snow," the number of specific radicals (i.e., word-bases whose meaning applies uniquely to some form of snow) denoting this natural element (about ten of them) is somewhat higher than it is in English, French, or most other European languages.

3 Componential analysis (see Goodenough 1968) consists of describing the various submeanings coexisting within a lexeme. The word "father," for example, implies the ideas of "male" and "older generation."

4 Cognitive anthropology (see Tyler 1969) is the elicitation of the semantic classifications – or taxonomies – present in the minds of those speaking a specific language.

5 Denny (1981b) gives an excellent example of this phenomenon in his analysis of the semantic changes occurring when the affixes *-tuaq-* ("unique") and *-innaq-* ("only") combine into *-tuinnaq-* ("only real one"). For additional examples, see Therrien (1996).

6 Native speakers are rarely conscious of this structure. Its elicitation thus enables us to reach a particularly deep level in the semantic organization of social and cultural images.

7 However, these lexemes may have had understandable meanings in Proto-Eskimo or Proto-Eskaleut.

8 That the general notion of being born refers to the son rather than the daughter – and also that the word for "brother," *ani*, means "the one who exits (i.e., is born)" – may mean that the prototypical newborn is conceived of as male. The analysis of other terms tends to confirm this idea of the male gender as a human prototype (Dorais 1986b).

9 Semiotics and semiology study all types of symbols, linguistic or otherwise.

10 Personal communication, 30 January 2009.

11 First Nations people are called *allait* in Nunavik, Nunatsiavut, and the Baffin region, but west of Hudson Bay (i.e., in Kivalliq, the Kitikmeot region, Nunaqput, and northern Alaska) Dene Indians are dubbed *itqilgit* ("those with louse-nits"), while the Cree (only known in Kivalliq)

are called *unallit* ("the killers"). In Greenland the name of the North American Indians, *indianerit*, is a Danish loan-word.

12 The terms *angun/angut* and *arnaq* also apply to male and female animals. According to Guemple (1975), they are used under their basic form for human beings, spirits, dogs, and large land mammals and under a derived form for sea mammals (*angusarluk/arnaluk*) and birds (*angutiviaq/arnaviaq*).

13 Two examples are *uigu*-, "to lengthen something," and *uivaq*-, "to go round an obstacle."

14 For instance, the word for "girl" (*niviaqsiaq*) probably means "the one who is thrown back" (presumably to copulate, thus making a complete woman out of her).

15 A distinction must be made here between biological and social gender. A child who has received the name of someone whose sex is different from his or her own is often reared (at least until puberty) as though he or she were of that sex (see Saladin d'Anglure 1977).

16 For example, brothers and sisters are distinguished from nephews and nieces, as are grandparents from great-grandparents and so on.

17 The body is perceived as a habitat and a universe (Therrien 1982). By way of metaphors, plural meanings, and semantic change, the Inuit language expresses the vision of a universe shaped in the image of the human subject. Linguistic investigation thus puts into light aspects of Inuit traditional cognition that would otherwise remain unknown.

18 Saladin d'Anglure (1993) has shown that the Igloolik Inuit believe that human beings possess within themselves an air bubble (*sila*), a microcosmic version of the universe (*silarjuaq*, "the immense *sila*"), thanks to which they are reasonable persons living in harmony with the cosmos.

19 Comparing Briggs's data with his own northern Alaskan material, McNabb (1989) concludes that affects cannot be distinguished from their linguistic expression, both being intimately linked to the same social conventions.

20 In some dialects of Inuktitut (Nunavik, for instance), this way of proceeding has now been abandoned in favour of a system based on addition and subtraction: "they are three once again" (six); "they are not quite four once again" (seven); "they are four once again" (eight); "they are not quite ten" (nine); "they are five once again" (ten).

21 Up to the 1950s, counting was done in German in Nunatsiavut, under the influence of Moravian missionaries originally from Germany.

22 At the beginning of the twentieth century, Inuit men from Nunavik sometimes held competitions whose winner was the one who could

reach the highest number in counting. It is reported that the most skilful mathematicians could not count beyond the number sixty (Baillargeon et al. 1977, 101).

23 This does not mean that no distinction is made between past, present, and future. In some dialects (Nunavik Inuktitut, for instance), the moment of occurrence of an event can be expressed in a very precise way, thanks to lexical affixes whose respective meanings imply that something happened or will happen shortly, today, yesterday, tomorrow, or whenever. Time can thus be conceived of in a complex way. For example, the Nunamiut Iñupiat from northern Alaska establish a distinction between three types of past: the very first days of the universe, the original times (related through stories considered to be true, or not), and the period covered by the speakers' personal memories (Gubser 1965).

24 For the Inuit, in contrast with common European perceptions, the past (what came before) is in front of us, and the future (what will come after) is at our back.

25 Everywhere across the Inuit area, toponyms usually consist of generic geographical terms (e.g., *tasiq*, "lake"; *qikiqtaq/qiqirtaq*, "island"; *kuuk*, "river") followed by a qualifying affix denoting some ecological characteristic of the place thus named (e.g., *tasikallak* applies to a deep lake where there is fish, according to Vézinet 1975), or they may consist of lexemes expressing the presence of an unusual topographic characteristic or game species (e.g., the Greenlandic toponym *nanurtalik*, "where there are polar bears"). Gazeteers of Inuit place names such as the one edited by Müller-Wille (1987) offer good examples of the toponymic richness of a given region.

26 For instance, the demonstrative *una* would show the position of something easily accessible and/or visible.

27 An example is *qaqqartivap saani*, "in the front of the big hill."

28 A much more general introduction to the Inuit perceptions of what "the North" is can be found in Dorais (2008).

29 For instance, *ununga* (or *samunga*) ("toward down there") would always point to the direction of water. If one is inland or on the coast, it would refer to the sea (or river) shore. In a boat or on the sea-ice, it would point out to open water opposite the shore.

30 Like many other languages, most Inuit dialects do not distinguish between "green" and "blue," both being called *tungujuqtuq* or *tungujuqtaq*.

31 Dogs (*qimmiit*) and lice (*kumait*) are not considered *uumajuit* (i.e., animals) because they are equal to humans (dogs) or generated by them (lice).

32 It is mostly in the area of culture that newly introduced objects and concepts are found. Other major semantic fields (e.g., forms and categories, nature, and human beings) were barely affected by neology.

33 Onomatopoeias are the only lexemes created out of nothing. Their occurrence is very infrequent. To name new realities, Inuit prefer to use linguistic materials pre-existing in their language (lexeme-coining and semantic change) or in another tongue (borrowing).

34 These objects are considered larger or smaller than the traditional implement or are seen as being part of it.

35 The only difference is that borrowed words may start and, much more rarely, end with a consonant that the traditional language never allowed in the word-initial or word-final position (e.g., *l̲aija*, "lion"; *paisikal̲*, "bicycle").

36 Newly coined lexemes that include a borrowed radical (e.g., *tiiliuruti*, "teapot," based on the borrowed radical *tii-*, "tea") are regarded here as belonging to the first mode of designation, lexeme-coining.

37 German words were introduced by Moravian missionaries, who came from Germany. Almost all of these lexemes refer to measuring time. Originally, they were probably used in the context of church activities and the ecclesiastical calendar. Only one German loan-word is known outside Labrador, *luivi*, "lion" (*Loewe* in German), which is also in usage in the Tarramiut subdialect.

38 The only French word in Nunavik Inuktitut is fairly recent: *uiguit* ("the *oui-oui*"), the name given to francophones. This ethnonym has spread to southern Baffin Island as *uiviit*.

39 All types of illicit drugs are now called *aangajannatuq*, "that which makes one intoxicated."

40 The word for "computer," *qaritaujaq* or *qarisaujaq*, "which looks like a brain," might be a semantic borrowing from English, where computers are sometimes called electronic brains.

41 Objects and concepts belonging to actantial fields tend to be designated with newly coined lexemes expressing their function, and those that are linked to classificatory fields are usually named according to their appearance.

42 Petersen (1976a) points out that most Danish loan-words were initially adapted to Greenlandic phonology but that later on they were pronounced as in Danish. The term for "motor oil," for instance, originally pronounced *uulia*, is now written and pronounced *olie*, as in Danish. Other examples include current loan-words such as *feberi* ("fever"), *filmi* ("film"), *hesti* ("horse" [Danish *hest*]), *inspektøri* ("inspector"), *religioni* ("religion"), and *ækvatori* ("equator").

43 In my own study (Dorais 1983), these lexemes were not distinguished from other newly coined words.

44 Inupiaq possesses only one word that might be Dene: *naraji* ("frog").

45 These three words are *mantiikaq* ("lard or fat"; itself borrowed from Spanish *manteca*), *palayaq* ("boat"), and *pilip'iinaq* ("Filipino"). These loan-words seem to have been introduced by Filipino workers of the Bristol Bay fish canneries at the beginning of the twentieth century (Jacobson 1984).

46 However, modern Kalaallisut includes English loan-words linked to world culture (hip-hop, CD-ROM, etc.), as well as lexemes introduced through Danish (*jazzi*, "jazz"; *whisky*, "whisky"; etc.). An older loan-word is *tuluut* ("British, anglophone"), which probably stems from the phrase "how do you do?".

47 This could be a contraction of Hawaiian *paritanik* ("British, English"). At the turn of the twentieth century, Inuit from the Alaskan North Slope were in contact with Hawaiian sailors on American whaling ships.

48 American whalers operating in the area at the end of the nineteenth century often hired Portuguese-speaking Africans from the Cape Verde Islands, off the coast of Senegal.

49 At the beginning of the twentieth century, Alaskan Yupiit and Inuit were in contact with Saami brought there to teach them reindeer herding.

50 In various regions of the Arctic, there exist language committees that include translators and elders. Their task is to coin new Inuit words in different fields: medicine, justice, mechanics, and so on. These committees often publish thematic lexicons (e.g., Hugo et al. 1991; Pastori 1994; Sammons 1994). There also exists a transnational (Canada-Greenland) Internet discussion group on Inuit neology and other linguistic matters.

51 Unlike many other peoples, however, they did not have proverbs, common sayings, riddles, fables, or poems that were not sung.

52 Stories about Tuniit or Tunrit (Turnit in Greenland) constitute a good example of legends with a historical base. Most of them appear to describe prehistoric contacts between Paleo-Eskimo (the Tuniit) and Neo-Eskimo (the Thule ancestors of present-day Inuit). Of a historical nature too are Greenlandic legends about Kalaallit and Norsemen meeting during the Middle Ages as well as South Baffin Inuit stories telling about Frobisher's visits in 1576 and 1578.

53 In current speech, a visitor is invited to start a conversation by being asked *unikkaalaurit* ("please tell a story").

54 See, for instance, Boas (1964), Jenness (1922, 1924), Nelson (1899), Rasmussen (1929, 1939, 1931), Rink (1875), and Thalbitzer (1929). More recently, see the anthologies by Métayer (1973), Nungak and Arima (1969), Savard (1966), and Spalding (1979a).

55 The moon-man later became the protector of hunters and of mistreated women. Shamans went to visit him when the weather was bad and impeded hunting.

56 This girl has different names, according to the region were the myth is told: Nuliarjuk ("the immense spouse"), Sannaaluk ("the big one down there"), Takannaaluk ("this big one down here"), Kannakaffaaluk ("this big one who is down here"), and so on. In ethnographic literature, she is generally called "Sedna." In 2003 this name was given to a newly discovered asteroid.

57 Inuit believe in the existence of three separate souls: *atiq* (name), *tarniq* (immortal), and *anirniq* (breath, which disappears at death).

58 For the Nunavik Inuit, this lake is situated near Ivujivik, Quebec's northernmost village.

59 Several examples of Inuit songs can be found in Boas (1964), Hauser (1992), Jenness (1925), Pelinski et al. (1979), and Victor (1991). Traditional music, almost entirely vocal, has been the object of a number of recordings. For a discography valid up to the beginning of the 1980s, see Nattiez (1985).

60 This derives from the refrain common to this type of song: *ajaa ajaa* or *ajii ajii.*

61 In a famous song, Angutinnguaq threatens to throw into the river the Anglican missionary newly arrived in Kuujjuaq (Fort Chimo). In another composition, he claims a food allowance before leaving the Hudson's Bay Company trading post to go back home: *Aullalangasigama qaqqujanik pilaurlanga* ("Because I am about to leave, may I get biscuits?!"). Songs by and about Angutinnguaq were heard in Kuujjuaq in 1966, from the late Jiimi Kuuttuq Qungiaq.

62 Caribou, who migrate by the thousands, are to the earth what lice are to the human body.

63 Boot soles are made from the skin of the bearded seal.

64 These practices also include recent creations adhering to an ancient style. In Alaska and the western Arctic, some "traditional" songs were composed less than fifteen or twenty years ago.

65 Myths and legends have not really been replaced. The role they formerly played is now held, on the one hand, by Christian Scriptures (available in a written form) and, on the other hand, by truncated tales

without any canonical form that tell about various manifestations of the supernatural (dwarves, witches, ghosts, invisible beings, devils, etc.).

66 On Moravian Inuit music in Nunatsiavut, see Gordon (2007).

67 The Canadian Broadcasting Corporation's Northern Service has done a lot to disseminate contemporary Inuit music, producing its own cassettes and records or contributing to their production.

68 On modern Greenlandic music, see Johansen (2001).

69 This is the case if one also takes into account the etymological constraints that tend to preserve entirely or in part those already existing lexemes that denote a new reality seen as similar, in form and function, to its traditional equivalent.

CHAPTER SEVEN

1 In Kleinschmidt's time, the Greenlandic realization of an etymological *J* was *ʃ [sh]*, but by the mid-twentieth century this phoneme had merged with *s*, except in the speech of some older persons (Petersen 1976b).

2 In 1982 Greenland's Home Rule government established an official Language Commission (Oqaasileriffik, "The place where language is dealt with") responsible for the survival and development of Kalaallisut (see Oqaatsinut 2001). It has been allotted the task of preparing a general computerized dictionary of Greenlandic (Petersen 1990, 306).

3 On what is involved in imposing West Greenlandic on other dialectal areas, see Petersen (1977).

4 This arrangement is known as the Nunatsiavut Inuit Standardised Spelling System.

5 In Alaska, however, the Unangan and some Yupiit (the Alutiit in particular) had been taught to read in the Cyrillic alphabet by Russian Orthodox missionaries as early as the first half of the nineteenth century.

6 Evans had been trained as a commercial clerk in his native city of Kingston-upon-Hull, England. This is probably where he learned the so-called "Taylor shorthand," in use in his time (Lewis and Dorais 2004, 278).

7 Syllabic fonts have been adapted to the Internet, and many Inuit websites offer an Inuktitut syllabic version, but when composing e-mail, people usually prefer to write in the Roman script – or, more often, in English – because they may not know whether their correspondents possess the software necessary for deciphering syllabic messages.

8 One should read *suinnanginnik* (the modalis case of the nominal declension). The author has made a grammatical error.

9 For example, all consonant clusters – except for the uvuC – were to be written as though they were geminates.

10 The only major text ever published in that orthography was a compendium of practical information, *Qaujivaallirutissat* (Things That May Serve for Increasing Knowledge), published by the Canadian Department of Northern Affairs in 1964.

11 The standard was not able to render accurately the Siglitun and Uummarmiutun dialects and – as was discovered later on – Natsilingmiutut, whose phonology had not yet been thoroughly analyzed in 1976.

12 This led to erroneous transcriptions. When the village of Coppermine was renamed, its Inuit appellation, pronounced *qurluqtuq* ("waterfall"), was transcribed *kugluktuk* ("the two of them double themselves length-wise"), which became the official name of the place.

13 The symbol *H* is found in syllabics, but it is used only for transcribing the initial consonant of some words borrowed from English, such as *h̲amlit* ("hamlet") and H̲ari ("Harry").

14 This pictographic system was thus invented after the arrival of missionaries and other Europeans, and its creators knew about the existence of alphabets and literacy.

15 The Greenlandic orthography and ITC's Roman standard do not need any special adaptation because they make exclusive use of current keyboard characters.

16 One should also mention the Herzen Pedagogical Institute of Saint-Petersburg (Prosveshchenie Publishing), which publishes school materials in the languages of Russia's northern peoples, including Central Siberian Yupik.

17 In Nunavik, for instance, a survey conducted in the early 1980s (McGoldrick 1984) showed that 82.5% of all Inuit adults knew how to read Inuktitut. Almost half of them (36.7% of the sample) could not read any other language, while 16.5% of the surveyed population read only English. Readers of French accounted for a meagre 2.7% of the sample, while 45.8% read both Inuktitut and English. At the end of the 1980s, Donald M. Taylor (1990) found that Inuit residents of Kuujjuaq (Nunavik) estimated that their writing abilities in Inuktitut reached eight on a ten-point scale.

18 It can be hypothesized that in Canada at least, Inuit communication is still dominated by orality. English would be considered the only genuine

and efficient written medium, Inuktitut or Inuktun literacy thus playing a subsidiary role.

19 A stable form of bilingualism is one that would not be detrimental to the aboriginal language.

20 Such education projects were also overseen in Chukotka by the Soviet state and its Russian successor.

21 However, this may be changing with younger, formally educated mothers, according to Crago et al. (1993).

22 Two examples are *piipiiraaluga una* ("here is my big baby!") and *aalummiapik* ("poor little thing!").

23 Some linguistic aspects of language acquisition have been analyzed by Allen and Crago (1992), Allen (1996), Crago and Allen (1998), Allen and Schröder (2003), and Swift (2004).

24 At that time, East Greenland and the Thule district had not yet been reached by Europeans. As soon as these regions were included in the Danish colonial system (1895 in East Greenland; 1910 in Thule), schools were established and children started being taught to read and write in West Greenlandic Kalaallisut, the official language of the colony.

25 Generally speaking, this means Danes who speak Kalaallisut fluently.

26 Classes on Kalaallisut and Danish dealt with pedagogy and included eighteen lessons each.

27 The founder and first rector of the university was Robert Petersen, a native Greenlandic intellectual and former head of the Institut for Eskimologi at the University of Copenhagen, who has published extensively on anthropological and linguistic topics.

28 Ilisimatusarfik has been unable to fill all its faculty-level positions with Greenlanders. This means that a number of courses are taught in Danish or even in English when it is impossible to find enough professors from Denmark. Danes and foreigners living in Greenland are encouraged to learn Kalaallisut (among available teaching methods, see Pedersen 1977 and Janussen 1987), but few manage to achieve this goal.

29 In 2007 Nuuk's teacher training college (Ilinniarfissuaq) was attached to Ilisimatusarfik.

30 The teachers were Inuktitut-speaking missionaries or lay Inuit. Besides literacy, arithmetic, and religion, they taught basic notions of history and geography (see, e.g., Martin 1899). In 1914 the Moravians were operating eight schools, including one boarding school. Up to 1949 these offered a curriculum corresponding to the first three elementary grades (Jenness 1965).

31 Outside of Labrador, there were seven missionary schools in 1937 and some thirty of them in 1950 (Jenness 1964).

32 During the 1950s and 1960s, boarding schools or hostels adjoining secondary schools were in operation in Inuvik, Iqaluit, Chesterfield Inlet, and Fort Churchill, Manitoba (vocational school).

33 In 1965 forty federal schools were in operation in the Canadian Arctic. By 1970 almost 100% of all Inuit school-age children were going to school.

34 These schools operated alongside the federal establishments. They never enrolled more than 20% of the school-age population.

35 Two communities, Puvirnituq and Ivujivik, refused to recognize the validity of the James Bay Agreement and, as a consequence, the authority of the Kativik School Board. They opened their own schools under the direct supervision of Quebec's minister of education and arranged to have their teachers trained by Université du Québec en Abitibi Témiscamingue (see Maheux et al. 2004). On the history of education in Nunavik, see Vick Westgate (2002).

36 The Second World War had allowed Canada to discover the economic and strategic potential of its arctic regions and, in turn, to realize that those who lived there should become part of Canadian society.

37 A southern-style formal education was introduced that would be available in the local communities rather than in boarding schools or outlying institutions.

38 This education system, completely oriented toward southern values, had negative effects on the students: language problems (teachers spoke only English); frequent academic lags (two years on average during the mid-1960s); contempt for their language and culture (Brant and Hobart 1968).

39 However, several among them are unable to write Inuktitut because neither their parents nor the school taught them syllabics.

40 This deparment took the place of the Northwest Territories Department of Education when Nunavut seceded from the territories in 1999. On education in the Northwest Territories, see Benoit (1992).

41 The Education Act also provides for the establishment of a francophone school board to serve Nunavut's tiny French-speaking minority.

42 The college also occasionally holds classes in other communities.

43 In Nunavut as well as in Nunavik, Inuit interpreters and translators have their own professional association, which supervises translation and interpretation work for the government – for instance, simultaneous translation at the Legislative Assembly of Nunavut – and other

public agencies. On Inuit translation in Canada, see Harper (1983) and Sammons (1993). An interesting development in the field of translation is the recognition that deaf Inuit persons have the right to be interpreted in their own language (Inuit Sign Language) whenever necessary (see Macdougall 2001; Minogue 2005; Canadian Deafness Research and Training Institute 2006).

44 John Abbott College (English) and Cégep Marie-Victorin (French) have developed special programs for Nunavik students at the junior-college level.

45 The basic course is in the North Baffin dialect, but versions also exist for Inuinnaqtun (Harnum et al. 1982), Aivilik, Nunatsiavut, and Nunavik (Mallon 1992). This last is also available in French (Mallon 1993). In Ottawa, Inuktitut courses are offered by Janet McGrath of Tamalik and Associates.

46 At Institut des Langues et Civilisations Orientales (INALCO) in Paris, France, Inuktitut has been taught for many years by the ethnolinguist Michèle Therrien (Therrien 1989–92).

47 The University of Alaska was founded as early as 1917, in Fairbanks.

48 However, there are critics too. Bernadette Alvanna-Stimpfle (personal communication, 1987), who was teaching Inupiaq as a second language in Nome, considered bilingual education to be useless because most parents did not address their children in that language. In her opinion, teaching Inupiaq was primarily a political gesture of ethnic assertion.

49 The Yupik educator Oscar Kawagley has proposed a high school science curriculum based on aboriginal knowledge and teaching methods (Kawagley 1995), but it does not seem to have ever been implemented.

50 Webster (1968) and Panigeo (1979) have published self-teaching methods for learning Inupiaq.

51 The British sociolinguist Basil Bernstein has proved that it is important to respect the linguistic code (i.e., the actual use of lexical material and syntactic rules) of schoolchildren in order to facilitate their learning process.

52 There has also been a rapid increase in morphological change, as shown in Spada and Lightbown (2002) and in Allen et al. (2006).

53 For analyses of Berger's report, see Gallagher-Mac Kay (2007) and Bainbridge (2008).

54 This research would benefit from being resumed anew, most available data proceeding from studies conducted between the late 1970s and early 1990s.

55 Berthelsen (1983) has published an anthology of Greenlandic literature in a Danish translation.

56 This journal is still in existence. Its first editor was Rasmus Berthelsen.

57 Texts of local interest were usually written by Greenlanders, especially by catechists and schoolmasters, but sometimes too by ordinary hunters.

58 According to Petersen (1990, 303), publishing these legends, which closely followed oral expression (they included many elliptical sentences), influenced the Greenlandic literary language, which has remained, up to now, very close to the spoken language. For a theoretical view on this question, see Thisted (1992).

59 The emergence, since Home Rule, of administrative and political texts in Kalaallisut must be mentioned here. They are often characterized by a clumsy style and usually appear in a bilingual Greenlandic-Danish version, which makes it difficult to determine in which language they have originally been written (Fortescue 1990, 155).

60 These titles are also often read in their Danish or even English version.

61 There also exists an Inuit poetic tradition, which, except for songs, is conducted largely in English.

62 Even though she tells a fictitious story, Mitiarjuk resorts to the same style, as though she were relating real events (or a myth), often using the suffix *-guuq* ("it is said"), for instance, to give the impression that she is recounting facts known by hearsay.

63 On Alootook Ipellie, see Kennedy (1996).

64 It would probably also be useful to translate into Inuktitut a number of important Greenlandic titles.

65 Contrary to what happens in Greenland, fewer than a half-dozen non-Inuit literary works have been translated into Inuktitut. These include John Bunyan's *Pilgrim's Progress* and Robert L. Stevenson's *Treasure Island*.

66 In collaboration with local schools, the Alaska Native Language Center has published a lot of material in aboriginal languages. In the Inuvialuit region, one booklet has appeared in Uummarmiut (Albert et al. 1987).

67 Woodbury (1984b) has done something similar in the Hooper Bay/ Chevak Yup'ik dialect. In Unangax the principal bilingual title is the edition by Bergsland and Dirks (1990) of a corpus of tales and stories collected at the beginning of the twentieth century by the Russian anthropologist W. Jochelson. In Saint Lawrence Island Siberian Yupik, Koonooka (2003) has published a bilingual anthology of traditional legends.

68 Like those of Alaska, the Chukotka Eskimos do not really have a literature of their own, except for about sixty school booklets published since 1930, as well as a few articles in Siberian Yupik released in the local media. Menovshchikov (1990a) mentions two Eskimo poets

(Y. Anko and T. Gukhuv'e) and notes that several Russian classics have been translated into Yupik. More recently, a Yupik educator, Natalia Rodionova, published an anthology of classical and modern literary texts translated into Yupik from Russian (Rodionova 2007b).

69 The weekly paper *Sermitsiaq* is also available online in Greenlandic, Danish, and English (http://sermitsiaq.gl).

70 By publishing poems, songs, and short stories, these media also allowed local talents to express themselves freely. Due to the exorbitant cost of Inuktitut books, most Canadian Inuit writers still publish in community, governmental, or cultural media.

71 These periodicals with Inuit content included twenty-one newsletters and newspapers, sixteen magazines, and five scholarly journals (Rankin 2008).

72 The use of aboriginal languages is infrequent even in the *Tundra Times*, the most prestigious Alaskan native periodical.

73 According to Baunbæk (2007), in 2006 only 265 of 4,385 hours of television broadcasts, or 6%, were in Greenlandic, for an average of five hours a week.

74 Besides their community radio station, most Inuit villages host an internal network of citizens' band amateur radio sets. This system enables residents to communicate from one home to another and to stay in touch with individuals travelling or camping on the land. In contrast with the telephone, the internal radio network allows everyone to take part in collective conversations, thus reviving some sort of traditional sociability.

75 This might be linked to the advent of the videocassette recorder and, later on, of the Internet and DVDs, now available in all Inuit communities.

76 On the impact of the Internet on youth culture in Greenland, see Rygaard (2004).

77 This visibility was greatly enhanced by the foundation of the Inuit Circumpolar Conference (now the Inuit Circumpolar Council) in 1977. This international organization, recognized by the United Nations as one of its official partners, conveys the Inuit and Yupiit points of view to the non-Inuit world.

CHAPTER EIGHT

1 In Russian Chukotka, contacts were more frequent between Yupiget and Chukchi.

2 However, Indian-Inuit hostility should not be exaggerated. In southern Kivalliq, for instance, there were several cases of collaboration and mutual support between the two groups (Csonka 1999).

3 An exception is found in Chukotka, where many Yupiget also speak – or spoke – Chukchi.

4 A few Saami families from Norway had been brought to Alaska to teach reindeer herding to local Inupiat. During the first half of the twentieth century, Saami herders were similarly brought to the Mackenzie Delta and southern Baffin Island, but their stay there does not seem to have left linguistic traces.

5 Communication is easier within dialectal groupings (Inuktitut, Inuktun, etc.) than it is between two different linguistic subdivisions. In any case, many speakers now prefer to resort to English rather than trying to understand someone speaking another dialect.

6 Scandinavians from Greenland had encountered aboriginal *Skrælingar* ("Pagans") when visiting Newfoundland-Labrador at the end of the tenth century, but these were presumably Amerindians, not Inuit.

7 Missionaries chose the central west coast dialect of Nuuk, their headquarters, as the standard language. This dialect thus became quasi-official, as well as the only written form of Kalaallisut.

8 Up to 1953 no alien ship could land in Greenland without having previously received permission from the Danish administration.

9 In order to encourage bilingualism, a monetary bonus was offered to Danish-speaking Greenlandic employees.

10 Up to then, Greenland had been a colony whose native residents were not full-fledged Danish citizens. After 1953 the island became an integral part of Denmark.

11 For the same jobs, for instance, Greenlanders were paid much less than their Danish co-workers.

12 Some Basque whalers and fishermen came from Spain, and others from the French Basque Country (Pays basque). They had been frequenting the gulf and estuary of the Saint Lawrence River since the sixteenth century, and their presence is confirmed there until around 1730. According to Bakker (1989), the pidgin here mentioned could have originally included a majority of Basque words, before being restructured along a French pattern when the Basque ceased visiting Labrador.

13 It consists of a short memoir on the Labrador Coast, written by François-Étienne Cugnet (National Archives of Quebec, Fonds Pierre-Georges Roy, AP-G 239). A photocopy of this document was graciously sent to me by Charles Martijn, formerly of Quebec's Ministry of Culture.

14 Traditional Inuit politeness may explain why Amargo seems to be addressing Le Cour in the third person, as it is extremely embarrassing to ask someone his or her name in a direct way. It should be noticed that *kellanoré* could reflect either Inuktitut *kinaunali* ("but who is he?") or the French phrase *quel nom est?* ("what name is [that]?").

15 Around 1820 the traveller John West met Nunavik Inuit who yelled at him: "*Chimo! Chimo! Pillataa!*" (Bakker 1991). This simplified Inuit sentence – the word-base *saimuq-* (*chimo*) means "to greet each other, to shake hands," and *piliqta* (*pillataa*) means "let's do it" – seems to have been used for inviting Europeans to trade goods.

16 The whalers (chiefly American) and Inuit who visited the mouth of the Mackenzie River and the northern coast of Yukon (at Herschel Island) at the turn of the twentieth century communicated in a pidgin comprised of Iñupiat (and probably Siglitun), English, and possibly Hawaiian words (Stefansson 1909). American whaling captains often embarked Hawaiian sailors before reaching the arctic seas by way of the Pacific Ocean.

17 Almost 15% of all Nunatsiavut words denoting objects and concepts introduced by Europeans have been borrowed from English (Dorais 1983). As Settlers are concerned, they have adapted a number of Inuit words to their language (Ben-Dor 1966): *kamotik* (*qamutiik*, "sled"); *utuks* (*uuttuit*, "seals basking on the ice during spring"); *polaking* (*pulaak-*, "to visit," followed by the English suffix "-ing"); and so on.

18 According to Ben-Dor (1966), in Makkovik even the elders did not oppose the expansion of English because they did not consider Inuktitut adequate for communicating modern ideas.

19 This simplified language generally consisted of Inuit lexemes and morphemes combined along a syntactic structure shaped on that of English (Dorais 1979b), as in *uvanga taku ivvit* ("me see you") rather than *takuvagit* ("I see you"); or *uvanga naja nipi amisut* ("me sister voice many") instead of *najaga uqaqtualuk* ("my sister talks a lot"); or again *ivvit atausiq umiaq?* ("you one boat?") rather than *umiaqtututuanguvit?* ("are you alone in your boat?").

20 The proportion of native-language speakers circa 2000 was much higher on Saint Lawrence Island (71%), but very low (17%) among the Yupiget of Chukotka.

21 However, they often preserve a passive knowledge of Danish (understood without being spoken), which is fed by television and contacts with Danes living in Greenland (Langgaard 1992). But Kalaallisut is sufficient for performing adequately in all circumstances.

22 Greenland's Home Rule Working Group for Language Policy Review (Oqaatsinut 2001, 10) states that: "The language that is common to all Greenlanders is the Greenlandic standard language. The Greenlandic language, in the form it is now, does not belong to any specific dialect even though it originated in central-west Greenland. It is the language that all Greenlanders, whatever their own dialect, use when writing. However, the oral language is unregulated. Everyone can use his or her own dialect when speaking."

23 As can be seen in the next chapter, where more detailed language statistics are discussed, this figure is markedly higher (by some 10%) than the figure for Inuit-mother-tongue individuals, showing that knowledge of Inuktitut and Inuktun is not restricted to those who have learned it from birth.

24 On bilingualism as seen from a female perspective, see Mancini Billson and Mancini (2007, 132–6).

25 The exception was a few English-first-language young Inupiat who had regained their native tongue by learning it at the University of Alaska. Among the Yupiit and Unangan, bilingualism is universal, the exceptions being a few elderly Saint Lawrence Island Yupiget and some speakers of Central Alaskan Yup'ik over seventy years of age, who are still monolingual.

26 This research was summary because of its very small samples of respondents: fourteen individuals in Igloolik, twenty-two in Ammassalik.

27 Research was conducted in Puvirnituq and Ivujivik (Nunavik), as well as in Kimmirut, Igloolik, and Iqaluit (Baffin region of Nunavut). It comprised a questionnaire on sociolinguistic behaviour and a lexicometry component, where students were asked to write all the words that came to their minds, first in their mother tongue and then in their second language, on fifteen different topics.

28 Bilingualism is subtractive when the mother tongue is partly pushed aside by the second language. It is additive when learning another language leads to an enrichment of knowledge that is not detrimental to the mother tongue.

29 Iqaluit has been the capital of Nunavut since 1999. It is Nunavut's largest and most ethnically heterogeneous community.

30 Iqaluit is home to a small francophone community, which amounted to 290 individuals in 2006.

31 A total of 191 individuals of both genders and all age groups – comprising 153 native speakers of Inuktitut, 27 native anglophones, and 11 francophones – were interviewed in Iqaluit; 58 Inuit speakers were met

in Igloolik and 35 in Kimmirut. Moreover, the language behaviour was observed directly in several Iqaluit schools, homes, and workplaces.

32 On language choice and gender differences by topics of conversation in Iqaluit, as well as on language use at home, see Dorais (2002b).

33 Discourse practices are the culturally relevant ways by which various individuals and groups communicate linguistically among themselves within the confines of their community of residence (see Gumperz 1992).

34 Some youngsters mentioned that they dared not address elders anymore because they felt their Inuktitut was not adequate for communicating with monolingual speakers.

35 On code-mixing as an effect of Inuktitut-English bilingualism, see Allen et al. (2002). In 2001, 78.3% of bilingual Inuit adults in Nunavut reported mixing English words "often" or "all the time" with their Inuktitut, and the remaining 21.7% did it "occasionally" (Nunavummit Kiglisiniartiit 2001, 52).

36 In 2006 an international comparative survey of language attitudes among young Inuit, Yupiit, and Scandinavian Saami (the LPEASL Project) was launched by Shelley Tulloch (Canada), Karen Langgaard (Greenland), and others as an official activity of the 2007–2009 International Polar Year.

37 In 1988, 75% of Kuujjuaq's 1,100 residents were native speakers of Inuktitut, 15% native francophones, and 10% native anglophones.

38 These students also prefer reading in Danish.

39 The northernmost town in Alaska, Barrow is the state's second largest Inupiaq community (after Kotzebue).

40 A parser is a computer program that divides words into their component morphemes.

41 On Inuit tutelage and internal colonialism in the Arctic, see Paine (1977).

42 In Russian Chukotka, the same process led to the extinction of Sirenikski and to a severe decrease among speakers of Naukanski and Central Siberian Yupik.

CHAPTER NINE

1 Demographic data on Unangax and the Yupik languages can be found in chapter 1.

2 This refers to individuals born in Greenland (among a Greenlandic population of 56,648 in 2006), nearly all of them being of Inuit or part-Inuit ancestry.

3 For comparison's sake, the world Eskimo population was estimated at 131,000 individuals (including 102,000 Inuit and 29,000 Yupiit and Yupiget) in 1991 (Dorais 1996b, 23).
4 Diversified statistics on language use across the North can be found in the report of the Survey of Living Conditions in the Arctic (SLiCA 2007).
5 The proportion falls to 62.6% when Yupiit, Yupiget, and Unangan residing outside their native territory are included.
6 However, as seen in the study by Harcharek (2001), quoted in chapter 8, that 86% of Alaskan Inupiat are reported not to speak their aboriginal language does not mean they know nothing about it. Many have some passive knowledge of the language or are able to say a few words or sentences in Iñupiaq.
7 This refers to individuals speaking an Inuit dialect, in percentage of persons of Inuit ancestry.
8 According to statistical research conducted in 1999, 97% of all people born in Greenland reported speaking Kalaallisut (Oqaatsinut 2001, 37). The same percentage of speakers was applied to Kalaallit residing in Denmark.
9 This is the number of individuals who reported being able to hold a conversation in Inuktitut or Inuktun, according to the Canadian census of 2006. It should be noted that 1,575 of these persons did *not* identify themselves as Inuit (they might have been Euro-Canadians – Nunatsiavut Settlers or part-Inuit individuals, for instance – or members of a First Nation with some knowledge of Inuktitut). The proportion of respondents with an Inuit identity who reported knowing their ancestral language was 68.7% (34,685 of 50,480 Canadian Inuit).
10 Krauss (2007, 407–17). Krauss's data concern only Inupiat residing within Alaska. His reported proportion of 14% of speakers was applied to the estimated 3,140 Inupiat living outside the state.
11 At publishing time, available statistics from the 2006 Canadian census were extrapolations from a 20% sample of census respondents. Figures are rounded up to zero or five, often resulting in arbitrary numbers. For example, the quoted figure of fifteen Inuktitut-mother-tongue individuals in Prince Edward Island (PEI) stands for an estimated number of between ten and twenty speakers and for an actual number (when total census data become available) probably hovering between one and thirty. This means that percentages based on small numbers (e.g., 50% of Inuit-mother-tongue individuals in PEI) are indicative at best.

12 Of this total, 32,380 individuals reported Inuit as their unique first language, and 585 reported Inuit and English or French as multiple first languages.

13 Nunaqput comprises the Inuvialuit settlement region.

14 Cross-checking allows us to estimate the proportion of Inuit living outside *Inuit nunaat* at 11% in Quebec, 15% in Newfoundland, and 34% in the Northwest Territories. Nunavut lies entirely within *Inuit nunaat*.

15 These flights go to Ottawa and Edmonton.

16 Yukon lies outside *Inuit nunaat* except for its northern coast, which belongs to the Inuvialuit settlement region but hosts no permanent population.

17 "Mother tongue" is defined as the first language learned and still understood by someone. Southern Canadian Inuit may tend to lose their proficiency in Inuktitut or Inuktun after some time or may never have acquired any in the case of Inuit or part-Inuit individuals born or reared outside *Inuit nunaat* or adopted by non-Inuit parents.

18 These Settlers are thus technically considered to be "Inuit."

19 In a somewhat parallel way, 710 census respondents reported having Inuktitut as their first language without identifying themselves as Inuit.

20 Of the 230 speakers whose first language was not Inuktun, 150 reported an aboriginal identity to census takers.

21 Comparative figures on language use from 1981 to 2001 can be found in Senécal (2007).

22 Unfortunately, this is not the case during international meetings (those of the Inuit Circumpolar Council, for instance), where it is generally English that serves as the medium of communication among Inuit coming from different regions of the North American Arctic.

23 This is especially true for the North Slope and Kotzebue regions. On Seward Peninsula, many older people no longer speak Inupiaq.

24 However, a few individuals who usually speak the Inuit language at home may have had it as a second language rather than as their mother tongue.

25 This refers to the percentage of all Inuit speakers (all those able to hold a conversation in the aboriginal language) who have Inuktitut or Inuktun as their home language.

26 An interesting source of detailed language statistics on Nunavut is the Bureau of Statistics' report on language use (Nunavummit Kiglisiniartiit 2001), with very specific – although, sometimes, questionable as to their real accuracy – data (e.g., the language most frequently used for thinking when one is involved in subsistence activities).

27 For comparison's sake, detailed language data on *Inuit nunaat* based on the 1986 Canadian census can be found in Dorais (1996b, 24–6, 57–8). Comparable data for Alaskan and Greenlandic Inuit communities in 1980–81 have been published in Dorais (1996a, 58–9, 67).

28 In the two villages of Nain and Hopedale, however, where a majority of the aboriginal population is of Inuit (rather than Settler) heritage, the combined proportion of Inuktitut-mother-tongue residents reaches 32%.

29 In Iqaluit, Inuktitut-mother-tongue residents accounted for a mere 49% of the population in 2006.

30 Arviat (Kivalliq) constitutes an exception. With 2,060 residents in 2006 – it was Nunavut's third largest community – all of its 1,915 Inuit had Inuktitut as their first language, and 95% of them spoke the language at home.

31 However, as already mentioned, census data for 2006 available at publishing time were based on 20% samples and rounded out at random, with the result that smaller numbers may be inaccurate and yield slanted percentages.

32 Uummarmiut is a subdialect of the Alaskan North Slope Iñupiaq dialect.

33 The proportions for Uummarmiut and Siglitun are, respectively, 20% and 27% (1986) and 18% and 18% (2006).

34 The rates have decreased from 95% for all three to 90% (Kivalliq), 89% (Aivilik), and 91% (South Baffin).

35 However, the objectives of the government were somewhat contradictory: public education was aimed at enabling Inuit to become full members of Canadian society while also preserving their traditional way of life (Forgues 1987; see also Damas 2002 and Vick Westgate 2002).

36 This law allows all Canadians to preserve their ancestral culture, including their original language. Aboriginal rights in this domain are specifically mentioned in the Constitutional Law of 1982 and in a federal policy statement (Secretary of State 1985) issued three years later (Trudel 1996).

37 The "Bathurst Mandate" took its name from an orientation meeting of the first government of Nunavut, held in Bathurst Inlet in 1999 (see Government of Nunavut 2000; Jull 2000).

38 This is also the case in Greenland, where all former Danish village names have been replaced by Kalaallisut toponyms (Kleivan 1990).

39 French-Inuit toponyms were also adopted, as in Notre Dame de Koartac ("Our Lady of the Intestinal Worm"; the Inuit place-name Quaqtaq – Koartac in French – refers to this body parasite). As early as 1970 the Quebec government had started to make official use of

Inuktitut place-names (collected during a survey conducted in 1968; see Saladin d'Anglure et al. 1969) without an already existing equivalent in another language.

40 Müller-Wille (1983) gives the example of the community of Akilasakallak (the name used by its original residents), which became George River when a trading post of the Hudson's Bay Company was established there in the nineteenth century, then Port-Nouveau-Québec at the beginning of the 1960s, and finally Kangiqsualujjuaq after the signing of the James Bay Agreement.

41 Restrictions on English elementary and secondary education in Quebec (only children with at least one parent already schooled in English in Canada are allowed to enter anglophone schools) do not apply to the Cree and Inuit.

42 "High" functions include writing, reading, being schooled beyond grades 2 or 3, and communicating with official governmental or administrative bodies.

43 "Low" functions include private conversations, oral literature, and the lower school grades.

44 No West Greenlanders speak the Thule or East Greenlandic dialects.

45 However, local authorities tend increasingly to give more exposure to their language, using it for public bill-posting, for instance.

46 The decline of Inuktitut was also precipitated by forcing the young to use an Inuit orthography that was both obsolete and uselessly complex.

47 It is interesting to note that in Nunatsiavut, the internal division within Inuktitut (church versus spoken) seems to have contributed to the predominance of English, whereas in Nunavik the presence of two competing European languages (English and French) appears to have helped with the preservation of Inuktitut, still spoken by the vast majority of the population.

48 In 2006, 76% of the Kuujjuaq Inuit still had Inuktitut as their usual home language. However, the type of research conducted by Taylor and Wright (1989) in the 1980s needs to be resumed and updated.

49 The predominant position of English stems from the historical development of social and ethnic relations in Canada.

50 Their opinions, idealistic and realistic at the same time, are not so far from those expressed by Dorais and Sammons's Iqaluit respondents, mentioned in chapter 8 (see Dorais 2006a).

51 All Canadian Inuit communities, even the smallest, need more than one language in order to function adequately.

52 In 2006, according to census data, 100% of the Quaqtaq Inuit had Inuktitut as their home language.

53 According to Bourdieu (1991), languages are monetarily valued commodities whose mastery endows speakers with more or less social (or sociolinguistic) capital on the economic market.

54 English words are also used because children and young adults were schooled mostly in English, never being taught how to communicate in Inuktitut about present-day life (Dorais 2006a). This shows that bilingual education in its northern version contributes largely to diglossia.

55 By way of illustration, in 2001, 67% of Inuktitut-first-language Nunavut Inuit reported that it was very important to speak English in the territory today (Nunavummit Kiglisiniartiit 2001, 60). One-third of them (33%) felt they were losing their ability to speak their mother tongue (ibid., 51), while 34% of adult Inuit living in Iqaluit reported having difficulty receiving services from community businesses in their preferred language (ibid., 68).

56 According to Julie-Ann Tomiak (2003), by redefining and reconstructing symbolic capital, government policies such as Inuit Qaujimajatuqangit (making use of traditional knowledge in the governance of Nunavut) allow for the incorporation of some elements of the alternative Inuktitut language market into the dominant English one.

57 The third language, French, chiefly present in Iqaluit, serves mostly to preserve and transmit ethnic identity and group culture within the francophone community.

58 Moreover, the official version of the transcription of these debates is the English one.

59 The status of Inupiaq and Yupik was thus completely reversed. From indispensable but poorly valued languages, they became quasi-useless speech forms with a high symbolic value.

60 Data from the Nunavut Household Survey of 2001 show that 80% of the territory's Inuit residents state that it is "very important" to speak Inuktitut/Inuinnaqtun today, and another 16.8% find it "somewhat important" (Nunavummit Kiglisiniartiit 2001, 36).

61 An example of one such initiative is the Inuktitut or Inuktun translation by public organizations of hundreds of pages of ultraspecialized texts (legislation, technical and administrative data, etc.) that nobody is interested in reading in a language other than English.

62 In its proposition for a comprehensive arctic policy, for instance, the Inuit Circumpolar Council (1992) states that language plays a central

part in ensuring the continuity of Inuit culture and cultural identity. But among the 592 clauses in this proposition, only 9 (1.5%) concern linguistic questions.

CHAPTER TEN

1 In Alaskan Inupiaq, besides *uqaq-*, the radical *nipli-/nivli-* also denotes the action of talking. In Canada and Greenland, this radical means "to utter a sound, to shout."

2 Taamusi Qumaq (1914–93) was a self-taught (he never went to school) thinker and scholar from Puvirnituq, Nunavik, who, among other achievements, wrote the first dictionary of definitions in Inuktitut. In 1990 he was awarded the Canadian government's Northern Science Award.

3 Even liars (*sallutujut*), whose speech is not in accordance with their thoughts, "say that they tell the truth." If this were not the case, they would not be telling lies. The practical joker (*lannguatuq*, "one who pretends to say something") lets it be rapidly known that he or she is "pretending to say," which re-establishes the balance between thinking and speaking.

4 Like humans, however, they have a voice, *nipi*, of which Qumaq (1991, 352) states: "Humans and animals, all of them have a voice, each having a different voice."

5 Only dogs, too, possess their own name: Taqulik ("The one with a white spot"), Qirniq ("The black one"), Kajualuk ("Big brown"), and so on.

6 At the suprahuman level, a special tongue, the shaman's language, was also used for communicating with spirits (see chapter 6).

7 One may wonder which meaning of *uqaq-* came first: "tongue" or "to talk?" In the Yupik languages, the word for "tongue" is *ulu*. Interestingly enough, in the Inuit dialects, *ulu* denotes the semi-lunar woman's knife, whose shape can recall that of a tongue. In Yupik the woman's knife is called *uluaq* or *ulaaq* ("little tongue") (Fortescue et al. 1994, 367). *Ulu* might thus have originally meant "tongue." When, in Proto-Inuit, its meaning would have shifted to that of "woman's knife," the tongue had to be called something else. This is when the radical *uqaq-* ("talk") would have started being used as a noun (*uqaq*, "tongue") meaning literally "the talker."

8 Speech reflects thinking (*isuma*), whose function is to regulate life in a sensible way (Qumaq 1991, 45): "It [*isuma*] cannot be seen. It is thought by the human intellect [*isumauti*, "which is used for thinking"].

Without uttering any sound, thinking can regulate many things, even if it is just an idea."

9 Qumaq's thinking is thus close to that of Bourdieu (1991), for whom it is useless to hear a language if nobody values it enough to listen to it.

10 For example, the North Baffin myth explaining how the alternation of day and night appeared tells about a raven and a fox who argued about the relative importance of light and darkness. The raven shouted "*Qau, qau*" ("Light, light"), and the fox replied "*Taaq, taaq*" ("Darkness, darkness"). Daylight then started to alternate with night (Rasmussen 1929, 253).

11 The shaman's language allegedly shows that males are at the origin of things, whereas females are containers that simply receive what is laid down in them.

12 According to the East Greenlander Asineq (quoted in Collis 1990, 5), "The word is the greatest power human beings have. With words, you can wound others or make them happy – for life."

13 The need to use language with care gave rise to linguistic taboos: one should not speak inconsiderately about anything. Silence is preferable to useless babbling, and children who talk too much are considered less intelligent (Crago 1988). Inuit conversations are often interspersed with long periods of silence, sometimes interrupted by a greeting formula ("Hi, you!") addressed to the interlocutor and showing that communication has not been broken despite the absence of words.

14 This is the case because a polysynthetic language constructs words as they are needed.

15 There are also words that must be pronounced in specific circumstances of ordinary life: *qaqaqa* when a stone bursts asunder (Natsilingmiut), *mura* when one has farted (Aivilik), *qauq* when one farts or sneezes (Igloolik), and so on.

16 See Kublu and Oosten (1999) for a detailed description of how one Inuk from Igloolik addresses the members of her family and is addressed by them.

17 These are resources and techniques that they are able to name – and thereby to know – very precisely.

18 Thus there is an unfortunate tendency to use English as the means of communication among people who speak differing dialects, and in Canada and Alaska, it is impossible to unify the language by making one dialect official, as was done in nineteenth-century Greenland.

19 Many anthropologists equate this cognitive system with culture (see Tyler 1969).

20 "Ancestral community" refers to any societal grouping based on a real or presumed common origin, whether it be genealogical (common ancestors), geographical (shared territory), cultural (shared culture), or a mix of all three.

21 In contrast, among Europeans, according to Inuit perceptions, everything must be paid for.

22 *Siqiniq* ("sun") also expresses a way of thinking akin to the scientific explanation of solar radiation emanating from unceasing atomic explosions within the star.

23 Let it be recalled that in the Inuit language the notions of time and space are usually expressed by the same affixes, as in *quviasugvik*, which can mean "time for rejoicing" (i.e., Christmas and the New Year) or "place for rejoicing" (e.g., a feasting or dancing hall).

24 Inuktun then played an important part in socializing children because education often resorted to oral literature. It was also in Inuktun that people joked, discussed, or negotiated the resolution of conflicts.

25 The Dene too benefited from similar allocations.

26 Although Inuit from Alaska and Canada do not have any problem saying they are Americans or Canadians, most Kalaallit consider themselves Greenlanders, never Danes nor Danish nationals.

27 In Russian Chukotka the Yupiget have long been recognized as a national minority, although this has not allowed them to achieve any real measure of economic, administrative, or political autonomy. Nevertheless, they have been able to preserve their ethnic identity, a component of which is their ancestral language (Morgounova 2007).

28 A Kalaaliq may also be someone born in Denmark of Greenlandic parents.

29 These Inuit-led governments and administrations, of course, also seek to redress a special history of internal colonization by the Canadian government.

30 An exception, perhaps, is Nunatsiavut, where the Anglo-Saxon Settlers joined the Labrador Inuit Association and became beneficiaries of the Nunatsiavut Agreement. It remains to be seen, however, whether a cleavage of some sort does not subsist between them and the descendants of the original Labrador Inuit.

31 This may be the result of contemporary economic and political developments, namely the rise of regional native corporations in Alaska and separate land claims agreements in the various regions of arctic Canada.

32 The use of local variants (i.e., "rural" or "village" English) of the majority language is also important in identifying aboriginal Alaskans (Schafer 1977; Kwachka 1992a; Kaplan 2001).

33 They also manipulate the use of some semantic fields (see Morrow and Hensel 1992).

34 One Eskaleut language, Sirenikski, even became extinct in 1997 when its last speaker died.

35 An exception, perhaps, is the capital, Nuuk, where a sizeable minority of young, educated Kalaallit are unable to speak Kalaallisut (Yvon Csonka, professor, University of Greenland, personal communication, 4 April 2008).

36 Such barriers include the astronomical costs involved in implementing immersion programs in the language, as well as the prevalent sentiment that English is much more useful for performing in the contemporary world.

37 There is a slight difference in Nunavik, where some students learn French, although they seem to acquire an informal knowledge of English at the same time as they are formally taught French at school.

38 Inuktitut might also survive as a kind of intellectual hobby for a few individuals who learn it as a second language to expand their knowledge and strengthen their ethnic identity. This is what has happened with Cornish, a Celtic language formerly spoken in southwest England, whose last native speaker died in 1891 but which has since been kept alive by a small number of persons, for whom learning and speaking Cornish constitute a leisure activity (Grenoble and Whaley 2006, 45–8).

References

Adam, Lucien. 1884. "En quoi la langue esquimaude diffère-t-elle grammaticalement des autres langues de l'Amérique du Nord?" In Lucien Adam, ed., *Compte-rendu de la cinquième session du troisième Congrès international des Américanistes, tenu à Copenhague en 1883*, 337–55. Paris, France: Société des Américanistes.

Ajaruaq, John. 1970. *Jaani Ajaruap inuusinga* [The life of John Ajaruaq]. Ottawa: Government of Canada, Department of Northern Affairs.

Ajnana, Lyudmila I. 2003. *Kartinnij slovar' eskimosskogo iazika* [Picture dictionary of the Eskimo language]. Saint Petersburg, Russia: Prosveshchenie.

– and G.A. Nakazik. 1987. *Anxaq* [The little spark]. Leningrad, Russia: Prosveshchenie.

Alasuaq, Alacie. 1973. *Guide de la couturière*. Povungnituk, Nunavik, QC: Commission scolaire du Nouveau-Québec.

Alasuaq, Davidialuk. 1981. *Unikkaatuat ujaranngutitait* [Stories transformed into stone]. Inuksiutiit allaniagait 3. Quebec City: Association Inuksiutiit Katimajiit.

Albert, Rosie, Ronald Lowe, and Pierre Renaud. 1987. *Aakagiik niqaigutiruak* [A mother and her child have no food]. Quebec City: Association Inuksiutiit Katimajiit; Inuvik, NWT: Committee for Original Peoples' Entitlement.

Alia, Valerie. 1994. *Names, Numbers, and Northern Policy: Inuit, Project Surname, and the Politics of Identity*. Halifax: Fernwood.

– 2006. *Names and Nunavut: Culture and Identity in the Inuit Homeland*. Oxford, UK, and New York: Berghahn Books.

Allen, Shanley E.M. 1996. *Aspects of Argument Structure Acquisition in Inuktitut*. Amsterdam, Netherlands: John Benjamins.

– 2007. "The Future of Inuktitut in the Face of Majority Languages: Bilingualism or Language Shift?" *Applied Psycholinguistics* 28, no. 3: 515–36.

– and Martha B. Crago. 1992. "First Language Acquisition of Inuktitut." In M.J. Dufour and F. Therien, eds, *Regards sur l'avenir/Looking to the Future*, 273–81. Inuit Studies Occasional Papers 4. Quebec City: Association Inuksiutiit Katimajiit.

– Frank H. Genesee, S.A. Fish, and Martha B. Crago. 2002. "Patterns of Code Mixing in English-Inuktitut Bilinguals." In M. Andronis, C. Ball, H. Elston, and S. Neuvel, eds, *Proceedings of the 37th Annual Meeting of the Chicago Linguistic Society*, vol. 2, 171–88. Chicago, IL: Chicago Linguistic Society.

– and H. Schröder. 2003. "Preferred Argument Structure in Early Inuktitut Spontaneous Speech Data." In J.W. Du Bois, L.E. Kumpf, and W.J. Ashby, eds, *Preferred Argument Structure: Grammar as Architecture for Function*, 301–38. Amsterdam, Netherlands: John Benjamins.

– Martha B. Crago, and Diane Pesco. 2006. "The Effect of Majority Language Exposure on Minority Language Skills: The Case of Inuktitut." *International Journal of Bilingual Education and Bilingualism* 9, no. 5: 578–96.

Alvanna-Stimpfle, Bernadette. 1987. "King Island Inupiaq Course." Typed manuscript, Northwest Community College, Nome, Alaska.

Amagoalik, John. 2007. *Changing the Face of Canada*. Ed. Louis McComber. Life Stories of Northern Leaders 2. Iqaluit, NU: Nunavut Arctic College.

Amos, Muriel M., and Howard T. Amos. 2004. *Cup'ig [Nunivak Island] Eskimo Dictionary*. Fairbanks, AK: Alaska Native Language Center.

Andersen, Catharyn, and Alana Johns. 2005. "Labrador Inuttitut: Speaking into the Future." *Études/Inuit/Studies* 29, nos 1–2: 187–205.

Andersen, Thomas. 2001. "Statistik og sprogpolitik" [Statistics and language policy]. Paper read at the "Conference on Language Policies," Kangerlussuaq, Greenland.

Angilirq, Paul Apak, Norman Cohn, and Bernard Saladin d'Anglure. 2002. *Atanarjuat the Fast Runner*. Toronto: Coach House Books; Igloolik, NU: Isuma Publishing.

Angulalik, Gwen, Margo Kadlun, and Betty Harnum. 2000. *Inuinnaqtun-English Dictionary*. Cambridge Bay, NU: Nunavut Arctic College.

Anonymous. 1949. *Service Book of the Western Eskimos*. Toronto: Society of the Church of England in Canada.

Anonymous. 1971. *The Moravian Mission in Labrador/Moraviamiut Missioningat Labradoremiut Akkorngane*. Happy Valley, NL: Moravian Mission.

Anonymous. 1984. *TNI-NNBAP Audience Research Preliminary Report (Television)*. Montreal: Quithe Communications.

Anonymous. 2008. "Namminersorneq nammineersinnaatitaanerlu" [Self-rule and self-determination]. *Suluk* 4: 18–19.

Arnakak, Jay. 1994. "Use of Demonstratives in the Baffin Island Dialects." Paper read at the "9th Inuit Studies Conference," Nunavut Arctic College, Iqaluit, Nunavut.

Avataq. 1984. *Deliberations of the Inuit Language Commission*. Inukjuak, Nunavik, QC: Avataq Cultural Institute.

– 1990. *Nunavik Inuit Language Survey Results*. Inukjuak, Nunavik, QC: Avataq Cultural Institute.

– 2006. *Inuttituurniup Saturtauninganut Planning Committee Meeting Report*. Inukjuak, Nunavik, QC: Avataq Cultural Institute.

Aylward, M. Lynn, Millie Kuliktana, and Rosemarie Meyok. 1998. *Report of the Kitikmeot Language Research Project*. Cambridge Bay, NU: Kitikmeot Board of Education.

Badten, Linda Womkon (Aghnaghaghpik), Vera Oovi Kaneshiro (Uqiitlek), Marie Oovi (Uvegtu), and Christopher Koonooka (Petuwaq). 2008. *St Lawrence Island/Siberian Yupik Eskimo Dictionary*. 2 vols. Ed. Steven A. Jacobson. Fairbanks, AK: Alaska Native Language Center.

Baillargeon, Richard, Gérald Noelting, Louis-Jacques Dorais, and Bernard Saladin d'Anglure. 1977. "Aspects sémantiques et structuraux de la numération chez les Inuit." *Études/Inuit/Studies* 1, no. 1: 93–128.

Bainbridge, John. 2008. "A Response to Kelly Gallagher-Mackay." *Canadian Journal of Education* 31, no. 3: 761–6.

Bakker, Peter. 1989. "'The Language of the Coast Tribes Is Half Basque': A Basque-Amerindian Pidgin in Use between Europeans and Native Americans in North America, ca. 1540–ca. 1640." *Anthropological Linguistics* 31, nos 3–4: 117–47.

– 1991. "Trade Languages in the Strait of Belle-Isle." *Journal of the Atlantic Provinces Linguistic Association* 13: 1–19.

– 1996. "Language Contact and Pidginization in Davis Strait, Hudson Strait, and the Gulf of Saint Lawrence (Northeast Canada)." In E.H. Jahr and I. Broch, eds, *Language Contact in the Arctic*, 261–320. Berlin, Germany, and New York: Mouton de Gruyter.

Balt, Peter. 1977a. *Dictionary by Themes Inuktitut Qablunaatitut*. Rankin Inlet, NU: Community School.

– 1977b. *Body Parts Workbook: Timiup atingit*. Rankin Inlet, NU: Community School.

Barnum, Francis P. 1901. *Grammatical Fundamentals of the Innuit Language as Spoken by the Eskimo of the Western Coast of Alaska*. Boston, MA: Ginn and Co. Reprint, Hildesheim, Germany: Georg Olms Verlag, 1970.

Baunbæk, Lene, ed. 2007. *Greenland in Figures 2007*. Nuuk, Greenland: Greenland Home Rule Government, Statistics Greenland.

Beach, Hugh. 1986. "The Saami in Alaska: Ethnic Relations and Reindeer Herding." In H. Beach, ed., *Contributions to Circumpolar Studies*, 1–81. Uppsala Research Reports in Cultural Anthropology 7. Uppsala, Sweden: University of Uppsala, Department of Cultural Anthropology.

Béchard, Jean-Michel. 2006. "A Tongue in Search of Its Mother: Reversing the Language Shift in Cambridge Bay, Nunavut." MA thesis, Ludwig-Maximilians University, Germany.

Ben-Dor, Shmuel. 1966. *Makkovik: Eskimos and Settlers in a Labrador Community*. St John's, NL: Memorial University of Newfoundland, Institute of Social and Economic Research.

Benoit, France. 1992. "Education in the Northwest Territories: The 1990s." In M.J. Dufour and F. Therien, eds, *Regards sur l'avenir/Looking to the Future*, 231–9. Inuit Studies Occasional Papers 4. Quebec City: Association Inuksiutiit Katimajiit.

Berge, Anna. 1992. *A Comparison of Four Theories of Syntax and Their Relation to the Study of Inuktitut*. Iqaluit, NU: Nunavut Arctic College.

– 2005. "Eskimo-Aleut." In K. Brown, ed., *Encyclopedia of Language and Linguistics*, vol. 6, 219–23. Oxford, UK: Elsevier.

– and Moses Dirks. 2006. *Niigˆugˆis Mataliin Tunuxtazangis: How the Atkans Talk (A Conversational Grammar)*. Fairbanks, AK: Alaska Native Language Center.

Berger, Thomas R. 2006. *The Nunavut Conciliator's Final Report*. Ottawa: Indian and Northern Affairs Canada.

Bergsland, Knut. 1951. "Aleut Demonstratives and the Aleut–Eskimo Relationship." *International Journal of American Linguistics* 17: 167–79.

– 1955. "A Grammatical Outline of the Eskimo Language of West Greenland." Typed manuscript, University of Oslo, Norway.

– 1959a. "Aleut Dialects of Atka and Attu." *Transactions of the American Philosophical Society* 49, no. 3: 5–128.

– 1959b. "The Eskimo-Uralic Hypothesis." *Journal de la Société Finno-Ougrienne* 61, no. 2: 1–29.

– 1986. "Comparative Eskimo-Aleut Phonology and Lexicon." *Journal de la Société Finno-Ougrienne* 80: 63–167.

– 1994. *Aleut Dictionary: Unangam Tunudgusii*. Fairbanks, AK: Alaska Native Language Center.

– 1998. *Ancient Aleut Personal Names: Materials from the Billings Expedition, 1790–1792*. Fairbanks, AK: Alaska Native Language Center.

– and Hans Vogt. 1962. "On the Validity of Glottochronology." *Current Anthropology* 3, no. 2: 115–53.

– et al. 1978. *Qawalangim Tunugan Kaduugingin: Eastern Aleut Grammar and Lexicon*. Anchorage, AK: National Bilingual Materials Development Center.

– and Moses L. Dirks. 1978. *Niigugim Tunugan llakuchangis: Introduction to Atkan Grammar and Lexicon*. Anchorage, AK: National Bilingual Materials Development Center.

– and Jørgen Rischel, eds. 1986. *Pioneers of Eskimo Grammar*. Copenhagen, Denmark: The Linguistic Circle of Copenhagen.

– and Moses L. Dirks, eds. 1990. *Unangam Ungiikangin Kayux Tunusangin/Unangam Uniikangis ama Tunuzangis: Aleut Tales and Narratives*. Fairbanks, AK: Alaska Native Language Center.

Berliner, P. 1987. *Cognitive Style and Attitudes in Bilingual Inuits*. Copenhagen, Denmark: Danish Social Science Research Council.

Bernstein, Basil. 1971. *Class, Codes and Control*. London, UK: Routledge and Kegan Paul.

Berthelsen, Christian. 1976. *Oqaluttualiaativut taalliaativullu* [Our novels and our poetry]. Copenhagen, Denmark: Ministeriet for Grønland; Nuuk, Greenland: Det grønlandske Forlag.

– 1979. "What Conditions Does the Danish State Provide for the Existence and Development of the Greenlandic Language?" In B. Basse and K. Jensen, eds, *Eskimo Languages: Their Present-Day Conditions*, 11–20. Aarhus, Denmark: Arkona.

– 1983. *Grønlandsk Litteratur, en Kommenteret Antologi* [Greenlandic literature, an annotated anthology]. Viby, Denmark: Centrum.

– 1986. "Greenlandic Literature: Its Traditions, Changes and Trends." *Arctic Anthropology* 23, nos 1–2: 339–46.

– 1990a. "Greenlandic in Schools." In D.R.F. Collis, ed., *Arctic Languages: An Awakening*, 333–9. Paris, France: Unesco.

– 1990b. "Greenlandic Literature." In D.R.F. Collis, ed., *Arctic Languages: An Awakening*, 343–53. Paris, France: Unesco.

– Birgitte Jacobsen, Inge Kleivan, Frederik Nielsen, Robert Petersen, and Jørgen Rischel. 1990. *Oqaatsit Kalaallisuumiit Qalluunaatuumut: Grønlandsk-Dansk Ordbog* [Greenlandic-Danish dictionary]. Nuuk, Greenland: Atuakkiorfik.

Bethune, W.C. 1935. *Canada's Eastern Arctic, Its History, Resources, Population and Administration*. Ottawa: Department of the Interior.

Birket-Smith, Kaj. 1924. *Ethnography of the Egedesminde District*. Meddelelser om Grønland 66. Copenhagen, Denmark: Meddelelser om Grønland.

– 1928. *Five Hundred Eskimo Words*. Report of the Fifth Thule Expedition, vol. 3, no. 3. Copenhagen, Denmark: Report of the Fifth Thule Expedition.

– 1929. *The Caribou Eskimos: Material and Social Life and Their Cultural Position*. Report of the Fifth Thule Expedition, vol. 5, nos 1–2. Copenhagen, Denmark: Report of the Fifth Thule Expedition.

Bittner, Maria. 1987. "On the Semantics of the Greenlandic Antipassive and Related Constructions." *International Journal of American Linguistics* 53: 194–231.

Boas, Franz, 1964. *The Central Eskimo*. 1888. Reprint, Lincoln: University of Nebraska Press.

Bodfish, Waldo Sr. 1991. *Kusiq: An Eskimo Life History from the Arctic Coast of Alaska*. Fairbanks, AK: University of Alaska Press.

Bok-Bennema, Reineke. 1991. *Case and Agreement in Inuit*. Studies in Generative Grammar 38. Berlin, Germany, and New York: Foris.

Bordin, Guy. 2003. *Lexique analytique de l'anatomie humaine/Analytical Lexicon of Human Anatomy: Timiup ilangitta atingit Nunavimmilu Nunavummilu*. Louvain, Belgium, and Paris, France: Éditions Peeters.

Bourdieu, Pierre. 1991. *Language and Symbolic Power*. Cambridge, MA: Harvard University Press.

Bourquin, Theodor. 1891. *Grammatik der Eskimo Sprache* [Grammar of the Eskimo language]. London, UK: Moravian Mission Agency.

Brant, Charles S., and Charles W. Hobart. 1968. "The Educational System in the Western Arctic." In V. Valentine and F. Vallee, eds, *Eskimo of the Canadian Arctic*, 186–96. Toronto: McClelland and Stewart.

Brask, Per, and W. Morgan. 1992. *Aboriginal Voices: Amerindian, Inuit and Sami Theater*. Baltimore, MD: Johns Hopkins University Press.

Briggs, Jean L. 1968. *Utkuhikhalingmiut Eskimo Emotional Expression*. Ottawa: Government of Canada, Department of Indian Affairs, Northern Science Research Group.

– 1970. *Never in Anger: Portrait of an Eskimo Family*. Cambridge, MA: Harvard University Press.

– 1997. "From Trait to Emblem and Back: Living and Representing Culture in Everyday Life." *Arctic Anthropology* 34, no. 1: 227–35.

Brody, Hugh. 1975. *The People's Land*. Harmondsworth, UK: Penguin Books.

Bugge, Aage, et al. 1960. *Dansk-Grønlandsk Ordbog* [Danish-Greenlandic dictionary]. Nuuk, Greenland: Det Grønlandske Forlag.

Burch, Ernest S. 1998. *The Iñupiaq Eskimo Nations of Northwest Alaska*. Fairbanks, AK: University of Alaska Press.

Burnaby, Barbara. 1982. *Language in Education among Canadian Native Peoples*. Toronto: OISE Press.

Calvet, Louis-Jean. 1974. *Linguistique et colonialisme: Petit traité de glottophagie*. Paris, France: Payot.

Canadian Deafness Research and Training Institute (CDRTI). 2006. *Nunavut Deaf's Focus Group*. 2 DVDs. Montreal: CDRTI.

Carpenter, Edmund. 1973. *Eskimo Realities*. New York: Holt, Rinehart and Winston.

Christensen, Neil Blair. 2003. *Inuit in Cyberspace – Embedding Offline Identities Online*. Copenhagen, Denmark: Museum and Tusculanum Press and University of Copenhagen.

Coldevin, Gary O., and Thomas C. Wilson. 1983. "Longitudinal Influences of Satellite Television on Canadian Inuit Adolescents." In G.G. Valaskakis, ed., *Communication and the Canadian North*, 68–98. Montreal: Concordia University, Department of Communication Studies.

Collis, Dirmid R.F. 1969. "On the Establishment of Visual Parameters for the Formalization of Eskimo Semantics." *Folk* 11–12: 309–28.

– 1970. "Études philologiques et linguistiques des langages esquimaux." *Inter-Nord* 11: 263–82.

– 1971. *Pour une sémiologie de l'esquimau*. Paris, France: Université de Paris VI, Centre de linguistique quantitative.

– 1992. "Le statut des langues autochtones et leurs domaines d'utilisation au Québec." In J. Maurais, ed., *Les langues autochtones au Québec*, 115–49. Quebec City: Les Publications du Québec.

– and Louis-Jacques Dorais. 1983. "From Humiliation to Harmony: An Ethnolinguistic Analysis of Labrador Inuttut Customary Law Concepts." Unpublished report, Labrador Inuit Association, Nain, Newfoundland and Labrador.

– ed. 1990. *Arctic Languages: An Awakening*. Paris, France: Unesco.

Colombo, John Robert, ed. 1997. *Poems of the Inuit*. Toronto: Colombo and Company.

Consilium. 2005. *Report on Inuktitut and Other Indigenous Language Protection and Promotion Models*. Submitted to Avataq Cultural Institute. Ottawa: Consilium.

Cornillac, Guy. 1993. *Le mot en français et en esquimau: Étude de psychosystématique comparée*. Paris, France: Éditions Peeters.

Correll, Thomas C. 1974. "Language, Christianity and Change in Two Eskimo Communities." In J.J. Poggie and R.N. Lynch, eds, *Rethinking Modernization*, 292–331. Westport, CT: Greenwood Press.

– 1976. "Language and Location in Traditional Inuit Societies." In M.R.F. Freeman, ed., *Inuit Land Use and Occupancy Project*, vol. 2, 173–9.

Ottawa: Government of Canada, Department of Indian and Northern Affairs.

Couch, Donald. 1992. "Nunavut and Inuktitut: Language Planning and Implications for Education." Report presented to the Royal Commission on Aboriginal Peoples, Iqaluit, Nunavut.

Crago, Martha B. 1988. "Cultural Context in Communicative Interaction of Inuit Children." PhD dissertation, McGill University, Montreal.

– Betsy Annahatak, Mary Aitchison, and Donald M. Taylor. 1992. "Keeping It Alive: Linguistic, Cultural and Social Issues Related to Language Policy in Nunavik." Paper read at the conference "Language and Educational Policy in the North," University of California, Berkeley.

– Betsy Annahatak, and Lizzie Ningiuruvik. 1993. "Changing Patterns of Language Socialization in Inuit Homes." *Anthropology and Education Quarterly* 24, no. 3: 205–23.

– and Shanley E.M. Allen. 1998. "Acquiring Inuktitut." In L. Leonard and O. Taylor, eds, *Language Acquisition across North America: Cross-Cultural and Cross-Linguistic Perspectives*, 245–79. San Diego, CA: Singular.

Cranz, David. 1820. *The History of Greenland.* London, UK: Longman.

Creider, Chet. 1981. "Place of Articulation Assimilation and the Inuktitut Dialect Continuum." *Études/Inuit/Studies* 5 (supplementary): 91–100.

Crowell, Aron L., Amy E. Steffian, and Gordon L. Pullar, eds. 2001. *Looking Both Ways: Heritage and Identity of the Alutiiq People.* Fairbanks, AK: University of Alaska Press.

Csonka, Yvon. 1995. *Les Ahiarmiut à l'écart des Inuit Caribous.* Neuchâtel, Switzerland: Édition Victor Attinger.

– 1999. "A Stereotype Further Dispelled: Inuit-Dene Relations West of Hudson Bay, 1920–1956." *Études/Inuit/Studies* 23, nos 1–2: 117–44.

– 2007. "The Yupik People and Its Neighbours in Chukotka: Eight Decades of Rapid Changes." *Études/Inuit/Studies* 31, nos 1–2: 23–37.

Cummins, Jim. 1981. *Bilingualism and Minority Language Children.* Toronto: OISE Press.

– 1991. "Language Development and Academic Learning." In L.M. Malavé and G. Duquette, eds, *Language, Culture and Cognition: A Collection of Studies in First and Second Language Acquisition*, 161–75. Clevedon, UK: Multilingual Matters.

Curley, Tagak. 1975. *An Inuit Leader Speaks Out on Education.* Eskimo Point, NWT: Inuit Cultural Institute.

Damas, David. 2002. *Arctic Migrants/Arctic Villagers: The Transformation of Inuit Settlement in the Central Arctic.* Montreal and Kingston: McGill-Queen's University Press.

Daveluy, Michelle. 2004. "Language Policies and Responsibilities in the Canadian North." *International Journal of Canadian Studies* 30: 83–99.

– 2005. "Resilience and Language." In L. Kaplan and M. Daveluy, eds, *Resilience in Arctic Societies: Papers from the Third IPSSAS Seminar*, 89–94. Fairbanks, AK: University of Alaska Press.

Delanglez, Jean, ed. 1944. "Journal de Louis Jolliet alland à la descouverte de Labrador." In P.G. Roy, ed., *Rapport de l'archiviste de la Province de Québec*, 168–206. Quebec City: King's Printer.

Denny, J. Peter. 1981a. *Cultural Ecology of Mathematics: Ojibway and Inuit Hunters*. London, ON: University of Western Ontario, Department of Psychology.

– 1981b. "The Logical Semantics of *Only*, *Tuaq*, *Innaq* and *Tuinnaq*." *Études/Inuit/Studies* 5 (supplementary): 115–24.

– 1981c. *Semantics of the Inuktitut (Eskimo) Spatial Deictis*. London, ON: University of Western Ontario, Department of Psychology.

DeReuse, Willem J. 1994. *Siberian Yupik Eskimo: The Language and Its Contacts with Chukchi*. Salt Lake City: University of Utah Press.

Devillar, Robert A., Christian J. Faltis, and Jim Cummins, eds. 1994. *Cultural Diversity in Schools: From Rhetoric to Practice*. Albany: State University of New York Press.

Dikov, Nikolai N. 1979. *Drevnije Kultury Severo-Vostochnoj Azii* [Ancient cultures of Northeast Asia]. Moscow, Russia: Nauka.

Dorais, Louis-Jacques. 1971. "Some Notes on the Semantics of Eastern Eskimo Localizers." *Anthropological Linguistics* 13, no. 3: 91–5.

– 1973. "Les Inuit du Québec-Labrador: Distribution de la population, dialectologie, changements culturels." *Recherches amérindiennes au Québec* 3, nos 3–4: 82–102.

– 1975a. "Iqalungmiut uqausingit (Kingmirungmiullu Pangniqtuumiullu): Southeast Baffin Inuit Language/Le parler inuit de Baffin sud-est." Typed manuscript, Association Inuksiutiit Katimajiit, Quebec City.

– 1975b. "Kinngarmiut uqausingit: The Inuit Language in Cape Dorset N.W.T./Le parler inuit de Cape Dorset T.N.O." Typed manuscript, Association Inuksiutiit Katimajiit, Quebec City.

– 1975c. *Inuit uqausingit, manuel de langue inuit (Nouveau-Québec)*. Quebec City: Association Inuksiutiit Katimajiit.

– 1975d. "Le vocabulaire du calcul du temps chez les Inuit du Québec-Labrador." *Recherches amérindiennes au Québec* 5, no. 3: 70–3.

– 1975e. "Cours de langue inuit (Nouveau-Québec septentrional)." Typed manuscript and 32 audio tapes, Université Laval, Département d'anthropologie et Service des laboratoires de langues, Quebec City.

– 1975f. "Exercices de langue inuit (Nouveau-Québec)." Typed manuscript, Université Laval, Département d'anthropologie, Quebec City.

– 1976a. "Some Phonological Characteristics of Eastern Canadian Inuit." *Anthropological Linguistics* 18, no. 8: 387–92.

– 1976b. "Aivilingmiut uqausingit: The Aivilik Inuit Language/Le parler inuit aivilik." Typed manuscript, Association Inuksiutiit Katimajiit, Quebec City.

– 1976c. "Quelques aspects linguistiques du changement social chez les Inuit de l'Arctique oriental canadien." *Cahiers d'anthropologie de l'Université Laval* 1: 96–102.

– 1977a. "Le parler inuit de Rigolet (Labrador)." *Études/Inuit/Studies* 1, no. 2: 113–17.

– 1977b. *Inuit Kupaimmiut uqausingit: The Language of the Northern Quebec Inuit.* Quebec City: Association Inuksiutiit Katimajiit.

– 1977c. "La structure du vocabulaire moderne de la langue inuit du Québec-Labrador." *L'Homme* 17, no. 4: 35–63.

– 1978. *Iglulingmiut uqausingit: The Inuit Language of Igloolik N.W.T./ La langue inuit d'Igloolik T.N.O.* Quebec City: Association Inuksiutiit Katimajiit.

– 1979a. "Inu'juamiullu Kuu'juaraapimmiulu uqausingit: The Inuit Language in Inujjuaq (Port Harrison) and Great Whale River/Le parler inuit d'Inujjuaq et de Poste de la Baleine." Typed manuscript, Université Laval, Département d'anthropologie, Quebec City.

– 1979b. "The Influence of English and French on Northern Quebec Vocabulary and Semantics." In B. Basse and K. Jensen, eds, *Eskimo Languages: Their Present-Day Conditions*, 77–82. Aarhus, Denmark: Arkona.

– 1980. *The Inuit Language in Southern Labrador from 1694–1785.* Canadian Ethnology Service Paper No. 66. Ottawa: National Museum of Man.

– 1981a. "Some Notes on the Language of East Greenland." *Études/Inuit/ Studies* 5 (supplementary): 43–70.

– 1981b. "A Few Thoughts on the Language of the Inuit." *Canadian Journal of Native Studies* 1, no. 2: 303–9.

– 1983. *Uqausigusiqtaat: An Analytical Lexicon of Modern Inuktitut in Quebec-Labrador.* Quebec City: Presses de l'Université Laval.

– 1984. "Sémantique des noms d'animaux en groenlandais de l'est." *Amerindia* 9: 7–23.

– 1985a. "Regressive Consonant Assimilation in Eastern Inuktitut: Toward a Sociolinguistic Approach." *International Journal of American Linguistics* 51, no. 4: 390–3.

– 1985b. "Terminology and Lexical Structure: An Inuktitut Example." *TermNet News* 9: 11–18.
– 1986a. "Inuktitut Surface Phonology: A Trans-Dialectal Survey." *International Journal of American Linguistics* 52, 1: 20–53.
– 1986b. "Agiter l'homme pour attraper la femme: La sémantique des sexes en langue inuit." *Études/Inuit/Studies* 10, nos 1–2: 171–8.
– 1988a. "A Qairnirmiut (Baker Lake) Glossary." Typed manuscript, Association Inuksiutiit Katimajiit, Quebec City.
– 1988b. *Tukilik: An Inuktitut Grammar for All.* Inuit Studies Occasional Papers 2. Quebec City: Association Inuksiutiit Katimajiit.
– 1988c. "Inuit Identity in Canada." *Folk* 30: 23–31.
– 1988d. "Quelques aspects du comportement langagier inuit à Igloolik et Ammassalik." *Objets et Mondes* 25, nos 3–4: 97–102.
– 1988e. "Sois belle et tais-toi! La langue des Inuit dans le Canada actuel." *Études/Inuit/Studies* 12, nos 1–2: 235–43.
– 1989. "Bilingualism and Diglossia in the Canadian Eastern Arctic." *Arctic* 42, no. 3: 199–207.
– 1990a. *Inuit Uqausiqatigiit: Inuit Languages and Dialects.* Iqaluit, NU: Nunavut Arctic College.
– 1990b. *Inuit Uqausingit: 1000 Inuit Words/Mots inuit.* Inuit Studies Occasional Paper 3. Quebec City: Association Inuksiutiit Katimajiit.
– 1990c. "The Canadian Inuit and Their Language." In D.R.F. Collis, ed., *Arctic Languages: An Awakening*, 185–289. Paris, France: Unesco.
– 1991. "Language, Identity and Integration in the Canadian Arctic." *North Atlantic Studies* 3, no. 1: 18–24.
– 1993. *From Magic Words to Word Processing: A History of the Inuit Language.* Iqaluit, NU: Nunavut Arctic College.
– 1994. "À propos d'identité inuit." *Études/Inuit/Studies* 18, nos 1–2: 253–60.
– 1996a. *La Parole inuit: Langue, culture et société dans l'Arctique nord-américain.* Paris, France: Éditions Peeters.
– 1996b. *Language in Inuit Society.* Iqaluit, NU: Nunavut Arctic College.
– 1997. *Quaqtaq: Modernity and Identity in an Inuit Community.* Toronto: University of Toronto Press.
– 2002a. "Notes sur l'inuktitut parlé à Iqaluit (Nunavut)." *Études/Inuit/Studies* 26, no. 1: 193–201.
– 2002b. "Why Do They Speak Inuktitut? Discourse Practices in the Capital of Nunavut." *Zeitschrift für Kanada-Studien* 22, nos 1–2: 116–30.
– 2003. *Inuit Uqausigatigiit: Inuit Languages and Dialects.* 2nd ed. Iqaluit, NU: Nunavut Arctic College.

– 2006a. "Inuit Discourse and Identity after the Advent of Nunavut." Unpublished research report, Université Laval, Faculté des sciences sociales, Centre interuniversitaire d'études et de recherches autochtones (CIÉRA), Quebec City.

– 2006b. "Discours et identité à Iqaluit après l'avènement du Nunavut." *Études/Inuit/Studies* 30, no. 2: 163–89.

– 2008. "Terre de l'ombre ou terre d'abondance? Le Nord des Inuit." In D. Chartier, ed., *Le(s) Nord(s) imaginaire(s)*, 9–22. Montreal: Imaginaire/Nord.

– and Ronald Lowe. 1982. "Les dialectes de l'Arctique de l'ouest." *Études/Inuit/Studies* 6, no. 2: 127–33.

– and Dirmid R.F. Collis. 1987. "Inuit Bilingualism and Diglossia." Unpublished research report, Université Laval, International Centre for Research on Bilingualism, Quebec City.

– and Susan Sammons. 2000. "Discourse and Identity in the Baffin Region." *Arctic Anthropology* 37, no. 2: 92–110.

– and Susan Sammons. 2002. *Language in Nunavut: Discourse and Identity in the Baffin Region*. Iqaluit, NU: Nunavut Arctic College; Quebec City: Université Laval, Groupe d'études inuit et circumpolaires (GÉTIC).

Douglas, Anne. 1994. "Inuit Identity and the Qallunaat School: An Encounter between Two World Views." Paper read at the "9th Inuit Studies Conference," Iqaluit, Nunavut.

Drapeau, Lynn. 1993. "Language Birth: An Alternative to Language Death." In A. Crochetière, J.-C. Boulanger, and C. Ouellon, eds, *Proceedings of the XVth International Congress of Linguistics*, vol. 4, 141–4. Quebec City: Presses de l'Université Laval.

Dresher, B. Elan, and Alana Johns. 1995. "The Law of Double Consonants in Inuktitut." *Linguistica Atlantica* 17: 79–95.

– and Alana Johns. 1996. "Rigolet and Phonological Change in Labrador." *Études/Inuit/Studies* 20, no. 1: 113–21.

Dritsas, Polly. 1986. "Plants in Inuit Culture: The Ethnobotany of the Iglulingmiut." MA thesis, Université Laval, Quebec City.

Dufour, Rose. 1977. "Les noms de personnes chez les Inuit d'Iglulik." MA thesis, Université Laval, Quebec City.

Dumond, Don E. 1965. "On Eskaleutian Linguistics, Archaeology and Prehistory." *American Anthropologist* 67: 1231–57.

– 1984. "Prehistory: Summary." In D. Damas, ed., *Handbook of North American Indians*, vol. 5, *Arctic*, 72–9. Washington, DC: Smithsonian Institution.

– 1987. "A Reexamination of Eskimo-Aleut Prehistory." *American Anthropologist* 89, no. 1: 32–55.

Dybbroe, Susanne. 1991. "Local Organisation and Cultural Identity in Greenland in a National Perspective." *North Atlantic Studies* 3, no. 1: 5–17.

Dyck, Carrie J., and Jean L. Briggs. 2005. "Historical antecedents of /h/, /s/, /j/ and /r/ in Utkuhiksalik (Inuktitut)." *Études/Inuit/Studies* 29, nos 1–2: 307–40.

Egede, Ingmar. 1976. "Educational Problems in Greenland." *Pedagogik* 6, no. 2: 1–14.

Egede, Poul. 1750. *Dictionarium grönlandica-danico-latinum* [Greenlandic-Danish-Latin dictionary]. Copenhagen, Denmark: G.F. Kisel.

– 1760. *Grammatica grönlandica-danico-latina* [Greenlandic-Danish-Latin grammar]. Copenhagen, Denmark: G.F. Kisel.

Enel, Catherine. 1982. "Étude morphologique de quelques éléments de vocabulaire moderne ouest-groenlandais." DEA thesis, Université de Paris VII, France.

– 1984. *Élements de grammaire et de vocabulaire de la langue ouest-groenlandaise*. Documents du Centre de Recherches Anthropologiques No. 8. Paris, France: Musée de l'Homme.

Engell, M. 1982. "Et land – to sprog: Dansk i Grønland" [One country – two languages: Danish in Greenland]. Typed manuscript, University of Copenhagen, Denmark.

Erdmann, Friedrich. 1864. *Eskimoisches Wörterbuch gesammelt von den Missionären in Labrador* [Eskimo dictionary compiled from the missionaries in Labrador]. Budissin, Germany: E.M. Monse.

Eriksson, Björn. 1998. "Iqaluit: Diglossia and Language Identity among the Inuit." MA thesis, University of Vaxjö, Sweden.

Evans, Michael R. 2008. *Isuma: Inuit Video Art*. Montreal and Kingston: McGill-Queen's University Press.

Fabricius, Otto. 1801. *Forsøg til en Forbredet Grønlandsk Grammatica* [Essay toward a preliminary Greenlandic grammar]. Copenhagen, Denmark: C.F. Schubart.

Farrell, Siobhan. 1983. "Literacy and the Canadian Inuit." In G.G. Valaskakis, ed., *Communication and the Canadian North*, 1–22. Montreal: Concordia University, Department of Communication Studies.

Ferguson, Charles A. 1959. "Diglossia." *Word* 15: 325–40.

Fienup-Riordan, Ann, and Lawrence D. Kaplan, eds, 2008. *Words of the Real People: Alaska Native Literature in Translation*. Fairbanks, AK: University of Alaska Press.

Flint, M.S., ed. 1954. *Revised Eskimo Grammar.* From Rev. E.J. Peck's grammar of 1883. Toronto: Anglican Church in Canada.

Forgues, Louis. 1987. "L'action du gouvernement fédéral chez les Inuit du Nouveau-Québec: Le cas de l'éducation (1949–1975)." MA thesis, Université Laval, Quebec City.

Fortescue, Michael. 1981a. "Endoactive-Exoactive Markers in Eskimo-Aleut, Tungus and Japanese: An Investigation into Common Origins." *Études/Inuit/Studies* 5 (supplementary): 5–41.

– 1981b. "Den gamle verdens genopdagelse af den ny – og den ny verdens genopdagelse af den gamle" [The Old World's rediscovery by the New – and the New World's rediscovery by the Old]. *Grønland* 2: 41–7.

– 1983. *A Comparative Manual of Affixes for the Inuit Dialects of Greenland, Canada and Alaska.* Man and Society 4. Copenhagen, Denmark: Meddelelser om Grønland.

– 1984a. *West Greenlandic.* Croom Helm Descriptive Grammars. London, UK: Croom Helm.

– 1984b. *Notes on the Upernavik Dialect of West Greenlandic.* Copenhagen, Denmark: Institut for Eskimologi.

– 1984c. "The Origin of the I-Dialect Phenomenon in Greenland." *Études/Inuit/Studies* 8, no. 2: 91–8.

– 1984d. "Affixal-Inflectional Interaction in West Greenlandic in the Light of the Western Dialects of Inuktitut and the Thule-Copper Connection." Typed manuscript, Institut for Eskimologi, Copenhagen, Denmark.

– 1984e. *Some Problems Concerning the Correlation and Reconstruction of Eskimo and Aleut Mood Markers.* Tidskrift 12. Copenhagen, Denmark: Institut for Eskimologi.

– 1985a. "The Degree of Interrelatedness between Inuit Dialects as Reflected by Percentages of Shared Affixes." *International Journal of American Linguistics* 51, no. 2: 188–221.

– 1985b. "Learning to Speak Greenlandic: A Case Study of a Two-Year-Old's Morphology in a Polysynthetic Language." *First Language* 5: 101–14.

– 1986. "What Dialect Distribution Can Tell Us of Dialect Formation in Greenland." *Arctic Anthropology* 23, nos 1–2: 413–22.

– 1988a. "The Eskimo-Aleut-Yukagir Relationship: An Alternative to the Genetic-Contact Dichotomy." *Acta Linguistica Hafniensia* 21, no. 1: 21–50.

– 1988b. *Eskimo Orientation Systems.* Man and Society 11. Copenhagen, Denmark: Meddelelser om Grønland.

– 1990. *From the Writings of the Greenlanders: Kalaallit atuakkiaannit.* Fairbanks, AK: University of Alaska Press.

– 1991. *Inuktun: An Introduction to the Language of Qaanaaq, Thule/En introduktion til Thulesproget.* Copenhagen, Denmark: Institut for Eskimologi.

– 1998. *Language Relations across Bering Strait.* London, UK: Cassell.

– 2004. "How Far West into Asia Have Eskimo Languages Been Spoken, and Which Ones?" *Études/Inuit/Studies* 28, no. 2: 159–83.

– 2005. *Comparative Chukotko-Kamchatkan Dictionary.* Berlin, Germany: Mouton de Gruyter.

– 2007a. *Comparative Wakashan Dictionary.* Munich, Germany: Lincom Europa.

– 2007b. "The Trials and Joys of Comparative Dictionary Making." *Études/Inuit/Studies* 31, nos 1–2: 213–21.

– and Lise Lennert-Olsen. 1992. "The Acquisition of West Greenlandic." In D.I. Slobin, ed., *The Crosslinguistic Study of Language Acquisition*, vol. 3, 111–220. Hillsdale, NJ: Lawrence Erlbaum Associates.

– Steven A. Jacobson, and Lawrence D. Kaplan. 1994. *Comparative Eskimo Dictionary with Aleut Cognates.* Fairbanks, AK: Alaska Native Language Center.

Freeman, Minnie Aodla. 1978. *Life among the Qallunaat.* Edmonton: Hurtig.

Gad, Finn. 1971–82. *The History of Greenland.* 3 vols. Montreal and Kingston: McGill-Queen's University Press.

Gad, Ulrik P. 2009. "Post-Colonial Identity in Greenland?" *Journal of Language and Politics* 8, no. 1: 136–58.

Gagné, Raymond C. 1961. *Tentative Standard Orthography for Canadian Eskimos.* Ottawa: Government of Canada, Department of Northern Affairs and National Resources.

– 1964. *Eskimo Language Course Inuktitut.* 2 vols and 35 audio tapes. Ottawa: Government of Canada, Department of Northern Affairs and National Resources.

– 1968. "Spatial Concepts in the Eskimo Language." In V. Valentine and F. Vallee, eds, *Eskimo of the Canadian Arctic*, 30–8. Toronto: McClelland and Stewart.

Gallagher-Mac Kay, Kelly. 2007. "Review Essay on Conciliator's Final Report: 'The Nunavut Project.'" *Canadian Journal of Education* 30, no. 4: 1093–104.

Gedalof, Robin. 1979. *An Annotated Bibliography of Canadian Inuit Literature.* Ottawa: Government of Canada, Department of Indian and Northern Affairs.

– and Alootook Ipellie. 1980. *Paper Stays Put: A Collection of Inuit Writing.* Edmonton: Hurtig.

Geoghegan, Richard H. 1944. *The Aleut Language*. Washington, DC: Government of the United States, Department of the Interior.

Gessain, Robert, Louis-Jacques Dorais, and Catherine Enel. 1986. *Vocabulaire du groenlandais de l'est*. Documents du Centre de Recherches Anthropologiques No. 10. Paris, France: Musée de l'Homme.

Gilberg, A., L. Gilberg, R. Gilberg, and M. Holm. 1978. *Polar Eskimo Genealogy*. Man and Society 203/4. Copenhagen, Denmark: Meddelelser om Grønland.

Goddard, Ives. 1984. "Synonymy." In D. Damas, ed., *Handbook of North American Indians*, vol. 5, *Arctic*, 5–7. Washington, DC: Smithsonian Institution.

Golovko, Evgeni V., and Nikolai B. Vakhtin. 1990. "Aleut in Contact: The CIA [Commander Islands Aleut] Enigma." *Acta Linguistica Hafniensia* 22: 97–125.

Goodenough, Ward H. 1968. "Componential Analysis." In M. Fried, ed., *Readings in Anthropology*, vol. 2, 315–30. New York: Crowell.

Gordon, Tom. 2007. "Found in Translation: The Inuit Voice in Moravian Music." *Newfoundland and Labrador Studies* 22, no. 1: 287–314.

Government of Nunavut. 2000. *The Bathurst Mandate/Pinasuaqtavut: That Which We've Set Out to Do*. Iqaluit, NU: Government of Nunavut.

– 2002. *Nunavut Education Act*. Iqaluit, NU: Government of Nunavut.

– 2007a. *Proposed Inuit Language Protection Bill*. Iqaluit, NU: Government of Nunavut.

– 2007b. *Proposed Official Languages Bill*. Iqaluit, NU: Government of Nunavut.

Graburn, Nelson H.H. 1960. "Social Organization of an Eskimo Community: Sugluk, No. Quebec." MA thesis, McGill University, Montreal.

– 1964. *Taqagmiut Eskimo Kinship Terminology*. Ottawa: Government of Canada, Department of Northern Affairs and National Resources, Northern Co-ordination and Research Centre.

– 1965. "Some Aspects of Linguistic Acculturation in Northern Ungava Eskimo." *Kroeber Anthropological Society Papers* 32: 11–46.

– 1982. "Television and the Canadian Inuit." *Études/Inuit/Studies* 6, no. 1: 7–17.

Grann, Niels. 1988. "Lexical Innovation in East Greenlandic." Paper read at the "6th Inuit Studies Conference," Copenhagen, Denmark.

Greenberg, Joseph H. 1987. *Language in the Americas*. Palo Alto, CA: Stanford University Press.

Greenland Home Rule Government, Department of Culture and Education. 1980. *Training of Teachers for the Primary School in Greenland*. Circular 13/80. Nuuk, Greenland: Greenland Home Rule Government.

Grenoble, Lenore A., and Lindsay J. Whaley. 2006. *Saving Languages: An Introduction to Language Revitalization*. Cambridge, UK: Cambridge University Press.

Gubser, Nicholas J. 1965. *The Nunamiut Eskimos: Hunters of Caribou*. New Haven, CT: Yale University Press.

Guemple, Lee. 1975. "Marking and Sex Classification in Inupik Eskimo." In *Proceedings of the Second Congress CES*, 183–96. Ottawa: National Museum of Man.

Gumperz, John J. 1992. "Contextualization and Understanding." In A. Duranti and C. Goodwin, eds, *Rethinking Context: Language as an Interactive Phenomenon*, 229–52. Cambridge, UK: Cambridge University Press.

Gynther, Bent. 1980. *The Use of Greenlandic and Danish in Greenland Schools, 1950–1978*. Ottawa: Association of Canadian Universities for Northern Studies.

Hakluyt, Richard. 1904. *The Principal Navigations, Voiages and Discoveries of the English Nation*. Vol. 7. 1589. Reprint, Glasgow, UK: James MacLehose and Sons.

Hammerich, Louis L. 1936. *Personalendungen und Verbalsystem im Eskimoischen* [Person-endings and verbal system in Eskimo]. Copenhagen, Denmark: Levin and Munksgaard.

– 1951. "Can Eskimo Be Related to Indo-European?" *International Journal of American Linguistics* 17, no. 4: 217–23.

Hamp, Eric P. 1976a. "On Eskimo-Aleut and Luoravetlan." In Eric P. Hamp, ed., *Papers on Eskimo and Aleut Linguistics*, 81–92. Chicago, IL: Chicago Linguistic Society.

– ed. 1976b. *Papers on Eskimo and Aleut Linguistics*. Chicago, IL: Chicago Linguistic Society.

Harcharek, Robert C. 2001. *Summary Data Report: Iñupiaq Language Usage in Barrow, Alaska*. Barrow, AK: Ilisagvik College.

Harnum, Betty. 1989. "Lexical Innovation in Inuktitut." MA thesis, University of Calgary, Calgary.

– Janet McGrath, and Margo Kadlun. 1982. *Inuinnaqtun Lessons: Phase 1*. Cambridge Bay, NU: Kitikmeot Inuit Association.

Harper, Kenn. 1974. *Some Aspects of the Grammar of the Eskimo Dialects of Cumberland Peninsula and North Baffin Island*. Canadian Ethnology Service Paper No. 15. Ottawa: National Museums of Canada.

– 1979. *Suffixes of the Eskimo Dialects of Cumberland Peninsula and North Baffin Island*. Canadian Ethnology Service Paper No. 54. Ottawa: National Museums of Canada.

– 1983. "Writing Systems and Translations." *Inuktitut* (September): 3–103.

– 1985. "The Early Development of Inuktitut Syllabic Orthography." *Études/Inuit/Studies* 9, no. 1: 141–62.

– 1992. "Current Status of Writing Systems for Inuktitut, Inuinnaqtun and Inuvialuktun." Unpublished research report, Government of the Northwest Territories, Department of Culture and Communications, Yellowknife.

Harrison, B.G. 1981. "Informal Learning among Yup'ik Eskimos: An Ethnographic Study of One Alaskan Village." PhD dissertation, University of Oregon, Eugene.

Hauser, Michael. 1992. *Traditional Greenlandic Music*. Copenhagen, Denmark: Kragen Ulo.

Hawkes, Edward W. 1916. *The Labrador Eskimo*. Memoir 91. Ottawa: Geological Survey of Canada.

Heinrich, Albert C. 1971. "Some Borrowings from German into Eskimo." *Anthropological Linguistics* 13, no. 3: 96–9.

– 1972. "A Non-European System of Color Classification." *Anthropological Linguistics* 14, no. 6: 220–7.

– 1977. "Some Notes on Central Eskimo Color Terminology." In W.C. McCormack and S.A. Wurm, eds, *Language and Thought: Anthropological Issues*, 45–59. Paris, France: Mouton.

Hensel, Chase. 1996. *Telling Our Selves: Ethnicity and Discourse in Southwestern Alaska*. New York: Oxford University Press.

– 2001. "Yup'ik Identity and Subsistence Discourse: Social Resources in Interaction." *Études/Inuit/Studies* 25, nos 1–2: 217–27.

Hinz, John. 1944. *Grammar and Vocabulary of the Eskimo Language*. Bethlehem, PA: The Moravian Church.

Hofmann, T.R. 1978. "Equational Sentence Structure in Eskimo." In E.D. Cook and J. Kaye, eds, *Linguistic Studies of Native Canada*, 121–41. Vancouver: University of British Columbia Press.

Holm, Gustav. 1914. *Ethnological Sketch of the Angmassalik Eskimo*. Meddelelser om Grønland 39. Copenhagen, Denmark: Meddelelser om Grønland.

Holtved, Erik. 1951. *The Polar Eskimos: Language and Folklore*. Meddelelser om Grønland 152/1–2. Copenhagen, Denmark: Meddelelser om Grønland.

– 1956. "Remarks on Eskimo Semantics." In *Proceedings of the 32nd International Congress of Americanists*, 617–23. Copenhagen, Denmark: 32nd International Congress of Americanists.

– ed. 1964. *Kleinschmidts Briefe an Theodor Bourquin* [Kleinschmidt's letters to Theodor Bourquin]. Meddelelser om Grønland 140/3. Copenhagen, Denmark: Meddelelser om Grønland.

Honigmann, John J., and Irma Honigmann. 1965. *Eskimo Townsmen*. Ottawa: University of Ottawa, Canadian Research Centre for Anthropology.

Hot, Aurélie. 2008. "Un bilinguisme stable est-il possible à Iqaluit?" *Études/Inuit/Studies* 32, no. 1: 117–36.

Hugo, Beverly A., et al. 1991. *North Slope Iñupiaq Medical Terminology*. Barrow, AK, North Slope Borough: Iñupiat History, Language and Culture Commission.

Igloliorte, Nat. 1976. "My life in Nain." *Inuktitut* (Fall): 71–5.

– 1990. *Learn Inuktitut Fast*. St John's, NL: Self-published.

Immaroitok, Bernadette K., and Peter Jull. 1985. "Inuktitut: Surviving in the Arctic's New Age." *Inuit* (January-February): 14–15.

Immaroitok, Emile, et al. 1985. *Illingarumanaqtuit* [Things worth being considered important]. Igloolik, NU: Adult Education Centre.

Innuksuk, Rhoda, and Susan Cowan, eds. 1978. *We Don't Live in Snow Houses Now*. Ottawa: Canadian Arctic Producers.

Inuit Circumpolar Conference/Council (ICC). 1983. *Resolution 83 on a Standard Writing System*. Iqaluit, NU: ICC.

– 1992. *Principles and Elements for a Comprehensive Arctic Policy*. Montreal: McGill University, Centre for Northern Studies and Research.

Inuit Cultural Institute. 1978. "Inuit Language Commission." *Ajurnarmat* (Summer): 9–110.

Ipellie, Alootook. 1993. *Arctic Dreams and Nightmares*. Penticton, BC: Theytus Books.

Iutzi-Mitchell, Roy D. 1992. "Bilingualism and Educational Language Policy in the Far North: Framing the Issues." Paper read at the conference "Language and Educational Policy in the North," University of California, Berkeley.

Jacobsen, Birgitte. 1991. "Recent Phonetic Changes in the Polar Eskimo Dialect." *Études/Inuit/Studies* 15, no. 1: 51–73.

Jacobson, Anna W. 1990. *Elnguq*. Fairbanks, AK: Alaska Native Language Center.

– 1996. *Yup'ik Phrase and Conversation Lessons*. Booklet with 2 audio tapes. Fairbanks, AK: Alaska Native Language Center.

– 1998. *Yup'ik Stories Read Aloud: Yugcetun Qulirat Naaqumalriit Erinairissuutmun*. Booklet and audio tape. Fairbanks, AK: Alaska Native Language Center.

Jacobson, Steven A. 1995. *A Practical Grammar of the Central Alaskan Yup'ik Eskimo Language*. Fairbanks, AK: Alaska Native Language Center.

– 1998. *Yup'ik Dialect Atlas and Study*. Fairbanks, AK: Alaska Native Language Center.

– 2001. *A Practical Grammar of the St Lawrence Island/Siberian Yupik Eskimo Language*. Fairbanks, AK: Alaska Native Language Center.

– ed. 1984. *Yup'ik Eskimo Dictionary*. Fairbanks, AK: Alaska Native Language Center.

– ed. 1987. *A Dictionary of the St Lawrence Island/Siberian Yupik Eskimo Language*. Fairbanks, AK: Alaska Native Language Center.

– ed., with Elizaveta A. Dobrieva et al. 2004. *Naukan Yupik Eskimo Dictionary*. Fairbanks, AK: Alaska Native Language Center.

Janussen, Estrid. 1987. *Handbog i grønlandsk grammatik* [Handbook of Greenlandic grammar]. Nuuk, Greenland: Pilersuiffik.

Jeddore, Rose. 1979. "The Decline and Development of the Inuttut Language in Labrador." In B. Basse and K. Jensen, eds, *Eskimo Languages: Their Present-Day Conditions*, 83–91. Aarhus, Denmark: Arkona.

– ed. 1976. *Labrador Inuit Uqausingit*. St John's, NL: Inuit Committee on Literacy.

Jenness, Diamond. 1922. *The Life of the Copper Eskimos*. Report of the Canadian Arctic Expedition 1913–18, vol. 12. Ottawa: King's Printer.

– 1924. *Eskimo Folk-Lore*. Report of the Canadian Arctic Expedition 1913–18, vol. 13. Ottawa: King's Printer.

– 1925. *Songs of the Copper Eskimos*. Report of the Canadian Arctic Expedition 1913–18, vol. 14. Ottawa: King's Printer.

– 1928. *Comparative Vocabulary of the Western Eskimo Dialects*. Report of the Canadian Arctic Expedition 1913–18, vol. 15, part A. Ottawa: King's Printer.

– 1953. "Did the Yahgan Indians of Tierra del Fuego Speak an Eskimo Tongue?" *International Journal of American Linguistics* 19, no. 2: 128–31.

– 1964. *Eskimo Administration II: Canada*. Technical Paper 14. Montreal: Arctic Institute of North America.

– 1965. *Eskimo Administration III: Labrador*. Technical Paper 16. Montreal: Arctic Institute of North America.

Johansen, Brian A. 2001. "Contemporary Greenlandic Music." *Études/Inuit/Studies* 25, nos 1–2: 169–90.

Johns, Alana. 1987. "Transitivity and Grammatical Relations in Inuktitut." PhD dissertation, University of Ottawa, Ottawa.

– 1992. "Deriving Ergativity." *Linguistic Inquiry* 23: 57–88.

– 2007. "Restricting Noun Incorporation: Root Movement." *Natural Language and Linguistic Theory* 25, no. 3: 535–76.

– and Lydia Tuglavina. 2004. *Audio Files in Labrador Inuttitut*. http://www.chass.utoronto.ca/~inuit/materials.html.

Jull, Peter. 2000. "A Blueprint for Indigenous Self-Government: The Bathurst Mandate." *Indigenous Law Bulletin* 4, no. 27: 14–18.

Kalluak, Mark. 1987. *ICI Inuktitut Glossary.* Vol. 1. Arviat, NU: Inuit Cultural Institute.

Kalm, Pehr. 1772. *Travels into North America: Containing its natural history, and a circumstantial account of its plantations and agriculture in general: with the civil, ecclesiastical and commercial state of the country, the manners of the inhabitants, and several curious and important remarks on various subjects.* London, UK: T. Lowndes.

Kalmar, Ivan. 1977. "The Antipassive in Inuktitut." *Études/Inuit/Studies* 1, no. 1: 129–42.

– 1979. *Case and Context in Inuktitut (Eskimo).* Canadian Ethnology Service Paper No. 49. Ottawa: National Museums of Canada.

– 1982. "A Note on the Inadequacy of Modern Socio-Political Terms in the Inuit Language." Typed manuscript, University of Toronto, Department of Anthropology, Toronto.

Kaplan, Lawrence D. 1981a. *Phonological Issues in North Alaskan Inupiaq.* Fairbanks, AK: Alaska Native Language Center.

– 1981b. "On Yupik-lnupiaq Correspondences for ï: A Case of Inupiaq Innovation." *Études/lnuit/Studies* 5 (supplementary): 81–9.

– 1990. "The Language of the Alaskan Inuit." In D.R.F. Collis, ed., *Arctic Languages: An Awakening*, 131–58. Paris, France: Unesco.

– 1992. "A History of Language Policy in Alaska." Paper read at the "First International Congress of Arctic Social Sciences," Quebec City.

– 2000. "L'inupiaq et les contacts linguistiques en Alaska." In N. Tersis and M. Therrien, eds, *Les langues eskaléoutes*, 91–108. Paris, France: CNRS Éditions.

– 2001. "Inupiaq Identity and Inupiaq Language: Does One Entail the Other?" *Études/Inuit/Studies* 25, nos 1–2: 249–57.

– 2003. "Inuit Snow Terms: How Many and What Does It Mean?" In F. Trudel, ed., *Building Capacity in Arctic Societies: Dynamics and Shifting Perspectives*, 263–9. Quebec City: Université Laval, Faculté des sciences sociales, Centre interuniversitaire d'études et de recherches autochtones (CIÉRA).

– 2005. "Inupiaq Writing and International Inuit Relations." *Études/Inuit/Studies* 29, nos 1–2: 233–7.

– ed., with Margaret Yocom. 1988. *Ugiuvangmiut Quliapyuit/King Island Tales: Eskimo History and Legends from Bering Strait.* Fairbanks, AK: Alaska Native Language Center and University of Alaska Press.

Kawagley, A. Oscar. 1995. *A Yupiaq Worldview: A Pathway to Ecology and Spirit*. Prospect Heights, IL: Waveland Press.

Kennedy, Michael P. 1996. "Alootook Ipellie: The Voice of an Inuk Artist." *Studies in Canadian Literature* 21, no. 2: 155–64.

Kleinschmidt, Samuel. 1981. "A Grammar of the Greenlandic Language with Partial Inclusion of the Labrador Dialect." 1846. Translated from the German by Birger Andersen. Typed manuscript, University of Aarhus, Department of Greenlandic, Denmark.

Kleivan, Inge. 1970. "Language and Ethnic Identity: Language Policy and Debate in Greenland." *Folk* 11–12: 235–85.

– 1979. "Language and the Church in Greenland." In B. Basse and K. Jensen, eds, *Eskimo Languages: Their Present-Day Conditions*, 123–44. Aarhus, Denmark: Arkona.

– 1984. "History of Norse Greenland." In D. Damas, ed., *Handbook of North American Indians*, vol. 5, *Arctic*, 549–55. Washington, DC: Smithsonian Institution.

– 1990. "Debate and Linguistic Usage in Connection with Double Place-Names in Greenland." In D.R.F. Collis, ed., *Arctic Languages: An Awakening*, 341–3. Paris, France: Unesco.

Klokeid, Terry J., and Eugene A. Arima. 1977. "Some Generalizations about Antipassives in Inuktitut." *Études/Inuit/Studies* 1, no. 2: 85–95.

Koonooka, Christopher P. 2005. "Yupik Language Instruction in Gambell (Saint Lawrence Island, Alaska)." *Études/Inuit/Studies* 29, nos 1–2: 251–66.

– ed. 2003. *Ungipaghaghlanga/Let Me Tell a Story: Quutmiit Yupigita Ungipaghaatangit/Legends of the Siberian Eskimos*. Fairbanks, AK: Alaska Native Language Center.

Krauss, Michael E. 1973. "Eskimo-Aleut." *Current Trends in Linguistics* 10: 796–902.

– 1979. "The Eskimo Languages in Alaska, Yesterday and Today." In B. Basse and K. Jensen, eds, *Eskimo Languages: Their Present-Day Conditions*, 37–50. Aarhus, Denmark: Arkona.

– 1980. *Alaska Native Languages: Past, Present, and Future*. Research Paper 4. Fairbanks, AK: Alaska Native Language Center.

– 1997. "The Indigenous Languages of the North: A Report on Their Present State." In H. Shoji and J. Janhunen, eds, *Northern Minority Languages: Problems of Survival*, 1–34. Senri Ethnological Studies 44. Osaka, Japan: National Museum of Ethnology.

– 2001. "Mass Language Extinction and Documentation: The Race against Time." In O. Sakiyama, ed., *Lectures on Endangered Languages*, vol. 2, 19–39. Sapporo, Japan: Endangered Languages of the Pacific Rim (ELPR) Publication Series C002.

– 2006. "The Eskimo Language Work of Aleksandr Forshtein." *Alaska Journal of Anthropology* 4, nos 1–2: 114–32.

– 2007. "Native Languages of Alaska." In O. Miyaoka, O. Sakiyama, and M.E. Krauss, eds, *Vanishing Languages of the Pacific Rim*, 406–17. Oxford, UK: Oxford University Press.

– ed. 1985. *Yupik Eskimo Prosodic Systems: Descriptive and Comparative Studies*. Fairbanks, AK: Alaska Native Language Center.

– ed. 1995. *Inuit Nunait/Nunangit Yuget/Unangan Tanangin*. Map of the Eskaleut language area. Fairbanks, AK: Alaska Native Language Center.

Kristensen, Kurt. 2009. "Language Integration Is the Key." *News from Greenland*, February 9. http://sermitsiaq.gl/rss/en_newsletter.jsp.

Krupnik, Igor. 1991. "Extinction of the Sirenikski Eskimo Language: 1895–1960." *Études/Inuit/Studies* 15, no. 2: 3–22.

– and Mikhail Chlenov. 1977. "Dinamika ètnolingvisticheskoy situatsii u asiatskikh eskimosov" [The dynamics of the ethnolinguistic situation of the Asiatic Eskimos]. *Sovetskaya Etnografiya* 2: 19–28.

Kublu, Alexina, and Jarich Oosten. 1999. "Changing Perspectives of Name and Identity among the Inuit of Northeast Canada." In J. Oosten and C. Remie, eds, *Arctic Identities*, 56–78. Leiden, Netherlands: University of Leiden, CNWS Publications.

Kwachka, Patricia. 1992a. "Discourse Structures, Cultural Stability, and Language Shift." *International Journal of the Sociology of Language* 93: 67–73.

– 1992b. "Language Shift and Cultural Priorities." Paper read at the "First International Congress of Arctic Social Sciences," Quebec City.

Land Council of Greenland. 1973. *Land Council Regulation on Change in the Greenlandic Orthography*. Nuuk, Greenland: Land Council of Greenland.

Langgaard, Karen. 2001. "Discourse Practices in Nuuk, Greenland: Language Usage and Language Attitudes of the Students at the Gymnasium." *The Canadian Journal of Native Studies* 21, no. 2: 231–72.

– 2008. "Oral/Past Culture and Modern Technical Means in the Literature of the Twentieth Century in Greenland." *Acta Borealia* 25, no. 1: 45–57.

Langgaard, Per. 1990. *To Be a Very Small University in a Very Small Society*. Nuuk, Greenland: Ilisimatusarfik.

– 1992. "Grønlandsksproget – tosproget – grønlandsksproget: Nogle tendenser i det dansk-grønlandske sprogmøde blandt Nuuks skolebørn" [The Greenlandic language – bilingualism – the Greenlandic language:

Some tendencies in Danish-Greenlandic language contacts among schoolchildren in Nuuk]. In *Grønlandsk kultur- og samfunds forskning*, vol. 92, 104–28. Nuuk, Greenland: Ilisimatusarfik/Atuakkiorfik.

– 2008. "Taking the Tagger to the Next Level." Paper read at the "16th Inuit Studies Conference," Winnipeg, 23–25 October.

Laugrand, Frédéric, Jarich Oosten, and François Trudel. 2005. *Apostle to the Inuit: The Journals and Ethnographic Notes of Edmund James Peck – The Baffin Years, 1894–1905*. Toronto: University of Toronto Press.

LeBlanc, Sylvie. 2000. "Middle Dorset (1900–1100 BP) Regional Variability on the Island of Newfoundland and in Saint-Pierre et Miquelon." In M. Appelt, J. Berglund, and H.C. Gulløv, eds, *Identities and Cultural Contacts in the Arctic*, 97–105. Copenhagen, Denmark: Danish National Museum and Danish Polar Center.

Leer, Jeff. 1982. *A Conversational Dictionary of Kodiak Alutiiq*. Fairbanks, AK: Alaska Native Language Center.

Lefebvre, Gilles R. 1957. *A Draft Orthography for the Canadian Eskimo*. Ottawa: Government of Canada, Department of Northern Affairs and National Resources.

– 1964. "Le Nouveau-Québec dans la perspective de l'unité linguistique esquimaude." In J. Malaurie and J. Rousseau, eds, *Le Nouveau-Québec*, 277–313. Paris, France: Mouton.

Légaré, André. 2001. "The Spatial and Symbolic Construction of Nunavut: Towards the Emergence of a Regional Collective Identity." *Études/Inuit/Studies* 25, nos 1–2: 141–68.

Le Mouël, Jean-François. 1984. *Les 36 Eskimos de l'île aux mouettes*. Paris, France: Berger-Levrault.

Lennert-Olsen, Lise. 1987. *Lidt om grønlandske børns sprog* [Something on the language of the Greenlandic child]. Report. Copenhagen, Denmark: Institut for Eskimologi.

Lewis, Arthur. 1904. *The Life and Work of the Rev. E.J. Peck among the Eskimos*. London, UK: Hodden and Stoughton.

Lewis, R. Alison, and Louis-Jacques Dorais. 2004. "Two Related Indigenous Writing Systems: Canada's Syllabic and China's A-Hmao Scripts." *The Canadian Journal of Native Studies* 23, no. 2: 277–304.

Lipscomb, David R. 1993. "A Critique of the Nominal Hypothesis for Eskimo." *Études/Inuit/Studies* 17, no. 2: 127–40.

Louis, Winnifred, and Donald M. Taylor. 2001. "When the Survival of Language Is at Stake: The Future of Inuktitut in Arctic Quebec." *Journal of Language and Social Psychology* 20, nos 1–2: 111–43.

Lowe, Ronald. 1978. "Le mythe de l'ergatif en inuktitut." *Études/Inuit/Studies* 2, no. 2: 108–15.

– 1980. "De l'espace au temps en inuktitut." In A. Dugas, ed., *Inuktitut et langues amérindiennes au Québec*, 133–57. Cahier de Linguistique 10. Quebec City: Presses de l'Université du Québec.

– 1981. *Analyse linguistique et ethnocntrisme: Essai sur la structure du mot en inuktitut*. Canadian Ethnology Service Paper No. 70. Ottawa: National Museums of Canada.

– 1983. *Kangiryuarmiut uqauhingita numiktittitdjutingit: Basic Kangiryuarmiut Eskimo Dictionary.* Inuvik, NWT: Committee for Original Peoples' Entitlement.

– 1984a. *Uummarmiut uqalungiha mumikhitchirutingit: Basic Uummarmiut Eskimo Dictionary.* Inuvik, NWT: Committee for Original Peoples' Entitlement.

– 1984b. *Siglit Inuvialuit uqausiita kipuktirutait: Basic Siglit Inuvialuit Eskimo Dictionary.* Inuvik, NWT: Committee for Original Peoples' Entitlement.

– 1984c. "L'assimilation linguistique des Esquimaux de l'Arctique de l'ouest: La fin d'un début ou le début de la fin?" *Recherches amérindiennes au Québec* 14, no. 4: 54–7.

– 1985a. *Uummarmiut uqalungiha ilihaurrutikrangit: Basic Uummarmiut Eskimo Grammar.* Inuvik, NWT: Committee for Original Peoples' Entitlement.

– 1985b. *Siglit Inuvialuit uqausiita ilisarviksait: Basic Siglit Inuvialuit Eskimo Grammar.* Inuvik, NWT: Committee for Original Peoples' Entitlement.

– 1985c. *Kangiryuarmiut uqauhingita ilihautdjutikhangit: Basic Kangiryuarmiut Eskimo Grammar.* Inuvik, NWT: Committee for Original Peoples' Entitlement.

– 1988. "La forme déclarative et l'alternance des suffixes *-vu* et *-ju* dans les dialectes inuit de l'arctique canadien de l'est." *Revue québécoise de linguistique* 17, no. 1: 137–65.

– 1991. *Les trois dialectes inuit de l'Arctique canadien de l'Ouest: Analyse descriptive et étude comparative.* Quebec City: Université Laval, Groupe d'études inuit et circumpolaires (GÉTIC).

– 2001. *Siglit Inuvialuit Uqautchiita Nutaat Kipuktirutait Aglipkaqtat: Siglit Inuvialuit Eskimo Dictionary.* Quebec City: Éditions Nota Bene.

Macdonald, John. 1998. *The Arctic Sky: Inuit Astronomy, Star Lore, and Legend.* Toronto: Royal Ontario Museum; Igloolik, NU: Nunavut Research Institute.

Macdougall, James C. 2001. "Access to Justice for Deaf Inuit in Nunavut: The Role of 'Inuit Sign Language.'" *Canadian Psychology* 42, no. 1: 61–73.

Mackay, Ronald. 1986. "The Role of English in Education in an Eastern Arctic School." PhD dissertation, Université de Montréal, Montreal.

MacLean, Edna Ahgeak. 1979. "The Need for and Feasibility of Planning for a Coordinated International Auxiliary Inuit Writing System." In B. Basse and K. Jensen, eds, *Eskimo Languages: Their Present-Day Conditions*, 51–64. Aarhus, Denmark: Arkona.

– 1980. *Iñupiallu tannillu uqalunisa ilanich: Abridged Iñupiaq and English Dictionary*. Fairbanks, AK: Alaska Native Language Center; Barrow, AK, North Slope Borough: Iñupiat History, Language and Culture Commission.

– 1990. "Culture and Change for Inupiat and Yupiks of Alaska." In D.R.F. Collis, ed., *Arctic Languages: An Awakening*, 159–75. Paris, France: Unesco.

Madden, Ryan. 1992. "The Forgotten People: The Relocation and Internment of Aleuts during World War II." *American Indian Culture and Research Journal* 16, no. 4: 55–76.

Maheux, Gisèle, Yvonne da Silveira, and Diane Simard. 2004. "La question de l'inuttitut en formation des enseignants inuit: Analyse d'une expérience de travail depuis 1984." *Cahiers d'histoire* 24, no. 1: 107–29.

Mailhot, José. 1978. "L'étymologie de 'esquimau' revue et corrigée." *Études/Inuit/Studies* 2, no. 2: 59–69.

– Jean-Paul Simard, and Sylvie Vincent. 1980. "On est toujours l'Esquimau de quelqu'un." *Études/Inuit/Studies* 4, nos 1–2: 59–76.

Mallon, S.T. (Mick). 1977. "How Inuktitut Avoids Some Ambiguities that English Doesn't." *Études/Inuit/Studies* 1, no. 1: 149–53.

– 1979. "How Can an Alien Bureaucracy Safeguard a Language?" In B. Basse and K. Jensen, eds, *Eskimo Languages: Their Present-Day Conditions*, 65–8. Aarhus, Denmark: Arkona.

– 1985. "Six Years Later: The ICI Dual Orthography for Inuktitut, 1976–1982." In B. Burnaby, ed., *Promoting Native Writing Systems in Canada*, 137–57. Toronto: OISE Press.

– 1991. *Introductory Inuktitut*. Victoria, BC: Linguistic Programs.

– 1992. *Inuttitut ilinnialirta: Let's Start to Learn Inuttitut*. Dorval, QC: Kativik School Board.

– 1993. *Introduction à l'inuktitut*. Victoria, BC: Ittukuluuk Language Programs.

Mancini Billson, Janet, and Kyra Mancini. 2007. *Inuit Women: Their Powerful Spirit in a Century of Change*. Lanham, MD: Rowman and Littlefield.

Marcus, Alan R. 1995. *Relocating Eden*. Hanover, NH, and London, UK: University Press of New England.

Markoosie. 1970. *The Harpoon of the Hunter*. Montreal and Kingston: McGill-Queen's University Press.

Marsh, Gordon H., and Morris Swadesh. 1951. "Eskimo–Aleut Correspondences." *International Journal of American Linguistics* 17: 209–16.

Martin, A. 1899. *Unipkautsit attornartut ajokertûtsemut kaujijaksaujuni sunatuinarne* [Stories useful for teaching general knowledge]. Herrnhut, Germany: G. Winter.

Martin, Ian. 2000a. *Aaajiqatigiingniq: Language of Instruction Research Paper*. Iqaluit, NU: Government of Nunavut, Department of Culture, Language, Elders and Youth.

– 2000b. *Report of the Research Project: Language Attitudes, Ability, Use, Vitality and Sociolinguistic Trends Most Likely to Affect School-Based Language Planning and Promotion Policies*. Iqaluit, NU: Government of Nunavut, Department of Education.

Martin, Laura. 1986. "'Eskimo Words for Snow': A Case Study in the Genesis and Decay of an Anthropological Example." *American Anthropologist* 88, no. 2: 418–23.

Mary-Rousselière, Guy. 1980. *Qitdlarssuaq – l'histoire d'une migration polaire*. Montreal: Presses de l'Université de Montréal.

– 1992. "Language and Magic among Central Eskimos." 1966. Reprinted in *Eskimo* n.s. 42: 14–21.

Massenet, Jean-Marie. 1986. *Étude phonologique d'un dialecte inuit canadien*. Inuit Studies Occasional Papers 1. Quebec City: Association Inuksiutiit Katimajiit.

Mathiassen, Therkel. 1928. *Material Culture of the Iglulik Eskimos*. Report of the Fifth Thule Expedition, vol. 6, no. 1. Copenhagen, Denmark: Report of the Fifth Thule Expedition.

Mazurkewich, Irene. 1992. "Language Shift in the Inuit of Northern Labrador." Paper read at the "15th International Congress of Linguists," Quebec City.

McCarthy, S. 1991. "The Cree Syllabary and the Writing System Riddle: A Paradigm in Crisis." Typed manuscript, Timmins, Ontario, in possession of the author.

McComber, Louis. 2001. "Radio communautaire et ethnicité chez les Inuit du Nunavut." MA thesis, Université Laval, Quebec City.

McGhee, Robert. 1984. "Thule Prehistory in Canada." In D. Damas, ed., *Handbook of North American Indians*, vol. 5, *Arctic*, 369–76. Washington, DC: Smithsonian Institution.

McGoldrick, M. 1984. *Study on Inuit Print Media Needs in Northern Quebec*. Montreal: Makivik Corporation, Information Department.

McGrath, Robin. 1984. *Canadian Inuit Literature: The Development of a Tradition*. Canadian Ethnology Service Paper No. 94. Ottawa: National Museum of Man.

– 1986. "Inuit Community Newspapers." *Inuit* (Summer): 47–51.

McNabb, Steven. 1989. "Expressive Conventions in Inuit Society." *Études/Inuit/Studies* 13, no. 2: 49–67.

Mennecier, Philippe. 1995. *Le Tunumiisut, dialecte inuit du Groenland oriental: Description et analyse*. Paris, France: Klincksieck.

Menovshchikov, Georgii A. 1960. *Eskimosskiy yazyk* [The Eskimo language]. Leningrad, Russia: Uchpedgiz.

– 1964. *Yazyk sirenikskikh Eskimosov* [The language of the Sirenikski Eskimos]. Moscow and Leningrad, Russia: Nauka.

– 1969. "Les constructions fondamentales de la proposition simple dans les langues Eskimo-Aléoutes." *Langages* 15: 127–33.

– 1975. *Yazyk naukanskikh Eskimosov* [The language of the Naukanski Eskimos]. Leningrad, Russia: Nauka.

– 1978. "Emprunts lexicologiques russes dans les langues autochtones de l'Alaska et des îles aléoutiennes." *Inter-Nord* 15: 45–51.

– 1980. *Yazyk Eskimosov Beringova proliva (Inuitskii)* [The language of the Bering Strait Eskimos (Inuit)]. Leningrad, Russia: Nauka.

– 1990a. "Contemporary Studies of the Eskimo-Aleut Languages and Dialects: A Progress Report." In D.R.F. Collis, ed., *Arctic Languages: An Awakening*, 69–76. Paris, France: Unesco.

– 1990b. "Eskimo." In D.R.F. Collis, ed., *Arctic Languages: An Awakening*, 114–16. Paris, France: Unesco.

– and Nikolai Vakhtin. 1984. *Eskimosskii yazyk: Uchebnoe posobie dlya peduchilishch* [The Eskimo language: A teaching aid for pedagogical colleges]. Leningrad, Russia: Prosveshchenie.

Métayer, Maurice. 1953. "Dictionnaire esquimau-français, Aklavik et Cambridge Bay N.W.T." Typed manuscript, Oblate Archives/Archives Deschâtelets, Ottawa.

– 1973. *Unipkat, Tradition esquimaude de Coppermine, Territoires-du-Nord-Ouest, Canada*. 3 vols. Quebec City: Université Laval, Centre d'études nordiques.

Minogue, Sara. 2005. "Hear No Evil." *This Magazine*, May-June. http://www.thismagazine.ca/issues/2005/05/hearnoevil.php.

Mithun, Marianne. 1998. "Yup'ik Roots and Affixes." In O. Miyaoka and M. Oshima, eds, *Languages of the North Pacific Rim* 4, 133–212. Kyoto, Japan: Kyoto University Graduate School of Letters.

Miyaoka, Osahito. 1978. *Esukimo no gengo to bunka* [Language and culture of the Eskimo]. Tokyo, Japan: Kobundo.

Møller, Aqigssiaq. 1990. "Language Policy and Planning under the Home Rule Administration." In D.R.F. Collis, ed., *Arctic Languages: An Awakening*, 61–4. Paris, France: Unesco.

Morgan, Lael, ed. 1979. *Alaska's Native People*. Alaska Geographic, vol. 6, no. 3. Anchorage, AK: Alaska Geographic Society.

Morgounova, Daria. 2007. "Language, Identities and Ideologies of the Past and Present Chukotka." *Études/Inuit/Studies* 31, nos 1–2: 183–200.

Morrow, Phyllis, and Chase Hensel. 1992. "Hidden Dissension: Minority-Majority Relationships and the Use of Contested Terminology." *Arctic Anthropology* 29, no. 1: 38–53.

Müller-Wille, Ludger. 1983. "Inuit Toponymy and Cultural Sovereignty." In L. Müller-Wille, ed., *Conflict in Development in Nouveau-Québec*, 131–50. Montreal: McGill University, Centre for Northern Studies and Research.

– 1987. *Inuttitut Nunait Atingit Katirsutauningit Nunavimi (Kupaimmi Kanatami)/Gazetteer of Inuit Place Names in Nunavik (Quebec, Canada)/Répertoire toponymique inuit du Nunavik (Québec, Canada)*. Inukjuak, Nunavik, QC: Avataq Cultural Institute.

Murdoch, John. 1892. *Ethnological Results of the Point Barrow Expedition*. 9th Annual Report. Washington, DC: Government of the United States, Bureau of American Ethnology.

Nakashima, Douglas J. 1991. "The Ecological Knowledge of Belcher Island Inuit." PhD dissertation, McGill University, Montreal.

Nappaaluk, Salome Mitiarjuk. 1984. *Sanaaq*. Ed. B. Saladin d'Anglure. Inuksiutiit allaniagait 4. Quebec City: Association Inuksiutiit Katimajiit.

– 2002. *Sanaaq*. Transliterated from syllabics and translated into French by Bernard Saladin d'Anglure. Montreal: Stanké.

Nattiez, Jean-Jacques. 1985. "Le disque de musique amérindienne, IV: Nouveaux disques et cassettes de musique inuit." *Recherches amérindiennes au Québec* 15, no. 4: 67–77.

Nelson, Edward W. 1899. *The Eskimos about Bering Strait*. Washington, DC: Government of the United States, Bureau of American Ethnology; reprint, Washington, DC: Smithsonian Institution, 1984.

Newsweek. 1991. "The Melting of a Mighty Myth." *Newsweek*, 22 July, 63.

Nochasak, Zippora, and Paul Pigott. 2005. *On-Line Dictionary of Labrador Inuttitut*. http://www.labradorvirtualmuseum.ca/inuttut.php.

Nowak, Elke. 1987. *Samuel Kleinschmidts "Grammatik der Grönländischen Sprache"* [Samuel Kleinschmidt's "Grammar of the Greenlandic Language"]. Hildesheim, Germany: Georg Olms Verlag.

– 1993. "Through the Looking-Glass: Syntactic Structures of Inuktitut and Ergativity." *Études/Inuit/Studies* 17, no. 1: 103–16.

– 1995. "The 'Eskimo Language' of Labrador: Moravian Missionaries and the Description of Labrador Inuttut, 1733–1891." *Études/Inuit/Studies* 23, nos 1–2: 173–97.

– 1996. *Transforming the Images: Ergativity and Transitivity in Inuktitut (Eskimo)*. Berlin, Germany, and New York: Mouton de Gruyter.

– 2008. *Inuktitut: Eine grammatische Skizze* [Inuktitut: A grammatical sketch]. Languages of the World/Materials 470. Munich, Germany: Lincom Europa.

Nuligak. 1972a. *Moi Nuligak: Mémoires d'un Esquimau*. Trans. and ed. Maurice Métayer. Montreal: Éditions du Jour.

– 1972b. *Nuligak*. Trans. and ed. Maurice Métayer. 2nd ed. Toronto: Peter Martin Associates.

Nunavik Educational Task Force (NETF). 1992. *Silatunirmut: The Pathway to Wisdom*. Lachine, QC: Makivik Corporation.

Nunavummit Kiglisiniartiit. 2001. *Language Data from the 2001 Nunavut Household Survey*. Iqaluit, NU: Government of Nunavut, Bureau of Statistics.

Nunavut Tunngavik Inc (NTI). 2004. *An Annual Report on the State of Inuit Culture and Society, 2002–2003*. Iqaluit, NU: NTI.

Nungak, Zebedee, and Eugene A. Arima. 1969. *Eskimo Stories from Povungnituk, Quebec*. Ottawa: National Museum of Man.

Nuttall, Mark. 1991. *Arctic Homeland*. Toronto: University of Toronto Press.

– 2001. "Locality, Identity and Memory in South Greenland." *Études/Inuit/Studies* 25, nos 1–2: 53–72.

Okpik, Abraham. 2005. *We Call It Survival: The Life Story of Abraham Okpik*. Ed. Louis McComber. Iqaluit, NU: Nunavut Arctic College.

Olsen, Carl Christian. 1979. "The Status of the Greenlandic Language in Greenland Today." In B. Basse and K. Jensen, eds, *Eskimo Languages: Their Present-Day Conditions*, 161–5. Aarhus, Denmark: Arkona.

Oman, Lela Kiana. 1995. *The Epic of Qayaq: The Longest Story Ever Told by My People*. Ottawa: Carleton University Press.

Omura, Keiichi. 1997. *Basic Arviligjuaq Inuktun Dictionary*. Osaka, Japan: Pelly Bay Ethnological Research Project.

– 1998. "A Research Note on the Colour Terminology System in the Natsilingmiutut Dialect of Inuktitut." *Études/Inuit/Studies* 22, no. 1: 123–38.

Oosten, Jarich, and Frédéric Laugrand, eds. 2007. *Annaumaniq piqqusiqatigiinngittunik inuusirniit: Inuit piqqusituqangit tigujauvalliajut inuusuktunut innarnit/Surviving in Different Worlds: Transferring Inuit Traditions from Elders to Youth*. Iqaluit, NU: Nunavut Arctic College.

Ootoova, Elisapee, ed. 2000. *Uqausiit Tukingit: Inuktitut Dictionary: Tununiq Dialect*. Iqaluit, NU: Government of Nunavut, Qikiqtani School Operations.

Oqaatsinut politikkimik nassuiaasiornissamik suleqatigiit. 2001. *...oqaaserli: Oqaatsinut politikkimik nassuiaasiornissamik suleqatigiit innersuussutaat* [...but the word: Recommendations from the working group for language policy review]. Nuuk, Greenland: Oqaasileriffik/Sprogsekretariatet.

Ortiz, Dolores, with Luisa Kanarjuaq. 1993. *Conversation inuit: Inuktitut uqariursautiit*. Quebec City: Presses de l'Université Laval.

Orvik, J.M. 1977. "Definitions of Bilingual Education in Alaska." In R. Barnhardt, ed., *Cross-Cultural Issues in Alaskan Education*, 141–7. Fairbanks, AK: University of Alaska Press.

Ostermann, H. 1938. *Knud Rasmussen's Posthumous Notes on the Life and Doings of the East Greenlanders in Olden Times*. Meddelelser om Grønland 109/1. Copenhagen, Denmark: Meddelelser om Grønland.

Oswalt, Wendell H. 1979. *Eskimos and Explorers*. Novato, CA: Chandler and Sharp.

Owingajak, David. 1986. *Ukiuqtaqtumi Annaumanirmik Uqalimaaq: Arctic Survival Book*. Arviat, NU: Inuit Cultural Institute.

Padlayat, Jusipi, ed. 1974. *Tarramiut: The Northerners: Les Septentrionaux*. Montreal: Northern Quebec Inuit Association.

Paillet, Jean-Pierre. 1973. "Eskimo Language Animal and Plant Taxinomies in Baker Lake." Typed manuscript, Carleton University, Department of Linguistics, Ottawa.

Paine, Robert. 1977. "The Nursery Game: Colonizers and Colonized in the Eastern Arctic." *Études/Inuit/Studies* 1, no. 1: 5–32.

Pallascio, Richard, Richard Allaire, and Pierre Mongeau. 1993. "Spatial Representation of Geometric Objects: A North-South Comparison." *Études/Inuit/Studies* 17, no. 2: 113–26.

Panigeo, J. 1979. *Uqapiqta: Let's Speak Eskimo*. Barrow, AK: Iñupiat University of the Arctic.

Pasch, Timothy J. 2008. "Inuktitut Online in Nunavik." PhD dissertation, University of Washington, Seattle.

Pastori, Charles. 1994. *Kigutilirinirmut uqausiqarvingat: Dental Glossary/Glossaire dentaire*. Iqaluit, NU: Nunavut Arctic College, Nunatta Campus.

Patrick, Donna. 2003. *Language, Politics, and Social Interaction in an Inuit Community.* Berlin, Germany, and New York: Mouton deGruyter.

Peacock, F. William. 1974a. *Eskimo Affixes.* St John's, NL: Memorial University of Newfoundland.

– 1974b. *Eskimo-English Dictionary.* St John's, NL: Memorial University of Newfoundland.

– 1974c. *Eskimo-Synonyms Dictionary.* St John's, NL: Memorial University of Newfoundland.

Peck, Edmund J. 1925. *Eskimo-English Dictionary.* Hamilton, ON: Church of England in Canada.

Pedersen, K. 1977. *Grønlandsk for begyndere* [Greenlandic for beginners]. 2 vols. Copenhagen, Denmark: Arnold Busck.

Pelinski, Ramon, Luke Suluk, and Lucy Amarook. 1979. *Inuit Songs from Eskimo Point/Inuit imngiusingit ajajartut arviarmiutat.* Canadian Ethnology Service Paper No. 60. Ottawa: National Museums of Canada.

Perrot, Michel. 1986. "Les moyens de communication publique chez les Inuit: Étude anthropologique du développement de la radio et de la télévision au Groenland, au Canada et en Alaska." PhD dissertation, Université de Bordeaux III, Bordeaux, France.

Petersen, Robert. 1970. "On Phonological Length in the Eastern Eskimo Dialects." *Folk*, nos 11–12: 329–44.

– 1975. "On the East Greenlandic Dialect in Comparison with the West Greenlandic." *Objets et Mondes* 15, no. 2: 177–82.

– 1976a. "Nogle træk i udviklingen af det grønlandske sprog" [Some directions in the development of the Greenlandic language]. *Grønland* 6: 165–208.

– 1976b. *ʃ Kitaata qeqqani atorneqarnera dialektinullu allanut atassuteqarnera* [The use of ʃ in central West Greenland and its equivalents in other dialects]. Copenhagen, Denmark: Institut for Eskimologi.

– 1977. "On the West Greenlandic Cultural Imperialism in East Greenland." In C. Sandbacka, ed., *Cultural Imperialism and Cultural Identity*, 187–95. Helsinki, Finland: Finnish Anthropological Society.

– 1979. "Danish Influence on Greenlandic Syntax." In B. Basse and K. Jensen, eds, *Eskimo Languages: Their Present-Day Conditions*, 113–21. Aarhus, Denmark: Arkona.

– 1980. *Kalaallit oqaasiini nipit sivitsortarnerata ilisarnaatitut atorneqarnera* [The functional use of phonemic length in Greenlandic]. Nuuk, Greenland: Ilisimatusarfik.

– 1984. "Greenlandic Written Literature." In D. Damas, ed., *Handbook of North American Indians*, vol. 5, *Arctic*, 640–5. Washington, DC: Smithsonian Institution.

– 1985a. "Some Changes in the Greenland Inuit Language." Typed manuscript, Ilisimatusarfik, Nuuk, Greenland.

– 1985b. "The Use of Certain Symbols in Connection with Greenlandic Identity." In J. Brøsted et al., eds, *Native Power*, 294–300. Bergen, Norway: Universitetsforlaget.

– 1986. "Some Features Common to East and West Greenlandic in the Light of Dialect Relationships and the Latest Migration Theories." *Arctic Anthropology* 23, nos 1–2: 401–11.

– 1987. *Nunatta oqaluttuassartaanit* [From our country's material for stories]. Nuuk, Greenland: Pilersuiffik.

– 1990. "The Greenlandic Language: Its Nature and Situation." In D.R.F. Collis, ed., *Arctic Languages: An Awakening*, 293–308. Paris, France: Unesco.

Petitot, Émile. 1876. *Vocabulaire français-esquimau*. Paris, France: Ernest Leroux.

– 1888. *En route pour la mer glaciale*. Paris, France: Letouzey et Ané.

Petrone, Penny. 1988. *Northern Voices: Inuit Writing in English*. Toronto: University of Toronto Press.

Pitseolak, A. 1971. *Pictures out of My Life*. Toronto: Oxford University Press.

Pitseolak, Peter. 1975. *People from Our Side*. Edmonton: Hurtig.

Plumet, Patrick. 1979. "Thuléens et Dorsétiens dans l'Ungava (Nouveau-Québec)." In A.P. McCartney, ed., *Thule Eskimo Culture: An Anthropological Retrospective*, 110–21. Archaeological Survey Paper 88. Ottawa: National Museum of Man.

Prattis, J. Iain. 1986. "The Cultural Division of Labour in the Canadian North: The Implications for Multiculturalism Policy and the Inuit." Typed manuscript, Carleton University, Department of Sociology and Anthropology, Ottawa.

– and Jean-Philippe Chartrand. 1984. *Minority Language Bilingualism: The Case of Inuktitut in the Canadian North*. Departmental Working Paper 84–3. Ottawa: Carleton University, Department of Sociology and Anthropology.

Pullum, Geoffrey K. 1991. "The Great Eskimo Vocabulary Hoax." In *The Great Eskimo Vocabulary Hoax and Other Irreverent Essays on the Study of Language*, 159–74. Chicago, IL: University of Chicago Press.

Quinn, A. 1965. "Index." In R. Hakluyt, *The Principal Navigations, Voiages and Discoveries of the English Nation*, 967. Cambridge, UK: Hakluyt Society.

Qumaq, Taamusi. 1988. *Sivulitta piusituqangit* [The longstanding customs of our ancestors]. Inuksiutiit Allaniagait 5. Quebec City: Association Inuksiutiit Katimajiit.

– 1991. *Inuit uqausillaringit* [Real Inuit words]. Quebec City: Association Inuksiutiit Katimajiit; Montreal: Avataq Cultural Institute.

– 1996. "The Future of Inuktitut." In J. Maurais, ed., *Quebec's Aboriginal Languages: History, Planning and Development*, 256–61. Clevedon, UK: Multilingual Matters.

Randa, Vladimir. 1986. *L'ours polaire et les Inuit*. Paris, France: SELAF.

– 1989. "Esquisse du traitement lexical des catégories zoologiques dans la langue d'Igloolik." *Revue d'ethnolinguistique (Cahiers du LACITO)* 4: 147–68.

– 1990. "Note sur les méthodes d'analyse appliquées aux matériaux ethnozoologiques inuit." *Revue d'ethnolinguistique (Cahiers du LACITO)* 5: 203–11.

– 1994. "Inuillu uumajuillu: Les animaux dans les savoirs, les représentations et la langue des Iglulingmiut (Arctique oriental canadien)." PhD dissertation, École des Hautes Études en Sciences Sociales, Paris, France.

– 1996. "Différencier pour mieux rapprocher: Conceptualisation de la faune chez les Iglulingmiut et dynamique de la pensée analogique." In N. Tersis and M. Therrien, eds, *La dynamique dans la langue et la culture inuit*, 95–118. Paris, France: Éditions Peeters.

Rankin, Sharon, ed. 2008. *Caninuit: A Comprehensive Bibliography of Canadian Inuit Periodicals*. Teeswater, ON: Reference Press. http://www.libris.ca/caninuit.

Rasmussen, Jens Elmegaard. 1979. *Anaptyxis, Gemination and Syncope in Eskimo*. Copenhagen, Denmark: Linguistic Circle of Copenhagen.

Rasmussen, Knud. 1929. *Intellectual Culture of the Iglulik Eskimos*. Report of the Fifth Thule Expedition, vol. 7. Copenhagen, Denmark: Report of the Fifth Thule Expedition.

– 1930. *Igloolik and Caribou Eskimo Texts*. Report of the Fifth Thule Expedition, vol. 7, no. 3. Copenhagen, Denmark: Report of the Fifth Thule Expedition.

– 1931. *The Netsilik Eskimos: Social and Spiritual Culture*. Report of the Fifth Thule Expedition, vol. 8. Copenhagen, Denmark: Report of the Fifth Thule Expedition.

– 1942. *The Mackenzie Eskimos*. Report of the Fifth Thule Expedition, vol. 10. Copenhagen, Denmark: Report of the Fifth Thule Expedition.

– and H. Ostermann. 1941. *Alaskan Eskimo Words*. Report of the Fifth Thule Expedition, vol. 3, no. 4. Copenhagen, Denmark: Report of the Fifth Thule Expedition.

Ray, Dorothy J. 1981. "Picture Writing from Buckland, Alaska." *Arts and Cultures of the North* 5, no. 3: 339–44.

Reed, Irene, et al. 1977. *Yup'ik Eskimo Grammar.* Fairbanks, AK: Alaska Native Language Center.

Richards, Edward. 1913. "Vocabulary Prepared by Mr Richards of Rupert's House for Our Use with the Esquimaux." Hudson's Bay Company manuscript, Alaska Native Language Center, Fairbanks, Alaska.

Rink, Henry. 1875. *Tales and Traditions of the Eskimo.* Edinburgh, UK: Robert Brown.

– 1887a. *The East Greenland Dialect According to the Annotations Made by the Danish East Coast Expedition to Kleinschmidt's Greenlandic Dictionary.* Meddelelser om Grønland 39/4. Copenhagen, Denmark: Meddelelser om Grønland.

– 1887b. *The Eskimo Tribes.* Copenhagen, Denmark: Reitzel.

Rischel, Jørgen. 1974. *Topics in West Greenlandic Phonology.* Copenhagen, Denmark: Akademisk Forlag.

– 1975. "Asymmetric Vowel Harmony in Greenlandic Fringe Dialects." *ARIPUC* 9: 1–47.

– 1981. "Greenlandic as a Three-Vowel Language." *Études/Inuit/Studies* 5 (supplementary): 71–80.

Robbe, Pierre. 1977. "Orientation et repérage chez les Tileqilamiut (côte est du Groenland)." *Études/Inuit/Studies* 1, no. 2: 73–83.

– 1981. "Les noms de personne chez les Ammassalimiut." *Études/Inuit/Studies* 5, no. 1: 45–82.

– and Louis-Jacques Dorais. 1986. *Tunumiit oraasiat: Tunumiut oqaasii/Det østgronlandske sprog/The East Greenlandic Inuit Language/La langue inuit du Greenland de l'Est.* Quebec City: Université Laval, Centre d'études nordiques.

Robitaille, Norbert, and Robert Choinière. 1984. *An Overview of Demographic and Socio-Economic Conditions of the Inuit in Canada.* Ottawa: Government of Canada, Department of Indian and Northern Affairs.

Rodionova, Natalia. 2006. *Praktikim po eskimosskomu iazyku dlia studentov 1 kursa* [Eskimo language exercises for first-year university students]. Novosibirsk, Russia: University of Novosibirsk.

– 2007a. *Ukazatel' suffiksov eskimosskogo iazyka* [Index of suffixes in the Eskimo language]. Anadyr, Russia: Chukotskii mnogoprofil'nyi kolledzh.

– 2007b. *Sbornik rasskazov russkikh pisatelei, perevedennykh na eskimosskii iazyk* [Russian writers translated in the Eskimo language]. Anadyr, Russia: Chukotskii mnogoprofil'nyi kolledzh.

Rosing, Emil. 1978. *Qimusseq* [Sledging]. Copenhagen, Denmark: Ministeriet for Grønland.

Roth, Lorna. 2005. *Something New in the Air: The Story of First Peoples Television Broadcasting in Canada*. Montreal and Kingston: McGill Queen's University Press.

Rouland, Norbert. 1979. "Les modes juridiques de solution des conflits chez les Inuit." *Études/Inuit/Studies* 3 (supplementary).

Rubtsova, Ekaterina S. 1971. *Eskimossko-russkii slovar'* [Eskimo-Russian dictionary]. Moscow, Russia: Sovetskaya Entsiklopediya.

Ruhlen, Merritt. 1994. *On the Origin of Languages: Studies in Linguistic Taxinomy*. Palo Alto, CA: Stanford University Press.

Rygaard, Jette. 2004. "Youth Culture, Media and Globalization Processes in Greenland." *Young: Nordic Journal of Youth Research* 11, no. 4: 291–308.

Sadock, Jerrold M. 1972. "In Defence of Metathesis in Greenlandic." *Papers in Linguistics* 5, no. 1: 1–9.

– 1999. "The Nominalist Theory of Eskimo: A Case Study in Scientific Self-Deception." *International Journal of American Linguistics* 65, no. 4: 383–406.

– 2003. *A Grammar of Kalaallisut (West Greenlandic Inuttut)*. Languages of the World/Materials 162. Munich, Germany: Lincom Europa.

Saint-Aubin, Danièle. 1980. "English Loan-Verbs in the Inuktitut Speech of Inuit Bilinguals." MA thesis, McGill University, Montreal.

Saladin d'Anglure, Bernard. 1967. *L'organisation sociale traditionnelle des Esquimaux de Kangirsujuaaq (Nouveau-Québec)*. Quebec City: Université Laval, Centre d'études nordiques.

– 1977. "Iqallijuq ou les réminiscences d'une âme-nom inuit." *Études/Inuit/Studies* 1, no. 1: 33–63.

– 1978. *La parole changée en pierre: Vie et œuvre de Davidialuk Alasuaq, artiste inuit*. Cahiers du Patrimoine 11. Quebec City: Government of Quebec, Department of Cultural Affairs.

– 1993. "Sila, the Ordering Principle of the Inuit Cosmology." In M. Hoppal and K. Howard, eds, *Shamans and Cultures*, 210–25. Budapest, Hungary: Hungarian Academy of Science.

– 2006a. *Être et renaître inuit, homme, femme ou chamane*. Paris, France: Gallimard.

– 2006b. "The Construction of Shamanic Identity among the Inuit of Nunavut and Nunavik." In G. Christie, ed., *Aboriginality and Governance: A Multidisciplinary Perspective from Quebec*, 141–65. Penticton, BC: Theytus Books.

– Geneviève Malgrange-Saladin, and Louis-Jacques Dorais. 1969. "Enquête toponymique dans le Nouveau-Québec esquimau." Unpublished report, Commission de géographie du Québec, Quebec City.

Sammallahti, Pekka. 1981. "The Teachings of Eskimo: Alaska Native Languages in Transition." *Suomen Antropologi* 4: 177–201.

Sammons, Katherine. 1994. *Avatilirinirmut uqausiqarvingat/Environmental Glossary/Glossaire de l'environnement.* Iqaluit, NU: Nunavut Arctic College, Nunatta Campus.

Sammons, Susan. 1985. "Inuktitut in Rankin Inlet." PhD dissertation, University of Michigan, Ann Arbor.

– ed. 1993. *Meta, Translators' Journal* 38, no. 1 (special issue on "Translation and Interpretation in Northern Canada").

Sauvageot, Aurélien. 1924. "Eskimo et ouralien." *Journal de la Société des Américanistes* n.s. 16: 279–316.

Savard, Rémi. 1966. *Mythologie esquimaude: Analyse de textes nord-groenlandais.* Quebec City: Université Laval, Centre d'études nordiques.

Savoie, Donat, ed. 1970. *The Amerindians of the Canadian Northwest in the 19th Century, as seen by Emile Petitot*, vol. 1, *The Tchiglit Eskimos.* Ottawa: Government of Canada, Department of Indian and Northern Affairs.

Schafer, L. 1977. "Identity Symbols and Boundary Maintenance: Some Functions of Speech Forms in Rural Alaska." In R. Barnhardt, ed., *Cross-Cultural Issues in Alaskan Education*, 156–65. Fairbanks, AK: University of Alaska Press.

Schneider, Lucien. 1970. *Dictionnaire français-esquimau du langage de l'Ungava et contrées limitrophes.* Quebec City: Presses de l'Université Laval.

– 1972–76. *Inuktituorutit grammaire purement esquimaude.* 5 vols. Quebec City: Government of Quebec, Ministry of Natural Resources.

– 1979. *Dictionnaire des infixes de la langue esquimaude.* Dossier du Patrimoine 43. Quebec City: Government of Quebec, Ministry of Cultural Affairs.

– 1985. *Ulirnaisigutiit: An Inuktitut-English Dictionary of Northern Quebec, Labrador and Eastern Arctic Dialects.* Quebec City: Presses de l'Université Laval.

– 1986. "Inuit Chunks." Typed manuscript, Kativik School Board, Dorval, Quebec.

Schuhmacher, Wilfried W. 1975. "On the Liquidation of Indigenous Numerals in 'Primitive' Societies." *Dialectical Anthropology* 1: 94–5.

Schultz-Lorentzen, G.R. 1927. *Dictionary of the West Greenland Eskimo Language.* Copenhagen, Denmark: C.A. Reitzels Forlag.

– 1945. *A Grammar of the West Greenland Language.* Copenhagen, Denmark: C.A. Reitzels Forlag.

Searles, Edmund. 2001. "Interpersonal Politics, Social Science Research and the Construction of Inuit Identity." *Études/Inuit/Studies* 25, no. 1–2: 101–19.

Secretary of State. 1985. *Proposition for an Aboriginal Language Policy.* Ottawa: Government of Canada, Department of the Secretary of State.

Seiler, Wolf A. 2005. *Iñupiatun Eskimo Dictionary.* Kotzebue, AK: NANA Regional Corporation.

Senécal, Sacha. 2007. "Knowledge and Use of Inuktitut among Inuit in Canada, 1981–2001." Unpublished research report, Inuit Tapiriit Kanatami and Government of Canada, Department of Indian and Northern Affairs, Research and Analysis Directorate, Ottawa.

Shearwood, Perry. 1987. "Literacy among the Aboriginal Peoples of the Northwest Territories." *The Canadian Modern Language Review* 43, no. 4: 630–42.

– 2001. "Inuit Identity and Literacy in a Nunavut Community." *Études/Inuit/Studies* 25, nos 1–2: 295–307.

Sivuaq, Paulusi. 1972. *Ce qu'un chasseur doit savoir.* Povungnituk, Nunavik, QC: Commission scolaire du Nouveau-Québec.

– 1973. *Contes et légendes inuit.* 2 vols. Povungnituk, Nunavik, QC: Commission scolaire du Nouveau-Québec.

SLiCA. 2007. *Survey of Living Conditions in the Arctic.* Anchorage, AK: University of Alaska Anchorage, Institute of Social and Economic Research.

Smith, Lawrence R. 1975. "Labrador Inuttut Surface Phonology." *International Journal of American Linguistics* 43, no. 2: 97–105.

– 1977. *Some Grammatical Aspects of Labrador Inuttut (Eskimo): A Survey of the Inflectional Paradigms of Nouns and Verbs.* Canadian Ethnology Service Paper No. 37. Ottawa: National Museums of Canada.

– 1979. *A Survey of the Derivational Postbases of Labrador Inuttut (Eskimo).* Canadian Ethnology Service Paper No. 45. Ottawa: National Museums of Canada.

– 1981. "Passive as a Two-Cycle Process in Inuktitut." *Études/Inuit/Studies* 5 (supplementary): 101–13.

– and Sam Metcalfe. 1973. *Labrador Inuttut-English Glossary.* St John's, NL: Memorial University of Newfoundland.

Snigaroff, Cedor L., and Knut Bergsland. 1986. *Niigugis Maqaxtazaqangis: Atkan Historical Traditions.* Fairbanks, AK: Alaska Native Language Center.

Søby, Regitze M. 1979. "Language and Identity in Thule." In B. Basse and K. Jensen, eds, *Eskimo Languages: Their Present-Day Conditions*, 145–54. Aarhus, Denmark: Arkona.

Sonne, Birgitte. 1990. *The Acculturative Role of Sea Woman.* Man and Society 13. Copenhagen, Denmark: Meddelelser om Grønland.

Sontag, Natascha. 2007. *The Inuit Language in Inuit Communities in Canada*. Map. Fairbanks, AK: University of Alaska Press.

Sørensen, Bo Wagner, Hans Lange, and Hulda Zober Holm. 2003. "Nuuk: Fremmedgørelse i storbyen?" [Nuuk: Becoming a stranger in the big town?]. *Tidsskriftet Grønland* 51: 25–40.

Spada, Nina, and Patsy M. Lightbown. 2002. "L1 and L2 in the Education of Inuit Children in Northern Quebec: Students' Abilities and Teachers' Perceptions." *Language and Education* 16, no. 3: 212–41,

Spalding, Alex. 1959. "An Orthography for the Canadian Eskimo Language." *Northern Affairs Bulletin* 6: 22–6.

– 1969. *Salliq: An Eskimo Grammar.* Ottawa: Government of Canada, Department of Indian Affairs and Northern Development, Education Branch.

– 1979a. *Eight Inuit Myths/Inuit unipkaaqtuat pingasuniarvinilit.* Canadian Ethnology Service Paper No. 59. Ottawa: National Museums of Canada.

– 1979b. *Learning to Speak Inuktitut: A Grammar of North Baffin Dialects.* London, ON: University of Western Ontario, Centre for Research and Teaching of Canadian Native Languages.

– 1982. *Inuktitut Dictionary by Themes (Aivilik Dialect).* Ottawa: Government of Canada, Department of Indian and Northern Affairs.

– 1993. *Inuktitut: A Grammar of North Baffin Dialect.* 2 vols. Winnipeg: Wuerz.

– 1998. *Inuktitut. A Multi-Dialectal Outline Dictionary (with an Aivilingmiutaq Base).* Iqaluit, NU: Nunavut Arctic College.

Stairs, Arlene. 1985. "La viabilité des langues autochtones et le rôle de l'écrit: L'expérience de l'inuktitut au Nouveau-Québec." *Recherches amérindiennes au Québec* 15, no. 3: 93–5.

– and Betsy Annahatak. 1987. "The Impact of Early Primary Inuktitut-Language Education in Kativik Schools: Phase I, 1984–85." In W.P. Adams, ed., *Education, Research, Information Systems and the North*, 132–6. Ottawa: Association of Canadian Universities for Northern Studies.

Steckley, John. 2008. *White Lies about the Inuit.* Peterborough, ON: Broadview Press.

Stefansson, Vilhjalmur. 1909. "The Eskimo Trade Jargon of Herschel Island." *American Anthropologist* 11, no. 2: 217–32.

Swadesh, Morris. 1942. "South Greenlandic (Eskimo)." *International Journal of American Linguistics* 23: 30–54.

– 1962. "Linguistic Relations across Bering Strait." *American Anthropologist* 64, no. 6: 1262–91.

Swift, Mary D. 2004. *Time in Child Inuktitut: A Developmental Study of an Eskimo-Aleut Language*. Berlin, Germany: Mouton de Gruyter.

– and Shanley E.M. Allen. 2002a. "Contexts of Verbal Inflection Dropping in Inuktitut Child Speech." In B. Skarabela, S.A. Fish, and A.H.-J. Do, eds, *Proceedings of the 26th Annual Boston University Conference on Language Development*, 689–700. Somerville, MA: Cascadilla Press.

– and Shanley E.M. Allen. 2002b. "Verb Base Ellipsis in Inuktitut Conversational Discourse." *International Journal of American Linguistics* 68, no. 2: 133–56.

Tagoona, Armand. 1975. *Shadows*. Toronto: Oberon Press.

Taylor, Donald M. 1990. *Carving a New Identity: The Role of Language in the Education of Inuit Children in Arctic Quebec*. Dorval, QC: Kativik School Board.

– and Stephen C. Wright. 1989. "Language Attitudes in a Multilingual Northern Community." *Canadian Journal of Native Studies* 9, no. 1: 85–119.

– M. Caron, and Lynn McAlpine. 2000. "Patterns of Perceived Language Ability and Use in Arctic Quebec." *International Journal of Bilingual Education and Bilingualism* 3, no. 4: 283–96.

– and Stephen C. Wright. 2004. "Do Aboriginal Students Benefit from Education in their Heritage Language? Results from a Ten-Year Program of Research in Nunavik." *Canadian Journal of Native Studies* 23, no. 1: 1–24.

Tersis, Nicole. 1994. "Les phonèmes de la langue inuit sont-ils motivés?" *Bulletin de la Société de Linguistique de Paris* 89, no. 1: 337–57.

– 2003. "La langue inuit, permanence et innovation." In P. Huret, ed., *Les Inuit de l'Arctique canadien*, 49–62. Quebec City: CIDEF-AFI; Paris, France: Inuksuk.

– 2008. *Forme et sens des mots du tunumiisut: Lexique inuit du Groenland oriental*. Paris, France: Éditions Peeters.

– and Marc-Antoine Mahieu. 2006. "Sémantique des affixes incorporants en langue inuit (Groenland oriental)." *Études/Inuit/Studies* 30, no. 1: 157–81.

– and Michèle Therrien, eds. 2000. *Les langues eskaléoutes: Sibérie, Alaska, Canada, Groënland*. Paris, France: CNRS Éditions.

– and Marc-Antoine Mahieu, eds. 2009. *Variations on Polysynthesis: The Eskaleut Languages*. Amsterdam, Netherlands: John Benjamins.

Tester, Frank J., and Peter Kulchyski. 1994. *Tammarniit (Mistakes): Inuit Relocation in the Eastern Arctic, 1939–63*. Vancouver: University of British Columbia Press.

Thalbitzer, William. 1904. *A Phonetical Study of the Eskimo Language*. Reprint, New York: AMS Press, 1976.

– 1911. "Eskimo." In F. Boas, ed., *Handbook of American Indian Languages*, 967–1069. Bureau of American Ethnology Bulletin 40. Washington, DC: US Government Printing Office.

– 1921. *The Ammassalik Eskimo: Language and Folklore*. Meddelelser om Grønland 40/3. Copenhagen, Denmark: Meddelelser om Grønland.

– 1929. *Légendes et Chants esquimaux du Groenland*. Fontenay-aux-Roses, France: n.p.

– 1944. "Uhlenbeck's Eskimo-Indoeuropean Hypothesis." *Travaux du Cercle linguistique de Copenhague* 1: 66–96.

Therrien, Michèle. 1982. "La maison de neige (illuvigaq), une métaphore du corps humain." *Inter-Nord* 16: 121–6.

– 1987a. *Le corps inuit (Québec arctique)*. Paris, France: SELAF.

– 1987b. "La parole partagée: L'homme et l'animal arctiques." *Cahiers de littérature orale* 22: 105–30.

– 1989–92. *Ilisautiksait: Cours de langue inuit*. 4 booklets. Paris, France: Institut National des Langues Orientales.

– 1990. "Traces sur la neige, signes sur le papier: Significations de l'empreinte chez les Inuit Nunavimmiut." *Journal de la Société des Américanistes* 76: 33–53.

– 1995. "Corps sain, corps malade chez les Inuit, une tension entre l'intérieur et l'extérieur: Entretiens avec Taamusi Qumaq." *Recherches amérindiennes au Québec* 25, no. 1: 71–84.

– 1996. "Expériences premières et dynamique généralisée dans la culture inuit." In N. Tersis and M. Therrien, eds, *La dynamique dans la langue et la culture inuit*, 23–41. Paris, France: Éditions Peeters.

– 2000. "Nouvelles terminologies en inuktitut: Contraintes linguistiques, logiques, culturelles." In N. Tersis and M. Therrien, eds, *Les langues eskaléoutes*, 283–301. Paris, France: CNRS Éditions.

– and Frédéric Laugrand, eds. 2001. *Perspectives on Traditional Health*. Interviewing Inuit Elders 5. Iqaluit, NU: Nunavut Arctic College.

Thibert, Arthur. 1970. *English-Eskimo Eskimo-English Dictionary*. Rev. ed. Ottawa: Saint Paul University, Canadian Research Centre for Amerindian Anthropology.

Thisted, Kirsten. 1992. "Mundtlighed/skrift, en teoretisk indkredsning af 'det grønlandske' in grønlandsk litteratur" [Orality/writing, a theoretical deconstruction of "the Greenlandic" in Greenlandic literature]. In *Grønlandsk kultur- og samfunds forskning* 92, 195–226. Nuuk, Greenland: Ilisimatusarfik/Atuakkiorfik.

Thomsen, Bjarne T., ed. 2007. *Centering on the Peripheries: Studies in Scandinavian, Scottish, Gaelic and Greenlandic Literature*. London, UK: Norvik Press.

Thorleifsen, Daniel, ed. 1995. *Ilinniarfissuaq ukiuni 150–ini* [The Teacher College during 150 years]. Nuuk, Greenland: Ilinniarfissuaq/Atuakkiorfik.

Thrasher, Anthony A., with Gerard Deagle and Alan Mettrick. 1976. *Thrasher ... Skid Row Eskimo*. Toronto: Griffin House.

Tomiak, Julie-Ann. 2003. "Power, Identity and Discourse: The Politics of Language Choice in Nunavut." MA thesis, Freie Universität, Berlin, Germany.

Townsend, C.W., ed.. 1911. *Captain Cartwright and His Labrador Journal*. Boston, MA: Dana Estes.

Trinel, Ernest. 1970. *Atii, parlez esquimau*. Ottawa: Saint Paul University, Canadian Research Centre for Amerindian Anthropology.

Trudel, François. 1996. "Aboriginal Language Policies of the Canadian and Quebec Governments." In J. Maurais, ed., *Quebec's Aboriginal Languages: History, Planning and Development*, 101–28. Clevedon, UK: Multilingual Matters.

Tulloch, Shelley. 2004. "Inuktitut and Inuit Youth: Language Attitudes as a Basis for Language Planning." PhD dissertation, Université Laval, Quebec City.

Turner, Lucien M. 1887. "Eskimo-English Lexicon and Grammar." Manuscript, Smithonian Institution, Washington, DC.

– 1979. *Indians and Eskimos in the Quebec-Labrador Peninsula: Ethnology of the Ungava District*. 1894. Reprint, Quebec City: Presses Coméditex and Association Inuksiutiit.

Turquetil, Arsène. 1928. "Grammaire esquimaude." Typed manuscript, Oblate Archives/Archives Deschâtelets, Ottawa.

– 1968. "Religious Rituals and Beliefs." 1929. In V. Valentine and F. Vallee, eds, *Eskimo of the Canadian Arctic*, 43–8. Toronto: McClelland and Stewart.

Tyler, Stephen A., ed. 1969. *Cognitive Anthropology*. New York: Holt, Rinehart and Winston.

Uhlenbeck, C.C. 1905. "Uralische Anklänge in den Eskimosprachen" [Uralic echoes in the Eskimo language]. *Zeitschrift der deutschen morgenländischen Gesellschaft* 59: 757–65.

– 1935. *Eskimo en Oer Indogermansch* [Eskimo and early Indo-Germanic]. Mededelingen 77. Amsterdam, Netherlands: Royal Dutch Academy of Sciences and Literature.

Utatnaq, Alexis, et al. 1989. *Interpreter Translator Word List Book*. Iqaluit, NU: Nunavut Arctic College, Interpreter/Translator Program.

Vakhtin, Nikolai B. 1995. *Sintaksis iazika asiatskikh Eskimosov* [Syntax of the language of Asian Eskimos]. Saint Petersburg, Russia: Isdatelstvo Evropaiskogo Doma.

– 1998. "Endangered Languages in Northeast Siberia: Siberian Yupik and Other Languages of Chukotka." In E. Kasten, ed., *Bicultural Education in the North*, 159–73. Münster, Germany: Waxmann Verlag.

– 2005. "Two Approaches to Reversing Language Shift and the Soviet Publication Program for Indigenous Minorities." *Études/Inuit/Studies* 29, nos 1–2: 131–47.

– and N.M. Emelianova. 1988. *Praktikum po leksike Eskimoskogo iazika* [Exercises on the lexicon of the Eskimo language]. Leningrad, Russia: Prosveshchenie.

Valaskakis, Gail G. 1983a. "Communication and Participatory Development in the North: Inuit Interactive Experiments." In G.G. Valaskakis, ed., *Communication and the Canadian North*, 120–35. Montreal: Concordia University, Department of Communication Studies.

– ed. 1983b. *Communication and the Canadian North*. Montreal: Concordia University, Department of Communication Studies.

Vallee, Frank G. 1967. *Kabloona and Eskimo in the Central Keewatin*. Ottawa: Saint Paul University, Canadian Research Centre for Amerindian Anthropology.

Van der Voort, Hein. 1996. "History of Eskimo Interethnic Contact and Its Linguistic Consequences." In S.A. Wurm et al., eds, *Atlas of Languages of Intercultural Communication in the Pacific Hemisphere*, 1043–94. Berlin, Germany: Walter de Gruyter.

Vebæk, Mâliâraq. 2006. *The Southernmost People of Greenland: Dialects and Memories/Qavaat: Oqalunneri Eqqaamassaallu*. Man and Society 33. Copenhagen, Denmark: Meddelelser om Grønland.

Vermeulen, Dirk. 1989. *Report on the Native Language Communications Survey*. Beamsville, ON: Vermeulen Studios.

Vézinet, Monique. 1975. "Analyse sémantique des catégories de l'espace." *Recherches amérindiennes au Québec* 5, no. 3: 48–61.

Vibæk, Poul. 1905. *Contributions to the Study of the Eskimo Language in Greenland*. Meddelelser om Grønland 33/2. Copenhagen, Denmark: Meddelelser om Grønland.

Vick Westgate, Ann. 2002. *Nunavik: Inuit-Controlled Education in Arctic Quebec*. Calgary: University of Calgary Press.

Victor, Paul-Émile. 1963. *Boréal.* 1938. Reprint, Paris, France: Le Livre de Poche.

– with C. Enel and E. Maqe. 1991. *Chants d'Ammassalik.* Man and Society 16. Copenhagen, Denmark: Meddelelser om Grønland.

– and Joëlle Robert-Lamblin. 1994. *La civilisation du phoque 2: Légendes, rites et croyances des Eskimo d'Ammassalik.* Paris, France: Raymond Chabaud.

Webster, Donald H. 1968. *Let's Learn Eskimo.* Fairbanks, AK: Summer Institute of Linguistics.

– and Wilfred Zibell. 1970. *Iñupiat Eskimo Dictionary.* Fairbanks, AK: University of Alaska Fairbanks, Department of Education.

Williamson, Robert G. 1977. *The Boothia Peninsula People: Social Organization in Spence Bay N.W.T.* Spence Bay, NWT: Settlement Council.

– 1988. "Some Aspects of the History of the Eskimo Naming System." *Folk* 30: 245–64.

Willmott, William E. 1961. *The Eskimo Community at Port Harrison P.Q.* Ottawa: Government of Canada, Department of Northern Affairs, Northern Coordination and Research Centre.

Wilman, David. 1988. "The Natural Language of Inuit Children: A Key to Inuktitut Literacy." PhD dissertation, University of New Mexico, Albuquerque.

Wilson, Michael R. 1978. "Notes on Ethnobotany in Inuktitut." *Western Canadian Journal of Anthropology* 8, nos 2–4: 180–94.

Wilson, V.A. 1977. "Teaching Native Language as a Second Language." In R. Barnhardt, ed., *Cross-Cultural Issues in Alaskan Education,* 149–55. Fairbanks, AK: University of Alaska Press.

Woodbury, Anthony C. 1975. "Ergativity of Grammatical Processes: A Study of Greenlandic Eskimo." MA thesis, University of Chicago, Chicago, IL.

– 1984a. "Eskimo and Aleut Languages." In D. Damas, ed., *Handbook of North American Indians,* vol. 5, *Arctic,* 49–63. Washington, DC: Smithsonian Institution.

– ed. 1984b. *Cev'armiut Qanemciit Qulirait-llu: Eskimo Narratives and Tales from Chevak, Alaska.* Fairbanks, AK: Alaska Native Language Center.

Wright, Stephen C., Donald M. Taylor, and J. Macarthur. 2000. "Subtractive Bilingualism and the Survival of the Inuit Language: Heritage- versus Second-Language Education." *Journal of Educational Psychology* 92: 63–84.

Index

Adam, Lucien, 89
affix: lexical, 69; grammatical, 69–70
Aglait illunainortut, 209
Aivilik (Inuktitut dialect): dialectal classification, 40; geographical range, 38; subdialects, 38
Alaska Native Claims Settlement Act, 272
Alaska Native Language Center (ANLC), 20, 183, 199
Alasuaq, Davidialuk, 267
Aleut. *See* Unangan and Unangax
Allen, Shanley, 229
Altaic family, 91–4
Alutiiq: dialects, 16; literacy, 19–20; localization, 16; number of speakers, 21; orthography, 21
Amaohgak, Roy, 184
anatomy. *See* body (human)
antipassive, 77
Arctic Quebec Inuktitut. *See* Nunavik (dialect)
Arctic Small Tool Tradition, 95–6
attitudes toward language, 229
Atuagagdliutit, 203–4, 208
baby talk, 189
Bakker, Peter, 219
Barrow (Alaska), 231–2
Bergsland, Knut, 13, 15, 92, 104, 113
Beringian land bridge, 93
Bering Strait (Inupiaq dialect): geographical range, 29–30; phonology, 31–2; subdialects, 29–30
Bering Strait area, 93–4, 96–7
Berthelsen, Rasmus, 203
Big Diomede Island, 29
bilingualism: in the Baffin region, 226–7; in Barrow (Alaska), 231–2; in education, 191, 195, 198, 199–203, 228, 231; in Greenland, 239; how it works, 225–33; in Inuinnaqtun, 230; in Iqaluit, 228; in Nunatsiavut, 230–1; in Nunavik, 229–30; in Nunavut, 228–9; in other aboriginal languages, 216–17; percentage of bilinguals, 224–5; stable (additive), 228, 231, 277; subtractive, 201, 226, 251, 259
body (human): as anthropocentric model, 151; as basis for

numeration, 144–5; linguistic expression of, 141–2
borrowing (lexical). *See* loan-words
Bourquin, Theodor, 115
Briggs, Jean, 34, 142–3
Burnaby, Barbara, 187

Carpenter, Edmund, 264
change (linguistic): grammatical, 119–26; lexical, 118–19; phonological, 116–18. *See also* factors of linguistic change
Chukchi, 18–19, 97
Chukotko-Kamchatkan family, 93–4; hypothetical links with Eskaleut, 90–1, 93;
code-switching (code-mixing), 119, 239, 274
cognitive anthropology, 136, 149
Collis, Dirmid R., 137
colour terms, 149
componential analysis, 136, 140
computer: computerized linguistic tools, 232–3; Inuit fonts, 185–6
consonant assimilation (regressive), 57–8, 61, 116–17, 130
consonant clusters (types), 58
consonant weakening, 117–18; potential causes, 127–30
contact (linguistic): in Alaska, 222–3; in Canada, 219–20 (with Basque), 220–2 (with English), 220 (with German); in Greenland, 217–19 (with Danish), 217 (with Old Norse); with other aboriginal languages, 215–17
Correll, Thomas, 264
Crago, Martha, 189
Cree First Nation, 44, 216
creoles (Alaskan), 16
culture: Inuit definition, 269; and language, 268–70
customary law (linguistic expression of), 143

Daveluy, Michelle, 247
Davis, John, 108
declension (nominal). *See* Nunavik (dialect)
demonstratives. *See* localizers
Denny, J. Peter, 146, 148
dialect (definition), 3
dialectal distance (index of), 62
diglossia: definition, 249; as experienced by Inuit, 250–7; linked to politics, 258–9; linked to social dependence, 257–8
Dirks, Moses, 13
dog commands, 262
Dorset prehistoric culture. *See* Paleo-Eskimo
double consonants (law of), 68–9; its absence in eighteenth- and nineteenth-century Inuktitut, 111, 115, 118
double-person ending, 77
Dritsas, Polly, 150
drum-dancing, 166, 168
duality (expression of), 136, 146
Dybbroe, Susanne, 273

East Greenlandic (Kalaallisut dialect): death taboo (linguistic effects), 53, 132–3, 266; geographical range, 47; lexical innovation, 53–4, 133–4; subdialects, 47–9; vowel harmony, 52–3
education (formal): in Alaska, 197–9; in Canada, 192–7; and the future of the Inuit language, 276–7;

in Greenland, 190–2; impact on Inuit language, 199–203; perceptions of, 252; policies, 244, 246, 248–9; problems, 197
Egede, Hans, 113, 173
Egede, Ingmar, 199–200
Egede, Poul, 113
emotions (linguistic expression of), 142–3
ending (verbal), 81–2. *See also* affix (grammatical)
Enel, Catherine, 160
ergative, 77
Eriksson, Bjørn, 253
Eskaleut family: geographical range, 10; history, 88; hypothetical Indo-European influences, 90, 93; hypothetical links with Altaic languages, 91–3; hypothetical links with Chukotko-Kamchatkan, 90–1, 93; hypothetical links with Uralic languages, 91–3; impact of schooling, 26; not related to North American Indian languages, 89; number of speakers, 25–6; origins, 88–95; perspectives for the future, 275–7; rate of preservation, 25–6; split between the Eskimo and Aleut branches, 95–6, 101; split between Yupiit and Inuit languages, 97, 101; subdivisions, 9, 26; word structure, 9
Eskimo (current use of the term), 3
Eskimo-Aleut people: geographical range, 10; number, 236; prehistoric migrations, 95–101; subgroupings, 9
Eskimo languages: similarities with Unangax, 14–15; sub-branches, 15
ethnicity (ethnic identity): definition, 272; symbolized by language, 272–4
ethnolinguistics (definition), 4
etymological constraints, 159
Evans, Rev. James, 176–7
evolution (linguistic). *See* change (linguistic)

factors of linguistic change: cultural, 132–4; intermingling of factors, 134; linguistic, 126–7; social, 130–2; sociolinguistic, 127–30. *See also* change (linguistic)
field of experience, 157–9; actantial, 157–8; classificatory, 157–8
Fortescue, Michael, 62, 91–5, 102, 104, 138, 149
fourth person (reflexive), 74–5
fourth vowel, 56, 68, 107–8, 112, 126
French: official language in *Inuit nunaat*, 246–8; teaching in, 196; usage in Nunavik, 251
Frobisher, Martin, 88, 91, 106

Gagné, Raymond, 147–8, 179
gender (linguistic expression of), 139–40
glottal stop, 67
glottochronology, 95–6
Golovko, Evgeni, 14
Graburn, Nelson, 140, 153
Guemple, Lee, 140

Hall, Christopher, 106–8
Hammerich, Louis, 90
Hamp, Eric, 91
Harnum, Betty, 160

Harpoon of the Hunter (The), 206
Haven, Jens, 219
Heinrich, Albert, 149, 161
Hensel, Chase, 266
Home Rule (Greenland): impact on education, 191; impact on ethnicity, 272; language legislation, 245
Horden, Rev. John, 176
Hugo, Beverly A., 132
humanity (linguistic expression of), 138–9
hymns, 169

identity: definition, 268; and ethnicity, 274 (Alaska), 273–4 (Canada), 272–3 (Greenland); expressed through language, 252–3, 254–5, 258, 266–7, 269–74; expressed through syllabic writing, 179, 187
Igloolik Isuma Productions, 170, 211
Ilisimatusarfik (University of Greenland), 192
Imaruittuq, Emile, 132
Independence prehistoric culture. *See* Paleo-Eskimo
Indo-European family, 90, 93
Internet, 178, 213
Inuinnaqtun (Inuktun dialect): bilingualism, 230; geographical range, 33; subdialects, 33
Inuit: geographical range, 7; habitat, 7; number, 235–6; percentage of speakers, 236
Inuit Broadcasting Corporation, 211
Inuit language: dialects, 25, 27, 28–9; in the eighteenth century, 110–14; essential for being a genuine Inuk, 268; geographical range, 10, 27; as an ideological object, 258; linguistic change, 119–26 (grammatical), 118–19, 131–2 (lexical), 116–18 (phonological); linguistic unity, 25, 27; morphology, 62–4; in the nineteenth century, 114–16; number of speakers, 25, 27; percentage of speakers, 236; phonology, 55–61; similarities with Yupiit languages, 21–4; in the sixteenth century, 106–9; split with Yupiit languages, 97, 101; syntactic structure, 54–5. *See also* statistics
Inuit Language Protection Act (Nunavut), 247
Inuit nunaat: definition, 237; language statistics, 241–4, 292–5
Inuktitut: dialectal subdivisions, 36; phonology, 42–4, 45
Inuktitut magazine, 209
Inuktun: dialectal subdivisions, 29; phonology, 34–5
inungmariit, 267, 270
Inupiaq (Iñupiaq): dialectal subdivisions, 29, 32; phonology, 30–2
Inuvialuktun. *See* Siglitun
Ipellie, Alootook, 206
Iqallijuq, Rose, 265
Iqaluit (Nunavut): bilingualism, 228; dialectal mix, 41; diglossia, 253; home language, 242
Itivimiut subdialect. *See* Nunavik (dialect)
Iutzi-Mitchell, Roy, 275

Jacobson, Anna, 208
Jacobson, Steven, 102
James Bay and Northern Quebec Agreement: impact on education,

193, 248; impact on ethnicity, 272; impact on toponymy, 247
Japanese language, 92–3
Jeddore, Rose, 250–1
Jenness, Diamond, 276
Jolliet, Louis, 110

Kalaallisut: dialectal subdivisions, 47–9; in the eighteenth century, 113–14; grammatical change, 122; phonology, 49–53; in the sixteenth century, 108–9
Kalaallit (Greenlanders): contact with Norse, 46; origin of name, 46–7; prehistoric migrations, 46; self-definition, 273
Kalmar, Ivan, 162
Kaplan, Lawrence, 102, 248–9, 274
Kativik School Board, 193, 195–6, 248
Kerek language, 97
King Island (Alaska), 29–30
kinship (linguistic expression of), 140
Kitaamiutut. *See* West Greenlandic
Kivalliq (Inuktitut dialect): dialectal classification, 38–40; geographical range, 36–8; prehistoric migrations, 39–40; subdialects, 36–8
Kleinschmidt, Samuel, 173
Korean language, 92–3
Krauss, Michael, 14, 161
Krupnik, Igor, 256–7
Kuujjuaq (Nunavik): bilingualism, 229–30, 251; home language, 242
Kuujjuaraapik (Nunavik), 252
Kwachka, Patricia, 271

Labrador Inuktitut. *See* Nunatsiavut (dialect)
Langgaard, Karen, 239
language: agglutinative, 9; erosion, 5, 26; globalization, 4; Inuit conceptions about language and speech, 261–4; minority, 4–5; polysynthetic, 9
Language Bureau (Northwest Territories), 246
Language Commission: Greenland, 245; Inuit Tapirisat of Canada, 180; Inuvialuit, 181; Nunavik, 182
languages commissioner, 246
Lefebvre, Gilles, 179
legends: examples of, 164–5. *See also* literature (oral)
legislation (on language): in Alaska, 248–9; in Canada, 246–8; in Greenland, 244–6; in Russia, 249
Lennert-Olsen, Lise, 189–90
literacy: in Alaska, 183–5; Canadian standard orthography, 179–83; in the eastern Canadian Arctic, 176–8; effects of literacy, 186–8; in Greenland, 173–4; in Nunatsiavut, 174–6; in the western Canadian Arctic, 178
literature (oral): magic formulas, 167, 264; myths and legends, 162–5; present-day oral literature, 168–70; songs, 166–7
literature (written): in Alaska, 208; in Canada, 205–8; in Greenland, 203–5
loan-words, 24, 119, 151–2, 156–7; 160–2; Inuit loan-words in English, 160
localizers: morphology, 82–4; semantics, 147–8; in the sixteenth century, 109; used for expressing time, 147

Lowe, Ronald, 181
Luoravetlan. *See* Chukotko-Kamchatkan family

Macdonald, John, 148–9
MacLean, Edna Agheak, 269
Malimiutun (Inupiaq dialect): geographical range, 30; phonology, 31–2; subdialects, 30
Mallon, S.T. Mick, 197
market (language), 252–3
Markoosie, 206
Martin, Ian, 228, 229
Mary-Rousselière, Rev. Guy, 264
McGrath, Robin, 206, 207
media: electronic, 209–13; written, 208–9
Menovshchikov, Georgii, 13, 20, 160–1
metathesis, 50–1
migrations (prehistoric), 95–101
moods (verbal), 78–81
Moravian Brethren, 46, 161, 174–5, 185, 192, 220
morphosemantics, 136–8
myths: examples of, 163; philosophical and pedagogical function, 164. *See also* literature (oral)

name (personal): naming taboo, 266; rules of address, 265–6; transmission (eponymy), 265
Nappaaluk, Salome Mitiarjuk, 89, 206
Naskapi First Nation, 216
Natsilingmiutut (Inuktun dialect): geographical range, 34; phonological conservatism, 35; subdialects, 34
Naukan (Chukotka, Russia), 18
Naukanski: localization, 18; number of speakers, 18, 21
negation (verbal), 81
Neo-Eskimo. *See* Thule culture
neologisms: semantic structure, 157–9. *See also* neology
neology, 151–62; borrowing, 156–7; lexeme coining, 154–5; modes of designation, 153–4; semantic change, 155–6. *See also* loanwords
Nielsen, Frederik, 204
North Baffin (Inuktitut dialect): geographical range, 40–1; grammatical change, 121–2, 124–5; subdialects, 40–1
North Slope (Inupiaq dialect): bilingualism, 231–2; geographical range, 30–1; phonology, 31–2; subdialects, 30–1
noun incorporation, 54–5, 76–7
number (grammatical), 62–4, 71; in the sixteenth century, 108
numerals, 85–6. *See also* numeration
numeration (linguistic expression of), 144–6
Nunatsiaq News, 209
Nunatsiavut (Inuktitut dialect): bilingualism, 230–1; diglossia, 250–1; in the eighteenth century, 110–12; geographical range, 44–5; grammatical change, 121–2; literacy, 174–6; neology, 153–7; in the nineteenth century, 114–15; phonology, 45; subdialects, 44–5
Nunatsiavut Agreement (impact on education), 193, 248
Nunavik (Inuktitut dialect): bilingualism, 229–30; declension

(nominal), 71–4; diglossia, 251–3; geographical range, 44; grammar, 69–86; grammatical change, 122–4; lexicon, 86; localizers, 82–4; moods (verbal), 78–81; neology, 153–7; in the nineteenth century, 115–16; nouns, 70–6; number of speakers, 66; numerals, 85–6; personal pronouns, 75–6; phonology, 66–9; possessives, 74–5; qualifiers, 85; small words, 84–5; subdialects, 44; verbs, 76–82
Nunavik Agreement-in-Principle: impact on education, 193, 248; legislative limits of, 258
Nunavut Agreement, 229, 253
Nunavut Arctic College: book series, 132, 207; courses, 196, 197
Nunavut Tunngavik Inc., 229

official aboriginal languages (Northwest Territories), 246
Official Languages Act (Nunavut), 246–7
Omura, Keiichi, 149
Ootoova, Elisapee, 132
Oqaasileriffik. *See* Language Commission (Greenland)
orthography. *See* writing systems

Paillet, Jean-Pierre, 149
palatalization, 30, 43, 50, 56
Paleo-Asiatic. *See* Chukotko-Kamchatkan family
Paleo-Eskimo: disappearance, 100; language: 96, 102; prehistoric migrations, 96–7
Pan'kov, Ivan, 13
passive, 77
Patrick, Donna, 252–3
Peck, Rev. Edmund James, 69, 115, 177
Petersen, Robert, 205, 239, 250
Petitot, Rev. Émile, 33
phonological distance (index of), 61–2
pidgin trade language (Belle-Isle Strait), 219–20
place names. *See* toponymy
Polar Eskimo. *See* Thule dialect
polysynthetic languages, 9
possessives (nominal declension), 74–5
post-base. *See* affix
Prattis, J. Iain, 257–8
Pre-Dorset prehistoric culture. *See* Paleo-Eskimo
printing, 185–6
proficiency (linguistic): academic, 229; conversational, 229
pronouns (personal), 75–6
Proto-Eskaleut, 94, 101, 104
Proto-Eskimo: grammar, 103; lexicon, 103–4; phonology, 102–3; reconstruction by linguists, 101–2; spoken by Paleo-Eskimo, 96
Proto-Inuit: reconstruction, 104–5; split from Proto-Eskimo, 101; spoken by bearers of the Thule culture, 97

Qallunaat: definition, 88; mythical origin, 88–9
Qawiaraq (Inupiaq dialect): geographical range, 30; phonology, 31–2; subdialects, 30
qualifiers, 85
Quaqtaq (Nunavik), 252
Qumaq, Taamusi, 131–2, 207, 261, 264, 268–9, 277

radical, 69
radio: CBC northern service, 210; community radio, 210; *Kalaallit Nunaata Radioa*, 210
Randa, Vladimir, 150
Rasmussen, Knud, 266
Resolute Bay (Nunavut): mixed dialect, 217; percentage of speakers, 241
Rigolet: subdialect of Nunatsiavut, 45; phonology, 45
Rink, Henry, 103, 203–4
Rischel, Jørgen, 113, 126
Robbe, Pierre, 148

Saint-Aubin, Danièle, 160
St Lawrence Island (Alaska): number of inhabitants, 17; school, 19
Saladin d'Anglure, Bernard, 140, 164
Sallirmiut, 38
Sammallahti, Pekka, 255–6
Sanaaq, 89, 206
Sarqaq prehistoric culture. *See* Paleo-Eskimo
Sauvageot, Aurélien, 92
school. *See* education (formal)
Self Rule (Greenland), 245–6, 272
semantics, 135–7
Senécal, Sacha, 240
Sermitsiaq, 208
Settlers (Nunatsiavut), 220–1, 238
shaman, 167–8. *See also* shamanistic language
shamanistic language, 133–4, 167–8, 264
Shearwood, Perry, 187–8
Siglitun (Inuktun dialect): geographical range, 32; presumed extinction of its speakers, 32–3
singing duel, 166–7
single-person ending, 77
Sirenikski: differences with other Eskimo languages, 18; extinction, 15, 18, 256–7; prehistoric migrations, 96–7
snow (words for), 135–6
sociolinguistics (definition), 4
songs. *See* literature (oral)
South Baffin (Inuktitut dialect): geographical range, 41; grammatical change, 122, 125; in the sixteenth century, 106–8; subdialects, 41
space (linguistic expression of), 147–9
Spalding, Alex, 61
speech: as an identity marker, 266–7; Inuit conceptions about language and speech, 261–4; types of speakers, 267
statistics (Inuit language), 292–5; home language, 239–40; percentage of speakers, 236–9. *See also* *Inuit nunaat*
Sugpiat: localization, 16; number, 16
Swadesh, Morris, 90–1, 95–6
syllabics, 176–9, 180–1, 182–3; symbol of Inuit identity, 179, 187; usage of, 187–8

Taqramiut Nipingat Inc., 211
Tarramiut subdialect. *See* Nunavik (dialect)
tattooing, 172
taxonomy: of animals, 150–1; of plants, 149–50
Taylor, Donald, 251
teacher training, 191–2, 196, 197, 199, 201

teaching the Inuit language: to babies, 189–90; to non-Inuit, 197
television, 211–13
Tersis, Nicole, 137
Thalbitzer, William, 90
Therrien, Michèle, 138–9, 141–2, 264
Thule (Kalaallisut dialect), 47
Thule prehistoric culture: contacts with Paleo-Eskimo, 98; language spoken, 97, 104, 106; prehistoric migrations, 97–100; technology, 98
time (linguistic expression of), 146–7, 158–9
toponymy, 247
tree-line, 7
Tukak Teatret, 170
Tulloch, Shelley, 229
Tuniit (Tornit), 100–1
Tunumiisut. *See* East Greenlandic

Uhlenbeck, C.C., 90, 92
Unalakleet (Alaska), 17
Unangan: culture, 11; geographical range, 10–11; history, 11, 16; number, 11; Russian influence, 11; and Second World War, 11–13
Unangas, 10
Unangax: dialects, 11; geographical range, 10–11; grammar, 14; language loss, 13–14; literacy, 13; phonology, 14; school education, 13; similarities with Eskimo languages, 14–15; split with Eskimo languages, 96, 101
unikkaatuaq, 162–3
unikkausiq, 163
Uralic family, 91–4
Uralo-Siberian (linguistic mesh), 94, 101
Uummarmiutun: localization, 30–1; subdialect of North Slope Inupiaq, 31
Uvingajaq, David, 132

Veniaminov, Rev. Ioann, 13, 19
Vézinet, Monique, 148
vocalic length, 56
vowel harmony, 52–3

Watkins, Rev. Edwin A., 176
West Greenlandic (Kalaallisut dialect): geographical range, 47; sociolinguistic predominance, 250; subdialects, 47
Wilman, David, 189
Wilson, Michael, 149–50
word-base. *See* radical
Wright, Stephen, 251
writing systems: Avataq standard (Nunavik), 182; Canadian Roman standard (*qaliujaaqpait*), 180–1; common Inuit, 184–5; Cyrillic (Alaska), 183; Inuvialuit standard (Mackenzie region), 181–2; Kleinschmidt's (Greenland), 173–4; Lefebvre-Gagné (Canada), 179; Moravian (Labrador), 175–6; new Greenlandic, 174; non-standardized (Alaska), 183; non-standardized alphabetical (western Canadian Arctic), 178, 181; Nunatsiavut standardized, 176; picture writing (central western Alaska), 183; standardized (Alaska), 184; syllabic (Canada), 176–8; syllabic standard (*qaniujaaqpait*), 180–1

Yukaghir language, 93–4
Yupiget: cultural and social unity, 17–8; number, 17; schools, 19–20
Yupiit (people): number, 16; subdivisions, 15–16
Yupiit languages: distribution, 15–16; grammar, 22–3; loan-words, 24; number of speakers, 21; orthography, 20–1; similarities with Inuit language, 21–4; similitude with Proto-Eskimo, 102–3; split with Inuit language, 97, 101
Yup'ik (Central Alaskan): dialects, 17; geographical range, 16; literacy, 19–20; number of speakers, 21; orthography, 21
Yupik (Central Siberian): geographical range, 17; literacy, 19–20; orthography, 21